JONATHAN EDWARDS
CONFRONTS THE GODS

JONATHAN EDWARDS CONFRONTS THE GODS

Christian Theology, Enlightenment Religion,
and Non-Christian Faiths

GERALD R. MCDERMOTT

OXFORD
UNIVERSITY PRESS

2000

OXFORD
UNIVERSITY PRESS

Oxford   New York
Athens   Auckland   Bangkok   Bogotá   Buenos Aires   Calcutta
Cape Town   Chennai   Dar es Salaam   Delhi   Florence   Hong Kong   Istanbul
Karachi   Kuala Lumpur   Madrid   Melbourne   Mexico City   Mumbai
Nairobi   Paris   São Paulo   Singapore   Taipei   Tokyo   Toronto   Warsaw

and associated companies in
Berlin   Ibadan

Copyright © 2000 by Gerald R. McDermott

Published by Oxford University Press, Inc.
198 Madison Avenue, New York, New York 10016

Oxford is a registered trademark of Oxford University Press.

All rights reserved. No part of this publication may be reproduced,
stored in a retrieval system, or transmitted, in any form or by any means,
electronic, mechanical, photocopying, recording, or otherwise,
without the prior permission of Oxford University Press.

Library of Congress Cataloging-in-Publication Data
McDermott, Gerald R. (Gerald Robert)
Jonathan Edwards confronts the gods : Christian theology,
Enlightenment religion, and non-Christian faiths / Gerald R.
McDermott.
p.   cm.
Includes bibliographical references.
ISBN 0-19-513274-2
1. Apologetics—United States—History—18th century.   2. Deism—
History—18th century.   3. Edwards, Jonathan, 1703-1758—
Contributions in relations of Christianity and other religions.
4. Christianity and other religions—History—18th century.
5. Edwards, Jonathan, 1703-1758—Contributions in theology of
revelation.   6. Revelation—History—18th century.   I. Title.
BT1180.M34   1999
239'.7—dc21   99-26834

1 3 5 7 9 8 6 4 2

Printed in the United States of America
on acid-free paper

For Mary Kevin McDermott and Eileen McDermott,
two women with special gifts

PREFACE

This book began with a startling discovery during my dissertation research in 1987 at Yale's Beinecke Rare Book and Manuscript Library. While wandering in the vast labyrinth of Edwards's sermon and notebook manuscripts — most of them unpublished and scrawled in a hand that can reduce a scholar to tears — I came upon hundreds of folio pages of Edwards's notes on non-Christian religions. Besides being astonished that this theologian, known for his celebration of Christian particularity, had shown interest in the particularities of other religions, I wondered what this could possibly mean. What was the purpose of these ruminations? How did these religions fit into his theology? What was he planning to do with these notes? They seemed to be building toward something, as if he was collecting data for future use. But for what? And were there other notebooks with similar materials? I copied what I could and began a search that carried me into an enormous trove of fascinating materials from the American colonies and several continents. I came to see that Edwards had joined a spirited discussion that was changing the way many Europeans would think about God, and that he was using this discussion to rethink both Enlightenment religion and his own Reformed tradition. This book tries to explain what I found.

A variation of chapter 11 appeared in the *New England Quarterly* in December 1999. I am grateful to the editors of the *Quarterly* for permission to use this material. Other versions of several chapters in this book have also been used for articles in *Pro Ecclesia*, *American Presbyterians*, and a chapter in Sang Hyun Lee and Allen C. Guelzo, eds., *Edwards in Our Time: Jonathan Edwards and the Shaping of American Religion* (Grand Rapids: Eerdmans, 1999). I am grateful to the editors of these journals and to Eerdmans for permission to draw from these materials.

Along the way I have incurred many personal and pleasant debts. Ken Minkema, executive editor of *The Works of Jonathan Edwards*, was unfailingly generous with his time and encyclopedic knowledge of Edwards. His suggestions and criticisms helped sharpen the argument in a legion of ways. George Marsden's careful reading of the manuscript prevented it, I think, from saying more than the evidence warrants. Skip Stout's advice was critically helpful at several important stages along the way. My department chair, Robert Benne, not only supported this project throughout its course but also smoothed its progress along the way with his counsel. Thanks also to the following scholars, who offered suggestions, criticisms, and encouragement: Doug Sweeney, Alan Pieratt, Avihu Zakai (whose camaraderie has been so much fun), Dan Hardy (who saw promise in this project and enabled me to devote a sabbatical year to it), Steve Chase, Leanne Van Dyk (who patiently read early and very imperfect versions of the manuscript), George Hunsinger, Victor Nuovo, Sang Hyun Lee, Wilson Kimnach, and David Dawson.

This book would not have been written without the generous support of the Center of Theological Inquiry, which provided me and my family with an idyllic year at Princeton and a perfect setting for study and writing. I am also grateful to Roanoke College for giving me several summer research grants and a Faculty Scholar award to support this project.

All scholars know how much they depend on librarians, and (now) computer and other technology experts. Pat Scott at Fintel Library was unceasingly cheerful and helpful; Karen Harris's expertise expedited manuscript preparation and rescued me from several near disasters; Bill Harris at Luce Library and Kate Skrebutenas at Speer Library (Princeton Seminary) helped me track down many a book and article; and Maureen Montgomery, Kate Le Van, and Linda Sheldon were particularly responsible for making my twelve months at CTI both productive and delightful. Finally, thanks are due to Chriss Davies-Ross for proofreading and Ryan McDermott for preparing the index.

Jean McDermott, my best friend and wife, provided more than she knows. Without her this book could not have been written.

July 1999 G.R.M.
Salem, Virginia

CONTENTS

Abbreviations xi
Introduction: A Strange, New Edwards 3

Part I: The Challenge

1. Deists and the Scandal of Particularity 17
2. Edwards's War against Enlightenment Religion 34

Part II: Strategies of Response

3. Our Noblest Faculty: The Promise and Limits of Reason in Religion 55
4. Signatures of Divine Majesty: The Reason and Mystery of Revelation 71
5. Trickle-Down Revelation and Religious Entropy: The Nature and History of Religion 87
6. Parables in All Nations: Typology and the Religions 110
7. A Possibility of Reconciliation: Salvation and the "Heathen" 130

Part III: Strategies Applied

8. Judaism: A Light among the Nations 149
9. Islam: The Left Arm of Antichrist 166

10. Greece and Rome: Very Noble and Almost Divine Truths   176
11. American Indians: The Devil Sucks Their Blood   194
12. The Chinese Philosophers: Shadows of the Trinity   207

Conclusion: Confounding the Enlightenment   217

Selected Bibliography   229

Index   241

ABBREVIATIONS

AF	*The Author's Farewel*, by Thomas Chubb
AW	*Apocalyptic Writings*, ed. Stephen J. Stein, vol. 5 of *The Works of Jonathan Edwards*
BC	"Book of Controversies," Edwards Papers, Beinecke Rare Book and Manuscript Library, Yale University
CAO	*Christianity as Old as the Creation*, by Matthew Tindal
CNM	*Christianity Not Mysterious*, by John Toland
DB	*The Life of David Brainerd*, ed. Norman Pettit, vol. 7 of *The Works of Jonathan Edwards*
DCR	*A Discourse Concerning Reason*, by Thomas Chubb
DF	*A Discourse on Freethinking*, by Anthony Collins
DSL	"Divine and Supernatural Light," by Jonathan Edwards, in Harold P. Simonson, ed., *Selected Writings of Jonathan Edwards*
EccW	*Ecclesiastical Writings*, ed. David D. Hall, vol. 12 of *The Works of Jonathan Edwards*
End	*The End for Which God Created the World*, by Jonathan Edwards, in EW
EW	*Ethical Writings*, ed. Paul Ramsey, vol. 8 of *The Works of Jonathan Edwards*
FW	*Freedom of the Will*, ed. Paul Ramsey, vol. 1 of *The Works of Jonathan Edwards*
HWR	*History of the Work of Redemption*, ed. John F. Wilson, vol. 9 of *The Works of Jonathan Edwards*
IW	*The Independent Whig*, by Thomas Gordon and John Trenchard
LPW	*Letters and Personal Writings*, ed. George S. Claghorn, vol. 16 of *The Works of Jonathan Edwards*

MNB	"Man's Natural Blindness in the Things of Religion," by Jonathan Edwards, in Edward Hickman, ed., *The Works of President Edwards*, vol. 2
NS	*Notes on the Scriptures*, ed. Stephen J. Stein, vol. 15 of *The Works of Jonathan Edwards*
OS	*Original Sin*, ed. Clyde A. Holbrook, vol. 3 of *The Works of Jonathan Edwards*
RA	*Religious Affections*, ed. John E. Smith, vol. 2 of *The Works of Jonathan Edwards*
SDK	*Sermons and Discourses, 1720–1723*, ed. Wilson H. Kimnach, vol. 10 of *The Works of Jonathan Edwards*
SDM	*Sermons and Discourses, 1723–1729*, ed. Kenneth P. Minkema, vol. 14 of *The Works of Jonathan Edwards*
SPW	*Scientific and Philosophical Writings*, ed. Wallace E. Anderson, vol. 6 of *The Works of Jonathan Edwards*
TM	"Types of the Messiah," by Jonathan Edwards, in *TW*
TV	*The Nature of True Virtue*, by Jonathan Edwards, in *EW*
TW	*Typological Writings*, ed. Wallace E. Anderson and Mason I. Lowance Jr., with David H. Watters, vol. 11 of *The Works of Jonathan Edwards*

JONATHAN EDWARDS
CONFRONTS THE GODS

INTRODUCTION

A Strange, New Edwards

Eighty years ago Karl Barth stunned Europe with his re-presentation of the "strange, new world" of the Bible.[1] For two hundred and fifty years Jonathan Edwards has horrified readers with his description of a god who dangles sinners by a spider-thread over the flames of hell. Few have known that this most famous sermon in American history was rather uncharacteristic of Edwards, who was obsessed not by the wrath of the divine but by its beauty. Fewer still have known his declaration that those whom terror has driven to religion are probably unconverted.[2] Most have assumed that for Edwards only Christians—and perhaps only Calvinist Christians—had religious truth.

They have assumed wrongly. This book is about a strange, new Edwards unfamiliar to generations of readers and scholars. It is the story of America's most frightening preacher who—strangely—was fascinated by other religions and religious others. It will startle those who know Edwards from their American literature surveys to learn that he believed there was true revelation from God in non-Christian religions. Those who have been schooled in the stereotypical Edwards will find it even more remarkable that he believed that some non-Christians worshiped, perhaps without knowing it, the true god.[3] A son of the Enlightenment who adopted

---

1. Karl Barth, "The Strange, New World within the Bible," in Barth, *The Word of God and the Word of Man*, 28–50.
2. This is the clear implication of the eighth "negative" sign and second and third "positive" signs of true religious affections. See RA, 155–57, 240–53, 253–66.
3. *An Humble Inquiry into the Rules of the Word of God, Concerning the Qualifications Requisite to a Complete Standing and Full Communion in the Visible Christian Church*, in EccW, 300.

key Enlightenment assumptions, Edwards nevertheless spent his life fighting Enlightenment religion. This battle reshaped his own understanding of the divine and its ways with human beings. And like some of the better-known thinkers of the Enlightenment, he was mesmerized by non-European religions and scoured New England for books on unfamiliar faiths.

From at least the Middle Ages it had been taken for granted in the West, both in popular and learned culture, that there can be no ultimate meaning without reference to the particular historical figure of Jesus Christ. There was plenty of disagreement over what this meant and how the relationship between meaning and Christ was to be worked out, but all agreed that final significance was related to him alone.

Toward the end of the seventeenth century, however, this assumption came under fire. More and more intellectual leaders challenged the old assumption with a new one: whatever delivers ultimate significance must be available to all human beings. Therefore final meaning cannot be tied to a particular person.

The deists were the first to make public arguments stemming from this new assumption, and they went on to reject most traditional Christian dogma. The assumption was accepted later even by those who did not reject Christianity outright—such as Lessing, Herder, Kant, and Hegel—but they agreed with the deists that ultimate meaning must be expressed in general rather than particular terms. As Lessing put it, "Accidental truths of history can never become the proof of necessary truths of reason."[4]

The result was a radically revised Christianity in which the idea of redemption was retained but without the indissoluble connection to the person of Jesus previously assumed. For Kant, significance comes from the moral rules we can find through reason alone; for Hegel, the reconciliation of the absolute with its natural and historical objectification must be grasped conceptually rather than through any representation and therefore must be freed of the limitations of particularity. Even for Schleiermacher, the great father of liberal Christian theology, the ideas of redeemer and redemption are found uniquely and unsurpassably in Jesus, but have no logically necessary reference to Jesus.[5]

Some of this story has been known for some time. But what is not generally well known is that the French and German Enlightenments, of which these later

---

In this passage Edwards claims that "Socrates . . . worshipped the true God, as he was led by the light of nature." It is not clear that Edwards believed Socrates was regenerate and had true virtue, but as we shall see, he believed that the conditions for the possibility of salvation were present in many religious traditions and recognized something approximating true virtue in individuals—such as Melchizedek and the Onohquaga Indians—who were neither Jews nor explicit disciples of Jesus.

4. Gotthold Lessing, "On the Proof of the Spirit and of Power," in Chadwick, *Lessing's Theological Writings*, 53.

5. The literature on this shift in thinking about religion is extensive; some of it is cited in the chapters that follow. For an introduction that has proved to be a seminal work for other scholars, see Frei, *Eclipse of Biblical Narrative*; for an insightful analysis of the turn in seventeenth-century theology, see Placher, *Domestication of Transcendence*. These paragraphs are indebted to the excellent introduction in Marshall, *Christology in Conflict*, 1–14.

figures are representative, owed a substantial debt to English deism.[6] It is even less known that the discovery of new lands (and hence new religions) in the sixteenth and seventeenth centuries played a significant role in the rise of deism, which formed the basis for the most trenchant critiques of the Christian faith in the eighteenth century. John Toland, Matthew Tindal, and other deists focused on the problem of particularity, which in their case meant the realization that only one-sixth of the world had heard the gospel (this was based on a seventeenth-century geographer's estimation and was quoted repeatedly), and that according to Calvinism the other five-sixths were damned. This threatened traditional notions of God's goodness and justice and led deists to reshape God and religion in ways that undermined both Catholic and Protestant understandings of revelation.

This is a study of how Jonathan Edwards responded to the radical Enlightenment's challenge to Reformed orthodoxy—a challenge that squared off over the issue of God's fairness toward non-Christians. Previous studies of Edwards and the Enlightenment have focused on Edwards's appropriation of Locke and Newton, England's stellar proponents of a *moderate* Enlightenment that claimed, sometimes disingenuously, to support traditional Christian dogma. But deism was a more radical form of Enlightenment. It self-consciously questioned the epistemological and theological foundations of all Christian thinking that appealed to written revelation. It was this form of Enlightenment that most worried and engaged Edwards.[7]

Edwards considered this the gravest threat facing Christian faith and marshaled his prodigious powers to combat it. More than twenty-five percent of his private notebook entries (357 of 1412)—and many entries comprise thousands of words—are devoted to explicit consideration of challenges raised by the deist agenda. Over sixty entries, some of the longest in all his notebooks, focus precisely on the contents of non-Christian religions. Far more than scholars have ever realized, many of his major treatises were targeted at problems raised directly or indirectly by deists.

The voluminous notebook entries on other religions indicate that as he grew older, Edwards became more and more intrigued by religious others. By the time of his death he had left a manuscript corpus devoted to the question of other religions at least as large as any other colonial thinker. Not until James Fenimore Cooper's *Last of the Mohicans* (1826) do we find anything in American popular literary culture as persistently fascinated by cultural difference.

---

6. Torrey, *Voltaire and the English Deists*; on d'Holbach's debt to Toland, see Jacob, *The Radical Enlightenment*, 27, 262; see also Harrison, '*Religion*' *and the Religions*, 176 n.4.

7. Scholars have discussed Edwards and Enlightenment, but none have focused on Edwards's principal Enlightenment nemesis—deism—and the question of Edwards and other religions has been ignored. Norman Fiering, for example, rightly acknowledged that Edwards grew up in a more cosmopolitan intellectual environment than is usually recognized but focused on the English sentimentalists rather than the deists. In his excellent study Robert Jenson notes that Edwards warred with deism and was nearly alone in recognizing the possibilities of salvation for "pagan religionists." But deism is in the background of Jenson's work and functions principally as the architect of American public policy. Alfred Owen Aldridge has recognized Edwards's opposition to deism, but he also fails to place Edwards's larger theological projects into the context of his life-long struggle with deism. Fiering, *Jonathan Edwards's Moral Thought*; Jenson, *America's Theologian*; Aldridge, "Enlightenment and Awakening," in Oberg and Stout, 27–41; Aldridge, *Jonathan Edwards*.

Edwards was not the first colonial to show interest in other religions, but he appears to have pursued this interest further than anyone else. Most regarded religious others with a combination of contempt and apprehension. New Englanders in the seventeenth century were aware of Muslims because corsair fleets of the Barbary pirates were harassing American shipping and capturing American sailors, whom they held as slaves until ransomed. When the turn of the eighteenth century brought an escalation of pirate attacks on American ships, distant "Turks" became something of a commonplace in the New England imagination—not unlike "Muslim terrorists" in the American mental landscape at the end of the twentieth century.[8] Cotton Mather owned a copy of the Qur'an, happily noted that it regarded Jesus as a messiah, and commended its condemnation of idolatry. But he found Islam's chief significance to be its use as an instrument of divine wrath. The Puritan poet Edward Taylor went even further, regarding Muslims as peculiar objects of wrath, singled out for Revelation's fifth vial of divine displeasure.[9]

Edwards's clerical contemporaries in the eighteenth century wrote very little about other religions. But when they did, they did so in a manner that was thoroughly traditional. They referred to "Mahometan impostures" and "Jewish errors" and believed the only hope for Native Americans was to follow Christian light out of their heathen darkness.[10] Liberals like Ebenezer Gay, who put far more stock than Edwards in the religious potential of nature and reason, preached that "the heathen were blind in religion" despite their impressive moral achievements. Liberal luminaries Charles Chauncy and Jonathan Mayhew appear reactionary on the matter of other religions when compared to Edwards.[11]

The only other colonial in Edwards's lifetime who approached his passion for other religions was Benjamin Franklin. Franklin was fascinated by China as a boy and published extracts from the works of Confucius in his *Pennsylvania Gazette*. He admired American Indian culture, was familiar with its creation myths, and on

---

8. Isani, "Edward Taylor and the Turks," 120–23; Isani, "Cotton Mather and the Orient," 46, 51.

9. Cotton Mather, *Magnalia Christi Americana* (Hartford, Conn., 1853), 2:663; Lovelace, *The American Pietism of Cotton Mather*, 42, 47; Isani, "Edward Taylor and the Turks," 120; see also Reiner Smolinski, ed., *The Threefold Paradise of Cotton Mather: An Edition of "Triparadisus"* (Athens: University of Georgia Press, 1995).

10. See, for example, Benjamin Wadsworth, "An Essay for the Charitable Spreading of the Gospel" (Boston, 1718), 12, 21; Nathanael Appleton, "How God Wills the Salvation of All Men" (Boston, 1753), 18; and Dexter, *The Literary Diary of Ezra Stiles*, 1: 385–86, 3: 339, 354, 386, 396, 403, 508, 538. All references to Native American religion in Stiles's *Diary* are derogatory.

11. Ebenezer Gay, "Natural Religion as Distinguished from Revealed" (Dudleian Lecture at Harvard, May 9, 1759), 21. Mayhew went to great pains to show that a premier mission society had not (but should have) preached the gospel to the Indians. Jonathan Mayhew, *Observations on the Charter and Conduct of the Society for the Propagation of the Gospel in Foreign Parts* (Boston, 1763). In all of his voluminous writings on God's final treatment of human beings (published posthumously), Chauncy never showed the least interest in non-Christian faiths. One could conclude from his published writings that none but Christians enjoy religious truth. See Charles Chauncy, *The Benevolence of the Deity* (Boston, 1784), *The Mystery Hid from Ages and Generations* (London, 1784), *The Salvation of All Men* (Boston, 1782), and *Divine Glory Brought to View in the Final Salvation of All Men* (Boston, 1783).

several occasions published accounts of its virtues.[12] But his enthusiasm for religious others was never expressed in any of his major works. There was no American Sinophile (or American champion of any non-Western culture, for that matter) on the order of Voltaire or Leibniz, who publicly and repeatedly praised Chinese culture in France and Germany.[13]

No one in colonial America—other than Edwards—reflected persistently and systematically on religious others. Only Edwards developed an elaborate scheme for the role other religions had played in the grand scheme of redemptive history. Others denounced non-Christian religions as various shades of darkness, but Edwards regarded them as actors in the grand historical drama. They were not the main players, to be sure, and not the heroic protagonists, but they were important to the story. Apart from them, the narrative did not cohere; without their mediation, it did not make sense. In Edwards's history of the world, the non-Christian religions were not merely appendices or afterwords, but integral chapters that answered important questions about God and his revelation to creation. In other words, Edwards may have been the first American intellectual to give non-Christian religions positive significance in a Christian understanding of God and history.

My purpose here is to show how America's greatest colonial thinker responded to the radical Enlightenment—in particular how this philosopher-theologian sorted out the relationship of Christianity to other world religions. In contemporary theological terms, I describe his response to what is now dubbed "the scandal of particularity." Part I (Chapters 1 and 2) analyzes the deism Edwards faced and argues that it was this radical rejection of the very concept of revelation that Edwards considered his greatest challenge. Previous scholars have portrayed the colonial theologian as fighting intramural skirmishes with Arminians, thinkers who rejected Edwards's Calvinism but still believed that the Bible was God's word. I argue in these chapters that Edwards considered deism to be Christianity's most formidable opponent, and that the better part of his theological project was a direct or indirect response to it.

Part II outlines the most important theological tools Edwards used to undermine deism, which had become the Enlightenment religion for many of the eighteenth-century intellectual elite. Chapters 3 and 4 focus on the relationship between revelation and reason, the most immediate line of attack by deism against Christian orthodoxy. They profile Edwards's defense of revelation against deism's religion of nature, which deists conceived as a universal genus of religion, given by the light of reason alone, of which each world religion is an imperfect species. Edwards tried to disable the deist attack on revelation by proposing that its definition of reason was narrow and finally unreasonable.[14]

---

12. Aldridge, *The Dragon and the Eagle*, 25, 77, 25, 32, 67, 71–72; Aldridge, *Benjamin Franklin and Nature's God*, 120.
13. Aldridge, *The Dragon and the Eagle*, 268.
14. Strangely, none of the major recent interpreters of Edwards have focused on Edwards's battle with the deists over revelation. Morris, Jenson, Fiering, Daniel, Lee, Guelzo, and Cherry mention the subjects of reason and revelation separately and somewhat tangentially. None discusses at length

Scholars have never before considered Edwards's proposal for reason and revelation in the full context of the deist challenge. Indeed, this may be the first time that Edwards's vision of reason and revelation has been drawn from such a wide array of his unpublished notebooks. In these four chapters I reconstruct a theology of revelation and religion that was left in pieces in his notebooks, some parts of it reworked for use in treatises on the will, original sin, and virtue—and others awaiting the day when he would complete the massive *apologia* he had been planning for decades.[15] Herein I hope to suggest what Edwards might have one day published on reason, revelation, and other world religions—if he had survived the smallpox outbreak at Princeton.

Because scholars have never imagined that Edwards considered the possibility of revelation in other religions, no one has ever studied his understanding of religion as a human phenomenon involving anything other than the Christian Bible. But when we examine his corpus with an understanding of the radical deist claims in its polemical background, we can see his daring attempt to comprehend an extraordinary range of religious traditions for the purpose of commending Reformed Christianity among an emerging pantheon of deities. In other words, not only did Edwards accurately foresee that Christianity's greatest nemesis would be a religion that denies revelation, but he also saw the need to defend the Christian god in the new global arena where a host of gods competed for the world's loyalties. In Chapter 5 I unfold Edwards's understanding of religion *qua* religion—that is, what is really going on when people of other faiths worship a god other than the god of Christians. I also outline the startlingly different answers that deism and Edwards proposed for this question: for deism, religion is static and moralistic, while for Edwards religion is dynamic and draws the believer into mystical participation in the divine. In this chapter I demonstrate that Edwards perpetuated what scholars thought had been lost—the *prisca theologia*, a tradition dating back to the early church fathers that looked for elements of true religion in non-Christian traditions and thinkers—in his efforts to defend revelation against its detractors.

Chapter 6 shows how Edwards employed his massive and intricate typological system to defend revelation. Here I argue that he saw non-Christian religions as

---

the relationship between the two of them as a central problem for Edwards. See Morris, *Young Jonathan Edwards*; Jenson, *America's Theologian*; Fiering, *Jonathan Edwards's Moral Thought*; Daniel, *The Philosophy of Jonathan Edwards*; Lee, *The Philosophical Theology of Jonathan Edwards*; Guelzo, *Edwards on the Will*; and Cherry, *Theology of Jonathan Edwards*. John H. Gerstner, in volume 1 of *The Rational Biblical Theology of Jonathan Edwards*, addresses the issue at some length, but generally ignores scholarship since the 1960s, which limits the value of its discussion. Michael McClymond, in *Encounters with God: An Approach to the Theology of Jonathan Edwards*, makes an important contribution to Edwards studies by recognizing the apologetic nature of the Edwardsean project. But while McClymond acknowledges Edwards's interest in the revelation and reason debates, he focuses on Edwards's differences with Paley and Schleiermacher (both of whose works were published long after Edwards's death), not on the content of his arguments with the deists over revelation and reason.

15. See Edwards's letter to the trustees of the College of New Jersey, October 19, 1757, in *LPW*, esp. 727–28. Unless otherwise indicated, Edwards's letters are in *LPW*.

partly God-given images of divine truths portrayed more fully and distinctly in Christian revelation. Others have shown that Edwards pushed beyond the boundaries of traditional Christian typology to include history and nature; I propose that he went even further to bring other religions into his system.

Typically Edwards has been seen as preaching that there is no salvation for those who do not confess Jesus during their earthly sojourns. Edwards indeed suggests this in many of his explicit declarations on the "heathen"(the commonly used eighteenth-century word for those outside the worlds of Judaism, Christianity, and Islam[16]): they were blessed with considerable moral and religious truth but usually failed to take advantage of it. Yet Chapter 7 shows an extraordinary tension in his thinking. While preaching that the heathen were generally lost in darkness, he also located human "disposition" at the center of his soteriology and posited a temporal lag between regeneration and conversion, thus opening the door for the regeneration of some who did not confess Jesus. By this means he affirmed the salvation, for example, of the Canaanite priest Melchizedek and the regeneration of Cornelius the centurion as well as that of some of the apostles before they heard the gospel message. He also argued that Christ was present in all Old Testament theophanies to those who did not know the name Jesus, and that God's expectations varied according to the degree of revelation a people had received. So while Edwards usually stopped short of declaring the salvation of non-Christians, he laid a theological foundation for its possibility.[17]

Part III examines his material deliberations on the non-Christian religions he knew either through reading or observation. It illustrates how he applied the strategies of Part II to actual religions. Chapter 8, for example, reveals that while Edwards was traditionally supersessionist in his view of Judaism, his treatment of the relationship between the covenants was more subtle than that of most of his predecessors in Christian theology, and his typological understanding of Israel as true religion's city on a hill—an inspiration to the heathen—was distinctive. Unlike Enlightenment religionists, Edwards refused to sever the covenantal link between the two religions.

Chapter 9 argues that Edwards's vitriol against Islam can be explained by deism's use of that religion as a weapon against Christian orthodoxy. Edwards folded Islam into his elaborate eschatological vision and showed a knowledge of Muslims and their faith that was sophisticated by eighteenth-century standards.

The "heathen" Edwards knew best were the Greek and Roman philosophers (Chapter 10). He held classical religion in contempt but prized classical philosophy—especially Platonic—as an apologetic weapon for use against the radical Enlightenment and employed classical mythology for similar polemics.

---

16. Most frequently this meant classical Greeks and Romans; less frequently, Buddhists, Hindus, the Chinese, and assorted animists.

17. That Edwards saw religious truth among the heathen was not a novel move for a Reformed thinker. Calvin himself had noted the religious perception of the likes of Cicero and Plato; Calvin, *Institutes* 1.3.1; 1.3.3. But, to use Calvin's terms, while Edwards's Reformed predecessors had seen religious knowledge of God the *Creator* among pagans, Edwards expended considerable energy uncovering their knowledge of God the *Redeemer* as well.

The heathen closest to view, however, were the Native Americans, whom Edwards served as missionary pastor for seven years (Chapter 11). In them he saw a portent of the future of the work of redemption. They may also have helped influence his views of the heathen more generally: typically lost in darkness despite having been given revelation, but still the object of God's redemptive activity.

Chapter 12 demonstrates that Edwards held a remarkably generous view of God's revelation in Chinese culture. It places Edwards in the context of Western understandings (in the early modern period) of China by arguing that at a time when many of his contemporaries had nothing but contempt for the Middle Kingdom, Edwards perpetuated the Sinophilic tradition begun by the seventeenth-century French Jesuits.

Finally, in the conclusion I reflect on the implications of this study for our understanding of Edwards and the Enlightenment. I suggest that Edwards's confrontation with the Enlightenment was one of critical appropriation: he adopted Enlightenment presuppositions and spoke in terms best understood by other disciples of the Enlightenment. I also show that deism may have helped shape his thinking by setting part of his agenda. That is, his reflections on truth in the religions were prompted in part by deist questioning of traditional Christian thinking on the subject.

Yet I also argue that Edwards creatively coopted Enlightenment assumptions to serve Reformed theology (and not without refashioning Reformed theology in the process). He attempted to explode deist notions of reason as common sense, for instance, by arguing the dependence of reason on revelation and the inability of deist reason to deal with the complexities of human existence. And he sought to displace the deist attack on God's justice in revelation by proposing that God is a communicating being who has revealed his truths to nearly all religionists of the world.

Of course, this story is only another of the many stories that scholars have been reconstructing recently in their depiction of early modern cultural encounters between the West and the rest of the world.[18] The Edwards story—if you will—illustrates several trends that have emerged in the telling of many other stories. First, as is often the case, Edwards's encounter with religious others is important for what it tells us about the observer rather than the observed. As for so many other Westerners from the sixteenth to eighteenth centuries, the encounter with others often amounted to self-congratulation and self-projection rather than reliable description of the other.[19]

Second, there were gradations of otherness.[20] Deists, for example, divorced their perception of Jews from the concept of covenant, which increased the deist sense

---

18. A large number of studies of the development of concepts of alterity among Europeans has emerged in the 1980s and 1990s. For starters, see Schwartz, *Implicit Understandings*; Greenblatt, *New World Encounters*; Gernet, *China and the Christian Impact*; Boon, *Other Tribes, Other Scribes*; James and Marcus, *Writing Culture*; Fagan, *The Clash of Cultures*; Geertz, *Interpretation of Cultures*; Lach, *Asia in the Making of Europe*; Mason, *Deconstructing America*; Pagden, *European Encounters with the New World*; and White, *Tropics of Discourse*.

19. Pagden, *European Encounters with the New World*, 183–89.

20. Schwartz, "Introduction," in *Implicit Understandings*, 7–8.

of Jewish estrangement from non-Jewish society. Edwards, in contrast, retained the idea of covenantal connection between Jews and Christians and therefore felt more affinity for Judaism than the deists did. But there were also grades of otherness within Edwards's thinking about religion. Muslims seemed more alien to Edwards than Greeks and Romans, despite the fact that he believed Muhammad knew that Jesus was the Christ. American Indian culture, which he knew from personal experience, was repulsive to him, while Chinese high culture, which was removed from him by centuries and thousands of miles, seemed strangely familiar.

Third, Edwards also illustrates the finding of more recent studies that Western observers were influenced by their observations of other cultures.[21] Despite his preconceptions and his attitude of cultural superiority, his encounters with non-Christian religions seem to have caused him to rethink some of his theological presuppositions. In other words, earlier scholarly presumptions that Western attitudes of cultural superiority completely determined Western understanding of cultural alterity are "somewhat simplistic."[22] The process of cultural contact and reinterpretation was often "messy," involving change over time and mutual interaction.[23] In Edwards's case, his defense of Reformed doctrines in the face of deist challenges conditioned his understanding of non-Christian religions, but his encounters with these religions also influenced his reconfiguration of Reformed theology.

Ours is not the first century in which Western Christians have thought seriously about religious others. Nor is this the first era in which the Reformed tradition has questioned the presumptive doom of those without the gospel. We need to be reminded that, as Frank Manuel put it, "the gods were ubiquitous" in the eighteenth century.[24] The Enlightenment was awash in dictionaries and encyclopedias of religion. Intellectuals in Britain and on the Continent had available a profusion of empirical data on world religions, from travelers' accounts to translations of sacred texts from the East and descriptions of exotic mythologies.

Manuel is wrong, however, to conclude that America was "ill-prepared" for serious reflection on these data.[25] Edwards knew as much about other religions as most of the British thinkers reflecting on the gods and in several respects matched their reflections with meditations at least as original. He shared Voltaire's cosmopolitan fascination with other lands and their religions, but of course for different reasons. The New England theologian eagerly sought out information on other religions, reflected deeply and often on the data he found, and incorporated these reflections into his grand vision for the history of the work of redemption. Therefore the image of Edwards as colonial provincial, probably uninformed and certainly uninterested in the wider intellectual debates of the Enlightenment, must

---

21. See, for example, Willard J. Peterson, "What to wear? Observation and participation by Jesuit missionaries in late Ming society," in Schwartz, *Implicit Understandings*, 378–402.
22. Schwartz, "Introduction," in *Implicit Understandings*, 6.
23. Ibid.
24. Manuel, *The Eighteenth Century Confronts the Gods*, 5.
25. Ibid., 10.

be laid to rest. Edwards was thoroughly immersed in a transatlantic culture of learning that was far more interested in religious and cultural others than most scholars have imagined.[26]

And like the seventeenth- and eighteenth-century European divines using the *prisca theologia* whom D. P. Walker has described as generally liberal in their views of salvation,[27] Edwards in his private notebooks emphasized similarities rather than differences between religions. He viewed non-Christian religions not as netherworlds of unmixed darkness but as traditions once visited by and still retaining traces of the light of revelation. Indeed, he believed that some non-Christians possessed more religious truth and saw more clearly the outlines of virtue than many of the saints of the Old Testament.

At the same time, Edwards was not really open to other religions as viable, living faiths. He was interested in them primarily because they provided both ammunition for his battles with deism and support for other polemical claims made on behalf of Reformed Christianity. Perhaps because of these restricted purposes, Edwards labored under some serious misunderstanding of these faiths. Despite having seen a copy of the Qur'an, for example, he followed his era's conventional use of the term "Mahometan," as if Muslims worshiped Muhammad. In his voluminous writing on Greek and Roman thought, he followed his sources rather uncritically—often ignoring the contexts of the passages he cites, interpreting them in a literalist fashion that almost certainly was not the original intent.

Edward Said has observed that Westerners have gotten away with such misrepresentations because they had so little contact with religious others. Because Flaubert's Egyptian courtesan never spoke, Said points out, Flaubert felt free to describe her as "typically Oriental."[28] But what if the courtesan had the freedom to define herself? Until he moved to Stockbridge in the last years of his life, Edwards had probably never had any serious personal encounters with "heathen." Perhaps if he had, he would have read his sources more critically. Then again, the private notebooks of his final years may reflect just this kind of encounter. For it is in these notebooks that he reflects most generously and expansively on the religious state of the heathen. This was also the period that, for the first time in his life, he came to know and converse with people who had grown up outside Christendom. The result—as a reading of these massive notebooks demonstrates—is a remark-

---

26. For some of the recent literature that has unearthed this seventeenth- and eighteenth-century web of cultural connections, see David Hackett Fischer, *Albion's Seed: Four British Folkways in America* (Oxford, 1989); David Cressy, *Coming Over: Migration and Communication between England and New England in the Seventeenth Century* (New York, 1987); Jack P. Greene, *Pursuits of Happiness: The Social Development of Early Modern British Colonies and the Formation of American Culture* (Chapel Hill, N.C., 1988); Francis J. Bremer, ed., *Puritanism: Transatlantic Perspectives on a Seventeenth-Century Anglo-American Faith* (Boston, 1993); and Michael J. Crawford, *Seasons of Grace: Colonial New England's Revival Tradition in Its British Context* (New York, 1991).

27. Walker, "Orpheus," 120; Walker, *Ancient Theology*, 228–30. The *prisca theologia* is an apologetic tradition dating back to the early church that claimed Jewish sources for the best of classical culture. Chapter 5 describes this tradition in some detail.

28. Said, *Orientalism*, 6.

able intellectual drama. Colonial America's greatest mind, of whom it has often been said that his thinking changed little over the course of his career, seems to have been a work in process on the question of the world religions. In the midst of the enormous scribbled entries on revelation and truth among "the heathen wise men," one detects a determined struggle to come to terms with truth found in unexpected places. Edwards seems to have tossed and turned, as it were, trying to reconcile those truths with a theological tradition that had relegated other traditions to irrelevance. The result was a remarkable achievement for Christian theology in its struggle with Enlightenment religion: Edwards found a way to acknowledge genuine religious truth outside the Judeo-Christian world while at the same time holding fast to a particular and historical revelation. In the process, Edwards opened his own intricate system to the possibility of salvation for those outside the Christian church. Like Barth on universalism, Edwards could deny that he ever explicitly conceded what until then was heterodox while nevertheless constructing a system that could permit its entrance.[29]

In short, this book is the result of a discovery that rather startled me. My forays into his private notebooks, and then my explorations of his published works guided by what I had uncovered in the notebooks, led me to an Edwards whom I and other scholars had never met—a colonial theologian fascinated by religions and worlds far removed from his own. I think the result is a new perspective on the thinking of America's greatest theologian. At the same time, this Edwards opens a window on how Christians of another era responded to a scandal of particularity not unlike the one that bedevils their successors at the dawn of the twenty-first century.

---

29. Barth denied universalism but created a theological system that permitted hope for it. Similarly, Edwards usually referred to the heathen as damned, but at the same time he opened theological space for the possibility that some could be saved.

I

THE CHALLENGE

1

DEISTS AND THE SCANDAL OF PARTICULARITY

For some time now, historians have regarded the first half of the eighteenth century in England as an "Age of Reason"[1] that fairly overwhelmed visions of faith inherited from the Reformation and before. While there is much to be said for this perspective, we permit it to mislead us if we overlook the fact that even the shrillest arguments of the time for the supremacy of reason were grounded in a religious view of reality. A recent historian has noted that John Locke bequeathed to the age "an almost pathological fear of religious emotion."[2] True enough, but Locke also assumed the divine origin of the New Testament, and all who claimed his mantle—which includes nearly everyone who published on religion and philosophy in the eighteenth century—were as committed as he to the principle that the stability of society depends on religion.

Indeed, the early eighteenth century in England can be viewed as a grand debate over what it means for God to be just and good. Although polemicists not infrequently branded their opponents as atheists, none accepted the name. All publicly affirmed the existence of God but disputed his nature. This was an age in which secularism as a principle of separation of church and state began to emerge, but it was not a secular age in the sense that God was excluded from public discussion. In fact, the most celebrated debates were contests between rival portraits of God, all of which claimed for the deity justice and goodness. The real disagreement was not about whether or not God existed, or whether or not belief in his

---

1. See, for example, Cragg, *The Church and the Age of Reason*, and Mossner, *Bishop Butler*.
2. Cragg, *Reason and Authority*, 10.

existence was essential to a healthy polity (nearly all agreed that it was), but about the nature of goodness and justice—and, consequently, the nature of God.

Although the English debate about goodness and justice revealed many disparate positions and parties (e.g., orthodox of various stripes, latitudinarian, deist, Arminian, Arian, and Socinian), most arguments were based on one of two convictions. The first assumed that one could start with abstract reason and then proceed from an abstract ("self-evident") principle to conclusions about goodness, justice, and God (in that order). One could, for instance, assume that God is a perfect being and that a perfect being does not need compensation for wrongs done to it to be happy. Hence the satisfaction theory of the atonement makes no sense. Since the deity is perfect, it does not need its wrath "satisfied" by sacrifice in order to forgive wrongs done to it.

The second conviction (perhaps "basic assumption" is more accurate) was that one should start with traditions rooted in the testimony of preeminent religious progenitors. Recent historical accounts of this period have usually called this an appeal to "authority."[3] Those who made this appeal did indeed refer to "authority," but usually only because they considered such an appeal reasonable. But unlike those of the first conviction for whom "reasonable" meant starting with abstract principles, these thinkers considered authority (the Bible and orthodox tradition) reasonable because it was derived, they believed, from apostolic experience.

The two most prominent proponents of these convictions were the deists,[4] who held to the the first conviction, and those calling themselves orthodox,[5] who held to the second. These groups, and their positions, best isolated what was at stake in the eighteenth-century English debates over religion. For it was finally a debate about the relationship between "natural religion" based on abstract principles and "revealed religion," said to be rooted in the religious experience recorded in Scripture.

Jonathan Edwards joined this debate, which was at the center of the English Enlightenment and profoundly influenced both the French and German Enlightenments,[6] far more actively and with far more urgency than scholars have acknowledged. Students of Edwards typically consider Arminianism to have been his principal nemesis, and not without reason. There were many more Arminians than deists in eighteenth-century New England, and the Northampton theologian often attacked them in his writings. But though three thousand miles away, Edwards followed keenly the intellectual conversation in England, where in the first three

---

3. For example, Cragg in *Reason and Authority*.

4. For secondary treatments of deism, see Cragg, *Reason and Authority*; Sullivan, *John Toland and the Deist Controversy*; Byrne, *Natural Religion*; Harrison, *"Religion" and the Religions*; Champion, *The Pillars of Priestcraft Shaken*; Mossner, *Bishop Butler*; Daniel, *John Toland*; Redwood, *Reason, Ridicule and Religion*; Aldridge, "Deism," in Stein, *The Encyclopedia of Unbelief*; Stephen, *English Thought*; and Manuel, *The Changing of the Gods*, esp. 5–129. The best contemporary account is John Leland's *View of the Principal Deistical Writers*.

5. Admittedly, there are problems with this term, because like "deism" it was a catch-all that subsumed many disparate positions. The differences among the orthodox were far greater than those which separated its followers from their enemies. I use the word to refer to those who saw the need for revelation beyond reason and accepted the Bible as divinely inspired. See Stephen, *English Thought*, 91.

6. See Introduction, note 3.

decades of the century deism kept orthodoxy on the defensive. Edwards soon realized that deism was a more dangerous enemy than Arminianism, if only because it was a ruthless application of Arminian presuppositions and therefore a more radical attack on the Reformed tradition.[7]

The deists were more consistent in their use of the abstract principles that inspired Arminians, Socinians, and Arians. The last three groups used those principles to question traditional claims deriving from Scripture, but only the deists attacked the validity of Scripture itself. Hence deism, by Edwards's lights, was the terminus of all roads that departed from Reformed orthodoxy and meandered through the way stations of latitudinarianism, Arianism, and especially Arminianism. Edwards believed that New England in the first half of the century was infested with Arminians and feared that if they remained unchecked, his "land" would be overwhelmed by the deist catastrophe that had already "overrun" England. That would mean a denial "of the whole Christian religion."[8]

Because this book is an account of how Edwards responded to problems posed by deists, we will spend the next four chapters laying out the basic outlines of the deist challenge and Edwards's most direct responses to it. If at times protracted, this format is nevertheless necessary for two reasons: first, because only a comprehensive tracing can adequately communicate the eighteenth century's most incisive critique of the radical Enlightenment; and second, because it is only through an ordered exposition of both the deist and Edwardsean projects that we can appreciate the full force of each.

The Historiographical Problem

But first, a detour into historiography. The "deists" did not all think alike, and so historians have debated what "deism" really was. So while I reify the term throughout this book, I do so with the realization that there are problems in doing so. The first problem is that some of those I call deists rejected the label. Charles Blount (1654–93) and John Toland (1670–1722), for example, claimed to be fighting deism, and Anthony Collins (1676–1729) never confessed to being a deist. William Wollaston (1660–1724) insisted that his intent was not to undermine true "revealed religion" but only to "pave the way for its reception."[9]

No doubt this was because "deist" was something of a dirty word, which polemicists of the period used as a weapon against their opponents. It had the effect

---

7. Margaret Jacob has also called the deists the radicals of the Enlightenment, but primarily for political and metaphysical reasons—they advocated republicanism and (some, like Toland) pantheism or materialism in contrast to the "moderate Newtonian" Enlightenment that supported the political status quo and held to a distinction between matter and spirit. Although I focus on the *theological* radicalism of the deists, Jacob and I agree that they represent the sharpest attack on Christian orthodoxy during the English Enlightenment. See Jacob, *Radical Enlightenment*, 22, 143–44, 263.
8. HWR, 432.
9. Charles Blount, *An Appendix Concerning the Modern Brachmins in the Indies*, in *Miscellaneous Works*, 87; Toland, CNM, 12; Sullivan, *John Toland and the Deist Controversy*, 215; Wollaston, *Religion of Nature Delineated*.

in the eighteenth century that "nazi" and "fundamentalist" have at the end of the twentieth—branding their recipients as enemies of humanity. The word was coined by Pierre Viret in 1564 to designate anything that fell between atheism and Christianity and was used with similar imprecision in the early eighteenth century.[10]

Another problem is that there was minimal intellectual coherence among those I call deist. The Arian Samuel Clarke (1675–1729) recognized this even at the time, distinguishing four different sorts of so-called deists: those who believed in a clockmaker God who created the world but left it to run on its own, those who believed in the Creation and general providence but no moral government (the notion that God rewards good and punishes evil), those who believed in God as creator and moral governor but not in the immortality of the soul, and those who believed in the Creation and moral government but not in special revelation (in the Bible).[11]

The disparity among these thinkers is even more apparent to the historian. Some, such as Toland, Thomas Chubb (1679–1746), and the earl of Shaftesbury, doubted the immortality of the soul and a future existence,[12] but others like Blount and Wollaston considered it essential.[13] Matthew Tindal (1657–1733) believed that future retribution was fundamental to faith, while Lord Bolingbroke (1678–1751) thought it dubious. Most believed that morals could be deduced from abstract principles of reason, but Shaftesbury and Bolingbroke laughed at this notion. Shaftesbury and Tindal were convinced that humans are innately benevolent, and Bolingbroke was just as convinced that they are controlled by self-love.[14] Toland was a materialist[15] and pantheist,[16] whereas Tindal and most other deists believed in souls distinct from God. Most of these thinkers also believed in free will, but Collins denied it. Finally, while deism is commonly defined today as a denial of providence, some of those in this intellectual family steadfastly affirmed the role of providence in human affairs.[17]

It is no wonder that historians refer to the "elusiveness of deism," preferring to call it a temper rather than a creed, and suggesting that it is a label of covenience for the historian of ideas rather than a precise term of analysis.[18] But this has not stopped them from stipulating working definitions for their historiographical purposes. Peter Byrne, for instance, has defined deism as the negative criticism of claims for the

---

10. Sullivan, *John Toland and the Deist Controversy*, 12.

11. Clarke, *Discourse*, 12–25.

12. Daniel, *John Toland*, 97; Leland, *Principal Deistical Writers*, 198, 66.

13. Charles Blount, *Anima Mundi; or, an Historical Narrative of the Opinions of the Ancients Concerning Man's Soul After This Life According to Unenlightened Nature*, in *Miscellaneous Works*, 120; Wollaston, *Religion of Nature Delineated*, 193ff.

14. Leland, *Principal Deistical Writers*, 243; Stromberg, *Religious Liberalism*, 66.

15. See Toland, *Two Essays*.

16. Toland, *Pantheisticon*, 16–17.

17. Sullivan, *John Toland and the Deist Controversy*, 259; Wollaston, *Religion of Nature Delineated*, 93, 96–100.

18. Sullivan, *John Toland and the Deist Controversy*, 205–34; Cragg, *Reason and Authority*, 66; Byrne, *Natural Religion*, xiii.

uniqueness and divine character of any revealed religion (including Christianity) and the positive affirmation that a religion based on reason and nature is sufficient for salvation. Robert E. Sullivan has taken a very similar approach.[19]

For the sake of greater precision, I add the following methodological component: all of these thinkers rejected a simple appeal to authority precisely because their own understanding of what is reasonable—and of course they differed on what accords with the "common sense" of reason—was their final test of what is divine. That is, the location of a doctrine in the Bible was not reason enough for it to be declared divine; it had to meet the approval of what their eighteenth-century reason considered acceptable.

Furthermore, for all the thinkers I call deists the end or purpose of religion is morality. Not only is the function of true religion moral and social—that is, its role is to show the way to a good society—but in its very essence religion is morality. Some denied the validity, others just the importance, of what might be called the doxological character of religion, or its capacity for worship of the divine, and for that matter its mystical dimension as well.

The Origins of Deism

The first impulses that later became what we recognize as a deist sensibility emerged as a reaction to the religious wars of the seventeenth century. Lord Herbert of Cherbury, who is widely regarded as a progenitor of deism, proposed his five "common notions," which he hoped would help bring the wars of religion to a close, particularly France's war against her Protestants.[20] He and his successors believed that appeals to religious authority, which emphasized differences rather than similarities among religions, were singularly responsible for the intellectual and political violence of the seventeenth century. There was a new determination "in the air" to rely on evidence from nature and reason rather than tradition because all human beings were thought to share a common nature and reason. Lord Herbert and those influenced by him cautiously hoped that a religion of reason, common to all, could orient future political activity toward the attainment of peace in an enlightened society.[21]

For other discussions of the definition of deism, see Walsh, "A Note on the Meaning of 'Deism'"; Gay, *Deism*, 12–13; Carabelli, "Deismo inglese e dintoni"; Winnett, "Were the Deists 'Deists'?"; Lovejoy, "The Parallel of Deism and Classicism," 78 and passim; Stromberg, "Lovejoy's 'Parallel' Reconsidered," 383–84; Stromberg, *Religious Liberalism*, 52–69; Wessell, "Rejoinder to Stromberg's 'Reconsideration'"; Sullivan, *John Toland and the Deist Controversy*, 205–34; and Byrne, *Natural Religion*, xiii–xiv.

For additional literature that sheds light on the deists' place within the Enlightenment, see Goldmann, *Philosophy of the Enlightenment*; Crocker, *Age of Crisis*; and Jacob, "John Toland and the Newtonian Enlightenment," esp. 329–31.

19. Byrne, *Natural Religion*, xiv; Sullivan, *John Toland and the Deist Controversy*, 213–15.
20. Herbert, *On Truth in Distinction from Revelation*, 58–60.
21. Cragg, *Reason and Authority*, 2; Daniel, *John Toland*, 4.

Newton's new science and Locke's new philosophy encouraged the hope that truth could be established by the enlightened mind emancipated from the shackles of tradition. Locke's emphasis on reason as a clear and distinct idea may have helped initiate a reaction against mystery in religion, and his linkage of truth in religion to the generality of human knowledge[22] probably encouraged deists who winnowed truth from error in the Bible by exposing its content to their notions of reason. Progress in a variety of disciplines seemed to provide hope that life and society could be brought under human control: Newton had brought a rational and simple order to physics; Pufendorf and Montesquieu had done the same to law; Richard Simon to biblical criticism; Locke to philosophy; and Shaftesbury would later do something similar to ethics.[23]

The Cambridge Platonists (of the seventeenth century) had encouraged a complementary hope that human reason can recognize and appropriate divine truth.[24] Ralph Cudworth, whose *True Intellectual System of the Universe* (1678) was "the longest and the most revered book of the seventeenth century dedicated to the refutation of irreligion,"[25] claimed to have proved that the "Gentiles and Pagans, however Polytheists and idolaters, were not unacquainted with knowledge of the true God."[26] Benjamin Whichcote proclaimed that reason is the divine governor of human life and the "very voice of God." Henry More pronounced that reason connects human beings to God. While Protestants in the sixteenth and early seventeenth centuries had interpreted Proverbs 20:27 ("The spirit of man is the candle of the Lord") as emphasizing the inadequacy of natural knowledge, the Cambridge Platonists used this passage to teach the opposite: human reason is, as More put it, "divine sagacity."[27]

The Cambridge Platonists also brought morality to center stage, in reaction to nearly a century of wars over doctrine. They linked morality to religion by making a moral disposition a precondition for true spiritual experience: to see the divine, they preached, one had to be an "intensely loving soul." Reason, they said, is enlivened and enlightened by a moral disposition, and without a moral life there is no insight into divine truth.[28]

Deists secularized the Cambridge Platonists' view of religion. For the former, reason was not a mode of revelation, as it was for the Cambridge dons, but a le-

---

22. Locke wrote in his *Essay Concerning Human Understanding* that "analogy is the great rule of probability," meaning the analogy between reports of an event by human testimony and our "common experience" of "the ordinary course of things." Locke said miracle stories are an exception to this rule, but deists denied his claim that some of them were "well-attested." *Essay*, 4.16.12–13.

23. Stromberg, 18; Byrne, *Natural Religion*, 97; Cragg, *Reason and Authority*, 2–4, 19–20.

24. In other words, reason has "an intuitive power as well as a discursive one." Beiser, *The Sovereignty of Reason*, 165.

25. Redwood, *Reason, Ridicule and Religion*, 51. For an excellent introduction to the Cambridge Platonists, see Howe, "Cambridge Platonists." See also Beiser, *The Sovereignty of Reason*, chap. 4; Cragg, *Cambridge Platonists*; Patrides, *Cambridge Platonists*; Cole, *Light and Enlightenment*; and De Boer, *Theory of Knowledge*.

26. Cudworth, *True Intellectual System*, 623.

27. Cragg, *Cambridge Platonists*, 17; Patrides, *Cambridge Platonists*, 10.

28. Patrides, *Cambridge Platonists*, 13; Cragg, *Cambridge Platonists*, 19.

gitimate source of knowledge in itself. The Platonists' reasonableness of religion became the rationalism of the deists. Deists also inverted the role of morality. While for the Platonists morality was a precondition for experiencing the divine, the deists insisted that God fit their ideas of what is moral. The focus of religion was no longer on divine being but on moral rules contained in the human subject.

It wasn't only the Cambridge Platonist focus on reason and morality that prepared the way for deism. There were other factors as well. Ecclesiastical corruption, for instance, exasperated many: Vicar of Brayism (changing one's principles to suit the times),[29] pluralism, moral turpitude, general crass neglect of spiritual needs in the parish, the establishment of the Scottish Kirk (which led to a loss of prestige for the Church of England), and relaxation of church discipline. When, in addition, clergymen were given to political wrangling and theological disputation, deists found a ready audience for their denunciations of "priestcraft."[30]

What Jürgen Habermas has called the emerging "public sphere" of the early eighteenth century was another factor in the rise of deism.[31] With the decline of the absolute monarchy in Western Europe, and the simultaneous diminution of its bureaucratic control over social and religious life, "individuals increasingly came to identify themselves as active subjects . . . [whose] own enterprise and ability mattered."[32] Scientists, writers, and other "men of wit and fashion" gathered in coffeehouses, inns, taverns, beer houses and brandy shops to discuss ideas and nearly invariably engage in theological and political debate. Religious and political questions, to be avoided at dinner and at church, were to be discussed primarily in coffeehouses, England's most popular locus for this new public culture.[33]

Stephen Daniel has shown that John Toland (the best-known early deist) preferred the irreverent environment of the coffeehouse to discuss and develop his ideas. Here his anticlericalism and advocacy of natural religion were tolerated. And here, with "men of taste and policy," public opinion could be shaped apart from the narrow strictures of official Anglicanism.[34]

Political control, then, was another factor. John C. Biddle makes a persuasive argument that behind Locke's epistemology lay the insistence on persons' fundamental right to understand the truth for themselves. According to Biddle, Locke feared that without that autonomy people would be susceptible to political control by Roman Catholics using implicit faith and papal infallibility and enthusiasts

---

29. The term comes from a popular song that told of a "vivacious vicar" who held the benefice from the reign of Henry VIII to that of Elizabeth I, and "was twice a Papist and twice a Protestant" (OED, 1971, s.v. "vicar").

30. Mossner, *Bishop Butler*, 25.

31. Habermas, *Structural Transformation*.

32. Kramnick, *Republicanism and Bourgeois Radicalism*, 8.

33. Daniel, *John Toland*, 145. See also Gerald Cragg, *From Puritanism to the Age of Reason*, 138–47; Lillywhite, *London Coffeehouses*; Ashton, *Social Life in the Reign of Queen Anne*; and Becker, *Emergence of Civil Society*.

34. Daniel, *John Toland*, 145–46. Margaret C. Jacob has recently shown the connection between coffeehouses, Masonry and the rise of republicanism, which she calls the "radical Enlightenment." Jacob, *The Radical Enlightenment*.

using immediate inspiration. This was why Locke insisted that reason can and must judge the content or parts of a revelation as well as the whole.[35]

Daniel argues that for Toland, self-determination was a fundamental human value, which religious mystery only undermined. J.A.I. Champion makes the same case for the deist movement as a whole—it was more interested in challenging the church's monopoly on truth than in repudiating any set of doctrines. Deist writers attacked what they perceived to be an unjust distribution of authority in society, so that the heart of their project was not irreligion but anticlericalism. Their radicalism consisted in an attempt not to destroy religion but to deprive a corrupt priesthood of all independent political power.[36] I think Champion overstates his case and underestimates the gravity of the deists' theological arguments. But his book does demonstrate that the political situation helps explain both the origin of deist thinking and its enthusiastic reception in some quarters.

Yet there is still another factor that has not received due attention from scholars, and which helps us understand Edwards's approach to other religions. This is the fact that some of the most important proto-deists and deists were reacting against what theologians now call the scandal of particularity—the notion, galling to many, that God revealed himself to particular peoples at particular times rather than to all human beings from the very beginning.[37] Herbert of Cherbury confessed at the beginning of his *Antient Religion of the Gentiles* that he wrote his treatise because of the way "very many Fathers of the Church" had interpreted particularity. They had concluded, he wrote, that "the far greatest part of Mankind must be inevitably sentenced to Eternal Punishment. This appearing to me too rigid and severe to be consistent with the attributes of the *Most Great and Good God*." This was abhorrent to one who was familiar with many reports, coming out of the East in the preceding century, of "heathen" who lived "most innocent and commendable Lives." Therefore he was confirmed in what he had earlier argued in his *On Truth* (1624): that "only that which is universal can be true."[38]

This was the first of many attacks on received doctrines that Herbert and his disciples made on the basis of new reports about the heathen and appreciation for their moral virtues.[39] As Leslie Stephen put it, deists kept taunting Christians with the existence of 300 million Chinese whose case could not be squared with Christian theories. The old formula "quod ubique quod semper quod ab omnibus creditum est" [that which has been believed everywhere, at all times, and by every-

---

35. John C. Biddle, "Locke's Critique of Innate Principles and Toland's Deism," in Yolton, *Philosophy, Religion and Science*, 413–17.

36. Daniel, *John Toland*, 5, 18–19; Champion, *The Pillars of Priestcraft Shaken*, 9, 11, 18, 24, 229–30.

37. Originally, as first posed by Lessing, the scandal was the unreliability of truths derived from history. He was convinced that the accidental truths of history can never prove the necessary truths of reason—that there was an "ugly, great ditch" between reason and history that could not be jumped; Chadwick, *Lessings's Theological Writings*, 51–56. For a review of the development of this scandal since Lessing, including Christian responses, see Marshall, *Christology in Conflict*, 1–14.

38. Herbert, *Antient Religion of the Gentiles*, 1–2, 4, 77.

39. For a review of this literature, see Lach, *Asia in the Making of Europe*, 3:549–97.

one, is true doctrine]⁴⁰ was now applied with new power, but this time to undermine orthodoxy. Blount, for example, used the Jesuit travelogues from China to rail against "particular religions" and stipulate that revealed religion cannot be true because it was not received by all human beings. Toland insisted that the orthodox God is not good if he requires some to believe what they have never heard. Collins protested the idea that God has favorite nations and peoples without considering their merits. This, he complained, puts some at a great disadvantage. He pointed out that other religions have different scriptures with different notions of God—presumably ones that don't make God out to be so arbitrary.⁴¹

Matthew Tindal protests against Christian particularity on the title page of his great work, *Christianity as Old as the Creation* (1730). Under the title he inscribed Acts 10:34–35, which was a favorite proof-text for deists: "God is no Respecter of Persons; but in every Nation, he that feareth him, and worketh Righteousness, is accepted with him." The burden of his argument in this work is that since God always wanted all human beings to know his truth, he must have given them the means to do so from the very beginning of time. What is finally important, then, is the sincerity of the heart, which notion "place[s] all Religions on a Level." For God to present a revelation some time after the Creation would be "unfair" to those who had lived before that time. And the traditional Christian notion of revelation through Jesus Christ is unfair to "the greatest part of mankind." If this God is good only to a few, then he is "cruel and unmerciful." Chubb makes a similar argument in his *Discourse Concerning Reason*. If reason were defective, as the orthodox claim, and God gave revelation to remedy the defect, then he should have given this revelation to the whole species. But since he did not, this God cannot be the true God, who would have revealed himself equally to all.⁴²

The scandal of particularity, then, was an important stimulus to deism. It was a principal reason why they judged the orthodox God to be a monster in whom they could not believe. And the religions of non-Christians, of which they learned from sixteenth- and seventeenth-century reports coming out of voyages to the New World and the East, provided the background against which the God of orthodoxy stood out as arbitrary and therefore cruel.⁴³ These reports portrayed millions of non-Christians as religious souls who often seemed more moral than their European contemporaries. The idea that they could be consigned to an eternal hell simply because they had never heard the gospel was too much for deists and many others to accept. The true God, they concluded, must be of a different sort from

---

40. This was known as the "Vincentian canon," named after Vincent of Lérins, an early fifth-century opponent of Augustinianism. OED, 2d ed. (1983).

41. Stephen, *English Thought*, 81–83; Blount, *Modern Brachmins*, 81, 89, 198 (also see his *Great Is Diana of the Ephesians*, 3, in *Miscellaneous Works*); CNM, 134; DF, 39, 52–53.

42. CAO, 4, 2, 49, 250, 401; see also 135, 196, 374–75, 399; DCR, 12–13, and passim.

43. This is not to say, of course, that it was only religious knowledge that shaped understanding of other peoples and their religions. For a fascinating look at the role played by Europeans' understanding of their own technological superiority in shaping their attitudes toward other peoples, see Adas, *Machines as the Measure of Men*.

what tradition had delivered. And his revelation could not have been restricted to a chosen few.

The Nature of Deism

The God who restricted salvation to a chosen few was especially associated by deists with the "partial and arbitrary" God of Calvinism. Herbert and his successors were enraged by the orthodox generally, and the Calvinists in particular, who seemed to promise eternal damnation to those who disagreed with them. Herbert himself raged that the "peremptory decrees" of Calvinism impugn God's justice (since they deny the means of salvation to so many) and goodness (since they imply a god that created people only to damn them, without their knowledge and against their will). Blount agreed that Calvinism denies God's goodness, and Toland, who tried to rehabilitate Druidism and showed interest in continental freemasonry, nevertheless inveighed against Christian mysteries, of which the decrees of Calvinism were the most notorious.[44]

Deists also rejected the notion of a mediator (Christ) who atoned for human sin—a doctrine shared by Calvinists and other orthodox as well. Blount was the first to sound the battle cry. "Miserii cordia Dei sufficiens Justitia suae" [The compassion of God's heart is sufficient to satisfy his justice], he announced. If God had to appoint a mediator, he must have already wanted reconciliation. And if that was true, then why did he not grant reconciliation without a mediator? The notion of mediation only detracts from God's infinite mercy and smacks of ancient heathen sacrifices.[45]

All the deists were revolted by the satisfaction theory of the atonement, which requires sacrifice by a mediator to win God's forgiveness. Thomas Chubb, echoing many, stated peremptorily that repentance and reformation are the proper grounds of forgiveness. Tindal added that if God required reparation or satisfaction, that would imply that he could be hurt. But since God is perfectly happy in himself, and the capacity to be hurt implies weakness and imperfection, which God cannot have, God cannot require either reparation or satisfaction.[46]

The rejection of particularity also, and perhaps more tellingly, implied the rejection of a mediator. To accept a mediator would have meant accepting orthodoxy's claim to Jesus as Mediator. But this was impossible because Jesus was a latecomer to the history of humanity. To accept a central role for him would have opened the door to orthodoxy's claim that some times and places were privileged over others. It also would have opened the door to the claim that the Jews were the Chosen People, an idea that deism rejected with remarkable vehemence.

---

44. CAO, 409; Herbert, *Antient Religion of the Gentiles*, 58, 4–5; see also Herbert, *De Religione Laici*, 119; Blount, *Miscellaneous Works*, 198; Sullivan, *John Toland and the Deist Controversy*, 202; CNM, 89.
45. Blount, *Miscellaneous Works*, 89; Blount, *Great Is Diana*, 14–15.
46. DCR, 21; CAO, 38–39.

As Frank E. Manuel puts it, for deists Judaism was worthless. The religion was an outlandish example of the heavy encrustation of man-made ceremonials and priestly imposture. One of the cruelest religions ever, its miracles were frauds and its prophecies superstitious. In deist hands, Jews were transformed from a nation with a special religious identity to an isolated and irrelevant remnant of barbarian tribes, who still preserved their bizarre and fanatical customs. They worshiped dead, soul-less animals rather than a spiritual divinity, and their sacrificial rites were like those of the natives of India, America, and West Africa.[47]

Thomas Chubb, for example, said that Jewish law was completely unrelated to the gospel and argued that the preservation of the Jews over the centuries was not miraculous because they were told by their leaders not to mix with the Gentiles. Their belief that they were God's chosen people was egotistical, and arbitrariness (a word always used by deists with contempt) was the Jewish principle. Anthony Collins called the Jews an "illiterate, Barbarous and Ridiculous People," whom God picked only to show his patience with the world. Thomas Morgan (d. 1743) explained that the Jewish god was a cheat and an idol, and the Jewish religion a foul source of everything in Christianity that is contrary to a pure, simple, and reasonable natural religion. The deist newspaper *The Independent Whig* broadcast to its readers that Moses gave the Jews a "Law of Bondage . . . [with] statutes which were not good, and Judgments by which they could not live."[48]

According to Manuel, the deists were the leaders of the Enlightenment's radical re-evaluation of Judaism. Voltaire learned from them when he was in London in the 1720s. He eventually became obsessed with anti-Semitism, always calling them the "execrable Jews," and once wrote that a Jew is someone who should have engraved on his forehead, "Fit to be hanged." His *philosophe* confreres attacked the Hebrew Bible with zeal, reasoning that if Christianity is as old as the Creation, there was no need for Judaism. It simply serves as an illustration of "detested priestcraft."[49] In the mid- and late-eighteenth century the Holbachians still made it a practice to adapt the deist writings of the early eighteenth century for their own anticlerical and anti-Semitic crusades.[50] Manuel concludes that the emergence of anti-Semitism as a "scientific doctrine" at the end of the nineteenth century can be traced to these eighteenth-century sources.[51]

Among other reasons, Jews were considered execrable because their religion was not accessible to all. But the moral dictates of reason, supposedly inscribed on every human mind, *were*. And for deists morality was the essence of religion. As William Wollaston put it, "By *religion* I mean nothing else but our obligation to

---

47. Manuel, *The Broken Staff*, 191, 179.

48. *AF*, 111, 161–67, 166–67, 203, 307, 314; *DF*, 121; Morgan, *The Moral Philosopher*, 19; Leland, *Principal Deistical Writers*, 147; *IW*, 1:328.

49. Manuel, *The Changing of the Gods*, 112–16.

50. The Holbachians were disciples of Baron d'Holbach, a militant atheist who opposed both Christianity and deism (because it was theistic). "He and his aristocratic atheist circle" were influential in Paris in the 1760s. May, *Enlightenment in America*, 118.

51. Manuel, *The Broken Staff*, 166.

do (under which I comprehend acts both of body and mind. I say *to do*) what ought not to be omitted, and to *forbear* what ought not to be done."[52]

Although Locke never identified religion with morality in simplistic fashion, his presentation of true religion in *The Reasonableness of Christianity* could have encouraged deists to do so. As Leslie Stephen observed, for Locke Christianity is in effect a new promulgation of the moral law. It is a great legislative reform, enforced by sanctions previously unavailable, thus providing new authority for the dictates of reason about the moral life. Christ's purpose was to teach the old moral law with new force; he alone possessed the authority to teach and enforce it, since reason takes too long and is too intricate for the masses to follow. It was Locke who started the suspicion that Christ was unnecessary for salvation, for not only does he avoid in *The Reasonableness of Christianity* any mention of atonement, but he asserts outright that reason alone teaches those who will listen that repentance is sufficient for reconciliation with God.[53]

Tindal, who was even less subtle than Locke, states plainly that "the Religion of Nature consists in observing those things, which our Reason . . . demonstrates to be our duty." For Chubb as well, religion was little more than morality, good only for its social function. Even the Arian Samuel Clarke believed that "Moral Virtue is the Foundation and the Sum, the Essence and the life of all true Religion." For Clarke and the deists who often quoted him, moral law outweighed all creeds because religion at its heart was simply a set of moral dictates.[54]

These moral dictates are known, for most deists, a priori. Herbert of Cherbury's famous five common notions (the existence of God; God ought to be worshiped; the necessity of moral virtue and piety; sin is to be expiated by repentance; there is reward and punishment after death) were declared by Herbert to be known by all human beings by a priori intuition. Cherbury's disciple Blount had similar confidence that morality can be known apart from tradition or society. Reason, he said, is the "first revelation of God . . . full of its own light shining always in us." Toland assumed that we can know a priori right from wrong before we read the Bible and use that knowledge to separate true from false in Scripture. For Tindal as well, we can know the will of God "antecedent" to going to external revelation by considering the "invariable perfections of God."[55]

Tindal's notion of "invariable perfections" was a commonplace for deists. God and true religion were thought to be absolutely invariable since the beginning of history. In this sense, deism was a-historical. Deists were adamant about the static nature of both God and religion because they rejected particularity. Since they had decided a priori that revelation must have always been available equally to all human beings from the very beginning of history, and that to admit anything otherwise

---

52. Wollaston, *Religion of Nature Delineated*, 25.
53. Locke, *The Reasonableness of Christianity*, 163–81; Stephen, *English Thought*, 98–100; Locke, *The Reasonableness of Christianity*, 162–63.
54. *CAO*, 13; *AF*, 370–71, 72–73; Clarke, *Discourse*, 90.
55. Herbert, *On Truth in Distinction from Revelation*, 56; Blount, *Miscellaneous Works*, 92; *CNM*, 157ff.; *CAO*, 66. Chubb taught that God is known to be wise and good independently of revelation because every person's heart contains the divine law; *AF*, 6; *DCR*, 15. See also Collins, *Discourse*, 99.

would be to conceive an unjust and malevolent God, they found it necessary to insist on the unchanging character of both true religion and its deity.⁵⁶

This is the thinking that undergirds Tindal's *Christianity as Old as the Creation; or, the Gospel, a Republication of the Religion of Nature*. The second quotation on the title page is from Grotius: "Est autem jus naturale adeo immutabile, ut ne quidem a Deo mutari potest" [There exists a natural law that is absolutely unchanging, so that not even by God can it be changed].⁵⁷ In the opening pages Tindal asserts that God's will is "unchangeable." Therefore revelation, which may have come later, can be no different from natural religion. The point in contention is whether "a Religion absolutely perfect [can] admit of any Alteration; or be capable of Addition, or Domination . . . Can Revelation, I say, add anything to a Religion thus absolutely perfect, universal and immutable?"⁵⁸

Tindal answered his question in the negative by appealing to God's perfection. Any change would imply imperfection: "The Religion of Nature was so perfect it needs no addition." Since God is not arbitrary, and his perfection precludes change, Tindal concluded that true religion is the same in all times and all places. Otherwise God would not have given all humans equal means of knowing the truth, and to admit otherwise would diminish God's justice and goodness.⁵⁹

For the deists, then, true religion has no history and little or no relation to culture. All religions connected to history are necessarily suspect and products of an arbitrary god who is not God. All changes in history are unrelated to religious or even philosophical truth. As Ernest Campbell Mossner has observed, in the Age of Reason nature stood for uniformity, and history was relatively unimportant. It was only in the Romantic period that nature would come to represent diversity and history become the key to knowledge.⁶⁰

Since moral truth has always been known to human beings, and no religious doctrine has been known universally, deists commonly averred that sincerity is all that matters for divine acceptance. Only the sincerity of an honest heart is required for proof of devotion to truth. As John Trenchard and Thomas Gordon expressed it in the *Independent Whig*, "God puts upon no Man the Aegyptian task of making Bricks without straw; nor requires anything which you cannot perform . . . So that the Gentiles themselves are to be judged by their Sincerity, and not condemned for involuntary errors."⁶¹

Therefore differences of religious opinion are no longer germane to the final estimation of things. Let a person be orthodox, heterodox, or heretic—it does not matter so long as one is sincere in one's beliefs: "Every honest man will be saved, let his Opinion and Mistakes be what they will." According to Tindal, this doctrine of sincerity rendered all religions relative. None was better than another at

---

56. CNM, xiii, 63; AF, 378.
57. Grotius, *De Jure Belli et Pacis*, 1.1, c.1, S.101.5.
58. CAO, 2–4.
59. Ibid., 69.
60. Mossner, *Bishop Butler*, 25.
61. IW, 1:334.

reconciling the individual to the divine. For the key to religious success was not doctrine or belief but sincerity and "disposition" of heart.[62] Again, what was critical was not the notions of the mind but the moral character of the heart.

Deists never stopped boasting that their religious scheme was superior to the orthodox plan precisely because it focused on moral character, which was accessible to all, rather than doctrinal belief, which was restricted to the minority of human beings who had heard the doctrine. Yet they also evinced a curious elitism, both in their thinking and practice. Most of them believed that the truth can be understood in its full clarity only by the educated who can follow rational argument, but that the uneducated masses are able to comprehend only fables and religious allegories.[63] Like Benjamin Franklin, they thought Christianity useful for teaching the untutored hordes for the purpose of social control. These slow, unenlightened commoners had neither training nor leisure to learn the religion of nature, so it was best to indoctrinate them in what was finally misleading if only because it taught them morality. Collins, for example, sent his domestics to church so they might learn not to rob him or cut his throat. Franklin had seen in his youth that while deism was true it was not socially useful; so he felt obliged throughout his life to encourage a Christianity that he considered useful but probably not true.[64]

Some of the deists even regarded the *hoi polloi* with unabashed hostility. Toland, for instance, confessed in his *Pantheisticon*, "We shall be in Safety if we separate ourselves from the Multitude; for the multitude is a proof of what is worst."[65] Others, like Conyers Middleton, took a more paternalistic approach, regarding most of the uneducated as simple minds who could not comprehend abstract reason. Hence it was fitting for them to learn Christianity, which though untrue was useful for those who needed mystery in their religion. As Tindal remarked, citing a Greek proverb, "Miracles for fools and reasons for wise men."[66]

Those who recognized the absurdity of trusting in mysteries, on the other hand, knew what was reasonable because it was self-evident to them. It was as apparent as common sense—at least to them. As Chubb confidently declared, reason was neither defective nor fallen but perfectly capable of discerning between good and evil, truth and error, simply by appealing to what is intuitively obvious—or, as deists often put it, "common sense." In fact, proclaimed Chubb, Adam's reason was improved by the Fall. With this powerful ability to distinguish what is true, it was immediately evident to Chubb that the New Testament was not divine. For

---

62. *IW*, 2:13; *CAO*, 2; *CAO*, 413–14, 415.

63. See, e.g., Manuel, *The Changing of the Gods*, 34–35.

64. Cragg, *Reason and Authority*, 15; Stromberg, *Religious Liberalism*, 69. Toland's *Pantheisticon* contains the following passage taken from the ritual for what was probably a Masonic meeting:

PRESIDENT: Keep off the prophane People.

RESPONSE: The Coast is clear, the Doors are shut, all's safe.

Jacob, *The Radical Enlightenment*, 153.

65. Toland, *Pantheisticon*, "To the Reader." This was a quotation from Seneca's *De vita beata*, chap. 1; cited in Manuel, *Changing of the Gods*, 36.

66. Stromberg, *Religious Liberalism*, 75–77; *CAO*, 192.

it did not conform to what common sense had shown to be true. It contained commands that, to Chubb, seemed to violate common sense. Since God could not command what was unfit or unreasonable, it was clear to him that these commands and indeed the whole New Testament could not have been inspired by God.[67]

Sometimes common sense was interpreted by deists as whatever was consistent with their own experience. Chubb rejected the New Testament stories of angels conversing with human beings because there was no analogue for such a thing in human history. For the same reason he held that the accounts of graves opening and Christ's appearing to people after his resurrection, and healings by contact with handkerchiefs and aprons (Acts 19:12) had to be spurious.[68]

When Chubb and other deists spoke of reason as common sense, they usually did not mean knowledge that was gained from everyday experience. More often than not they were applying abstract principles of reason divorced from experience and traditions claiming to be grounded in religious experience. Most deists, for example, rejected Christ's resurrection as inherently unlikely because of the abstract principle that the course of nature is never altered. Chubb refused to countenance anything smacking of election and reprobation because the principle was already obvious from reason that repentance and forgiveness are the proper grounds of forgiveness. He was also convinced that Confucius had a better interpretation of how we should relate to enemies because reason showed him immediately that Jesus' command to love our enemies was improper. Tindal agreed.[69]

We have already seen how Tindal handled the satisfaction theory of the atonement. Like nearly all deists, he rejected it, principally because it conflicted with the principle that what is perfect can admit no change, for change implies imperfection. There were other problems as well. Human sacrifice is inherently abhorrent and so could never serve as an expiation for sins. Free pardon of sins by definition would not need expiation; otherwise it would not be free. And how could it be "mere Mercy, and pure Forgiveness, after a full Equivalent paid, and adequate Satisfaction giv'n?" The principle of free pardon could never be conjoined with the need for a sacrifice to effect that pardon.[70]

Tindal insisted that all orthodox disagreements with his reasoning were results of anthropomorphism. They represented a stubborn refusal to follow the logic of reason and an authoritarian defense of mythology. For similar reasons, orthodox devotion to the Sabbath was silly. A perfect being needs no worship to keep it happy. Sabbath observance had no foundation in reason but was maintained simply for the benefit of priests. And as we have seen, reason showed that the concept of mediation was wrongheaded. Only a weak deity would need a mediator, and to retain such a notion would only diminish our love for the Creator. Even the heathen would never imagine a mediator or the still sillier concept of incarna-

---

67. DCR, 8; AF, 132, 335. On reason as common sense, see also CNM, xiii, 145; Herbert, *De Religione Laici*, 91, 99; and DF, 93.68. AF, 197, 201, 215.

68. AF, 197, 201, 215.

69. Stromberg, *Religious Liberalism*, 75; DCR, 21–24, 274; CAO, 341–42.

70. CAO, 38–39, 419.

tion. All these ridiculous concepts were shown to be illusory by the clear principles of abstract reason.[71]

Because they emphasized abstract principles, deists could insist that their religion of nature was based on certitude rather than the grossly inferior foundation of mere probability. This was an age in which mathematics served as the model for reasoning. Truth was typically thought to be found in the form of a set of propositions that could be "demonstrated" or proven with certainty. The deists dismissed scholastic jargon that relied on authority and mystery with contempt; they gave preference to argument and proof, following the clear and simple methods of mathematicians and scientists. In their opinion it was possible to condense the essence of religion into a few, simple propositional statements.[72]

Hence reason, when understood as simple and clear abstract principles that seemed obvious to deists, became the final arbiter of everything in religion. It had the authority to determine not only whether a certain book was revelation from God, but also whether a particular doctrine in that book was inspired.[73] John Locke spoke for most of the age, and certainly for deists, when he pronounced that "reason must be our last judge and guide in everything." Chubb spoke for all deists when he made the following statement the thesis of his *Discourse Concerning Reason*: reason is or ought to be a sufficient guide in matters of religion. That meant that deist reason defined the parameters within which God was permitted to act. As Chubb expressed it, God always makes the "reason of things" the rule and measure of his actions. Toland demanded, "To what end should God require us to believe what we cannot understand?" Nothing could be true of God that exceeded the limits of his understanding.[74]

Not surprisingly, what was self-evident to the deists was less clear to others. Collins joked that no one had doubted the existence of a deity until Samuel Clarke tried to prove it, and Leslie Stephen wryly added that "nobody doubted the doctrine of the Trinity until William Sherlock tried to demonstrate it mathematically." But in a similar turn of events, as Paul Ramsey observed, "Nobody doubted the religion of nature until the deists undertook to say what it was." John Locke was the first great thinker to argue that Herbert's five common notions were not in fact common at all. And the more the deists identified their abstract principles, the more commonly other English thinkers concluded they were not all as self-evident as deists proclaimed.[75]

---

71. Ibid., 46–47, 116, 86.
72. CNM, xiii; Cragg, *Reason and Authority*, 28–31.
73. For Tindal, reason is the means to discover true Christianity, and all probability or certainty depends on self-evident truths; CAO, 2, 6, 182–83, 189.
74. Locke, *Essay*, 4.19.4; DCR, 14 and passim, 55; CNM, 143.
75. Stromberg, *Religious Liberalism*, 10–11; Stephen, *History of English Thought* 1: 80; FW, 68; Locke, *Essay*, 1.3.15–20. Among the 150 replies to Tindal were William Law (*The Case of Reason*, 1731) and Joseph Butler (*The Analogy of Religion*, 1736), who argued along this line. David Hume (*Dialogues Concerning Natural Religion*, 1779) finally laid to rest the presumption that reason alone can establish faith in his argument that reason by itself leads only to skepticism.

Deists were not unduly alarmed by such responses. They attributed ignorance of natural religion to a conspiracy of priests, who had, for the sake of selfish gain, purposely distorted or destroyed the original knowledge given by reason and intuition to all human beings. In a Golden Age at the beginning of creation the first generations practiced a simple and clear religion of nature. But there arose a class of priests who used fraud, imposture, and mystery to make the people dependent on them for access to the newly created sacred rites. Priests had perpetuated this fraud ever since, claiming a monopoly on truth and using the state to enforce their self-interested dictates. Toland's ditty caught the flavor of the unending deist attack on priestcraft:

> Natural religion was first easy and plain
> Tales made it mystery, offerings made it gain;
> sacrifices and shows were at length prepared.
> the priests ate roast meat and the people starved.[76]

For Toland, the priests' (he meant primarily the Anglican priests of the seventeenth century) greatest sin was to prevent people from thinking for themselves. Self-determination was divinity's greatest gift to humanity, so priestly deception threatened to reduce its victims to something less than fully human. For Tindal, priests were responsible for the worst aberrations in the history of religion. Sacrifice, originally a heathen custom, was imported to Christianity by priests who wanted the best part of the offerings for themselves. The law of nature would be clear to all but for the obfuscation taught by priests. Most corruption in church history had been committed by priests and permitted by a blindly deferential laity.[77]

For Chubb and Tindal, the deists best-known to Jonathan Edwards, priestcraft was a cardinal impediment to true religion. Chubb believed that priests prevented people from using reason to think for themselves, which was the proper way to understand true religion. Tindal preached that priests' imposture led people to neglect the rational religion they could find in their minds and hearts.

---

76. Harrison, "*Religion*" *and the Religions*, 73–83; Champion, *The Pillars of Priestcraft Shaken*, 9, 24, 229; CNM, 130.

77. Daniel, *John Toland*, 18–19, 26, 33; CAO, 59, 379, 311, 107–8. See also Beiser, *The Sovereignty of Reason*, 223–25.

2

EDWARDS'S WAR AGAINST ENLIGHTENMENT RELIGION

Deism was the religion of the Enlightenment. Of course it was not the only religion of the Enlightenment. Both Locke and Newton, for example, departed from orthodox Christology without discarding what deism rejected—the inspiration of the Bible.[1] But deism was the religion that took the Enlightenment presupposition of intellectual autonomy most seriously. And it was deism that most effectively transmitted Enlightenment religious sensibilities to later generations.

Jonathan Edwards recognized, perhaps more acutely than any other American thinker in the eighteenth century, that if Christian thinking seriously entertained the most elemental deist presumptions, the Reformed faith would collapse. To him deism epitomized the most pernicious philosophical and theological trends of his day. He also believed, rightly or wrongly, that it was actually tempting the minds of his colonial compatriots. As a result he dedicated his career to its destruction. In his philosophical treatises he set out to explode the arguments of the deists. In his theological works he sketched portraits of a religious beauty that would, he hoped, convince observers of the ugliness of the deist alternative.

Ironically, however, deism enjoyed a victory of sorts. By the very gravity of its allegations, it compelled Edwards to reconstruct Reformed theology in ways that would, he thought, respond to its challenges. In significant respects, deism set the agenda. Edwards replied to deist charges with sophistication and often turned deist arguments back against themselves, but usually it was deism not Reformed theology that chose the battleground and set the conditions for victory.

1. Both took an Arian view of Christ. Arius was an early fourth-century Alexandrian priest who taught that Jesus was more than just a man but less than fully God.

In order to see all this, we must first look at the two deists whom Edwards knew best, Thomas Chubb and Matthew Tindal.[2]

Edwards's Deists

Thomas Chubb (1679–1746), a Salisbury tallow chandler and glove-maker who confessed he knew no languages but his own, was the least educated of all the deists; Paul Ramsey called him an "interloper among scholars." He began as a disciple of Arians William Whiston and Samuel Clarke, then became a deist. According to Ramsey, "from the Trinitarian controversy to the evident disorder and lack of positive content in deism, Thomas Chubb summed up in his person most of the currents of the age." And he was able to express those currents in a vigorous and accessible fashion; more than anyone else, Chubb took deism to the common people.[3]

We have already seen Chubb's basic rule of thinking, that reason either is or ought to be a sufficient guide in matters of religion. He taught that all persons have the divine law in their hearts, so they can easily determine if something purporting to be divine is truly so. Religion is valuable only as it serves human morality; far from central, life after death is at best uncertain and prayer is unnecessary.[4]

The difference between Chubb's method and Edwards's can be illustrated by comparing their interpretations of John 21:25 ("And there are also many other things which Jesus did, the which, if they should be written every one, I suppose that even the world itself could not contain the books that should be written"). Chubb simply denied that this statement could possibly be true. To the Salisbury candle-trimmer, the idea that there could be enough books to fill the world, much less books about one subject, was self-evidently false.

Edwards, on the other hand, took this verse to refer not only to things done by Christ but also to things accomplished by Christ's actions. In addition it referred to the "internal manner of doing" or "the design with which" these things were done, influences on Christ, and Christ's purposes and motives in all that he did. In other words, this passage had in mind "all the glorious, wise purposes and designs of God's wisdom and grace, and the love of Christ, and all that belongs to

---

2. Edwards knew of and was familiar with the basic arguments of all of the best-known thinkers associated indirectly or directly with deism: Thomas Hobbes, Herbert of Cherbury, Blount, Toland, the earl of Shaftesbury, Collins, Chubb, Thomas Woolston, Thomas Morgan, Tindal, Lord Bolingbroke, and David Hume. Most of these figures he probably knew only through secondary sources such as Leland's *Principal Deistical Writers* (1745) and Philip Skelton's *Deism Revealed* (1748).

There are indications in his writings, however, that he had firsthand knowledge of the principal works of Chubb and Tindal. Edwards quoted Chubb at length on the atonement in *Misc.* 1213 and paraphrased Leland's treatment of him in *Misc.* 1297. In *Freedom of the Will* Chubb was one of Edwards's principal antagonists; FW, 132, 232–33, 226–38, 343–48, 418. Chubb's complaints about Calvinism's unfairness to the heathen are in DCR, 1–6, 12, 22, 71, 209. Similar sentiments can be found in IW, 1:333–34, 2:13.

3. Stephen, *English Thought*, 87; FW, 75, 68.

4. DCR, 14 and passim; AF, 60–72; Leland, *Principal Deistical Writers*, 196–200.

that manifold wisdom of God, and those unsearchable riches of wisdom and knowledge, in the work of redemption, that we read of in the Scripture."[5]

Edwards apparently assumed the inspiration and therefore truth of the passage on aesthetic and suprarational grounds, as well as rational ones, and approached the text with faith seeking understanding. Chubb decided on the basis of his preconceived notions of what is possible that the assertions of this text could not be true.

Chubb also took the position, common to deism and the Age of Reason, that the will is self-determining. Edwards took this notion to be "the breach through which deism poured, and the abandonment of Christianity . . . [For] by taking refuge in the autonomy of their wills . . . people . . . avoid full-scale confession of sin. . . . [O]nce they begin to search only for self-determined acts they are likely to find nothing at all to confess." Without understanding of depravity, he believed, one would see no need for a Mediator to do for the self what the self could not. In his *Freedom of the Will* Edwards claimed to reduce Chubb's notion of a free act to "a heap of contradictions." For one of those contradictions, the pastor at Stockbridge pounced on Chubb's statement, "When the self-moving power is exerted, it becomes the necessary cause of its effects." Edwards pointed out that this makes every choice necessary, both because of the plain face of the statement and because Chubb also proposed that every act of choice is commanded by a separate act of choice. So the freedom of choice, Edwards happily concluded, is only a chimera according to Chubb's own reasoning—it is contradicted and therefore swallowed up by necessary choice.[6]

Matthew Tindal (1657–1733) was the most learned of the British deists. His *Christianity as Old as the Creation* (1730) was not called "the Deists' Bible" without reason: it elicited more than one hundred fifty published replies. Despite having sat at Locke's feet as an admiring disciple, Tindal, like most deists, believed in a priori knowledge. His basic argument in *Christianity* began with the assumption that rational religion is clear, accessible, and perfect. If perfect, it cannot be made clearer. Any claim to make it clearer is therefore false. Since traditional Christianity makes that claim, it is false. Hence any pretenses to external (outside the human mind and heart) revelation owe to enthusiasm or imposture. To be governed by such revelation is to renounce reason and replace understanding with implicit faith.

In the second half of *Christianity*, which he wrote when he was seventy-five years old, Tindal systematically attacked the Bible by impugning the character of biblical heroes and the intelligence of the apostles, questioning the reliability of the prophecies and miracle stories, and challenging the limits of the canon. Much of the New Testament, he declared, was hyperbolic and parabolic, so its words must be interpreted in a contrary sense in order to make common sense. In contrast to the confusion elicited by the Bible, the light of nature clearly shows us the way to God by repentance and moral amendment.[7]

---

5. "Notes on the Bible," in Hickman, *The Works of President Edwards*, 2:794; hereafter referred to as "Hickman."
6. *FW*, 69, 70–71, 235.
7. *CAO* 204–22, 245, 261–62, 287, 334–37, 391–92.

Edwards ignored most of Tindal's detailed arguments, leveling his sights on a presumption at the heart of them all—that just because the law of nature is perfect we can assume that knowledge of that law is also perfect. The New England theologian also focused on Tindal's terms, charging that Tindal used the word "reason" in inconsistent and contradictory ways that obscure the reality of mystery in life. We will look more closely at these lines of argument in Chapter 4.

Fear of Deism

Jonathan Edwards attacked Chubb and Tindal because he considered deism dangerous. In this he was hardly alone. The period was flooded with an avalanche of paper attacking the deists; many Englishmen were apparently concerned that society as a whole was drifting toward deism and, so they said, atheism. John Redwood has written of a pervasive fear of deism that infected England in the late seventeenth and early eighteenth centuries. Many believed this was "the greatest controversy of the present age, and which ever was in the Christian world." Even in the fashionable literature of the day—*The Spectator* and *The Tatler*—deists were regarded with odium. An indication of the degree of fear can be seen in the 1697 hanging of Thomas Aikenhead, age eighteen, for professing deism and scoffing at the Old Testament. Francis Hutcheson was prosecuted for deism as late as 1738.[8]

Although historians have since concluded that deism was never an influential movement in America until after the Revolution,[9] there were not a few colonials who took fright. A Philadelphia newspaper column worried in 1735, for example, that deism was poisoning the minds of the young. In the following decade evangelist George Whitefield noted anxiously that deists were trying to convert "moral men" and seemed relieved when a deist yielded to his evangelical preaching. At about the same time Jonathan Dickinson, the New Side Presbyterian pastor, was concerned that guests at inns and coffeehouses were entertaining deistic notions.[10]

In eighteenth-century England deists were safe as long as they refrained from open blasphemy or extremely immoderate expressions. Free thought and heterodoxy met little real persecution. By the last third of the century deism had finally failed, both intellectually and spiritually, so that in 1790 Edmund Burke remarked

---

8. Redwood, *Reason, Ridicule and Religion*, 10, 16, 134ff; Dr. William Harris's preface to Simon Browne, *A Defense of the Religion of Nature and the Christian Revelation*, iii, cited in Cragg, *Reason and Authority*, 63; Stromberg, *Religious Liberalism*, 4.

9. Turner, *Without God, Without Creed*, 44–49, 52. More recently, however, A. Owen Aldridge has argued that two tracts published in 1771 and 1772 contained deistical beliefs; Aldridge, "Natural Religion and Deism in America before Ethan Allen and Thomas Paine," *William and Mary Quarterly*, 3d ser., 54, no. 4 (October 1997): 836–48.

10. *The American Weekly Museum*, October 9–16, 1735 (no. 824); Whitefield, *A Continuation of the Rev. Mr. Whitefield's Journal. etc.* (London, 1744), 66–67; Dickinson, *Familiar Letters* (Glasgow, 1775), 2. Cited in Morais, *Deism in Eighteenth-Century America*, 79–80.

that no one read the deists anymore.[11] Nevertheless, between 1700 and 1733 it had orthodoxy on the ropes; the agenda had shifted to dealing with its concerns, and many feared that the church would be overwhelmed by its way of thinking.

Edwards was also alarmed. In a June 1743 sermon he referred to "robbers, pirates and deists" with, as John Gerstner puts it, implied apologies to the robbers and pirates for putting them in such company.[12] Six years earlier, in a public lecture on 2 Peter 1:19, Edwards described deists as those who regarded the Bible as a "mere human book," rejected all revelation, and thought of Christ as "a cheat." Lately they had made "amazing progress in our nation," as their beliefs had "grown fashionable," so that a "great part of the nation are become deists."[13]

As a result, Edwards lamented, "The Bible is derided, Christ openly blasphemed, and all doctrines and miracles ridiculed in publick Houses and open streets." Almost as bad, deists promoted outlandish doctrines (for example, that "men die like bruits") and outrageous morals. They were teaching that "there is no more evil in murder and robbery than in a deed of Charity," and they "plead for the lawfullness of drunkenness and fornication—adultery—murder & Robbery. Yea they plead it Lawfull to kill their own children and have of late practiced upon it and done it in cold blood."[14]

There is no indication in the historical record that I have seen that Edwards was speaking accurately at this point. And Edwards never came close to these rhetorical excesses again—at least in his private notebooks and published writings. But this and many other digressions on deism make it clear that for Edwards deism was not just a threat but in fact a clear and present danger to England and her colonies. It had gone so far as to "prevail" in Britain and would continue to drive out true religion if not checked.[15]

Deism in the Edwards Corpus

Allusions to deism and its dangers, both implicit and explicit, show up throughout Edwards's written remains. Much that formerly seemed obscure and apparently antiquarian suddenly re-emerges with new clarity and relevance when viewed in the context of his perception of a deist menace. For example, Edwards filled scores and scores of pages in his *Miscellanies* with tedious and dauntingly detailed ruminations on the etymologies of Greek and Roman mythical figures—pages that are impossible to fathom without the realization that the deists used Greco-Roman

---

11. Stromberg, *Religious Liberalism*, 65. "Who, born within the last forty years, has read one word of Collins, and Toland, and Tindal, and Chubb, and Morgan, and that whole race who called themselves freethinkers? Who now reads Bolingbroke? Who ever read him through? Ask the booksellers of London what is become of all these lights of the world. In a few years their few successors will go to the family vault of 'all the Capulets'" (Burke, *Reflections on the Revolution in France*, 101).
12. Sermon on Romans 2:5, [p.] 4, in Gerstner, *Rational Biblical Theology*, 1:118.
13. Lecture on 2 Peter 1:19, August 1737, Edwards Papers, 22, 23.
14. Ibid., 23, 24.
15. Lecture on 2 Peter 1:19, 30.

mythology and philosophy to argue the independence of the best pagan wisdom from revelation. Edwards's counterarguments were intended to show that the finest pagan thinking was in fact dependent on revelation.

As we shall see, deism played a critical role in shaping the mind of Jonathan Edwards. It served as both background irritant and open antagonist in his private ruminations (both experimental and developmental, as seen in his private notebooks), spoken addresses (his sermons and lectures, where he seemed to feel freer to indulge his polemical apprehensions), and major treatises (where his reflections on deism are more measured but no less grave).

Edwards's first explicit reference to deism in the *Miscellanies* came early, when he was only twenty-one or twenty-two years old (Misc. 127). To the deist challenge that revelation has nothing to add to natural religion and organized worship is unimportant, Edwards responded that without revelation there is nothing to direct even deists how to worship. Revelation is absolutely necessary for "right social worship."

An astonishing twenty-five percent of the 1412 entries in the *Miscellanies* relate directly or indirectly to issues raised by the deist challenge. That is, more than 357 entries (and there are many more, if other topics that bear indirectly on the deist agenda are included)[16] discuss the superiority of the "Christian religion" to other religions, or "deism," or revelation and its necessity, or the reasonableness of the doctrine of satisfaction.

Thirteen entries are titled "DEISM" and attack the claims of the freethinkers directly, usually employing extracts from Skelton's *Deism Revealed* or Leland's *View of the Principal Deistical Writers*. The greatest number of entries falling under the same head are titled "CHRISTIAN RELIGION." There are approximately one hundred of these, nearly all of which defend the necessity of (Christian) revelation or the integrity of the Bible. For example, Misc. 128 asserts that the Christian religion is the only religion that teaches us a host of important doctrines, such as the nature of God, monotheism, God's Creation and works, God's government and designs and will, reward and punishment, morality, and life after death. The very next entry (Misc. 129) makes two arguments for the necessity of revelation: first, humanity was darkened religiously and morally because of the Fall and is blind without revelation; second, since humankind was created for a particular religious end, "it is a strange thing that there should be no mutual communion between him and God."

---

16. Such as Misc. mm and Misc. 40, which defend the office of the ministry against what seem to be deist diatribes against priestcraft; Misc. 40, which supports Sabbath-keeping in the face of deist trivialization of the same; Misc. 246 ("GOSPEL"), which denies the deist claim that Christ taught nothing new; Misc. 265 ("CHRIST'S DEATH"), which contends with deist claims that Christ's death was not the kind of punishment humans deserved; Misc. 326 ("OLD TESTAMENT DISPENSATION"), which defends the Old Testament sacrifices (only deists attacked them); and Misc. 352, Misc. 358, and Misc. 359, which argue for the "INSPIRATION OF THE SCRIPTURES." It was the deists who most famously attacked it. Even Misc. 292 ("SUPRALAPSARIANS"), which betrays Edwards's infralapsarianism, is indebted to Turretin and Mastricht but may have been strengthened by deist complaints that the supralapsarian God is arbitrary and cruel. There are probably many more that were partly or wholly inspired by the deist controversy.

The reference to deism is implicit but clear; Edwards's comments were direct rejoinders to deist denials of both Christianity's uniqueness and humanity's need for revelation.

Several years later (in 1728 or 1729) Edwards addressed the deist challenge at greater length. In a "CHRISTIAN RELIGION" entry that outlined the themes he would use for the rest of his career to attack deism, he argued that without revelation much that now seems clear in natural religion would be shrouded by darkness, doubt, and endless dispute. Men would be "like a parcel of beasts." This can be seen now, he maintained, in places that have not received the Christian gospel; they toil in "gross darkness" and "brutal stupidity." Yet contrary to deist claims, there has never been a people without any revelation at all. For the wiser forefathers gathered up "remains of truth" and "relics of revelation" they had heard from other countries, especially Judea. China, for example, learned from Noah, who in fact settled in its western regions and ruled over it for "many hundred years."

Scores of other entries with this heading respond to deist claims. Misc. 1170, for instance, defends the "necessity of revelation" by quoting an extract from the Reformed scholastic Johann Friedrich Stapfer (1708–1775), who defended revelation by pointing to the slowness with which humans find truth, "as in the instance of the roundness of the earth." Misc. 1309, written during the Stockbridge years, endorses the "divine authority of the Book of Daniel," a book deists had ridiculed.

The heading with the second largest number of entries (31) is "TRINITY." These entries were probably not directed solely against deists, for there was a bitter controversy over the Trinity among Anglicans and dissenters toward the end of the seventeenth century. Then in 1712 Samuel Clarke published an Arian tract under the title *Scripture–Doctrine of the Trinity*. Moderates Hubert Stogdon and Isaac Watts joined the controversy in 1719 and 1722 with works criticizing any attempts to make foundational to faith doctrines not "plainly revealed" in the Bible.[17] The implication, of course, was that one such doctrine not plainly revealed is that of the Trinity.

Edwards apparently regarded these new developments with impatience. He saw no reason to be so timid about defending a doctrine that for him was absolutely central to Christian faith. "There has been much cry of late," he noted at the end of 1723, "against saying one word, particularly about the Trinity, but what the scripture has said; judging it is impossible but that if we did, we should err in a thing so much above us." The young theologian thought the real error was in failing to take seriously the implications of scriptural statements—a failure that under the cloak of scholarly caution proceeded to gut true religion. A determination to take those things seriously could empower reason to discover truths like the Trinity that would stand deism on its head. Or as Edwards put it:

---

17. Hubert Stogdon, *Seasonable Advice Relating to the Present Disputes about the Holy Trinity* (London, 1719); Isaac Watts, *The Christian Doctrine of the Trinity* (London, 1722).

But ... I am not afraid to say twenty things about the Trinity which the scripture never said. There may be deductions of reason from what has been said of the most mysterious matters, besides what has been said, and safe and certain deductions too, as well as about the most obvious and easy matters. I think that it is within the reach of naked reason to perceive certainly that there are three distinct in God. (Misc. 94)

These remarks of course were not directed only at deists. For Edwards knew that there were Arians and Socinians who also questioned the Trinity. But he certainly had deists in mind as well, for they were the most notorious opponents of Trinitarianism, and they often cited the Trinity as an egregious example of how priestcraft had imposed mysterious doctrines that violated common sense.

The next largest series of entries (27) in the Edwards notebooks is titled "HEATHEN PHILOSOPHERS." The first one, written in 1742 or 1743, states the theme that runs throughout these entries:

that the HEATHEN PHILOSOPHERS had their notions of the unity of God[,] of the Trinity[,] of the immortality of the soul[,] the last judgment[,] the general conflagration, &c—by TRADITION from the first ages of the world and from the Jewish nation is manifested by their own testimony and many things thay say shew [sic] that they suppose that they had these things by traditions from those that were divinely instructed and inspired of God. (Misc. 953)

In an addition to this entry, Edwards adds by way of support for his thesis, that "Plato in his Philebus acknowledges that the report or tradition he had received of the unity of God as to his essence and plurality of persons and decrees was from the antients who dwelt nearer the gods and were better than they."[18]

The next twenty-six entries under this heading develop this theme, that the heathen received their wisdom not from reason alone, but by tradition from revelation given to the fathers of their nations. We know this, Edwards told himself, by their own testimony and by seeing the conformity of their doctrines to those of Reformed Christianity. Since deists denied Reformed doctrines and the notion that reason could prove Reformed doctrines, the presence of these doctrines in heathen traditions proved for Edwards both their truth and the likelihood that they derived these truths not from reason but revelation passed down by tradition.

In these entries Edwards recorded Hugo Grotius's claims that Greek and Roman laws were taken from the laws of Moses (Misc. 1012), and that the "HISTORY OF THE OLD TESTAMENT from Moses's time" was confirmed by heathen traditions (Misc. 1020).[19] From Grotius he also learned that the heathen taught "Christian duties": Ovid and Seneca knew that one can commit adultery in the heart, Plato enjoined the forgiveness of injuries and love for enemies, and Euripides recommended

---

18. Edwards took this information from Theophilus Gale's *Court of the Gentiles* (1669–1677), a massive four-volume work dedicated to the proposition that all ancient languages and learning, particularly philosophical, were derived from the Jews.

19. Edwards kept another notebook, entitled by a later copyist "Defense of the Authenticity of the Pentateuch as a work of Moses," presumably stimulated by deist attacks on the same. Currently in the Edwards Papers, Beinecke Library, Box 15, f. 1204, Edwards intended it to be a continuation of what is now no. 416 in his *Notes on the Scriptures*.

monogamy (Misc. 1023). Chevalier Ramsay showed Edwards that Chinese philosophers believed in the Trinity, paradise, the Fall, redemption by a messiah, and the nature of true religion (Misc. 1181). And from Skelton's *Deism Revealed* he discovered that Lao-zi held to something like a Trinity (Misc. 1236).

Lest Edwards concede the deist argument that all truth is found in the beginning before Christianity, however, he penned just before the end of his life an extract from John Brine that detailed the "defects of heathen morality." They had not true love for God but merely honor for demons and heroes; they abstracted virtue from the will of God; they showed too much self-reliance and too little humility; and they neglected many of the essentials of virtue. For example, Cicero and others countenanced fornication and idolatry (Misc. 1357).

Edwards also gave considerable attention to the "ETERNITY OF HELL TORMENTS" (17 entries) and "CHRIST'S SATISFACTION" (12 entries). In the series on hell, deists are never mentioned explicitly. But it was the deists who voiced the loudest opposition to traditional notions of hell, suggesting that an eternal hell of horrific intensity was cruel and unusual punishment. So there is little doubt that he addressed these entries to challenges raised principally by deists. And significantly, deism appears obliquely in a definition of hell found in what is perhaps the most famous *Miscellanies* entry—Misc. 782 on the "SENSE OF THE HEART." In this exposition of what could be called Edwards's canon within the canon, the Northampton divine opines that only those with "sensible" (as opposed to "speculative") knowledge of God's excellency can imagine the "dreadfulness of the wrath of such a Being" and therefore understand the "natural agreement between affronts of such a majesty and the suffering of extreme misery; it appears much more credible to them that there is indeed an extreme misery to be suffered for sin." This lack of sensible knowledge also explains, according to Edwards, why many are "blind to the suitableness of Christ's satisfaction." They don't see that this is a "divine contrivance" (Misc. 782).

As we have already seen, deists universally rejected the doctrine of Christ's satisfaction for sin. Edwards undertook to formulate a response to their arguments at the very beginning of his career. His second entry in the *Miscellanies* (Misc. b), written when he was twenty, focuses on satisfaction. Just a short time later, probably in the same year, the young polemicist noted the deist argument against satisfaction: "Now some may say, why could not God, of his mercy, pardon the injury only upon repentance without other satisfaction, without doing himself any hurt?" Edwards's method in his reply is to underline God's transcendence and imply that deists reduced it to human proportions: all the repentance humanity is capable of "is no repentance at all. . . . [I]t is as little as none in comparison of the greatness of the injury, for it cannot bear any proportion to it." If God were to pardon simply on the basis of human repentance, it would be "dishonorable to God, just as dishonorable if he pardoned without any repentance at all" (Misc. oo).[20]

---

20. Curiously, there is some indication that deists may have influenced Edwards's understanding of the atonement, which eventually included aspects of the governmental theory to supplement his more Anselmian satisfaction theory. At Stockbridge Edwards quoted Thomas Chubb on the atonement without refuting him. The Chubb selection in Misc. 1213 states that an innocent

In his eleven entries devoted to the topic "THE END OF CREATION" Edwards expressed perhaps the pithiest rejoinder to the deist attack on revelation: "God is a communicating being" (Misc. 332). In other words, while deists condemned God to silence outside the secret dictates of the inner mind, Edwards proclaimed that God was forever communicating, and through many and diverse media—not only Scripture but also through nature, history, and the history of religions. Much of this communication was in typological form, but it was vivid communication nonetheless. And not only communication, but revelation. Edwards insisted that human beings before the advent of Christ and outside the borders of Christian nations were not and are not deprived of revelation, as deists claimed, but have been fairly inundated with the voice of God calling to them from many different directions.

A principal theme of these entries on the end of creation is the problem of God's selfishness. As we have seen, deists complained that a god who insists on being praised by his creatures is egotistical, unworthy of worship. Edwards used most of these entries to wrestle with this charge. In Misc. 445 he denies that God's end (purpose) of communicating happiness is subordinate to making his own glory appear. In Misc. 669 he argues that God glorifies himself because God's glory is in itself an excellent thing that ought to be cultivated for its own sake: "God don't seek his own glory for any happiness he receives by it, as men are gratified in having their excellencies gazed at[,] admired and extolled by others[,] but God seeks the display of his own glory as a thing in itself excellent. . . . The excellency of God's nature appears in that that [sic] he loves and seeks whatever is in itself excellent."

In Misc. 704 Edwards tries to negotiate the deist complaint that God created human beings with the intention of damning them. Taking an infralapsarian approach, he decided that God's decree of reprobation "is not to be conceived of as prior to the fall[,] yea and to the very being of the persons, as the decree of the eternal glory of the elect is . . . there is nothing but the ultimate end of all things[,] viz. God's glory and the communication of his goodness that is prior to all."[21]

Edwards apparently concedes to the deists the point that supralapsarianism would be impossible to defend as just and good. So he resorted to an understanding of some decrees as being conditioned upon others: "Decrees may in some sort be conditions of decrees so that it may be said that God would not have decreed some things had he not decreed others" (Misc. 704).

In Misc. 1218 Edwards returns to the issue of egotism in God. Specifically, the question was whether the Calvinist God acts "justly only for the sake of the honour of his justice." This time the response focuses on God's concern with objective

---

person cannot be punished for the sake of the guilty; God is not thereby required to forgive the sins of the guilty. Therefore God's pardon of sinners is wholly free. The passion moved God to forgive, but not by satisfying God's wrath. For more on Edwards's atonement theory, see Rudisill, *Doctrine of the Atonement*.

21. This was the approach taken by most Reformed theologians after Calvin; Heppe, *Reformed Dogmatics*, 143–47, 156–58, 162.

justice. "Justice itself is an inclination to do justly[,] which must exist before God is inclined to honour it." So God's "glorifying himself" is not seeking his own honor but doing what is objectively just.

Furthermore, Edwards emphasizes, God creates beings to communicate His goodness to them. But this goodness is infinitely different from all human conceptions of goodness. It is that part of God's character which Edwards understood to be His "glory" that is disposed to display each part of God's perfections. And it is that, God's glory, which is actually the reason for which God displays His perfections to creatures, which is the same thing as a communication of His goodness. So it is a desire to do what is most excellent in and of itself, which is the display of God's perfections, that moves God to seek his glory, not a selfish desire for personal gratification as humans conceive it.[22] Even altruistic goodness as humans think of it is too humanocentric to represent this disposition of God to seek his glory; for this reason Edwards refused to use the word "goodness" for God's disposition to create new beings to whom he would communicate his very being. Instead he chose to express it as "the disposition that is in the infinite fountain of good and of glory and excellency to shine forth or flow out[. This] shining forth or flowing out of Gods [sic] infinite fullness is called Gods [sic] glory in Scripture" (Misc. 1218).

In the nine entries titled "REVEALED RELIGION" Edwards develops his most basic lines of argument against the deists, often mentioning the movement by name. Contrary to what freethinkers say, he charges, philosophy has given little or no knowledge of the true God, and what true knowledge existed among the heathen had come from revelation (Misc. 986). The history of religion is a history of degradation, decline, and the corruption of an original pure deposit of revelation (Misc. 986). He quotes Clarke to the effect that the wisest heathen (Cicero is named) always confessed their ignorance and blindness in morals and divine things (Misc. 977) and cites Samuel Shuckford's claim that Plato, Cicero, and others confessed their native inability to know the nature and attributes of God (Misc. 979). Reason alone, he insists, can never provide assurance that repentance is enough for reconciliation with the divine (Misc. 1239). The deists are prone to greater error than the ancient heathen because they do not acknowledge the possibility of revelation (Misc. 1298). Finally, in Misc. 1338 Edwards makes two arguments we shall explore more closely in the next two chapters. Reason, he argues, may be sufficient to confirm the reasonableness of a notion already discovered but is usually unable to discover that notion in the first place; and most of the heathen have been exposed to revelation by tradition coming from the first fathers of the nations and borrowing from the Jews.

There are also a number of topics that, while not developed with a large number of entries, are the loci for pointed refutation of key deist positions. For instance, four entries defend biblical prophecies against deist ridicule, six entries contend for the importance of mystery in religion, six argue for the authenticity

---

22. In this entry Edwards speaks of God's glory as both his disposition to display his attributes and the effect of that display.

of the biblical miracle accounts, four refute deist attacks on the New Testament (Misc. 842 argues that Paul did not expect the parousia in his lifetime, Misc. 1198 and Misc. 1199 maintain that Christ did not expect the imminent end of the world, and Misc. 276 contends for the reliability of the gospels), ten attempt to prove life after death, and four justify faith in Christ as Mediator. Four more defend the Calvinist notion of decrees. In Misc. 273 the young Edwards tries to vindicate the notion that God loves some and not others before there are any differences among them. It "may appear reasonable" by recognizing that God knows the reprobate will never be his (presumably because they choose to reject him), and so he has no love for them—just as we have no disposition to love those whom we know will never be ours.

There are other headings to which Edwards devoted only an entry or two: "CHRIST NOT AN IMPOSTER," "FAITH AND REASON," "ATONEMENT," "SALVATION OF THE HEATHEN," "MORAL GOVERNMENT," and the like. All of these were integral to the deist rejection of revealed religion, and Edwards apparently felt obliged to prepare an apologetic response at each point of attack.

Finally, one of Edwards's longest entries in the Miscellanies (1069), which runs to 133 pages in the Yale edition, was also directed in part to the deist challenge.[23] Under the title "TYPES OF THE MESSIAH," it is an extensive (sometimes tedious) analysis of the types of Christ Edwards found in the Old Testament. Now Edwards seemed to revel in typology, which he found in nature and history as well as in the Bible. So this enormous exercise no doubt brought him scholarly and religious pleasure. But there were polemical purposes also at work. Several prominent deists had proclaimed for all to hear the Marcionite charge that the New Testament is cut of a completely different cloth from the Old. They recommended that the Old Testament be discarded from not only Christian but human use. Against both of these charges, the demonstration of Christ and the gospel in the warp and woof of the Hebrew Bible was a powerful retort. Furthermore, demonstration of the types in the Old Testament was a clever riposte to the deist complaint that the heathen and all before Christ had been deprived of the most important part of revelation. Edwards could proudly rejoin that the gospel of Christ was present and active among the Jews before Christ, if only in typological disguise, and news of this went out to the heathen, as their mythology clearly shows.[24]

We have already seen that the discovery of new lands in the sixteenth and seventeenth centuries played a significant role in the rise of deism. We have also seen that deists used these discoveries to undermine orthodoxy's claim to be preaching a good and just God; deists questioned how the restriction of revelation to a small minority in history could be consistent with goodness and justice. In his

---

23. TW, 191–324.
24. Edwards also kept a notebook, "The Harmony of the Genius, Spirit, Doctrines, & Rules of the Old Testament & the New," which further reinforced his argument for the unity of the Testaments. Edwards Papers, Box 15, f. 1210.

oral ministry Edwards used these same discoveries to subvert deist claims for the universality of natural religion. Why in this age of discovery of new parts of the world, he asked, has no nation been found with knowledge of this natural religion? One finds this question at several different junctures in his sermon corpus, particularly when he discusses the relationship of reason to revelation, which we will explore more thoroughly in the next two chapters.

A good example of this line of questioning can be found in three sermons he gave in February 1740 titled "Man's Natural Blindness in the Things of Religion."

> If human reason is really sufficient, and there be no need of anything else, why has it never proved so? Why has it never happened, that so much as one nation, or one city or town, or one assembly of men, have been brought to tolerable notions of divine things unless it be by the revelation contained in the Scriptures?[25]

In these sermons he playfully reminds his auditors that all the people of these new lands "had the same natural reason that the deists have." Yet they do not have true notions of the divine being and his perfections "by virtue of that human reason they have been possessed of so many thousands of years" (MNB, 253).

It is also clear from Edwards's sermons that he considered deism Reformed Christianity's foremost nemesis. Several times he listed deism alongside Roman Catholicism and Islam as enemies of the church. Yet it was plain to him and his auditors that the last two were not credible threats to New England religion. Only deism could be seen on the New England horizon, if usually only in the form of its underdeveloped cousin Arminianism. In his 1737 lectures on 2 Peter 1:19 Edwards explains that there are three groups at large in the world that reject revelation: Muslims, Catholics, and deists. Then in January 1740, while explaining that the "papist and the mahometan religions [are] . . . the fruit of the inventions and Imaginations of superstitious men," he told his hearers that the deists were wrong to claim the same for the Christian Bible. There is no mention of any other adversaries. In an ordination sermon from several months later Edwards uses the first twelve pages of his sermon to delineate three uses of reason in an attempt to show that the deists' use of reason was one-dimensional and clumsy.[26]

Deism was also a principal antagonist for the great works of the Stockbridge period, even though by then deism had lost its momentum in England. Edwards evidently believed that it was still a threat to New England, for it looms in the background of each of his most memorable treatises from that period.

This is true even of *Freedom of the Will* (1754), the great philosophical treatise that more than anything else has led historians to believe that Edwards's principal antagonist was Arminianism. Seven years before its publication Edwards had written his friend Joseph Bellamy that he was working on "the Arminian controversy," and the following year he wrote his Scottish minister friend John Erskine asking for "the best books that have lately been written in defense of Calvinism" on "the

---

25. MNB, in Hickman, 2:253.
26. Sermon on Matthew 12:7, [pp.] 20–23, 36; sermon on 1 Corinthians 2:11–13, May 7, 1740, for the ordination of Mr. Billings. Unless otherwise stated, all sermons by Edwards are from the Edwards Papers, Beinecke Library, Yale University.

Arminian controversy."[27] Such remarks would seem to suggest that Arminianism was indeed central to Edwards's concern and deism at best tangential.

Yet there are clues even within this correspondence that Edwards's struggle with Arminianism was but a battle in a life-long war with deism. For example, Edwards made it clear in a 1752 letter to Erskine that Chubb and Anglican Daniel Whitby were to be his principal antagonists in *Freedom of the Will*, though neither was "properly Pelagian, nor Arminian." And in his preface to the work Edwards explained that the Arminian notion of free will, which is the manifest object of his attack, "if pursued in its consequences, will truly infer, or naturally lead to all the rest" of Chubb's deist conclusions. The design of this great philosophical work, then, was to prevent the disaster of deism, which would obliterate Christian faith, by disarming its progenitor, which imitates Christian faith.[28] As Perry Miller put it, the freedom of the will, which Arminians championed, was "the breach through which deism poured, and the abandonment of Christianity."[29]

Arminianism was perilous indeed because by logical implication it led to the collapse of Christian thinking; but deism was worse because while few Arminians followed their beliefs to their logical conclusions, all deists explicitly and self-consciously rejected both the foundation (revelation) and superstructure (doctrine) of Christian faith. Arminianism was the path to unbelief for those who wished to take it; but deism was unbelief itself—no more travel was necessary. Furthermore, while Arminianism subtly undermined Christian thinking by penetrating faith at one point (the ability of the will to determine itself), deism openly abused Christian thought with a wide-ranging series of assaults. Chubb, Tindal, and their cohorts assailed not just Christian understandings of the will, but also revelation, atonement, Christ's deity, and a host of other notions at the heart of traditional Christian theology. God's very goodness and justice were at issue. Hence the Arminian challenge could be met with one book (*Freedom of the Will*), but the deist enterprise required a series of treatises that would take a lifetime to complete.

Original Sin was a rebuttal to the Enlightenment charge of injustice in the God of traditional orthodoxy. The God who imputed Adam's sin to his unwitting descendants seemed to most Enlightenment thinkers arbitrary and unfair. Why blame a person for the sin committed by someone else? A major argument of this treatise is that we descendants of Adam are looked upon by God as sinning in and with our common ancestor because of the "consent and concurrence of the hearts of the members with the head in that first act."[30]

Edwards explains that when a sinner first approves of Adam's sin as Adam himself approved of it, it was not a

> consequence of the imputation of that first sin [but] . . . the *coexistence* of the evil disposition, implied in Adam's first rebellion, in the root and branches, [which] is a consequence of the union, that the wise Author of the world has established be-

27. *LPW*, 217, 249.
28. *FW*, 6, 132.
29. Ibid., 69.
30. *OS*, 387.

tween Adam and his posterity.... The evil disposition is *first*, and the charge of guilt *consequent*, as it was in the case of Adam himself.[31]

Repeatedly in this treatise Edwards uses the word "consent," with the intention of proving that Adam's sin was also the sin of his posterity: "By virtue of the full consent of the hearts of Adam's posterity to that first apostacy ... the sin of the apostacy is not theirs, merely because God *imputes* it to them; but it is truly and *properly* theirs, and on that ground, God imputes it to them." At the Judgment, he explains, each person will be judged for "the sin of his own wicked heart, or sinful nature or practice."[32]

Edwards's principal antagonist in *Original Sin* was the dissenter John Taylor (1694–1761), whose Arminianism Clyde A. Holbrook identifies with "a complex of notions involving an elevated confidence in freedom of choice, a sharply upward revised estimate of human nature, and a form of commonsense moralism, all of which were related to an acute dissatisfaction with Calvinism" (OS, 4). These views did not separate him from the deists. In fact, John Wesley said Taylor's views were "old deism in new dress" (OS, 69). However we label his views, they were similar to those of the deists insofar as both they and Taylor rejected received notions of religion if they conflicted with moralism and Enlightenment theism. Taylor differed from the deists by retaining belief in the prevalence of sin and the sovereignty of God, but they shared an "emphasis on the moral aspects of Christianity and distaste for the niceties of theological disputation ... well attuned to the commonsense rationalism and moralism of the Enlightenment" (OS, 70). In *Original Sin*, then, Edwards confronts an Enlightenment religion very much like the theism he describes in his more directed attacks on deism. He was challenging positions that, while not unique to deists, were close to the heart of the deist project.

Edwards's other great treatises from this period were the companion pieces *The End for Which God Created the World* and *Nature of True Virtue*, published together posthumously in 1765. It is striking that all of the objections Edwards poses to his thesis in the *End* are typical deist arguments. Most revolve around the criticism that the God of orthodoxy is an egotistical being obsessed with applause. One of Edwards's answers to this criticism uses the concept of "true value." We think egotism is wrong, he begins, because it conflicts with the nature of things—that which indeed is of the greatest value. An egotist has a "disposition to prefer self as if it were more than all." We recognize this as vicious because we know that no individual can possibly be of greater worth than the whole system of beings. But God is so great that all other beings are as nothing to him, and all other excellency is as nothing, even less than nothing, in comparison. And God knows that he is infinitely the most valuable being. So it is fitting that other beings should recognize this with praise, because it conforms to the "true nature and proportion of things."[33]

Another answer hangs on the notion of the public good. In created beings self-interest can be opposed to the public welfare. But this cannot be so with respect

---

31. Ibid., 391.
32. Ibid., 391, 407–9.
33. End, 451.

to the supreme being, who is the fountain of being and goodness to the whole. He alone is good for the whole system, so it is appropriate that worship should be given him (EW, 451–52).

True Virtue's very first chapter singles out "the more considerable Deists" as the ultimate proof of universal agreement among religious thinkers "that virtue most essentially consists in love" (EW, 541). This treatise is essentially an attack on "schemes of religion or philosophy" that are concerned with ethics but "have not a supreme regard to God, and love to him." In all such schemes, Edwards pronounced peremptorily, "there is nothing of the nature of true virtue or religion in them" (EW, 560). In other words, this work wants to expose the religious vacuity of all theological or philosophical proposals that separate morality from its integral dependence on religion. Arminian schemes tended in that direction, but for Edwards the deists made it a *fait accompli*.

It was not only in the Stockbridge period, however, that deism appears as a principal antagonist. The Edwardsean philosophy of history, developed in the late 1730s, also gave considerable prominence to deism. The series of sermons that eventually became the *History of the Work of Redemption* was meant to show that "'tis the gospel, and that only, that has actually been the means to bring the world to the knowledge of the true God" (HWR, 398). Only deists—not Arminians—were disputing the importance of the traditional Christian gospel for knowledge of true religion.[34] Arminians disputed the shape of the gospel and the interpretation of its scripture, but only the deists in principle rejected any need for the scripture and the gospel derived from it.

The *History of the Work of Redemption* portrays the church besieged by a number of enemies, but deism is preeminent. In sermon 24 Edwards describes the "corrupt opinions" Satan was using to oppose the church. After describing the beliefs of Anabaptists, enthusiasts, Socinians, Arminians, and Arians, he focuses on the deists.

> The deists wholly cast off the Christian religion, and are professed infidels. They ben't like the heretics, Arians and Socinians, and others, that own the Scriptures to be the word of God, and hold the Christian religion to be the true religion, but only deny these and these fundamental doctrines of the Christian religion; they deny the whole Christian religion. Indeed, they own the being of God but deny that Christ was the son of God, and say he was a mere cheat, and so they say all the prophets and apostles were. And they deny the whole Scripture; they deny that any of it is the word of God. They deny any revealed religion, or any word of God at all, and say that God has given mankind no other light to walk by but his own reason. (HWR, 432)

Not only did Edwards consider deism qualitatively worse than Arminianism and other heresies, but he also thought it was more active. Arminianism had "spread greatly in New England as well as Old," but deism had "overrun" England and was growing: it "prevails more and more" (HWR, 432). It was also, he thought,

---

34. Arminians accepted the inspiration of Scripture and other orthodox doctrines such as the deity of Christ and satisfaction theory of Christ's atonement. But they rejected Calvinist doctrines such as predestination, total depravity, and limited atonement.

the most representative form of anti-Christian thought. When in sermon 21 Edwards surveys the opposition Christianity had faced in the Roman empire, he singles out deism as the best example of anti-Christian philosophy. Celsus and Porphyry "wrote books against the Christian religion with a great deal of virulence and contempt, much after the manner that the deists of the present age do oppose and ridicule Christianity" (HWR, 388).

In sermon 25 Edwards declares that the preceding argument provides evidence that the Scriptures are the word of God (HWR, 442). No one but deists—certainly not Arminians—were denying this. In sermon 26, when describing the great work of God's Spirit that would come at the end of the age, Socinians, Arians, Quakers, and Arminians are listed together. Only deism is listed separately and with a distinctive adjective: "Deism that is now so *bold* shall be crushed and driven away and vanish to nothing" (HWR, 467; emphasis added). And in the following sermon, when picturing the final judgment, only deists are mentioned by name. All other heresies are lumped together in several nondescript phrases: "There will doubtless at the introducing of this dispensation be a visible and awful hand of God against blasphemers, *deists*, and obstinate heretics, and other enemies of Christ, terribly destroying them with remarkable tokens of wrath and vengeance" (HWR, 475; emphasis added). Perhaps he was reluctant to assign Arminians to the pit publicly; but he had no such hesitance with deists.[35]

Finally, all of sermon 13 seems to have been directed at deist principles. The entire sermon is a defense of the inspiration of the Old Testament, the loudest detractors from which were deists. On the first page he draws a conclusion from the preceding sermons, "From what has been said we may strongly argue that Jesus of Nazareth is indeed the Son of God, and the Savior of the world, and so that the Christian religion is the true religion" (HWR, 281). No group with any strength in England or New England denied these doctrines except the deists—certainly not the Arminians. The sermon proceeds to argue that the "vast variety of types and figures" in the Old Testament proves that Jesus is the Christ and therefore "the unreasonableness of deists that deny revealed religion" (HWR, 282). Christ and his redemption are the subject of every part of the Bible, the Old Testament included (HWR, 289). Even the histories of the wars and civil transactions of the kings and people "show forth Christ" (HWR, 283–84). Those who don't see Christ in the Old Testament "do but superficially read" it (HWR, 290). They are "like a man that has a box full of silver and gold, and don't know it, don't observe that it is anything more than a vessel filled with common stones" (HWR, 291).

Deism, Edwards, and Non-Christian Religions

As we have seen, deists used non-Christian religions as a powerful wedge to separate Christianity from what seemed to be reasonableness. Even more powerfully,

---

35. In *Misrepresentations Corrected* (1752), Edwards named the two extremes outside true faith as atheists and deists, not Arminians. EccW, 485, 491.

they used the existence of other religions to distinguish orthodoxy from what they conceived to be goodness and justice. A god cannot be good and just if he gives his saving revelation to only a minority of human beings and sends a majority of them to an eternal hell. For the deists, particularity and goodness were mutually exclusive terms.

We have also seen that for Edwards deism was a major, perhaps the principal, ideological enemy of Reformed Christianity in the eighteenth century. He had heard most of the deist arguments, including the ones that used other religions to implicate orthodoxy in a conspiracy of priests against the better part of humanity. Edwards's recourse was not only to fight back but to use the very tool—other religions—the deists had employed. For example, he answered the deist charge that the Incarnation is unreasonable by pointing to Julian the Apostate's belief that Jupiter begat Esculapius and sent him to Epidaurus to heal humanity. Edwards added that many nations believed in the incarnation of Jupiter himself (*Misc.* 1233).

To support his arguments against deist attacks on revelation, Edwards pointed out that the heathen showed more humility than the deists by their willingness to accept mysteries above the comprehension of mere reason. The deists, he charged, "receive nothing but what they clearly see, and draw out the demonstrable evidence of, from the fountain of their own unassisted reason." But the heathen received many things that were "incomprehensible" and "above their comprehension" without objection. The ancient heathen did not disdain "all dependence on teaching, as our deists do ... out of an affectation of thinking freely, and independently, and singularly. ... They were willing to pick up some scraps of their truth which came from revelation, which our deists reject all in the lump" (*Misc.* 1297).

But the other religions of the world were more than just a club that Edwards and the deists threw back and forth at each other. They also stimulated serious rethinking or at least reformulation of old thinking on both sides. As we saw in Chapter 1, the deists were inspired in part by the discoveries of new peoples and their religions to reconsider old religious claims. For his part, Edwards was intrigued by other religions, as the readings listed in his catalogue indicate. Deist use of other religions to attack orthodoxy may also have influenced his project in a number of ways. His typological reading of the Old Testament may have been motivated in part by the desire to demonstrate the unity of the Bible against deists who denied that unity (Chapter 6). His consideration of the nature of religion *qua* religion, and its history, was if not shaped by deism, certainly formulated with the recognition that his conclusions challenged deist thinking at nearly every point (Chapter 5). There is some indication, as we shall see in Chapter 7, that his soteriology—at least when applied to non-Christians—was influenced by new knowledge of the other religions of the world that deism helped stimulate.

Perhaps most important, however, deism stimulated his thinking on the relationship of reason to revelation. For it was at this point that the deists and Edwards differed most. This relationship was at the heart of the deist critique of Christian orthodoxy, and for Edwards it was here that deism proved itself to be the precise antithesis of basic Christian claims.

II

STRATEGIES OF RESPONSE

3

OUR NOBLEST FACULTY

The Promise and Limits of Reason in Religion

One day New England's philosopher was musing about the deists' refusal to accept any Christian doctrine that seemed to contradict common sense. Deciding to conduct an experiment that would amount to a theological object lesson, he asked a thirteen-year-old boy in his parish if he believed that a two-inch cube was eight times as big as a one-inch cube.

When the boy replied that it seemed impossible, Edwards marched him out to his workshop and carefully cut out a two-by-two-by-two-inch block of wood. Then, to the boy's amazement, he cut the block into eight pieces, each measuring one inch on a side. But even then, the boy was not convinced. He continued to count the blocks, comparing them to another cube two inches on a side. The boy could not bring himself to believe it and wondered if magic had been at work.

Edwards concluded with satisfaction that the puzzle in this block of wood was a greater mystery to the boy than the Trinity "ordinarily is to men." Its apparent contradiction (a two-inch cube being eight times as large as a one-inch cube) was a greater difficulty than "any mystery of religion to a Socinian or Deist"[1]—clear evidence that if revelation contains mystery, so does the nature prized by deists.

The deists of the early eighteenth century somehow failed to see that it is not self-evident that all propositions must be self-evident in order to be true. But this failure may have been inevitable, given their understanding of knowledge. Following Locke, they conceived of knowledge as the agreement or disagreement of ideas. Edwards, however, said knowledge is the perception of the "union or disunion of ideas, or the perceiving whether two or more ideas belong to one an-

---

1. Misc. 652; SPW, 388.

other." That is, the soul naturally associates ideas that are similar because of mental dispositions that intuitively recognize the connections between things.[2]

In other words, while for deists knowledge was no more than a matter of the intellect, for Edwards it reached down to the most basic drives of the human self. This disagreement on the nature of knowledge was symptomatic of Edwards's fundamental criticism of deism. It was too shallow, he charged, because it too easily divorced head from heart, reason from the affections, and understanding from experience. When knowledge is thought to be disconnected from the inner psyche, both reason and knowledge are distorted. Reason takes on an inflated sense of its own powers, and knowledge limits itself to what is already familiar.

In order to understand Edwards's attacks upon the deist enterprise, it is necessary first to examine his more general understanding of the relationship between reason and revelation. His criticisms of deist declarations about reason and knowledge of God make sense only when seen in the context of his fuller understanding of the roles reason and revelation play in our knowledge of God.

What Reason Can Know about God

Edwards had a lofty view of reason, when considered in the abstract, apart from its fallen condition in the unregenerate. He considered the human capacity to reason "a participation of the divine essence," "the rational image of God in man"; the "noblest," "most excellent," and "highest" faculty that "is designed by our maker to ever rule and exalt sense, imagination, and passion, which were made to be [its] servants." It is what most essentially distinguishes us from beasts. He identified the soul as essentially rational: "that thinking being that is contained in the body of every living man."[3]

Edwards also had considerable faith in the power of reason—once again abstracted from its fallen state in the unregenerate—to know religious truth. First and foremost, it can prove the existence of God. In fact, this task is "short and easy and what we naturally fall into" (Misc. 268), for God has implanted within the human mind a principle of causation that points to the existence of God, and for that matter all other being as well.[4] His unshakable conviction that "whatever begins to be must have a cause," which he presumed to be self-evident because of its placement in the human mind by God, was the "foundation of all reasoning

2. CNM, 9–13; CAO, 181; Edwards, "The Mind," no. 71, in SPW, 329 (emphasis added).
3. Misc. 210; sermon on Job 31:3, in SDK, 195; Sermon on Romans 2:10, in Hickman, 2:907; SDK, 347, 195; OS, 168; SDK, 309. Edwards defined reason toward the end of his life as the faculty that judges the truth of a proposition either immediately by self-evidence or by inference from an intuitively self-evident proposition: "that power or faculty an intelligent being has to judge of the truth of propositions, either immediately by only looking on the propositions, which is judging by intuition and self-evidence; or by putting together several propositions, which are already evident by intuition, or at least whose evidence is originally derived from intuition" (Misc. 1340).
4. This, of course, is what later philosophers called the principle of sufficient reason.

about the existence of things" (FW, 181). Without it we could prove neither the existence of God nor anything else (FW, 183).

Now it is important to note at this point that Edwards believed not only in an inborn principle of causation which reason can use to prove God's existence but also in an innate, pre-reflective awareness of God: "that secret intimation and sort of inward testimony that men have upon occasion of the being of God, and is in the minds of all men, however they may endeavor to root it out" (Misc. 268). In other words, Edwards believed that although reason can prove God when it uses a divinely implanted structure of reasoning, the soul does not need rational argument to come to an awareness of God, for there is a "natural inclination" that "does as it were prejudice" the soul to believe in God (Misc. 268).[5] Thus the existence of God is both "demonstrable" by reason and intuitively "plain and manifest": "it is manifest in ourselves, in our own bodies and souls, and in every thing about us wherever we turn our eye, whether to heaven, or to the earth, the air, or the seas" (MNB, 252).

This belief in an inborn principle pointing to God and confidence that one can prove God's existence with ease were not new to the Reformed tradition. Calvin himself taught that "there is within the human mind, and indeed by natural instinct, an awareness of divinity," that there are so many "innumerable evidences [of God] both in heaven and on earth" that humans "cannot open their eyes without being compelled to see him," and that the Scriptures contain so many internal evidences of its divinity that "it is easy to see that [they] . . . breathe something divine."[6] Seventeenth-century Reformed scholastics had similar confidence in an implanted *semen religionis* and in the ability of reason working properly—which since the fall happens only if regenerated—to find God with ease.[7] If Edwards differed with them, it was only in his more plentiful use of philosophical arguments to prove divine truths, and in his confidence that arguments could prove not only God's existence but many other features of the divine as well.

Most of Edwards's arguments for God's existence are forms of the so-called ontological argument. In Wallace Anderson's words, Edwards's versions were not based on Anselm's most perfect or greatest conceivable being but emerged "from the conception of being per se, or being in general" (SPW, 69). Edwards argued that there is no chance that there is not a God because the only other option is Nothing. But we cannot conceive of Nothing except as something. Or, at least, we cannot conceive of nothing in an absolute sense—that is, as the opposite of all being. This, for Edwards, was a contradiction. So the idea of God must correspond to something real.[8]

---

5. Edwards also spoke of a "sense of conscience" that suggests "a superior power that would revenge iniquity" (Misc. 533).

6. Calvin, Institutes, 1.3.1; 1.5.1–2; 1.8.1. Calvin believed that knowledge of God that comes through natural revelation is useful only to deprive the unregenerate of an excuse, and that because of the noetic effects of sin there is no true knowledge of God apart from Scripture; Calvin, Institutes, 1.3–6. Most Reformed scholastics echoed this approach; Muller, *Post-Reformation Reformed Dogmatics*, chap. 5. As we shall see, Edwards held similar views.

7. Muller, *Post-Reformation Reformed Dogmatics*, 168, 243.

8. For a fuller discussion of Edwards's proofs of God's existence, see SPW, 68–75.

Edwards often appealed to cosmological and teleological arguments to confirm his ontological argument. In *Freedom of the Will*, he explained his method:

> We argue [God's] being from our own being and the being of other things, which we are sensible once were not, but have begun to be; and from the being of the world, with all its constituent parts, and the manner of their existence; all which we see plainly are not necessary in their own nature, and so not self-existent; and therefore must have a cause . . . [After saying that the weakness of the human intellect prevents us from knowing God's existence by intuition through a "clear idea of general and universal being," he explains that] the way that mankind come to the knowledge of the being of God, is that which the Apostle speaks of (Rom. 1:20), "The invisible things of Him, from the creation of the world, are clearly seen; being understood by the things that are made; even his eternal power and Godhead." We first ascend, and prove a posteriori, or from effects, that there must be an eternal cause; and then secondly, prove by argumentation, not intuition, that this being must be necessarily existent; and then thirdly, from the proved necessity of his existence, we may descend, and prove many of his perfections a priori. (FW, 181–82)

In a variation of the cosmological argument (which moves from the dependent or contingent character of the world to God as its noncontingent source), Edwards argued for God's existence on the basis of the existence of thought: "The mere exertion of a new thought is a certain proof of God." For it is a new thing, which must have a cause. "[The cause] is not antecedent thoughts, for they are vanished and gone" (Misc. 267).

His teleological arguments (moving from the apparent design of the world to a divine designer) for a divine being appealed to the generation of species (Misc. 269), the need of a "wise, just and good being to govern the world" (Misc. 274), the marvelous "workmanship" with which our souls have been crafted (Misc. 199), and the order and regularity in spirits and minds (Misc. 200). Similar arguments were used in a sermon to the Indians at Stockbridge in 1752. Preaching the doctrine, "There certainly is a God," Edwards presented four lines of evidence: the regularity of nature (the appearance of the sun, heat and light), the law of causation ("Who keeps the clouds that they don't fall? Who makes the thunder and lightning, and trees and grass?"), the "marks of God" in a single "leaf in a flower," and the design of the human body (ears that are made to hear, nostrils to breathe, trunk and legs to walk, teeth to eat, tongue to taste, bowels to eliminate waste, and the soul to think and understand).[9] Therefore, he concluded, the world is "full of evidence of final causes [that] show the Efficient Cause of the world must be an intelligent voluntary agent" (Misc. 749).

God's existence is only the beginning of things that reason can tell us about God. Reason can also tell us what God is like. First and foremost, it can tell us that God is a Trinity.[10] "I think that it is within the reach of naked reason[11] to perceive

---

9. Sermon on Psalm 14:1 [2], 1752.

10. Here Edwards went further than Calvin and Turretin. Turretin explicitly denies that natural theology can prove the Trinity; Turretin, *Institutes of Elenctic Theology*, 2.1.6.

11. By "naked reason" Edwards here means unprejudiced reason, or reason that is not hindered

certainly that there are three distinct in God, each of which is the same [God], three that must be distinct" (Misc. 94). Edwards reasoned that the divine must be plural in persons because a perfect being will have perfect knowledge of itself, and an absolutely perfect idea of a thing is the very thing. Thus the Son. The love between the Father and the Son infinitely loving and delighting in each other is the perfect act of God, hence a substantial act, "even the essence of God." Thus the Holy Spirit (Misc. 94).

Reason can also tell us about the end or purpose of creation. Edwards confidently declared the following "to be the dictates of reason": that there is no insufficiency, indigence, or mutability in God, or dependence of the Creator on the creature, for his perfection or happiness; what is good in itself is what God should value for itself; God's highest end must be what is superior in value to all other things; God himself is God's highest end, since he is infinitely the greatest and best of beings.[12]

Remarkably, Edwards even believed that reason alone—albeit when considered apart from its sinful corruptions—is capable of perceiving what is most important to know about God: his excellency and glory. What makes this remarkable is that for Edwards a vision of God's beauty or excellency is what finally distinguishes the saved from the damned, the saints from the demons. All, even the damned and demons in hell, will one day see God's holiness, but only the saints will see the *beauty* of that holiness. Yet Edwards preached in 1740 that natural reason, in and of itself and therefore apart from its sinful corruption but nevertheless without special illumination by the Holy Spirit, is as capable of knowing God's glory and excellency "as of any other knowledge whatsoever—and what is as plainly and abundantly manifested as anything whatsoever, innumerable ways, both in the word and works of God" (MNB, 252).[13]

Edwards taught that reason can prove a host of other things about God and divine things. For example, it is clear from reason that God punishes sin (Misc. 533); that God created humanity for happiness;[14] that Christians should have knowledge about the Creation, sin, and redemption and should know that what is revealed in the books of the Bible is necessary for God's intelligent creatures to know (HWR 286); that gratitude to God ought to be manifested at our own expense; that we should abstract our thoughts and affections from all earthly things— the "wise heathen plainly saw" this; that children should obey their parents—the

---

by sinful corruption. Only reason that has had its sinful prejudices removed by the light of a vision of Christ's excellency is capable of seeing such truths. See DSL, 74–75. Despite using the same term, Edwards means something else when he criticizes the deist use of the word "reason," as we shall see; there he means unregenerate reason, which is prejudiced by sin and without the assistance of revelation.

12. End, 420–21.

13. This seems to contradict Edwards's notion that only the regenerate can see God's beauty. But in this sermon Edwards means unprejudiced and regenerate reason when he says that reason can behold God's excellency. There he makes clear that although the unregenerate mind is "as capable of it, as of any other knowledge whatsoever . . . [it] can see nothing at all of it" (MNB, 252).

14. Sermon on Revelation 21:18, 19.

Native Americans know this; that God should communicate spiritual wisdom to his saints; and that self-denial is better than self-indulgence—even children know this.[15]

Edwards agreed with John Toland and Matthew Tindal that reason can prove whether or not Scripture is revealed and reliable. The doctrine for his sermon on 1 Corinthians 2:11–13 was, "'Tis by the faculty of reason that men know it to be a revelation and by that faculty that they know that a divine revelation is to be depended on." In a 1727 sermon he argued that miracles and prophecies are "evidence that the book where they are revealed is the Word of God."[16] Near the close of his career he wrote what was to be one of his most popular works in the twentieth century, *The Nature of True Virtue* (1755). Its companion volume, *The End for Which God Created the World* (1755), argues from both Scripture and reason, but *True Virtue* appeals only to reason. By the "light of nature" alone it asserts that true virtue is the cordial consent or union of being to Being in general (548), that "true virtue must chiefly consist in love to God" (550), and that true virtue is neither conscience nor moral sense nor self-love (589–627).

As Edwards grew older, however, he diverged somewhat from this "seemingly rationalist position." Wilson Kimnach has suggested recently that as a young man Edwards may have "wanted to demonstrate that he knew the way the world was going and that he could keep up with the best of the avant-garde if he so desired." He "apparently believed that he could effectively control people's minds and opinions by the sheer power of his arguments." But after reading John Locke and John Norris, he began to lose confidence in the adequacy of words and rational discourse in general to convey truths about divine things. Soon he allowed that arguments from reason were "only for those who are impressed with such proofs" and preached in 1727 that while reason and logical arguments can make theological dogmas seem *true*, they may not make them seem *real*. Dogma can point to an abstract principle, but it cannot impart the subtle and suprarational sense of the divine.[17]

Kimnach is undoubtedly correct in his appraisal. After the mid-1720s, one sees in Edwards less emphasis on the power of reason and more emphasis on the centrality of beauty in true religious experience. In sermons before 1724 Edwards frequently appeals first to reason and then to Scripture to prove a doctrine. But he reverses that order far more frequently after that date; in *A Divine and Supernatural Light* (1734), for example, he argues the doctrine by showing that "FIRST. It is scriptural" (77) and "SECONDLY, This doctrine is rational" (81).

---

15. SDK, 552n; sermon on Job 1:21; Hickman, 2:427; DSL, 84; Hickman, 2:59.
16. Sermon on Acts 17:11, "True Nobleness of Mind," in SDM, 233.
17. SDK, 195, 201. Very early in his career (1723), Edwards compared the sense of the *reality* of divine things to seeing a beautiful face. Arguments from reason alone are like knowing of a beautiful face by hearsay. One can be convinced that there is a beautiful face because of the reliability of testimony (convincing one that it is true that the face is beautiful), but only *seeing* the face "causes love to burn in the heart"—i.e., proves the *reality* of the claim. Edwards also described knowing the reality of divine things as "feeling" the truth "intuitively" so that one is "certain" of them. Knowing they are real transforms the heart, but knowing that they are only true does not. "A Spiritual Understanding of Divine Things Denied to the Unregenerate," in SDM, 79, 78, 81.

Religious Affections (1746), the theological work that sets out to portray true religion, places aesthetic vision at the center and claims that certainty comes not by rational proof but supernatural enlightenment. In his description of the fifth positive sign of grace—"a reasonable and spiritual conviction of the judgment, of the reality and certainty of divine things"—Edwards argues that apologetics will never lead a soul to regeneration. Only the intuitive knowledge of the beauty of the gospel that comes by revelation can do that: seeing that "God is God, and distinguished from all other beings, and exalted above 'em, chiefly by his divine beauty, which is infinitely diverse from all other beauty" (298). Arguments "fetched from ancient traditions, histories, and monuments" can give neither regeneration nor assurance of salvation (305).

Nevertheless, reason's natural capacity is considerable, and its product, knowledge, has important functions both before and after the reception of saving grace. Knowledge about God, gained by unregenerate reason reflecting on both being and Scripture, is a means of grace. It gives the unregenerate "the greatest advantage for the obtaining [of] grace" as "outward means that do most exhibit the truth to our minds" (Misc. 539). Similarly, false notions hinder grace. "A false notion gives no opportunity for grace to act, but on the contrary, will hinder its acting" (ibid). Insofar as knowledge can be a means of grace, faith can be built on rational arguments: "Rational arguments may savingly convince the soul of the truth of the things of religion" (Misc. 336).

Now these statements must be understood in their proper context. Edwards did not believe that rational arguments alone could move the heart and bring conversion. But like other means of grace such as reading the Scriptures, they could be used by the Spirit to convey spiritual truth. As he put it once in a series of sermons on Christian knowledge, there is no spiritual knowledge without rational knowledge. There can be no spiritual apprehension of divine things without some degree of rational perception. "No object can come at the heart but through the door of the understanding, and there can be no spiritual knowledge of that of which there is not first a rational knowledge." The more rational knowledge, "the more opportunity will there be, when the Spirit shall be breathed into your heart, to see the excellency of these things, and to taste the sweetness of them." Conversion comes by spiritual vision, not rational argument. But it does not take place in an intellectual vacuum. Rational argument is a means through which grace is given to see.[18]

By rational argument Edwards did not mean a medieval syllogism, or even one of his rational proofs. Instead he meant something close to what the Reformers meant when they insisted on the conjunction of Word and Spirit in conversion.[19] Edwards expanded "Word" to include not just preaching from the Bible but all evidences, concepts, and arguments that are drawn from Scripture or nature to present truths concerning the redemption. In other words, the mind is not disconnected from the affections. When the heart is given sight to see the beauty of

---

18. "Christian Knowledge," in Hickman, 2:158, 162; RA, 266–68.
19. See George, *Theology of the Reformers*, 315–16.

God, it sees something that the mind is able to imagine. Faith, then, contains an intellectual dimension. As examples of "rational arguments" Edwards cited Jesus' discussion with Nicodemus in John 3, Jesus' conversation with the Samaritan woman in John 4, John's testimony about Jesus throughout his gospel, Thomas's hand in Jesus' side, and the apostles' arguments for the resurrection in early church preaching (Misc. 636; Misc. 539).

In New Testament times, rational arguments consisted primarily of the words and deeds of Jesus and the apostles. Today they are usually based on the words of Scripture. The words in and of themselves, however, have no natural power. They are "only made use of to convey to the mind the subject matter of this saving instruction . . . [that] the seeing of the excellency of the doctrine may be immediately from the Spirit of God. . . . So that the notions that are the subject matter of this light, are conveyed to the mind by the word of God; but that due sense of the heart, wherein this light formally consists, is immediately by the Spirit of God" (DSL, 77).[20]

A second function of unregenerate knowledge about God is for condemnation. This knowledge will destroy excuses that could otherwise be made by the unregenerate at the day of judgment (Misc. 1338). This was routine in the Reformed tradition, but it was used less commonly by Edwards than by his scholastic predecessors. In fact, in a Miscellanies entry in which he reflects at length on why God gave religious knowledge by revelation to the heathen, Edwards suggested four uses for this knowledge, and not one is for condemnation (Misc. 1162). This suggests, as we shall see, that Edwards had more hope than some of his Reformed predecessors did for the salvation of the heathen.

After regeneration reason is a "great friend."[21] Assisted by revelation and the Spirit, it is freed to help the soul grow in knowledge of divine things. But it is significantly strengthened by the process of regeneration. In that process, the Spirit is united with the mind (DSL, 69), which is then drawn to the truth in objects of perception. The Spirit in a manner of speaking casts a light on "divine objects" so that their reality becomes alluring. Their "beauty and sweetness . . . draw forth" the exercises of the mind and thereby stimulate the mind to act as it should (DSL, 75). After first seeing the beauty of divine things reason acts to trust Christ (DSL, 85) and henceforth is regulated by the love of Christ (EW, 178, 185).

In the glorious age of the Spirit that will precede the millennium,[22] reason will be even further strengthened. There will be a new and glorious advancement of human learning, which will serve as a "handmaid to religion" to advance the kingdom that God is preparing for his Son (HWR, 441). Even now God is using printing and the great increase of learning during the Enlightenment "to prepare for the coming prosperity of the church" before and during

---

20. Turretin had a similar conception: "The Word acts objectively; the Spirit, efficiently. The Word strikes the ears externally; the Spirit lays bare the heart, internally." Turretin, Institutes of Elenctic Theology, 2.2.9.

21. "The Peace Which Christ Gives," in Faust and Johnson, Jonathan Edwards: Representative Selections, 139.

22. For a description of this period, see McDermott, One Holy and Happy Society, 77–82.

the millennium. "Thus the wealth of the wicked is laid up for the just, agreeable to Proverbs 13:22" (HWR, 441).

At first glance Edwards might seem to have perpetuated the celebration of reason that began with the Cambridge Platonists and culminated in the deists. Henry More's conviction that reason connects humanity to God and Benjamin Whichcote's contention that reason is the voice of God encouraged the hope that reason could recognize divine truth.[23] After Locke said that reason is the final judge of revelation, deists proclaimed that reason can know with certainty all religious truth. For example, said Thomas Chubb, reason was improved by the Fall, and can find forgiveness with certainty.[24] Matthew Tindal agreed that revelation was unnecessary to find forgiveness from God.[25]

Edwards, however, distinguished fallen reason from regenerate reason. The potential of reason to find God was indeed glorious—and on this point Edwards was not far from Calvin[26]—but its potential was fulfilled only when reason was reborn through aesthetic vision that recognized the christological meaning of the Scriptures. Edwards agreed with the Platonists that only the virtuous soul could recognize divine truth, and he charged the deists with failure to make this crucial distinction. Because they ignored the universal propensity of fallen reason to miss religious truth, he argued, they found not God but an idol constructed by their own imaginations.

The Limits of Reason

Despite the promise of reason, Edwards explained, human beings have not been able to find God and the fullness of truth through reason. This has not been the fault of reason, for it was given from God, but the fact remains that reason has failed. Edwards's description of this failure travels along two tracks; the first delineates precisely what reason has failed to accomplish, and the second explains why. In this section we shall look at reason's limits, or exactly what reason has failed to deliver.

---

23. More, *Cabbalah*, sigs. A7–A8, cited in Patrides, *Cambridge Platonists*, 11; Whichcote, *Moral and Religious Aphorisms*, no. 76. On Edwards and the Platonists, see Lowance, "Jonathan Edwards and the Platonists"; Gohdes, "Aspects of Idealism in Early New England"; Conkin, *Puritans and Pragmatists*; Watts, "Jonathan Edwards and the Cambridge Platonists"; Watts, "The Neoplatonic Basis of Jonathan Edwards's 'True Virtue'"; and Howe, "Cambridge Platonists."

24. Locke, *The Reasonableness of Christianity*, 205n; DCR, 8, 11.

25. CAO, 391–92.

26. Calvin also taught that if reason had not fallen it would have been able to reach true piety: "The natural order was that the frame of the universe should be the school in which we were to learn piety, and from it pass over to eternal life and perfect felicity. But after man's rebellion, our eyes—wherever they turn—encounter God's curse. . . . For even if God wills to manifest his fatherly favor to us in many ways, yet we cannot by contemplating the universe infer that he is Father. . . . This magnificent theater of heaven and earth, crammed with innumerable miracles, Paul calls the 'wisdom of God' (1 Cor. 1:21). Contemplating it, we ought in wisdom to have known God" (*Institutes* 2.6.1).

Edwards made an appeal to history for evidence of his contention that reason has failed to deliver what the deists have claimed it delivers. If there were some who thought reason had given knowledge of the true God and how sinful humanity could be reconciled to God, they were looking at a different history of the world from what Edwards had found.

> He that thinks to prove that the world ever did in fact by wisdom know God[,] that any nation upon earth, or any set of men ever did, from the principles of reason only, without any assistance from revelation, find out the true nature of the true worship of the Deity, must find out some history of the world entirely different from all the accounts which the present sacred and profane writings do give us; or his opinion must appear to be a meer guess, and conjecture of what is barely possible, but what all history assures us never was really done in the world. (Misc. 986)

Edwards was convinced that history proved that there had been no major moral reformation of the world before Christ. Even the Greek and Roman philosophers, despite flashes of brilliance, had missed the mark: "All the endeavors of philosophers had proved in vain, for many ages, to reform the world," either morally or spiritually before Christ (RA 140). The Greeks and Romans had "wise political rulers" and "excellent laws for regulating the civil state. . . . They excelled other nations in arts, government and civility, almost as much as men in common do beasts. Yet they could not deliver themselves from their heathenism" (MNB, 250).

God waited fifteen hundred years before he sent his Christ in order to prove that there was no other remedy for the world's darkness—that the "wisdom of the philosophers" had failed. By that time it was clear that human learning was finally futile when it comes to the moral and spiritual reformation of a society. And it was no wonder it failed: human beings cannot see the glory of God without knowing his design, which is revealed only in Scripture (HWR, 180, 440, 521).

The religion of the heathen was further proof of reason's failure. Even in their most flourishing state, the Greeks and Romans "worshipped innumerable gods . . . with most obscene and horrid rites. To some they offered human sacrifices"; even parents would offer their own "poor child [who] was laid naked in burning brass, and so burnt to death . . . . And thus many thousands of poor babes have been offered up" (MNB, 248). Others took on

> the most monstrous and horrible shapes . . . images of men openly exposing their nakedness. . . . One god they reckoned notorious for drunkenness; others notorious for uncleanness; to others they ascribed lying and stealing; . . . In matters of morality . . . many whole nations have professedly approved of many things directly contrary to the light of nature . . . such as revenge, cruelty and incest. Many nations have openly allowed the practice of sodomy . . . drunkenness and whoredom and the most abominable lewdness . . . being, if I may so speak, much more beastly than the beasts themselves. (MNB, 248)

There were exceptions; Socrates and Plato, for example, were the only heathen philosophers who based their morality on religious foundations. Yet even Plato failed to condemn publicly the idolatries of his day (Misc. 1238). In sum, the whole world lay in religious darkness until the coming of Christ. Despite the truths taught by the "wisest heathen," the Greek and Roman worlds generally embraced "the absurdest opinions and practices that all civilized nations now acknowledge to be crazy foolishness" (HWR, 400). This universal "darkness in religious things" proves that there was "no remedy before Christ" (MNB, 250). No nation ever freed itself from this state by its own wisdom. Indeed, it could not.

Toland and Tindal had boasted that reason alone had shown humanity the most basic religious truths. Edwards countered that reason had shown itself impotent to discover on its own the unity of God (Misc. 519), life after death (Misc. 514), the author and purpose of the world (End, 419),[27] the length of the sabbatical week, the final judgment, the nature of heaven, and sacrifice for sin.[28] These things had been shown by God to Adam and Noah, who passed them down by tradition to their descendants. Just because they appear reasonable in hindsight does not prove that reason originally discovered them.

Most important, reason was never able to show how sinful humans could be reconciled to their Creator. Locke and the deists may have been right to say that reason could show the necessity of repentance after sin, but they were wrong to believe that reason could show sinners how to achieve true repentance (Misc. 1304). So assurance of salvation was also impossible to find by reason alone (Misc. 1239). Since God is just as well as good, reason can never assure us that God is ready to forgive. What if he has greater regard for justice than mercy? Reason could never prove that he would forgive all sins, no matter how great. Nor could it prove how much repentance is necessary. Therefore the light of nature may show us the general shape of true religion, but it is unable to provide a religion of restoration. In other words, nature reveals God, but humans have not come to know the true God through nature. Even if they had come to this knowledge, they still would not have known if God wanted to save them or damn them (Misc. 1304).

Besides failing to provide a religion of restoration, fallen reason has been unable to show God's excellency or beauty, which is seen only in Christ. This means that even if a person by reason discovered all Christian doctrines and all the moral and natural attributes of God, she still would not have saving knowledge of God. For that knowledge comes through a vision of God's beauty, which is found most clearly in Christ. Reason abstracted from history and sin is capable of seeing God's beauty in Christ, but fallen reason as known in this world has proved itself incapable of this aesthetic vision (MNB, 252). As Kimnach noted, Edwards came to the conclusion that while fallen reason can prove religious propositions to be *true*, it cannot make them seem *real*.

Such vision is impossible without the knowledge of Christ that comes through revelation in Scripture. In fact, without knowledge of how it relates to Christ, *no* doctrine is known rightly (Misc. 519). Hence "the whole of Christian divinity depends on divine revelation" because even truths taught by the light of nature are not taught

---

27. Edwards believed that reason in the wake of revelation could show these things, but on its own could never reach "clear and established . . . settled judgments" about them. EW, 419.

28. "Perpetuity and Change of the Sabbath," in Hickman, 2:95; "The Final Judgement," in Hickman, 2:192; sermon on Revelation 21:18 [2]; HWR, 134, 137.

> in that manner in which it is necessary for us to know it, for the knowledge of no truth in divinity is of any significance to us any otherwise than it some way or other belongs to the gospel scheme, or has relevance to Christ the Mediator. It signifies nothing for us to know anything of any one of God's perfections unless we know them as manifested in Christ, and so it signifies nothing to us to know any part of our duty unless it will [bear] some relation to Christ. It profits us not to have any knowledge of the law of God, unless it be either to fit us for the glad tidings of the gospel or to be a means of our sanctification in Christ Jesus and to influence us to serve God through Christ by an evangelical obedience and therefore we stand in the greatest necessity of a divine revelation. (Misc. 837)

Hence deist knowledge of God is not true knowledge because it denies the revelation of Christ. Even their knowledge that God is one and not many is somehow distorted because it does not acknowledge that the one God was in Christ reconciling the world to himself. If God the Redeemer is not known, God the Creator is not known truly.

This also means that all knowledge of God short of regeneration, though that knowledge is propositionally correct, is nevertheless fundamentally distorted. For without a vision of Christ's beauty, which comes in regeneration, nothing is seen truly. In a passage perhaps emblematic of all his thought, Edwards insisted on the centrality of this vision to all true religious knowledge.

> He that sees the beauty of holiness, or true moral good, sees the greatest and most important thing in the world, which is the fullness of all things, without which all the world is empty, no better than nothing, yea, worse than nothing. Unless this is seen, nothing is seen, that is worth the seeing, for there is no other true excellency or beauty. Unless this be understood, nothing is understood, that is worthy of the exercise of the noble faculty of understanding. This is the beauty of the Godhead, and the divinity of Divinity (if I may so speak), the good of the Infinite Fountain of God; without which God himself (if that were possible to be) would be an infinite evil: without which, we ourselves had better not have been; and without which there had better have been no being. He therefore in effect has nothing, that knows not this. (RA, 274)[29]

For Edwards, then, reason can show many religious truths, but they are not known properly unless they are seen in relation to Christ and his redemption. Even knowledge of Christ and redemption is distorted and finally unhelpful unless it is known through aesthetic vision of God's beauty. So reason can provide mere "notional" knowledge of Christ through the words of Scripture but not knowledge of the true God in the absence of aesthetic vision. At this point the radical nature of Edwards's rejoinder to deism can be seen: he rejected not only the sufficiency of reason for knowledge of God but even the sufficiency of Scripture. Revelation is necessary, he contended, but in two senses. It is necessary in Scripture as the rational means by which spiritual knowledge comes; but spiritual knowledge comes only by revelation of the beauty of God in Christ. Written revelation is necessary for rational knowledge; spiritual revelation is necessary to give full meaning to that rational knowledge.

---

29. This vision of divine beauty is christological, as can be seen in RA, 258–59, 274, 344–57, and passim.

This is why even the devil can know about Christ and yet behave like the devil. It explains why he has "a great degree of speculative knowledge in divinity . . . concerning the nature and attributes of God [and] works of God" and indeed is "orthodox in his faith . . . [not] a Deist, Socinian, Arian, Pelagian or antinomian." Yet he sees no more of the "supreme holy beauty" than a man born blind sees colors.[30]

Similarly, a person can know the attributes of God and their harmony, the doctrine of the Trinity, the two covenants, the offices of Christ, salvation by Christ, justification, conversion, and the Spirit's work to apply Christ's redemption to the hearts of persons; may have more knowledge than hundreds of true saints; and may even see all the "external glory of Christ," yet not have saving grace. For "divinity . . is the doctrine of living to God by Christ. . . . There is no one doctrine, no promise, no rule, but what some way or other relates to the Christian and divine life, or our living to God by Christ." Reason can show all these truths about God and Christ, but it cannot show the beauty of God in Christ. Only with a vision of this beauty can one see the fullest meaning of all other truths.[31]

Why Reason Fails

Now we must look at the second track of Edwards's analysis of reason's failure. We have just seen *what* it fails to do; in this section we will examine Edwards's description of *why* it fails.

It is not surprising, given that he lived during the Age of Reason, that Edwards would insist that reason's failure could not be attributed to a defect within reason itself.[32] As we have seen, Edwards always maintained that reason as it proceeded from God's hands was (and is now when abstracted from the sinful human condition) fully capable of giving full knowledge of God and true religion, even of God's beauty, the key to all other knowledge of God. He did not attribute reason's failure to its finitude, as did Duns Scotus and other fifteenth-century scholastics.[33] Instead, he argued that reason had not been given the opportunity to do its proper work.

Occasionally, perhaps influenced by his reading of the Cambridge Platonists, Edwards attributed reason's inability to its union with bodily existence: "The body clogs and hinders the soul." More often, however, following his Reformed predecessors, he wrote that sin "stupefies" and "hinders" reason. Sin causes judgment to inquire not at the mouth of reason but at the mouth of inclination. Thus judgment is dominated by "wicked lusts" rather than reason; reason is prevented from exercising its proper rule over the soul. For example, carnal lust tells the

---

30. "True Grace Distinguished from the Experience of Devils," in Hickman, 2:43, 48.
31. Ibid., 43, 46; "Christian Knowledge," in Hickman, 2:158.
32. And, of course, this was a truism in the history of Christian thought. For example, see Thomas Aquinas, *Summa Theologica*, I, Q. 94.
33. Muller, *Post-Reformation Reformed Dogmatics*, 126.

soul that this world is all-important, while reason would say that eternal things are more important. Reason whispers to the soul that it should deny outward pleasures and redeem the time, but the will fights reason and continually wars against it.[34]

How does sin subvert reason so effectively? To answer this question Edwards turned first to epistemology. This is not the place to unpack all the complexities of Edwards's epistemology,[35] but I will describe his stipulation that human understanding of divine things depends on the "state of our minds" (FW, 146)—that is, a correspondence between those things outside the self and certain conditions (ideas) of the mind even before it perceives those things. To put it another way, Edwards claimed that we can apprehend only those ideas which find a corresponding idea in the "disposition"[36] of our minds. For example, we cannot comprehend the "complex idea" of benevolence unless our minds already contain the "simple ideas" (a simple idea is a "feeling or sense of the mind" [Misc. 123]) that combine to form the complex idea of benevolence.

Edwards derived the terms—simple and complex ideas—from Locke, but his use of them in this context was more subtle. Locke said that humans fail to find true religion because, among other things, priestcraft has kept them from using their reason. Edwards replied that with or without priests reason was too debilitated by sin to see what is essential in religion, because sin blocked the reception of the right simple ideas. On this point Edwards was closer to the Cambridge Platonists, whom he had read at Yale. Henry More and John Smith said that vision of the divine depended on the state of one's soul; one had to have a loving soul to understand the God of love. He was even closer to Clement and Plotinus, who believed that the soul cannot see beauty unless it possesses a measure of beauty itself.[37]

Simple spiritual ideas are experienced; they cannot be obtained by hearing or reading a description of them.[38] Their presence in the mind creates a disposition that resonates whenever it perceives something outside the mind that "harmonizes" with it. Edwards in fact compared the regenerate soul to a "musical ear" that naturally discerns spiritual "sounds" that harmonize with its disposition. Since the regenerate

---

34. "True Grace Distinguished from the Experience of Devils," in Hickman, 2:42, 47; sermon on Hosea 5:15, in Hickman, 2:833; sermon on Matthew 11:11–19, in Hickman, 2:919.

35. For excellent introductions to Edwards's epistemology, see William S. Morris, "The Genius of Jonathan Edwards," in Brauer, *Reinterpretation in American History*, 29–65; Anderson, "Introduction" to SPW, 111–36; and the Wainwright discussions listed in note 42.

36. This is different from Locke's conception of the mind having innate powers to ratiocinate based on step-by-step acquisition of concepts and knowledge. Edwards's disposition of mind is a capacity for direct and immediate apprehension that does not depend on prior reflection or conscious methodical procedure. John E. Smith points out that the difference is similar to F. H. Bradley's distinction between having something *before* the mind and having something *in* the mind. "The exercise of habit [disposition], for Edwards, is governed by a regular order in the mind, but it is not necessary for the structure embodied in habit to be *before* the mind in order for the person to follow the habit." Anderson, "Introduction" to SPW, 121–22; Smith, *Jonathan Edwards: Puritan, Preacher, Philosopher*, 24. For more on Edwards's use of "disposition," see Chapter 7.

37. Locke, *The Reasonableness of Christianity*, 165; Smith, *Select Discourses*, 2–3; More, *Mystery of Godliness*, v and "Preface," viii; Clement, *Stromata* 7.3; Plotinus 1.6.9.

38. In RA Jonathan Edwards calls spiritual perception "a new simple idea," 205; see also Locke's

soul is holy, it can discern holiness: "The soul distinguishes as a musical ear; and besides, holiness itself consists in spiritual harmony; and whatever don't agree with that, as a base to a treble, the soul rejects" (Misc. 141). Hence there is an "echo" or "consent" between divine things outside the self and the corresponding "affections of mind" that immediately recognize the "sweetness" of those divine things.

> The mind has those ideas of things spiritual, and therefore perceives what agrees and harmonizes with it; and if anything be mentioned that is congruous and harmonizes to it, the mind feels it immediately and echoes to it: it sees wherein the agreement is, and how it naturally falls in with it. And at such a time the soul, as soon as it looks into God's Word and sees a thing spiritual of which it has an idea, there mentioned, and reads the dependent passages, it sees that there is an exact correspondency, and that things consent in the same manner. (Misc. 126)

This is Edwards's first way of explaining why reason in the unregenerate is not able to do its proper work. To the unregenerate "the things of the gospel seem all so tasteless and insipid. . . . They are a parcel of words to which they in their own minds have no corresponding ideas. . . . This is why the Scripture is no more sweet to them." Their disposition of mind does not contain the simple ideas that correspond to the ideas of the gospel. Because they do not possess "faith, trust in God, holy resignation, divine love, [and] Christian charity, [they] can't have an idea of the excellencies and beauties of God and Christ, of which those things are the image" (Misc. 239).[39] Therefore even the most eloquent and diligent men of the world are not able to know the things of the gospel, "for the disposition, as we have shown, must necessarily be changed first" (Misc. 123).

Hence the first explanation of why reason fails is that understanding of divine things requires the presence of simple ideas that the unregenerate lack. Without those simple ideas, reason cannot function as it ought. Its proper operation depends on a certain disposition of the mind; without that holy disposition, reason is prevented from seeing the highest and most essential religious truths. These truths therefore cannot be communicated in simply propositional form to the unregenerate; they are "incommunicable" and "ineffable" because they depend on the presence of simple ideas and a resulting vision that issues from "ten thousand little relations and mutual agreements" (Misc. 201).

Edwards's second way of explaining reason's failure was to point to prejudice. Fallen humanity, he was convinced, tends to suspect and disbelieve anything that

---

Essay, bk. 2, chaps. 1–12. Locke said that we apprehend only ideas, not the things represented by the ideas. Edwards, however, posited a closer connection between the knowing mind and the object of experience by connecting the mind to nature via God's ordering: "God evidently designed such particulars to be together in the mind and in other things." That is, God designed both likenesses in things and the mind's ability to recognize those likenesses: he made "the soul of such a nature that those particulars which he thus made to agree are unavoidably together in the mind, one naturally exciting and including the others." Edwards, "The Mind," no. 37, in SPW, 355; Edwards, "The Mind," no. 43, in SPW, 362.

39. The preceding affections are not simple ideas *per se* but are founded upon and rooted in simple ideas that are received in a "discrete experience, incapable of reproduction through language." Cherry, *Theology of Jonathan Edwards*, 18.

is not immediately evident to the eyes. Human beings will generally "receive nothing but what they can clearly see, and draw out" (*Misc.* 1297). They are predisposed to doubt what is unfamiliar, even if it comes from a credible authority. This was especially true in the Age of Reason, when the opposite of Tertullian's motto came to be a article of faith: Credo quia non impossible est.[40]

Prejudice arises from education and custom. It is difficult to persuade people that a new way is better, particularly if it opposes the "general cry and fashion and vogue of an age," whose "exceeding strong influence [is] like a strong stream that carries all that way." Prejudice also favors "individual great men . . . in power, riches or honorable place . . . how much more weighty a man's sayings are after he becomes a bishop than before." Another prejudice is from "ridicule or an high, strong, overbearing, contemptuous style." And the strongest prejudices of all are religious (*SPW*, 387–88).

Indeed. The greatest demonstration of human prejuice, for Edwards, was a natural human propensity away from the true God. The fallen human mind, he declared, is "naturally" full of arguments against the gospel (*RA*, 307). It is prone to idolatry, with a disposition to act contrary to reason (*OS*, 147, 153). This propensity results not only from the absence of an inclination to truth but also from the presence of a positive "principle" or "cause" that "hinders the exercises of [human] faculties about the things of religion" (*MNB*, 247). This is a "depraved disposition" that overcomes "the greatest learning and the strongest natural reason" (*MNB*, 250; *OS*, 153).

The result is "a multiplicity of deceits . . . thousands of delusions" (*MNB*, 251). Human beings "rack their brains" to devise arguments that will stop their consciences and make them feel justified in their sin.[41] They do not act rationally and are incapable of seeing the beauty of divine things, which alone can free reason to work properly (*OS*, 157; *DSL*, 85).

Hence for Edwards, reason is capable of knowing God, but only when one's cognitive faculties are rightly disposed. God cannot be known by "objective" reason that has not been enlivened by spiritual experience. As William J. Wainwright has put it, "A suitably disposed natural reason is thus capable of establishing God's existence and general nature. Truths which depend on the ideas of holiness and true beauty can also be established by rational arguments, but the force of these can be appreciated only by people with spiritual frames."[42]

Therefore reason is not enough. According to Edwards, it can tell many true things about God. But without aesthetic vision it can never get at the reality it was meant to show. For that reason, revelation is necessary.

---

40. "I believe only that which is not impossible." For a fine introduction to this period, see the older but still reliable Cragg, *Reason and Authority*.

41. "Christian Cautions," in Hickman, 176.

42. Wainwright, "Nature of Reason"; see also Wainwright's excellent chapter on Edwards and reason in his recent *Reason and the Heart*.

4

SIGNATURES OF DIVINE MAJESTY

The Reason and Mystery of Revelation

More than anything else, it was its rejection of revelation that distinguished Enlightenment religion from all of its adversaries. Before the rise of deism, there were plenty of factions within what could be called orthodoxy that fought over the true form of orthodoxy and what the Bible really meant. But it was not until the rise of deism in the seventeenth century that substantial numbers of the intellectual elite openly denied the notion that God had spoken through the Bible. Soon "natural religion," which contended that God speaks only through nature and reason, became the most distinctive religious product of the Enlightenment.

Jonathan Edwards joined a host of orthodox thinkers who tried to defend the notion of revelation from its Enlightenment detractors. Edwards's arguments were not wholly dissimilar from those of his allies, but they showed greater subtlety and sensitivity to deist reasoning. He began his defense of revelation with a series of arguments for its necessity. Since he believed that reason was prevented by sin from leading human beings to the true God, he was convinced that revelation was necessary to supply what fallen reason could not. Only revelation had been able to provide true knowledge of God's nature and unity, God's works, Creation, government, his great designs, his will, rewards and punishments, the nature and end of human happiness, morality, life after death, the origin of sin, the future state, and the way of redemption (Misc. 128, Misc. 582).

The Necessity of Revelation

Edwards argued that deists misunderstood reason when arguing against revelation. They wrongly presumed they knew such a thing as "naked reason." In reality there is very little of such a thing. What they did not realize was that there is a much closer connection between reason and revelation than they ever acknowledged. Reason is dependent on revelation. It is formed and assisted by revelation in ways that are largely unrecognized. The original deposit of revelation given to Adam and Noah and their children offered notions and ways of thinking apart from which later philosophy would have been impossible. Following Locke and Samuel Clarke, Edwards explained that there were many notions people then took to be dictates of reason—such as the idea that happiness comes not from the world of sense but the world of spirit—which would have been hopelessly dark and mysterious if revelation had not unfolded them long ago.[1]

> We can give reasons for it [the origin of happiness] now that it is revealed, and it seems so rational, that one would think the light of nature sufficient to discover it; but we having always lived in the enjoyment of gospel light, and being accustomed to it, are hardly sensible how dependent we are upon it, and how much we should be in the dark about things that now seem plain to us, if we never had had our reason assisted by revelation.[2]

Since reason rested on a foundation of revelation, unbeknown to most, who boasted confidently of what naked reason supposedly showed, there was hardly anyone who had ever been without the effects of revelation. So Edwards very nearly agreed with Thomas Chubb's statement that if reason were defective, God would have given revelation to all the earth.[3] Edwards's only qualification was that God had given revelation to *nearly* all. As we will see, he didn't worry about the few who were cut off from all the effects of revelation—or if he did, he said little about their plight. What was important was the fact that God had provided abundant revelation to the vast majority of all who had ever lived on the planet.

But if revelation was the source of many doctrines thought to be derived from naked reason, it also was responsible—according to Edwards—for the very foundations of philosophy. It alone taught abstract thinking and basic principles, which are the basis for all philosophy. Only revelation teaches people that rational studies are worth their while, because it alone shows the end for which understanding should be sought. Only revelation gives a nation reason "to uphold an order of men who should make speculation the business of their lives" (*Misc.* 350).

Without revelation there would be endless disputes about God's existence, the eternity of the world, creation, the nature of the first cause, the future state, how to please God, and moral duties. How do we know this? Before Christ there were hundreds of theories about how to find happiness. "Indeed on no other subject was there so great difficulty among [philosophers]."[4] There was no consensus of opinion. Only with the introduction of revelation in the Christian religion was a general consensus achieved, and the course of human experience has proved it right.

---

1. Locke, *The Reasonableness of Christianity*, 171; Clarke, *Discourse*, 10.
2. Sermon on Matthew 5:8, in Hickman, 2:909.
3. DCR, 12–13.
4. Sermon on Matthew 5:8, 909.

Hobbes's materialism and Spinoza's pantheism illustrate what foolishness would reign in the absence of revelation. Humans would live like beasts, just as they do in those dark places where revelation has been absent (Misc. 1338; Misc. 350). But it was not only history that showed the necessity of revelation; reason itself told us that there ought to be a revelation from God. Surely the Creator would want to communicate the purpose of the Creation to his intelligent creatures (Misc. 129). He made them to be perceiving and conscious spirits, and it is the nature of spirits to communicate by conversation (Misc. 204; Misc. 749). It is reasonable that the Creator of history would want to explain the meaning and course of providence (Misc. 752). If he wanted his people to have true religion, reason would tell us that he would communicate to them his intentions (Misc. 1304).

Besides, God is a moral governor. In moral government there is always communication between the ruler and the ruled, so that the ruled may understand the rules by which they are to live. Hence it was reasonable that the mind of a ruler should declare his rules to his subjects (Misc. 1338; Misc. 864).

If reason tells us that revelation is necessary because of the need for communication, it also tells us that God's mercy requires revelation to his intelligent creatures. God has infinite concern for them (Misc. 544) and so would not leave them alone to reason. For it was painfully clear that fallen reason had failed to show the way to true religion (Misc. 249).

Yet reason informed by revelation and strengthened by the sense of the heart that comes with a vision of God's beauty can show that the Bible is just that revelation which was needed. On this, strangely enough, Edwards was in partial agreement with Locke and the deists, all of whom claimed that reason can and must show if there is to be a revelation. Locke said that reason proves that the Bible is God's revelation. Chubb and Tindal said that reason proved just the opposite. Edwards agreed with Locke but denied that reason must prove revelation if revelation is to be accepted.

In 1753 Edwards preached a sermon to the Stockbridge Indians proving that the Bible is the Word of God by reason alone. He gave ten lines of evidence: there is no comparable Word among the heathen, the Bible provides right notions of God (the way of forgiveness and salvation, God's rules and commandments, a Savior, end of the world and judgment), miracles and prophecies confirm it, the Bible has enlightened so many nations, the devil opposes it, it has prevailed against great opposition, no man could have written such a book, no book so reaches the hearts of people, and good people all love it (the more wicked they are, the more they are against it).[5]

Elsewhere Edwards gave other "rational proofs" of the Bible's unique inspiration. In the *Miscellanies* he cites the Jews' survival as a people across millennia (Misc. 1158), and in *Freedom of the Will* he proposes that the Scriptures are divine because they teach doctrines that wise and great men reject because of the blindness of their minds and the prejudices of their hearts, yet they are doctrines "exactly agreeable to the most demonstrable, certain and natural dictates of reason" (439).

---

5. Sermon on 2 Timothy 3:16, in Grosart, *Selections*, 191–96.

Finally, however, for Edwards as for Calvin, the rational proofs paled in importance beside the testimony of the Holy Spirit that is found by those with a rightly disposed mind in the pages of Scripture itself. Although we just saw a Stockbridge sermon in which Edwards argued from reason, his most vigorous arguments from reason for the Bible's inspiration are found closer to the beginning of his career. Even at Stockbridge, he argued for the self-validating character of the Bible as much as for its attestation by reason. As we have seen already, Edwards devoted less energy to rational proofs as he gained pastoral experience and concluded that the ultimate proof is the simple proclamation of the gospel. Already in 1727 the young pastor told his congregation that there are three ways to see that the Scriptures are the Word of God, and two of them circumvented reason. One was to see the "excellency" in the Bible, and the other was to receive true light into their minds from God's Word. After enumerating many "evidences" for the Bible's inspiration, he added, "Besides the stamps and Characters of divinity everywhere Appearing in the Bible[,] there are self-evident Proofs of its Coming from God."[6] Even in 1728–29 he was conceding that the saints' faith in the Bible as the Word of God is based on "the intrinsic signatures of divinity which they see in it . . . signatures of divine majesty . . . divine wisdom and of divine holiness. . . . They do as it were hear God speak, and they are assured of the divinity of his speech, for he speaks like a God. His speech is not like the speech of men, but like the speech of God: divinely excellent, holy, wise, awful and gracious."[7] In a 1740 sermon on the uses of reason, the maturing pastor preached that "divine revelation in these things don't go a begging for credit and validity by approbation and applause of our understandings."[8] Several years later, in his most important theological treatise, he once again proclaimed that the gospel "don't go abroad a begging for its evidence, so much as some think; it has its highest and most proper evidence in itself" (RA, 307).

In a series of sermons titled "The Wisdom of God Displayed in the Way of Salvation," Edwards explains the self-attestation of Scripture in terms reminiscent of Calvin. The gospel has no need of external evidences and arguments, he declares, for there is enough evidence within it for those who have been spiritually enlightened to distinguish it from "the effects of human invention." An enlightened mind will see "evident appearances of the divine perfections" and "the stamp of divine glory" in it. Just as persons of mature reason conclude that the sun is not a human invention when they consider "the nature of it, its wonderful height, its course, [and] its brightness and heat," so too if the "wisdom appearing in the gospel be truly considered, it will be seen as much to excel all human wisdom, as the sun's light excels the light of fires of our own."[9] The way of salvation is "so out of the

---

6. SDK, 193; sermon on Acts 17:11, 1727, 3–6. See also Calvin, Institutes, 1.7.4.
7. "Profitable Hearers of the Word," in SDM, 251–52. See also 252: "The knowledge and understanding of these great things of the Word of God are only given by the illumination of the Spirit of God. Men by study can make no approaches to such an understanding without God's teaching accompanying."
8. Sermon on 1 Corinthians 2:11–13, 32.
9. Turretin, whom Edwards read throughout his career, also compared Scripture to the sun; Turretin, Institutes of Elenctic Theology, 2.4.6.

way of all human thoughts, so different from all human inventions; so much more sublime, excellent and worthy, that it does not savour at all of the craft or subtlety of man; it savours of God only."[10]

A Confusion of Terms

Edwards's opposition to the deist project took the form of three distinct lines of attack. In the first he accused "freethinkers" of misunderstanding and misusing the word "reason." In the second he charged Matthew Tindal with overstating the perfection of the law of nature. And in the third he chided Tindal for failure to appreciate mystery.

In his first attack, that freethinkers confuse terms, Edwards zeroed in on the maxim, "Reason is a higher rule than revelation." This was a basic premise for Toland, Tindal, and Chubb, and one of the few rules on which almost all deists agreed.[11]

Edwards opens his argument with the claim that "freethinkers of late Ages" deceive themselves by "ambiguity or Equivocal use of the word REASON."[12] First, they state it is a rule of reasoning, but then they proceed to use it in two other, very different senses: sometimes as a faculty of judgment, and other times as an opinion that appears rational to us. Edwards's most basic argument in this section is that reason can never be used as a rule of thinking. To speak that way makes no sense. For reason is a faculty, not a rule. And to call a faculty a rule is a contradiction in terms. The faculty of reason in and of itself does not and cannot tell us what is true; that is the function of a rule.

Edwards illustrates this point by referring to the oft-used deist slogan, "One must doubt revelation because it does not agree with reason." An initial problem with this statement is that it imports yet a third meaning for reason: an opinion or set of opinions that one holds independent of revelation. It also reveals human prejudice. Edwards said that it is analogous to doubting a reliable friend's report after he has returned from a long journey because what he reports is strange and unfamiliar to us.

But the real problem with the deist slogan is that it ignores the critical distinction between reason as a faculty and reason as a rule. Edwards uses another analogy. To accept the deist slogan is like saying, "I'll never believe a telescope if it shows things different from what my naked eye sees, because my eye is the rule by which I see." This statement ignores the different senses in which the word "eye" is used: as a bodily organ and a faculty of seeing. To say that it is a rule is only to make the ridiculous assertion that I will refuse to accept as true anything I cannot see with my naked eye. No one actually intends that, but because they use the word "reason" carelessly, that is what their words actually amount to.

---

10. "The Wisdom of God Displayed in the Way of Salvation," in Hickman, 2:153–54. See also *Misc.* 333: "The Scriptures themselves are an evidence of their own divine authority."
11. CNM, passim; *CAO*, 222; *AF*, 131, 296.
12. BC, 190; see also "Efficacious Grace" notebooks, Edwards Papers.

In the case of the telescope, an acceptable *rule* could be to accept as true what the best instruments (including the eye and the best telescopes) affirm. This rule would also include correcting a perception of the eye with the best judgment of astronomers (for instance, discounting the eye's perception that the sun rises and sets). The eye, then, is not a rule but a faculty governed by the use of a rule.

Similarly, deists fail to make a proper distinction between the faculty of reason and the rule of reason. They fail to realize that the faculty of reason is a faculty of judgment—not only our highest but our only faculty of judgment. However, it is not and cannot be our highest *rule* of judgment. For the judge, and the rule by which he judges, are two different things, as are the judge and the faculty by which he judges. The eye is not a rule but a faculty governed by a rule. So too, the faculty of discerning truth, and a rule that regulates and determines the use of that faculty, are quite different things.

At this point, our previous analogy is instructive. The eye is the faculty not (as the deists say) the rule of seeing, that is to say, the way to use the eye to our best advantage. This would be like saying that sight is the best rule to regulate sight.

Again, the deists confuse faculty with rule. Reason is our faculty of judgment, Edwards argued, but not our rule. If it were, we'd be limiting ourselves once more in ridiculous fashion. We would have to say that we cannot believe that stars are round because they appear jagged to the naked eye. Or that we cannot believe that there are blood cells in the blood because they are not visible to the naked eye. If reason is a rule in this way, then we cannot believe anything that we don't already know (BC, 191–92).

There were even further confusions, Edwards continued, in the deist use of the word "reason." Sometimes they used the word to mean "argument" or "evidence." But, Edwards insisted, revelation is a kind of evidence. So when they say that reason is superior to revelation, they mean reason without revelation is superior to revelation. Or, all other testimony is superior to divine testimony. This often means that divine testimony is the very least and weakest of all arguments. But this contradicts their claim that God's testimony, which they find in nature and reason, is the strongest testimony of all (BC, 193).

Edwards then considered the objection, "I only mean evidence seen by reason, without dependence on the dictates of another; this is seeing things as they are in themselves. By this means we determine if there is a divine revelation."[13] Edwards inferred that the real objection here was against any medium of judgment in knowledge, so that the only true knowledge is self-evident, by intuition or immediate observation. But Edwards then observed that we judge reliably all the time by using media of judgment, and that in those cases we still see the things as they are in themselves. For instance, he suggested, consider the times when we use a measuring rod to judge distance, or a compass to find direction, or numerals to determine and calculate numbers. In all these cases we use a medium of judgment while at the same time seeing things as they are in themselves.

---

13. This was an objection to the use of testimony to support the authority of Christian revelation.

Edwards's last sally in this line of attack was a consideration of the associated maxim, "Reason is a superior rule to experience." What this often means, he suggested, is that reason is to be considered independent of experience. The problem with that, however, is that we evaluate experience by reason, comparing the testimony of our senses with testimony from other senses and other criteria of truth. Hence it is very difficult to separate reason from experience.

More to the point, reason includes experience, as the genus includes the species. Judging by experience is simply one way of judging by reason. Or, experience is one argument (or datum) which reason uses in judgment. So to say that reason is a more reliable rule than experience is to say that arguing is a more reliable rule than a particular way of arguing.

Now if by reason is meant the *faculty* of reason, Edwards continued, or the power of the mind to see the *force* of arguments, the statement is even more nonsensical. It is the same as saying that the mind's ability to see the force of arguments is a surer rule for judging truth than that particular argument: experience. Or, a man's understanding is a better rule to understand by than a particular means or rule of understanding. This, he insists, is an "abuse of language"! (BC, 195–96).

In sum, Edwards concluded, to say that reason is a superior rule to revelation is as foolish as to say that human reason is a test of truth superior to experience (BC, 196).

Is the Law of Nature Perfect?

Edwards's second line of argument was a forceful engagement with Matthew Tindal's *Christianity as Old as the Creation* (1730). He claimed that "Tindal's main argument against the need of any revelation is, that the LAW OF NATURE IS ABSOLUTELY PERFECT" (Misc. 1337). This was indeed Tindal's strongest contention, who assumed rather than proved the perfection of the law of nature, based on the a priori assumption that God's will is unchangeable and good.[14] Therefore God must have revealed his expectations to humans at the beginning; for he is good and therefore fair. And since Tindal was convinced that God's will is immutable, and God is perfect, the law of nature must be perfect. What was good for the original humans must be good for all human beings thereafter. Hence later revelation must be no different from the natural religion found in the law of nature that reason dictates. Revelation is simply the external manifestation of the internal law of nature. Therefore, the way to test the authenticity of a portion of supposed revelation is to measure it against what reason tells us of the law of nature.[15]

Edwards charged that Tindal made a false move when he inferred from the perfection of the law of nature that the light of nature is sufficient to see that law.

---

14. By "law of nature" Tindal meant the moral law, which he considered the essence of true religion.
15. *CAO*, 2–4, 4, 6.

To say that the law of nature is perfect only begs the question: what is the law? If it is self-evident, why do rational persons disagree about its nature?

Furthermore, according to Edwards, Tindal's assertion is a tautology; it says that what is right in itself (the law of nature) is right in itself (perfect). Or, what is good is good. What is, is, or is as it is.

The real question, which the perfection of the law of nature does not begin to answer by itself, is whether we have all the light we need from nature for a religion of sinners. That is, what do we need to do as sinners to obtain forgiveness, God's favor, and our happiness? The point, in other words, is that while a law of nature may indeed be perfect, our natural knowledge of this perfect law may be most imperfect.

So Edwards issued a challenge. If the light of nature, he asked, is sufficient to teach us all we need to know, then why do we need instruction about anything religious or moral? "Any additional instruction is needless and useless . . . all instruction in families and schools is needless and useless." All philosophy, all writing, and indeed all books "to promote any such knowledge as tends to make men good and happy . . . and then also all the pains the deists take in talking and writing to enlighten mankind, is wholly needless and vain; and all Tindal's own instructions, and particularly all the pains he takes to make men believe, that 'tis not best to give heed to pretended revelations and traditionary religion" (Misc. 1337; emphasis added).

In short, if Tindal is right, there is no need for the deist enterprise. Tindal himself was wasting his breath. For the need he sought to address was, by his own principles, not a need. But the fact that he addressed that need implied that there was after all a need, which is precisely what Edwards and Christian orthodoxy had always claimed.

Edwards proceeded to suggest that if we discount this inconsistency and give Tindal the benefit of the doubt that human beings need more instruction about the sufficiency of the law of nature from their fellow creatures, we might infer that further instruction from God is also called for. After all, if we need further instruction from creatures, wouldn't further instruction from the perfect instructor be of some use?

Then Edwards doubled back to look more closely at Tindal's original proposition, that the law of nature is perfect and the implication that the light of nature was sufficient "to know the way of duty and happiness." One of two things must be meant by this. Either it is (merely) *possible* to obtain this knowledge, or "these natural means have a sufficient tendency *actually* to reach the effect, either universally or at least generally, or at least in a prevailing degree, as the state of mankind is" (emphasis mine). In other words, either knowledge of the law of nature is only possible or is so easy to obtain that most have actually obtained it.

If only the first is true, Edwards reasoned, it is not proved that revelation is not needed. The vast majority of humankind may still be unaware of the law of nature. But if the second is true, that the light of nature is so strong and pervasive that most have actually obtained knowledge of the law of nature, then the way to test this proposition is to look at the historical record. We examine past and present experience to determine if this near-universal knowledge actually obtains.

But what is the knowledge to be found? Here Edwards differed from Tindal, for whom true religion consists in a sincere effort to live a moral life without the burden of worship or need for an atoning mediator.[16] Edwards granted that a part of true religion, which he called the "religion of nature," involved morality. But it also included something scarcely mentioned by Tindal: knowledge of our dependence on God and our duties to him. Edwards believed that no one had ever gained knowledge of this by reason alone. Those like Tindal who thought otherwise were confusing "the reasonableness of these things when pointed out" with "the sufficiency to find them out." In other words, it was easy to see the rationality of a religion of nature, but far more difficult to discover it from scratch. "None but either perfect dunces, or perfectly willful, will deny that there is a vast difference."

The other part of true religion that would be necessary to find in history was what Edwards called the "religion of a sinner." This consists in the duties becoming "depraved guilty and offending creatures." The light of nature, Edwards argued, has no tendency to reveal this to anyone; it never has, because such an understanding is beyond the capacity of a reason that has been tainted by sinful corruption. Edwards might have suggested that Tindal is an apt illustration of this failure, for Tindal himself never recognized either humanity's inherent corruption or reason's inability to obtain the fullness of religious truth. Edwards then suggested that even if the law of nature were known, it still would be insufficient to establish the religion of a sinner or provide any grounding for it (Misc. 1337).

Finally, Edwards entertained the objection raised by Tindal's book that if the orthodox view of revelation is correct, conversation between God and most of his creatures must be unnecessary because so few ever heard the gospel.[17] In other words, if we were to determine the necessity of revelation by observing the frequency of revelation in world history, we would conclude from the relative paucity of revelation among the peoples of the world that it must not be that important. Otherwise God would have provided it far more frequently than he had.

Edwards had four responses to this assertion. First, most human beings are rebels who have forsaken their lawful sovereign. So their deprivation of revelation is just, if they have indeed been so deprived. But second, actually they have not been deprived of revelation. It has come by tradition from their ancestors and from the Jews, so they have always had the "possibility of reconciliation" and the "equal possibility" of actually receiving the benefits of reconciliation. Third, the religious blindness and darkness of most societies have demonstrated the need for revelation. And fourth, the nations of the world have always had enough light to condemn them. In any event, their condemnation would always be "proportioned to the light" they received (Misc. 1338).

We see, then, that Edwards refused to concede the point that most of the world has been left without revelation. At issue was God's goodness and justice. While other Calvinists thought natural revelation through conscience and nature was

---

16. Ibid., 2, 13; 39, 86–87.
17. Ibid., 49, 196, 242, 250, esp. 374–75, 401.

enough to preserve God's justice,[18] Edwards used the *prisca theologia* tradition, as we shall see in Chapter 5, to insist that most of the world has actually heard the basics of the gospel. Hence God has been more than just. Not only has he given the religion of nature to all, but he has provided the religion of sinners to almost all as well.

Mystery

Edwards's third major assault on deism began by challenging Tindal's assumption that reason should be able to prove all particular propositions as well as the basic propositions from which particular propositions are derived.[19] Of course, Tindal was thinking of the Bible. Not only should reason be capable of determining whether or not the Bible as a whole is a revelation, but it should also have the authority to judge the authenticity of every proposition found within the Bible.[20]

Edwards retorted that this principle was contrary to the common sense that Tindal so famously championed. Edwards's common sense, which apparently was not common to Tindal, told him that a basic, general proposition may be evidently true, although the particular propositions that depend on it and follow from it are either not immediately evident or arguable when detached from the general proposition.

If Tindal is right, Edwards argued, we can no longer use our reasoning powers. We cannot derive particular propositions from general propositions, which is what we do in most of our reasoning. Nothing will be true except what appears to be immediately self-evident.

Edwards stipulated that some general propositions can be established by reason. From them are inferred by the "common consent of all mankind" and the "common and universal sense of the human mind" an "infinite multitude of other propositions" that cannot be known by reason independently of the general propositions. Edwards proposed five general propositions, which he asserted could be proved by reason, that numberless other propositions depended on. First was the proposition that we may rely on the testimony of our senses. Numberless propositions, he claimed, cannot be known without implicit faith in the testimony of the senses.

Next was the principle that the testimony of our senses is worthy of credit. Third was reliance on "the agreed testimony of all we see and converse with continually." Like the first two, this can be proved by reason, and there is an infinite number of propositions which cannot be verified independently of this kind of testimony. This includes "all occurrences, matters of fact, persons, things, actions, works, events and circumstances we are told of in our neighborhood and county or any part of the world that we are told of and haven't seen ourselves."

Fourth is the testimony of history and tradition, and fifth, the "experience of mankind." Edwards wrote that "no one doubts this"—that what the world finds

---

18. Muller, *Post-Reformation Reformed Dogmatics*, 119, 175.
19. Most of this section is derived from Misc. 1340, a 7,500-word entry at the end of his career.
20. *CAO*, 6, 66, 151, 182–83, 222.

to be true by experience is worthy to be judged true. He noted that this testimony of human experience is usually based on one of the other four—history and tradition, our conversation partners, memory, or sensory experience. Indeed, *all* that is known by human experience is known only by one or more of these testimonies—except those ideas that are now, as we read this sentence, immediately present to consciousness.

"How unreasonable it would be" to say that we must first know an idea to be true by reason before we give credit to our experience of its truth. In fact, we already accept as truths, from the common consent of all rational persons, many propositions that in themselves are difficult, even incomprehensible, and apparently irreconcilable with reason. Most human beings cannot explain them. For instance, Edwards suggested, take the proposition that our souls are united to our bodies, and that the two act on each other. This is a truth that reason can neither discover nor explain. How can what is immaterial act upon what is material? How can matter have perception?

Edwards went on to declare that there are innumerable propositions that we receive by the testimony of experience but which are above reason, and sometimes even paradoxical. His first example is the proposition that there is a material world. This is clear from the testimony of our senses, but its verification by reason is fraught with difficulties. For the world is either in the mind or outside the mind, independent of perception. If the latter, then it is material indeed and finally different from all the mental ideas we derive from our senses. Yet if we try to exclude from our thinking all ideas derived from our senses, we cannot imagine what the material world would be like. If on the other hand the world is only an idea in our mind, then the sense organs which we perceive with the mind must also exist only within the mind. The result is that the organs of sense then owe their existence to the organs of sense, and so are prior to themselves, causing their own existence. In what some would declare a display of sophistry, he declared this impossible.

Take the proposition that there exist such things as thought, love, and hatred. Where are they? If they exist, and yet in no place, this seems strange. Things must exist somewhere. If they do exist in some place, then they are not in others, and not in all places. Therefore they are confined at one time to one place or set of places, and that place or set of places must have limits. So thought and love and hatred must have shapes—perhaps round or square or triangular. This too is impossible to reconcile with reason.[21]

Then there is the proposition that something now exists. This too involves paradoxes contrary to reason, knots that reason cannot untie. For if something now is, it either was from all eternity, or began to be without cause. The latter defies all our natural sense of things. But the former implies infinite duration. Yet how can anything that is infinite be made larger? An infinite line cannot be made longer. But each year that which is becomes older. Infinite duration thus is made longer, for the whole is greater than a part. This seems paradoxical.

---

21. Of course this is paradoxical only if one begins with the presupposition that all is material.

Edwards then applied the last proposition to the existence of the world. That it has existed from eternity without cause seems inconsistent with reason, for nothing (but God) is necessary in itself, and this would involve an infinite succession of causes with no first cause. That it was created *ex nihilo* also seems unreasonable, and "many of the greatest philosophers agree." Reason cannot explain how something can be created out of nothing.

That a good and holy God presides over great evil is another proposition finally impervious to reason. But Edwards's response to this and all the preceding paradoxes is that mystery is to be expected in religion. If we are dealing with a revelation from God in heaven, we should expect things that "should be utterly beyond our understanding and seem impossible" (*Misc.* 583). Why? Edwards answers this question in four ways. Religion will necessarily involve mystery because of the nature of language, because there are mysteries in philosophy as well, because there are mysteries in nature also, and because religion is concerned with superior beings.

Ever since Toland's *Christianity Not Mysterious* (1696), Christian doctrines not transparently evident had been under attack. Toland had insisted that God has no right to require assent to what does not yield "clear ideas"; hence what the church has termed mysteries are to be rejected as remnants of paganism. Tindal had complained that a mystery that could not be translated into deist morality was really a code word for superstition, and that revelation by definition could not contain anything above human understanding.[22]

Edwards began his response by looking at human language. The nature of language will necessarily involve mystery in religion, he argued, because language uses signs taken from material reality while religion deals with immaterial realities. So words "are almost all borrowed" from their original material uses, and when pressed into the service of religion are "used in a sort of figurative sense." This occasions "a great deal of ambiguity and unfixedness in their signification," resulting in "innumerable doubts, difficulties and confusions in inquiries and controversies about things of this nature." The problem is even more severe when human language is used to try to describe "things in the mind of the incomprehensible Deity, precisely as they are" ("The Mind," no. 35, in *SPW*, 355).

Therefore in all discussions of divine things we must use "extreme caution" lest we speak "exceeding unintelligibly . . . contradicting ourselves." And it is no wonder "that the high and abstract mysteries of the Deity, the prime and most abstract of all beings, imply so many seeming contradictions" (ibid).

Mysteries in religion should not be surprising because there are so many mysteries in philosophy. Edwards asked, When was there ever a time when things in philosophy, "which are of a vastly lower nature and must be supposed to be more proportioned to our understandings," did not seem "absurd and impossible even to the learned, not just the vulgar" (*Misc.* 563)? If many of these notions had been revealed by God, he argued, they would have seemed mysterious and difficult,

---

22. CAO, 143, 23, 153–54; 168; 222.

and as impossible as most Christian doctrines do now. Even today, he went on, if heaven were to reveal these truths as they really are and not in accommodated form, many aspects of them would appear "absurd and contradictory" (Misc. 583).

Then Edwards related the story of the boy and the two-inch block of wood that we saw at the beginning of Chapter 3. Why can't there be truths as far above our understanding, he asked, as this was above the boy's? "Doubtless there is a vastly greater distance between our understanding and God's than between this boy's and [that] of the greatest philosopher or mathematician" (Misc. 652; SPW, 388). And suppose humankind were as developed intellectually as a typical seven-year-old, and truths on the order of what philosophers today consider undoubtedly true were introduced. Consider, Edwards hypothesized, what objections would arise from pride. Or suppose these same truths were presented in the time of Joshua, in ancient Israel. "How incredible would these truths have seemed!" (Misc. 1169).

A third reason Edwards gave for expecting mysteries in religion is that nature is full of mystery. In standard Reformed fashion, he believed that both nature and revelation are voices of God. But he emphasized mystery more than some of his predecessors. If one of these two voices is mysterious, he reasoned, one would expect the other to be as well.

In fact many things in nature, such as the union of body and soul, are more difficult to fathom than some things in the spiritual world (Misc. 1233). There are many contradictions in mathematics and science which are just as great or greater than the supposed contradictions in the Trinity (Misc. 1234). For instance, the effects of electricity and magnetism are very mysterious. But their mysteries were not objections, he boasted, to his faith in the accounts of the Philosophical Transactions of the Royal Society. To the contrary, they were to be expected "in a particular and exact observation of nature. . . . 'Tis to be expected that the further it is traced, the more mysteries will appear" (Misc. 1340).

And in mathematics, "there are many truths of which mathematicians are convinced by strict Demonstration, concerning many Kinds of Quantities, as said Quantities and Fluxions, concerning which they have no clear ideas." If this is true in mathematics, it is also true more generally that we can be "rationally convinced" of the truth of a proposition without having a clear idea of it.

We practice this, Edwards suggested, far more than we acknowledge. That is, we accept far more things on authority than by direct observation. When it comes to secular matters of nature and science, we are ready to trust someone of great repute if he is positive about something that seems to us very mysterious and is quite the opposite of what we had thought. We then tend to doubt our preconceptions, especially if it is a matter in which he seems to be an expert or has had greater advantages to know the truth.

Then Edwards posed a question. What if he were ten times greater a genius than any other man? Wouldn't we be ready to trust him, even if he said something we previously thought "perfectly incredible and absurd to suppose" (Misc. 770)?

Finally, Edwards said that mystery is to be expected in religion because religion is concerned with spiritual things that are not the objects of our senses. We can easily imagine that a revelation about the invisible God, and a future state when we are separated from the body, would contain mystery. Things of that world would be very different from things of this world, things of sense, and all that earthly language is meant to express (Misc. 1340).

At this point Edwards conducted a thought experiment. Imagine what it would be like, he wrote, if we were born without eyes or optic nerves. Suppose we were then told that some things can be perceived at a distance, and better than close up when touched. And that some things can be seen "that it would take millions of ages to travel to them." Undoubtedly this would seem incredible, just as descriptions of color would be utterly incomprehensible and mysterious. So would the statement that we can perceive at once the extent and shape of a tree, whose size and shape would take us many days to perceive by touch. All these would be impossible to reconcile with reason, without "very long and elaborate instruction." If we were rational, we would give full credit to the testimony of those who had experienced these things more directly. In other words, we would come to know these things "by the revelation of the word of them that see."

Now if God gives revelation not only about spiritual beings that we neither experience nor see but also about spiritual beings who are of a *superior* sort, then we may expect mysteries in that revelation. We can also expect that there will be difficulties in understanding.

Furthermore, if revelation is given about a Being who is uncreated and self-existent, "it would be very strange indeed, if there should not be some great mysteries, quite beyond our comprehension, and attended with difficulties which it is impossible for us fully to solve and explain." For example, the affairs of adults seem unexplainable to children; the affairs of learned philosophers and mathematicians seem inexplicable, impossible, and full of inconsistencies to untutored folks. And the reasoning of the best mathematicians contains mysteries concerning infinite lines and solids. Why should there not be mystery in infinite thought and love in *spiritual* beings?

Once Edwards completed his explanation of why mystery in divinity makes common sense, he turned, as he often did in his polemics, to address a relevant objection. As he put it, why should there be mystery in a book of revelation whose intent is to instruct? Isn't that inconsistent?

As usual, Edwards had more than one answer. His first reply was that we often understand basic propositions without understanding the manner in which they work. For example, we can perceive that the Trinity is one deity in three persons without having to understand the "manner of their distinction." We can accept the incarnation's union of human and divine natures without knowing "how it was effected." In other words, the presence of mystery in some of the propositions of revelation does not mean that there is not plenty that is rationally acceptable there as well.

His second reply begs the question. He says that understanding of revelation is progressive, so some of these mysteries may be understood in the future. His third reply throws the question back at the objector: if the mystery in revelation is a problem, what about the mystery in nature? If some parts of Scripture seem useless because they are impossible to fathom, so do some parts of the natural world. In a passage that calls to mind New England farmers' everlasting struggle with its stony soil, he wrote, "The innumerable stones and rocks that overspread so great a part of the land . . . [seem] altogether useless" (Misc. 1340). If God created the world and declared it good, why did he create rocks which seem not to serve the creation?

Then Edwards took the offensive. Mystery, he exulted, far from being a troublesome difficulty that threatens the authenticity of revelation, is actually a confirmation of revelation. If the difficulties of the Bible are no greater than what might be expected from a divine revelation, they are of no weight at all as objections against the revelation. On the contrary, they are confirmations and arguments in its favor.

For the identity of a thing is known by its properties. "Reason determines truth by things which reason determines to be the properties of truth." So if we did not find requisite difficulties and paradoxes, which even reason has now shown to be expected of a divine revelation, we would not be convinced of the authenticity of the Bible as revelation. If all in the Bible were self-evident, that fact alone would be a valid objection *against* the authority of Scripture!

Edwards's *coup de grace* was to point out that even deist notions were full of mystery and paradox. Think first, he reminded them, of the deist notion that there exists an unmade and unlimited Being. It is absolutely certain that this Being exists, yet it is full of mystery, and the very idea involves incomprehensible paradox and inconsistency. For this is a Being without a cause, omnipresent yet without extension, who experiences duration without succession. This last point is particularly difficult. "It seems as much as to say, an infinitely great or long duration all at once; or all in a moment; which seems to be saying, an infinitely great in an infinitely little; or an infinitely long line in a point without any length."

This is also a Being who has infinite understanding without mutation or succession of act and perfect knowledge of all things without receiving ideas from outside itself. Infinite knowledge implies knowledge of the whole to its limits, but in infinite space there are no limits. If there is no change in God, there are no new acts. Yet we know there are new effects (Misc. 1340). All of these notions were both held by deists and riddled with the very mystery deists publicly repudiated.

The doctrine of decrees, better known today as election, was Edwards's cardinal example of a notion rejected precisely because it was mysterious. Edwards's tack on this most notorious of all Calvinist doctrines was to argue that its opposite was more mysterious and plagued with greater difficulties and contradictions to reason. He argued in his *Freedom of the Will* (1754) that those who oppose the doctrine of decrees hold that the self-determining will chooses its first choice, because the will chooses all its actions. But Edwards asked, How can there be a choice before its first choice? For the will must choose to choose. And if a will must determine its own act by a prior act, this contradicts the supposition that the will determines itself even in its first act. Besides, for a will to determine itself is the same as saying that something makes itself, which is impossible to believe.[23] Even

---

23. FW, 172; BC, 274. An outline at the Beinecke for a projected treatise entitled "Of the Decrees of God" indicates that Edwards was planning to write an extensive treatment of the subject; box 20, folder 1240, Edwards papers. Thanks to Ken Minkema for this reference.

his writings on predestination, then, can be seen as moments in his long campaign against the deist denial of mystery.

Final Remarks

Leslie Stephen notes that John Locke was annoyed by John Toland's development of his ideas. But Locke shouldn't have been surprised, at least on the role of reason in religion. Locke's *Essay* had taught that we can judge the truth of an event by comparing it to our knowledge of the likelihood of that kind of event in general. Toland and other deists used this principle to deem miracles improbable from the start, despite Locke's suggestion that miracles are an exception to this rule. Although he conceded that some divine truths are above reason, in his *Essay* Locke had pronounced that reason is to be the last judge in every matter. Toland and Tindal took that maxim to heart when they asserted as a principle of knowledge that all certitude comes from self-evident demonstration. Toland, who tried to ban mystery from Christianity but labored to establish mystery in the earliest Masonic lodges, was the herald of an age that "prized clarity above profundity" and enthusiastically protested enthusiasm. Tindal and Chubb did theology by sound-bites; mystery was banished, and the depth and breadth of revelation were reduced to a few short propositions tied to a procrustean bed of bourgeois common sense.[24]

Jonathan Edwards accepted the Lockean and deist challenge to allow reason to determine the authenticity of a revelation. But at the same time he distinguished, as Locke and the deists did not, fallen reason from regenerate reason. With that distinction he was able to show why the force of regenerate reason's arguments to support the authenticity of the Bible were lost on those whose reason was unregenerate. The unregenerate could agree with the reasoning of the regenerate, but they could never feel its force. Others in the Reformed tradition had made a similar distinction, but Edwards's philosophical acumen used that distinction with unprecedented subtlety.[25]

Of course such a move had more polemical than practical value. Edwards was proposing a kind of reason that by nature (he believed) was inaccessible to his opponents. It was a speculative attempt to circumvent their reasoning—hardly persuasive to convinced freethinkers. Yet in the process he exposed the deist project as anthropocentric and doctrinaire. If deists rightly perceived that orthodox divines like Edwards were defensively committed to their "unreasonable" God, he unmasked their unreasonable reduction of reason to immediate intuition and their transmutation of God into an enlightened English squire.

---

24. Stephen, *English Thought*, 93–94; Byrne, *Natural Religion*, 96; Locke, *Essay*, 4.19.13–14; CNM, 59; CAO, 222; Harrison, *"Religion" and the Religions*, 89; Cragg, *Reason and Authority*, 22; AF, 131; CAO, 189, 222.

25. William Wainwright has written, "[Edwards's epistemology] is the most carefully articulated vision known to me of an epistemic theory deeply embedded in important strands of the Christian tradition." Wainwright, "Nature of Reason," 117.

5

TRICKLE-DOWN REVELATION AND RELIGIOUS ENTROPY

The Nature and History of Religion

The scientific study of religion originated not in the nineteenth and twentieth centuries, as scholars have often presumed,[1] but in the seventeenth and eighteenth centuries. The seeds were sown even earlier. During the Middle Ages "the religions" had been understood as the religious orders of the Roman Catholic church. But with German cardinal and philosopher Nicholas of Cusa (1401–64) and Italian humanist Marsilio Ficino (1433–99), philosophers began to think in terms of religion as a generic entity underlying all religious differences. Then in the seventeenth century the Cambridge Platonists spoke of a general human ability to find true religion by means of a priori ideas. Religious variations arose, they conjectured, when these innate ideas interacted with material conditions such as geography, custom, and habit.[2]

Deists appealed similarly to a priori ideas as a foundation for their "natural religion" but were far more exercised about the role of "sinister priestcraft" in concealing the truths of true religion. They accused the clergy of monopolizing the original monotheism dictated by nature and transforming it into polytheistic mysteries for the masses. The result was a "twofold philosophy" in which monotheistic truths were preserved in a secret language of hieroglyphs and symbols, accessible only to deceitful priests and the educated elite, while the rest of the

---

1. For example, see Jordan, *Comparative Religion*; Sharpe, *Comparative Religion*; and Küng, *On Being a Christian*, 89.

2. Harrison, *"Religion" and the Religions*, 11; on a priori ideas among the Cambridge Platonists, see, for example, Cudworth, *True Intellectual System*, 246–53, 625; and Harrison, *"Religion" and the Religions*, 27–46.

population succumbed to such monstrosities as human sacrifice and cabbage worship because of their "original imbecility."[3]

Later in the eighteenth century, Italian philosopher Giovanni Battista Vico (1668–1774) and David Hume (1711–1776) found the origins of religion not in the faculty of reason but in the constraints of human psychology. For Vico religious sentiment was not inborn but acquired in time by the fear and credulity of childlike primitives.[4] Hume argued that polytheism and idolatry, not monotheism, were most ancient, and that they were offspring of the passions—anxiety, dread of future misery, terror of death, and thirst for revenge.[5]

Edwards's Reformed predecessors, the seventeenth-century orthodox scholastics, resisted this trend to conceive of historical religions as derived from a common religion-in-general. For these Calvinists, historical religions were either the true (Christian) religion of grace and revelation or pagan heresy, which arose from human corruption. They used the Latin word *religio*, which means "to bind back or reattach," only for the true religion, which they thought was the only way for human beings to be brought back—or reattached—to God. Religion-in-general was excluded because it did not contain the historical particularities of the Christian faith, which alone could reconcile sinners to a holy deity. The religions could not be placed on a continuum with Christianity because without those historical particularities their nature and direction were fundamentally different. While in orthodox Christianity a holy God reaches down to save helpless sinners, in all other religions sinful humans try unsuccessfully to be reconciled to a holy God.[6]

For Edwards too all non-Christian religion showed the futility of human reason and will to find the true God. Although he believed that there were remnants of revelation in many non-Christian religions—as we shall see in this and the next chapter—and therefore that there are qualitative similarities between the Christian and other religions, he nevertheless concluded from the final form of these religions that they were just so many manifestations of the human proclivity to deny and distort the original revelations given to the fathers of the nations.

The Nature of Religion: Domesticated Divinity

As we saw in Chapter 1, the seventeenth- and eighteenth-century deists fairly identified religion with morality. They thought of religion in its essence as conformity to a set of moral propositions. In Chubb's words, "True religion, or that which is the ground of divine acceptance, does consist in doing what is right and fit, in the nature of things."[7] William C. Placher has recently described the trend in sev-

---

3. IW, December 31, 1720; Manuel, *The Eighteenth Century Confronts the Gods*, 65f., 80f.
4. Vico, *The New Science*.
5. Hume, *The Natural History of Religion*. For more on the origin of the scientific study of religion as a human phenomenon, see Pailin, *Attitudes to Other Religions*; Champion, *The Pillars of Priestcraft Shaken*, esp. 25–52, 99–169; and Manuel, *The Eighteenth Century Confronts the Gods*.
6. Muller, *Post-Reformation Reformed Dogmatics*, 113f., 118.
7. Chubb, *Collection of Tracts*, 1: 372. Edwards owned a copy of this work.

enteenth-century religious thought as an attempt to "domesticate" the divine. While confidence in human abilities burgeoned and the range of "acceptable reasoning" narrowed, there was less emphasis on revelation and grace, "decreasing attention [paid] to the Trinity," and a "shift to Christian reflection on a simply unitary God." Religion and theology were judged by their adequacy to fulfill objectives human beings set for them.[8]

Placher was describing a broad spectrum of religious thinkers—both deists and thinkers traditionally thought to be orthodox—but his description is particularly accurate for deists. Their religion so domesticated God that his existence at times seemed relevant only if it could serve the public order. Worship and praise for the deity were so far removed from true religion that they were sometimes regarded as unworthy of an acceptable deity. According to Chubb, worship "sets forth . . . the *weakness* or *unreasonableness* of the legislator."[9]

Edwards, however, placed worship at the heart of religion, both true and false. He conceived of all religion as a response to revelation, by worship either of the true God or of an idol. False religion worships creation rather than the Creator (*Misc.* 986), while true religion is a worshipful response of the soul to an aesthetic vision of divine excellence. It is a sincere conviction of the truth and reality of the gospel which issues both personally and "socially" in worship from the heart (DSL, 65–88; RA, 253–311).

While for the deists all religion was subordinated to morality, for Edwards morality served the higher end of worship. Personal "devotion" to God, or "beholding" and "admiring" and "contemplating" divine glories, is "the highest end of man" and his "principal business" (*Misc.* gg; *Misc.* kk). "Mutual love, charity, justice [and] beneficence" are subordinated to the higher end of devotion to the divine in worship. "For all justice, beneficence, etc. are good for nothing without [devotion] and are to no purpose at all." All morality and justice "are only for the advancement of the *great* business, to assist mutually each other to it" (*Misc.* kk). Morality in the absence of worship is finally immoral because it ignores true moral standards and the source of moral strength. And worse, it is blasphemous because it flouts the one who founded and sustains true morality (TV, 560, 609–18).

If Edwards's conception of religion scandalized deists because it elevated worship over morality, his notion of worship as participation must have seemed "enthusiastic" in the worst sense of the word. This age possessed a fanatical fear of religious and mystical emotion; deists were especially outraged by religious sentiment that extended beyond rational discussion of polite morality. For Edwards, on the other hand, true worship is not only praise of the divine but participation in the same. Worship consists of knowing God, loving God and one's neighbor in virtue and holiness, and rejoicing in God (End, 441–42). According to Edwards, all true knowing is participation in God's knowledge of himself, all true virtue is a sharing of God's love of himself, and all true joy is a partaking in God's rejoicing in his own excellence (End, 528). Hence in true religion God is both subject and

---

8. Placher, *Domestication of Transcendence*, 3, 14f.
9. Chubb, *Collection of Tracts*, 1:372.

object. The believer is not only an observer and worshiper of the divine but also a participant in the divine life. This was a far cry from the deist notion of religious knowledge as assent to moral propositions; deists would have—and indeed did when addressing similar schemes—dismissed this as mystical ("enthusiastical") nonsense.

Equally galling to deists was the notion that the deity desires praise from mortals. We have already seen that the deist attacks on the selfishness of the Calvinist God troubled Edwards, and we have looked at several of his replies to these charges. In fact, the *Miscellanies* notebooks demonstrate that Edwards worked on this problem throughout his career. Time and again he tried to pilot his notion of the "beautiful" God around the shoals of deist attacks on the worship of an egocentric deity. In the process Edwards refined his understanding of true religion as the worship of a God who is delighted by praise.

In 1724 Edwards co-opted the Enlightenment obsession with human happiness to argue for the disinterested virtue of the deity. In Misc. 104 he asserts that God created the world to make human beings happy. But this entry takes a christocentric turn. The Father, Edwards argues, completely communicated all of his happiness when the Father begat the Son. Why, then, the need for further creation, since this begetting was an infinite communication? Edwards's answer to his own question is that the Son also has an inclination to communicate himself "in an image of his person that may partake of his happiness." Therefore "this was the end of the creation, even the communication of the happiness of the Son of God." The young Edwards explains that this is what was meant by the passage in John's gospel, "As the Father has loved me, so I have loved you" (John 15:9).

By 1726, just two years later, Edwards had shifted the focus subtly back to the Father. Now the creation of the world was due to the Father's "propensity to goodness" to his son, "that he might prepare a spouse or bride for him to bestow his love upon [the church], so the mutual joys between this bride and bridegroom are the end of the creation." No longer was the immediate creator the Son; now the creator was the Father, who like many human fathers wants to give a gift to a son getting married. In this case, however, the purpose was not egocentric, for once again the Father was concerned with beings other than himself.[10]

Lest deists rest, Edwards highlighted what they typically omitted in their rather depersonalized accounts of the divine: God's delight in the Creation. It violated the deist notion of perfection for God to be happy in the act of creating, for that would seem to imply that God was not originally perfect before the Creation. Deriving new happiness from an act suggests less than perfect happiness before the act. Throughout the course of his career Edwards worked to accommodate God's delight to divine perfection.[11] In Misc. 271, an entry that contains most of the elements he would refine in later years, Edwards resolves that God was really happy in creating and then loving his creation not because they added to his perfections but because they provide him the opportunity to manifest those

---

10. Of course this description obscures Edwards's conception of the Son as one being with the Father; but it could serve to deflect deist criticisms.

11. Misc. 104, 271, 332, 448, 461, 679, 1091, 1139, 1275.

perfections. Loving his creation gratifies his natural propensity to goodness. He is delighted by their love and praise for him "not because he needs" anything but because he loves them. And it is the nature of a father to delight in the love of a child.

Two years later, in 1728, Edwards tried another tack. This time he argued that God created because it is his nature to "emanate," just as a fountain pours forth simply because it is its nature to do so. "God is a communicative being," Edwards wrote. It is his nature to give or "communicate" himself to others, so he created intelligent beings who could receive communications of his being. The Creation was for the "shining forth of his excellency and for the flowing forth of his happiness." It does not make God the "happier" to be praised; he "shines forth" not because it makes him happy but because it is his "excellency" to do so (Misc. 332).

The Miscellanies entries in later years reflect continued efforts to protect God from the accusations of egocentrism and imperfection. God's delight is in giving, not receiving (Misc. 448). He delights in goodness for its own sake, not simply because it glorifies him (Misc. 461). The glory of God is a manifestation and communication of God's goodness and happiness (Misc. 1091). God's pleasure in praise does not add to his self-sufficiency, as if he were not happy in himself; he delights in praise for his attributes because he knows his excellence is excellent in itself (Misc. 1139). And in *The End for Which God Created the World*, written just before his death, Edwards asserts that God's rejoicing is in his own acts for his creatures, so his joy is not derived from them.[12]

But at the same time Edwards refused to discard his notion—offensive to the deists[13]—that God is truly delighted in and by his creation, particularly by its praise for him. He linked God's happiness to goodness, as the eighteenth century required, but he never surrendered his conviction that the divine is personal, capable of delight: "God would be less happy if he was less good, or if it were possible for him to be hindered in exercising his goodness or to be hindered from glorifying himself" (Misc. 679).

Nor did Edwards yield to the Enlightenment's insistence that all notions of goodness and excellence were to be defined by eighteenth-century standards. God's glory is excellent in itself and is its own standard. Hence praise for it is fitting, even if praise does not comport with deist standards of excellence: "His glory is in itself excellent" (Misc. 699). If praise and God's delight in praise violate Enlightenment canons of decency, then, Edwards resolved, it was those canons which had to be refitted, not the truths of Reformed Christianity.

The History of Religion: Change and Progress

If Edwards differed with most Enlightenment understandings of the *nature* of religion, he also disagreed with them about the *history* of religion. In a sense, this was

---

12. End, 447; Lee, *The Philosophical Theology of Jonathan Edwards*, 207.
13. Chubb, *Collection of Tracts*, 1:372.

still an argument over the nature of religion: Edwards believed it was historical in its very nature, while deists refused to take history seriously. For the deists, religion "is perpetually and invariably the same,"[14] while for Edwards religion was a story of progressive development. But the upshot was a serious disagreement about the course of religion; deists saw religion as an unchanging record of priestcraft disguising the truths of natural religion, while Edwards sketched a long and complex history of both true and false religion continually evolving and developing.

In a curious way, however, Edwards's view of religion as historical and developmental bears some rhetorical resemblance to the deist account. Both are concerned to square the goodness of God with the limited reach of the Christian church. As we have seen, the growing recognition of religious pluralism was a serious intellectual problem for religious thinkers in the seventeenth and eighteenth centuries. How could God continue to be regarded as good and just if so many millions had never been exposed to what was thought to be true religion? Many of the orthodox simply ignored the problem or decided that ignorance of the gospel was prima facie evidence that God was just in damning them. Freethinkers and deists transformed true religion from historical revelation to innate dictates of reason that were accessible to every human being since the beginning. The Cambridge Platonists argued that the most important truths of Christianity had been propagated universally from the beginning. Jonathan Edwards made this argument as well.

Edwards was as fascinated as the deists by the flood of travelogues and other reports of heathen religions coming to England in the seventeenth and early eighteenth centuries.[15] His very first *Miscellanies* entry, written in 1722 or 1723 when he was about twenty years old, made mention of the "heathen" (Misc. a). In 1743 or 1744 he began writing detailed descriptions of non-Christian religious beliefs and practices (Misc. 953). Most of these entries were extracts he copied from seventeenth- and eighteenth-century Christian writers such as Theophilus Gale (1628–78), Hugo Grotius (1583–1645), Isaac Barrow (1630–77), Humphrey Prideaux (1648–1724), Samuel Clarke (1675–1729), Samuel Shuckford (c. 1694–1754), Isaac Watts (1674–1748), Philip Skelton (1707–1787), Chevalier Ramsay (1686–1743), and Johann Friedrich Stapfer (1708–1775).

Edwards seems to have become more interested in other religions as he grew older; most of the sixty entries devoted to this topic were written during his years at Stockbridge, in the last decade of his life. The majority of them purport to show that non-Christian thinkers and religions actually contain Reformed Christian doctrines. For example, Misc. 1181 is an extract from Chevalier Ramsay's *Principles of Natural and Revealed Religion* (Glasgow, 1749). It claims to find the Trinity in the Dao-de-jing, expectations of a suffering messiah in one of the Confucian classics, and a supposed statement by Confucius that a saint would come from the west to banish sin and suffering.

---

14. *AF*, 378.
15. For a review of this literature, see Lach, *Asia in the Making of Europe*, 3:549–97.

Edwards read voraciously about other religions; he knew of, tried to get, and perhaps read many of the travelogues, dictionaries, and encyclopedias of religion available in his time. The books cited in his "Catalogue" include George Sale's translation of the Qur'an, reports of the Jesuits in China, an analysis of the Qabbalah, comparative mythology, and a wide range of dictionaries and encyclopedias of religion—from skeptic Peter Bayle's *Historical and Critical Dictionary* to Daniel Defoe's *Dictionary of All Religions Antient and Modern*.[16]

Many of the writers whom Edwards read, particularly Skelton and Ramsay, understood other religions in terms defined by what was called the *prisca theologia* (ancient theology). This was a tradition in apologetic theology, resting on misdated texts (the Hermetica, Chaldean oracles, Orpheia, and Sybilline oracles), that attempted to prove that vestiges of true religion were taught by the Greeks and other non-Christian traditions. Typically it alleged that all human beings were originally given knowledge of true religion (monotheism, the Trinity, *creatio ex nihilo*) by the Jews or by traditions going back to Noah's good sons (Shem and Japheth) or antediluvians such as Enoch or Adam. This knowledge was subsequently passed down to Zoroaster, Hermes Trismegistus, Brahmins and Druids, Orpheus, Pythagoras, Plato, and the Sybils.[17]

The *prisca theologia* was developed first by Clement of Alexandria, Origen, Lactantius, and Eusebius to show that the greatest philosophers had borrowed from the Chosen People. It was revived in the Renaissance by Marsilio Ficino and Pico Della Mirandola to reconcile Neoplatonism and Christian dogma.[18] In the seventeenth and eighteenth centuries it was taken up again by the "Jesuit Figurists," who tried to win acceptance for their mission in China by claiming that China had worshiped the true God two thousand years before Christ, and by a number of other, mostly Protestant, thinkers, four of whom Edwards read carefully and took quite seriously. We have already mentioned Ramsay, who found trinitarian monotheism among the ancient Egyptians, Persians, Greeks, and Chinese. Ramsay tried to prove that God gave complete revelation of the essential Christian doctrines to the earliest patriarchs, so that most pagan religions teach a trinity similar to the Neoplatonic triad. Edwards also used extensively the work of Philip Skelton, a Church of Ireland divine and the author of the anti-deist work *Deism Revealed* (London, 1751).

---

16. He also read or tried to get a copy of William Turner's *History of All Religions* (1695), Isaac Watts's *Harmony of All Religions* (1742), Samuel Shuckford's *Sacred and Profane History* (1727), Ephraim Chambers's *Philosophical Dictionary* (1728), Broughton's *Bibliotheca Historico-Sacra* (1737), and Thomas Dyche's *A New General English Dictionary* (1725)—all of which featured articles on non-Christian religions. "Edwards' Reading 'Catalogue,'" Yale Divinity School.

17. On the *prisca theologia*, see Walker, "Orpheus," *Ancient Theology*, and *The Decline of Hell*; Yates, *Giordano Bruno*; Schmitt, "Perennial Philosophy"; Droze, *Homer or Moses?*; and Seznec, *The Survival of the Pagan Gods*.

18. Even Augustine seems to have been influenced by this tradition. In his *Retractions* he wrote, "What is now called Christian religion has existed among the ancients, and was not absent from the beginning of the human race, until Christ came in the flesh: from which time true religion, which existed already, began to be called Christian" (1.13).

Theophilus Gale and Ralph Cudworth (1617–88) are two earlier proponents of the *prisca theologia* who influenced Edwards. Gale's magnum opus, *The Court of the Gentiles* (1677), was a massive four-volume work dedicated to the proposition that all ancient languages and learning, philosophy in particular, were derived from the Jews. As Numenius of Apamea put it in a line noted by Edwards, "What is Plato but Moses speaking in the Attick language?" (Misc. 1355).[19] Cudworth, the great Cambridge Platonist, used much of his *True Intellectual System of the Universe* (1678) to show that the wiser pagans were trinitarian monotheists, not unacquainted with the true (Christian) God.

Edwards was clearly impressed by these proponents of the *prisca theologia*.[20] He copied enormous extracts from their works into his private notebooks. Yet as Diderot once said, imitation is continual invention. From his marginal notes and recapitulation of the tradition in other private notebooks, it is clear that Edwards was selectively and creatively refashioning the tradition to serve his own polemical needs. His principal purpose was to show, against the deists, that nearly all humans have received revelation, and therefore all knowledge of true religion among the heathen is from revelation rather than the light of natural reason.

Edwards went to great lengths detailing in his notebooks the religious truths possessed by the heathen. From Grotius he learned that the Greeks said that the Spirit moved on the waters at the beginning and knew that one can commit adultery in the heart and that one must forgive and love one's enemies (Misc. 1012; Misc. 1023). Virgil, Seneca, Juvenal, and Ovid, Edwards noted, confessed that our original nature was corrupt (Misc. 1073). Ramsay taught him that the Hindu Vedas and the Chinese I-Ching contain stories about a hero who expiates crimes by his own sufferings, and that many heathen from different traditions acknowledged a divine incarnation and realized that virtue comes only by an infusion of grace (Misc. 1351; Misc. 1355). Edwards noted in his Blank Bible[21] that heathen stories about gods and goddesses were actually distortions of Hebrew counterparts. Saturn, for example, is a transmutation of Adam, Noah, and Abraham; Hercules is a Greek rendition of Joshua, Bacchus of Nimrod, Moses, and the Hebrew deity; Apis and Serapis are Egyptian retellings of the story of Joseph (pp. 6, 11, 39).

In his own appropriation of the *prisca theologia*, Edwards said that the heathen learned these truths by what could be called a trickle-down process of revelation. In the "first ages" of the world the fathers of the nations received revelation of the great religious truths, directly or indirectly, from God himself.[22] These truths were then passed

---

19. Droze, *Homer or Moses?* 199; the quotation is cited by Edwards in his extract from Ramsay's *Philosophical Principles* on p. 942 of the Miscellanies notebook.

20. Edwards may have been introduced to the *prisca theologia* by Samuel Johnson, his tutor at Yale; Fiering, *Moral Philosophy at Seventeenth-Century Harvard*, 15.

21. A small copy of the King James Version interleaved with quarto-sized sheets of paper and bound in a large volume; Edwards Papers.

22. Misc. 953; Misc. 986; Misc. 984. Usually Edwards was ambiguous about the location of the original deposit of revelation. Only occasionally did he pinpoint Adam; in Misc. 884 he said that Adam learned the moral law from God and taught it with great clarity to his descendants. In *Original*

down, by tradition, from one generation to the next. Unfortunately, there is also a religious law of entropy at work. Human finitude and corruption inevitably cause the revelation to be distorted, resulting in superstition and idolatry.

From Ramsay Edwards learned that the breakdown was caused in part by a problem of language. All original peoples—even the Gauls, Germans, and Britons—shared hieroglyphs with the Egyptians to represent divine things taught by Noah. Over the course of time, pagans dissociated the symbol from its referent. "Men attached themselves to the letter and the signs without understanding the spirit and the thing signified" (Misc. 1255). This accounted for idols and "vile superstitions" (ibid.). It also accounted for the similarity between the stories of Christ's sufferings and the legends of pagan heroes: the heathen took the symbols of Christ's sufferings and applied them to their own champions. By this mechanism and others the original purity of divine truth was continually breaking down, corrupted by profane and demonic admixtures (Misc. 986). God used the Jews to retard the process of degeneration by periodically acting on their behalf with miracles, which reminded the heathen of the traditions they had once learned from their fathers but subsequently forgotten (Misc. 350).

In his private commentary on selected biblical passages Edwards recapitulated this drama.[23] "The knowledge of true religion was for some time kept up in the world by tradition. And there were soon great corruptions and apostasies crept in, and much darkness overwhelmed great part of the world." By the time of Moses, most of the truth that had previously been taught by tradition was now lost. So "God took care that there might be something new, [which] should be very public, and of great fame, and much taken notice of abroad, in the world heard, that might be sufficient to lead sincere inquirers to the true God." Hence the heathen nations in the Ancient Near East heard about the exodus of the Jews from Egypt, the miracles God performed for them in the wilderness, Joshua's conquests of the Canaanites, and how the sun stood still. The defeated Canaanites fled to Africa, Asia, Europe, and the isles of the sea "to carry the tidings of those things. . . . so that, in a manner, the whole world heard of these great things."

After these wondrous acts of God, knowledge of true religion was maintained for several generations. But by the time of David, much had been forgotten and distorted. So God acted once more, this time for David and Solomon, "to make his people Israel, who had the true religion, [be] taken notice of among the heathens." The diaspora after the Babylonian captivity spread knowledge of the true God even further abroad, so that "the nations of the world, if their heart had been well disposed to seek after the truth, might have had some means to have led 'em in their sincere and diligent inquiries to the knowledge of the true God and his ways."

Sin he wrote that Adam "continued alive near two thirds of the time that passed before the flood," so that most people alive until the Flood heard from Adam what "passed between him and his Creator in paradise" (OS, 170). Most often, however, he simply referred to the fathers of the nations as identical to or descended from Noah's sons.

23. Notes on the Scriptures, Acts 17:26f., no. 387; Edwards Papers. These are separate notebooks in which he commented on biblical passages; recently published as Notes on the Scripture [NS], vol. 15 of The Works of Jonathan Edwards.

And according to Edwards, God also saw to it that heathen philosophers came looking for news. Heathen "wise men" and "philosophers" obtained "scraps of light and truth . . . by travelling from one countrey to another," especially Judea, Greece, and Phoenicia (Lecture, August 1737 on 2 Peter 1:19, Edwards Papers). Edwards noted that Plato, for instance, had come to Egypt to learn what he could of the Jewish religion.

Edwards was always quick to note that heathen religion and philosophy contained "many absurdities" (e.g., Misc. 1350). But he learned from the *prisca theologia* that among the absurdities there were enough "scraps of truth" to show the way to salvation (Misc. 1297; NS, 387). Edwards found one way, then, to respond to the scandal of particularity the reports from the East had posed. He agreed with the deists that the problem could not be ignored and disagreed with earlier Reformed scholastics who saw nothing beyond knowledge of God the Creator in non-Christian religions.[24] God's justice and goodness were not sufficiently protected by the received tradition, so Edwards appropriated an old tradition to make Reformed history anew. In Edwards's new history God was still good, in the context of the new knowledge of pluralism, because knowledge of God the Redeemer had been available from the beginning.

If Edwards conceded, with the Enlightment, that traditional Christian historiography had been problematic, he also agreed with most eighteenth-century historians that religious history is replete with patterns. He rejected the Enlightenment contention that history's meaning was limited to recurring cycles of patterns but shared his age's fascination with them nonetheless. He saw in redemption history a number of recurring patterns: recurring degeneration, periodic revival, the repeated use of jealousy as a catalyst, and leadership by an eminent person.

Deists generally had little sense of history. Most posited an original Golden Age of natural religion that was subsequently corrupted by priests for their own gain.[25] Deterioration or degeneration, then, was the paramount principle of what little historiography they had. A similar principle of degeneration can be seen in the *prisca theologia* and Edwards's use of it.

There was a long tradition in the use of the *prisca theologia* that emphasized degeneration after the original deposit of revelation with the generations from Adam to Noah. According to this tradition, degeneration started with the sons of Noah, particularly Ham, who was said to have carried the spirit of Cain with him into the ark. Augustine saw Ham as prefiguring all heretics, and Shem and Japheth the Jews and Greeks respectively. Most who wrote in the tradition of the *prisca theologia* considered Ham the father of all the heathen. Peter Harrison explains that this principle of degeneration came in part from Renaissance pessimism, which had antecedents in both Christian and classical sources and was based on the presumption that change is

---

24. Following Calvin, they distinguished between knowledge of God the Creator, which is given through nature and conscience but has been distorted by sin, and knowledge of God the Redeemer, which is given through Scripture; Muller, *Post-Reformation Reformed Dogmatics*, 119.

25. Toland, for example, spoke of "the plain Easiness" of the religion of the ancient Egyptians, Persians, Romans, and Hebrews, which was subsequently corrupted; *Letters to Serena*, 71. See also Harrison, *"Religion" and the Religions*, 73–98.

always for the worse. This pessimism was softened somewhat in the eighteenth century by the growing success of the New Science, but it remained a cardinal postulate among deists, for instance, that only what is unchanging can be perfect.[26]

Edwards's philosophy of history was optimistic in its final outlook. Driven by the engine of religious revival, which he called "pourings out of the Spirit of God" (HWR, 146, 266), history will eventually culminate in the establishment of the kingdom of God on earth during the millennium. In the meantime one could plot the path to the eschaton by tracing the history of revival. In his *History of the Work of Redemption* (sermons preached in 1739) he describes revivals breaking out in the times of "Enos" (Enoch), the younger generation in the wilderness, Ezra, John the Baptist, Pentecost, and at Samaria in Acts 8. They continued all the way through church history, from the Reformation to the Great Awakening, propelling not only sacred but secular history as well.[27]

Final triumph lay ahead, but the road leading there was bumpy and winding. Throughout the work of redemption, degeneration set in whenever progress was made. By what I have called religious entropy, the revelations given to human beings were immediately and then continually attacked by corruption and distortion. God's intermittent recharging of the battery of revelation, as it were, was inevitably followed by loss of religious energy. The final result of thousands of years of such renovation and destruction was an entire world of heathen peoples hopelessly lost in idolatry.

Even the history of revival was punctuated regularly by deterioration and degeneration. In fact, God uses degeneration as an integral component of his method in redemption (Misc. 359; Misc. 986). His manner in almost everything was to "suffer 'em first to be undone, and then to build 'em up again in a more glorious [state]." For example, after the Reformation from "popery," God permitted the church to degenerate and "in a great measure to be destroyed by Deism[,] heresies, and cold dead formality, that he may make way for an immensely greater and more glorious reformation" (Misc. 907). It was common in history for a great spiritual darkness to precede a great revival (HWR, 195, 457).

Another pattern that Edwards found throughout the history of redemption was the principle of jealousy. God, he discovered, uses jealousy as a redemptive tool to disseminate knowledge of redemption and to stimulate revival (HWR, 179). Much of the religious truth possessed by the heathen, for example, was borrowed from the Jews, whose religion and way of life seemed attractive. Jewish idolatry made God jealous, but in disciplinary response God "will move them to jealousy in like manner by casting off them and taking other people that had not been his people in their room" (HWR, 189). God transferred his covenant to the Gentiles because the Jews' idolatry had made God jealous, and the Gentiles were jealous of the privileges of the covenant. At the end of the church age, just before the mil-

26. Harrison, *"Religion" and the Religions*, 106, 108. The apocryphal Esdras and St. Cyprian, on the Christian side, and Lucretius and Ovid, on the classical side; Harrison, *"Religion" and the Religions*, 102, 102–4.

27. HWR, 141, 190–91, 265, 314, 377.

lennium, the Jews will become jealous of the Gentile church, and all Israel will be converted (HWR, 469–70).

The end-time Jewish revival will follow the pattern of all previous revivals by issuing from the leadership of an "eminent person" who will serve as "an instrument of their reformation" (HWR, 195). Enoch, Moses, Ezra, John the Baptist, and Peter served as leaders of the revivals in their generations, and this is the pattern common to all redemptive history. "Time after time, when religion seemed to be almost gone and it was come to the last extremity, then God granted a revival and sent some angel or prophet or raised up some eminent person to be an instrument of their reformation" (ibid.). There is evidence in the Edwards corpus that he saw himself as one of these eminent persons called by God to lead a new reformation.[28]

Edwards's view of history, then, like that of the English Enlightenment,[29] is that it is a story of "periodic consummation" that retraces what has gone before. "Providence is like a mighty wheel," Edwards wrote, that returns to the "same point or place where [it] began." History waxes and wanes like the moon, seeming to progress for a time, but then appearing to regress shortly thereafter.[30]

According to Edwards, history was progress, but progress by a tortuous route through oft-repeating patterns and cycles.[31] Progress figures in deist accounts of history as well, as it does in the historiography of the Greeks and Romans, on which deist historiography was based.[32] But for the classical writers and the deists, whose view of history was basically cyclical, progress occurs within larger cycles, which recur endlessly. For Edwards, on the other hand, repeating cycles or patterns contribute to long-term historical progress.

Edwards implicitly acknowledged that the deist attacks on traditional Calvinist historiography had some merit—hence his appropriation of the *prisca theologia* to remedy its deficiencies. And his use of patterns in history was similar to the use made of them by the English Enlightenment. But his conception of the role of history in religion and being itself was a radical departure from deist conventions. While deists were barely able to conceive of a history of religion and generally regarded historical change as necessarily negative, for Edwards the historical view was critical to understanding the work of redemption, God's nature, and being itself.[33]

---

28. See McDermott, *One Holy and Happy Society*, 89–90.

29. Harrison, "*Religion*" *and the Religions*, 92–98.

30. Lee, *The Philosophical Theology of Jonathan Edwards*, 224; HWR, 517f.; Lee, *The Philosophical Theology of Jonathan Edwards*, 222f. Edwards was invoking the prophet Ezekiel's imagery of wheels within wheels; Ezekiel 1:15–21; 3:13; 10:6–19; 11:22.

31. For excellent critical analyses of Edwards's historiography, see Wilson, "Jonathan Edwards as Historian," and Wilson, "Introduction" to HWR, 1–109.

32. For deist reliance on classical sources, see Champion, *The Pillars of Priestcraft Shaken*, 35–7, 182–94, and Harrison, "*Religion*" *and the Religions*, 14–18. For the concept of progress in antiquity, see Dodds, *The Ancient Concept of Progress*, and Blundell, *Origins of Civilization*.

33. By 1739 Edwards had dropped his early plan to write a "Rational Account" of the Christian religion and preached the sermon series, "History of the Work of Redemption," that was to be the basis for a grand *summa* synthesizing his entire philosophico-theological vision. He never completed this work, but it is significant that at this mid-point in his career his vision took a markedly historical turn. See Schafer's introduction to Edwards, *Miscellanies, a-500*, 7n3.

History was such a basic category of thought for Edwards that he refused finally to separate time and space from eternity. Eternity, in Edwards's view, includes both time and space. It transcends and perfects them without being distinct from them. Eternity, then, is not timelessness, but a dimension that involves time and space while at the same time surpassing them both. Reality consists of a hierarchy of natures, one piled upon another, each supernatural to the one below. God is present throughout but manifests in a different way at each level. Thus eternity is not a nonsensuous realm beyond time and space but a realm of super-sense, super-space, and super-time.[34]

Deists attacked the Old Testament largely because it was a historical record of a particular people. They assumed that God would not teach truth through a historical medium. Since the Hebrew Bible was full of the histories of wars and "civil transactions," it could not have been inspired by God. Referring to these deist objections, Edwards commented, "Some say we find here among the books of a *particular* nation histories that they kept of the state of their nation from one age to another.... [W]hy then should we think that state histories that the Jews had are the word of God more than those that other people [had]?" (HWR, 283–84; emphasis added).

To Edwards this was a "silly objection" (284). For him it was obvious that this history was different from all others. It was the story of the "grand scheme of divine providence," written by "penmen" for whom there were "evident signs and testimonies of their being inspired by God" (286). Their subject, the work of providence, was greater than the work of creation, and "the Work of Redemption is the greatest of the works of providence" (286). What is found in history, then, was more important and revealing than what was given at the Creation. The deists' veneration for creation was misplaced and disproportionate; they had missed the grand show by their stubborn obsession with the previews.

They also missed the meaning of theology by their refusal to consider its historical development. For Edwards theology can be best understood from a historical perspective. For the subject of theology, God and all his glory, are too overwhelming for human beings to see all at once. This was why the kingdom of Christ had been established so slowly and gradually, lest the sight of it blind and obliterate finite creation. Only its gradual unfolding over the course of history could begin to show the fullness of God's glory in anything approaching its completeness. And by this slowly progressive unfolding, Satan was more gloriously defeated. For then the full extent of Christ's victory, in all of its aspects, could be made visible (HWR, 355–56).

Thus only by reviewing the history of the work of redemption can we see "the glorious majesty and power of God in this affair of redemption" (522), the "glorious wisdom of God" (524), "the stability of God's mercy and faithfulness to his people" (525), and "the beauty of God's works of providence" (519). History is also the best way to recognize "the happiness of the church of Christ" (526), "the misery of those without Christ" (527), and the inspiration of the Bible (520).

---

34. Lee, *The Philosophical Theology of Jonathan Edwards*, 211–41, esp. 237.

In his 1757 letter to the Princeton trustees Edwards explains his desire to write theology with a new, historical method. This was to be "a body of divinity in an entire new method, being thrown into the form of a history," considering each part of Christian theology in reference to "the great work of redemption by Jesus Christ," which is God's *summum* and *ultimum*. This method is "the most beautiful and entertaining, wherein every divine doctrine will appear to the greatest advantage, in the brightest light, in the most striking manner, showing the admirable contexture and harmony of the whole" (62–63).

For Edwards, then, history had both aesthetic and pedagogical value. Viewing God's redemption as a story rather than a timeless truth not only entertained and inspired but also clarified and revealed. Furthermore, history illuminates the organic nature of truth—the connectedness and interrelationships among all of its parts so that their sum is a systematic whole. Although, as we shall see, Edwards was not doing the kind of critical history that Hume and Voltaire professed to be doing, his sense of history as a medium for truth anticipated romantic currents in the nineteenth century.[35]

If God's work is best seen historically, it is because, in part, God himself delights in history. Far removed from the unblinking and impassive God of deism, Edwards's God exults in history because it is there that he can be himself. For history is an "increase, repetition or multiplication" of God's internal fullness (*End*, 433). The purpose of the Creation was the glory of God, which means the display of God's attributes, and these can be displayed fully only through the work of redemption in history. History gives God the opportunity to "exercise his goodness" (*Misc.* 679), which is his joy.[36] God's joy is rejoicing in his own acts (*End*, 447), and it is a rejoicing in *history* because it is there that his attributes are most fully manifested.

History was important to Edwards precisely because he thought God directed it at every moment toward an end of his design; the events of providence are "an orderly series of events, all wisely ordered and directed in excellent harmony and existence, tending all to one end" (*Misc.* 519). So history "makes a continual progress" (*Misc.* 547), using every event—no matter how indirectly—to further the ultimate end: "Nor yet are the past states of the world abolished by revolutions because they are in vain, or don't do anything towards promoting his design in creating the world; if so, providence would never have ordered them" (ibid.). The order was not immediately apparent; in fact most of the time history appeared to be as chaotic as the swirling eddies of a river: "The different streams of this river are ready to look like mere jumble and confusion to us because of the limitedness of our sight . . . but yet if we trace them they all unite at last and come to the same issue, disgorging themselves in one into the same great ocean. Not one of all the streams fail [sic] of coming hither at last" (*Misc.* 520). Every last moment and motion of history were orchestrated to progress toward the divine *telos*, so there was always "progression" and "eternal progress" (*End*, 534, 535).

35. See Barnes, "Romanticism and the Philosophy of History," and Hayden White's reference to the first half of the nineteenth century as "history's golden age," in White, *Tropics of Discourse*, 48.

36. Lee, *The Philosophical Theology of Jonathan Edwards*, 202f.

History's progress is a mirror of God's internal and infinite self-enlargement. Or to put it another way, history progresses only because God is pleased to enlarge himself in and through history. Recently Sang Hyun Lee has shown that Edwards's God progresses in his own being by ontological self-enlargement. Edwards was careful to protect God's perfection before the Creation by insisting that God's actuality in his internal being (ad intra) was absolutely complete, but suggested—in a novel move[37]—that history and the world are God's external repetitions (ad extra) of his being ad intra. That is, the temporal extension of God's actuality repeats in time God's internal actuality without improving it. The world is a temporal repetition of the divine fullness, which is inexhaustibly repeatable.[38]

Edwards saw a similar self-enlargement or progress in the being and life of Christ. After the Fall, he wrote, Christ took on a new role as intercessor for humanity, assuming "the care and burden of the government of the church and world" (HWR, 130). The Father no longer had direct contact with human beings, leaving that to the Son. So it was the second person of the Trinity who appeared to Moses, the seventy elders, Joshua, Gideon, Manoah, Isaiah, Daniel and the three Hebrew men in the fiery furnace (HWR, 239, 260). These various and "progressive" manifestations of the divine nature in Christ, including the Incarnation, "added to the finite holiness of the human nature of Christ" (Misc. 1005). So Christ progressed in holiness and ontological stature.

The church continued to add to the completeness of Christ by, paradoxically, increasing that completeness. In an early *Miscellanies* entry on the end of the Creation Edwards wrote that the world was created as a communication of the happiness and glory of the Son of God. In this entry Edwards alludes to "a kind of becoming . . . in the life of Jesus Christ himself."[39]

> Therefore the church is said to be the completeness of Christ (Eph. 1:23), as if Christ were not complete without the church, as having a natural inclination thereto. We are incomplete without that which we have a natural inclination to. Thus, man is incomplete without the woman, she is himself; so Christ is not complete without his spouse. (Misc. 104)

Christ's progression will continue even after the last judgment. Then "he will be admitted into a higher degree of enjoyment of the Father than before" (Misc. 957).

Progress is also the rule for the saints. They shall ever increase in (spiritual) beauty, knowledge, and holiness, "for as they increase in the knowledge of God, and of the works of God, the more they will see of his excellency; and the more they see his excellency, *caeteris paribus*, the more they will love him; and the more they love God, the more delight and happiness, *caeteris paribus*, will they have in him" (Misc. 105; Misc. 198). As Lee puts it, "The saint's eternal progress in his or

---

37. Lee suggests that while it was traditional in orthodox Western Christian theology to use the inside/outside distinction to hold to both God's transcendent and immanent relationships to the world, Edwards's innovation was to speak of God *ad extra* "not only as God's relation to the world but as *God's external repetition of his own being*." Lee, *The Philosophical Theology of Jonathan Edwards*, 204.

38. Misc. 448; End, 420, 448f.; Lee, *The Philosophical Theology of Jonathan Edwards*, 196–210.

39. Lee, *The Philosophical Theology of Jonathan Edwards*, 229.

her increase in beauty and being is a participation in God's own self-enlargement in time."⁴⁰

If the saint's progress is participation in God's self-enlargement, progress is also toward union. Saints continually approach union with divine being; but like an asymptote, their union with God "will become more and more strict and perfect" without ever "arriv[ing] at this infinite height" (*End*, 534).

Therefore heaven is progressive as well. The saints there continually increase in love and knowledge and never cease approaching nearer and nearer to the deity. And progress has always been the case for the church triumphant. In the Old Testament era, "the happiness of the departed saints . . . consisted much in the beholding the glory of God in the works of creation," but "since Christ's ascension . . . [their happiness consists] more in beholding the glory of God in the work of redemption" (*Misc.* 1137).⁴¹

A large part of that glory which the departed saints behold is the progressive development in the work of redemption. For instance, God's methods of redemption have changed over time. God raised up Abraham because true religion had gradually been corrupted after Babel, just as after the Flood, when God had to start over with Noah's family. But after the Flood, degeneration resumed. So after attempting to cultivate true religion in general humanity, God embarked on a novel procedure—the isolation of a chosen people (*HWR*, 158–59). After the Exodus, further separation (from the Palestinian tribes) was needed to preserve the integrity of the divine oracles (*HWR*, 177–80).

One could also see progress in the establishment of Christ's kingdom, which progresses through four phases: Christ's first coming, the destruction of the heathen Roman empire at the time of Constantine, the destruction of Antichrist just before the eschaton,⁴² and the last judgment (*HWR*, 351). Edwards believed that the church's conquest of Rome, or as he put it, Christ's "overthrow of heathenism" by the time of Constantine, was "the greatest revolution that ever was; the most like creating the world anew." By the triumph of the Christian faith, Christ had abolished idolatry in all the nations around Canaan, every heathen nation mentioned in the Old Testament, the isles mentioned in the Hebrew prophecies, and the countries subjected to the "four monarchies" (the Babylonian, Persian, Greek, and Roman empires), especially the greatest monarchy—Rome (*Misc.* 1327; *HWR*, 400–401).

Darkness and degeneration set in during the Middle Ages, before the revival of the Reformation brought a high tide of gospel truth and true religion. But degeneration set in again shortly after the Reformation, and continued until Edwards's day. This had been the time of the church's suffering, most of which it had endured from persecution by the Roman Catholic church. The Romanists' persecution was worse than that suffered by the early church at the hands of the heathen;

---

40. Ibid., 235.
41. For an overview of Edwards's conception of heaven as a progressive state, see Paul Ramsey, "Heaven Is a Progressive State," in *EW*, 706–38.
42. For a description of Antichrist and its destruction, see McDermott, *One Holy and Happy Society*, 81–82.

the worst of their persecutors were King Louis XIV of France and Queen Mary of England. Although persecution in the eighteenth century was less severe than what the church suffered in the first stage of the Reformation, unbelief was greater. The deists had been the most egregious heretics, and Edwards's era was the worst of all: "Never [was there] such a casting off the Christian religion and all revealed religion, never any age wherein was so much scoffing at and ridiculing the gospel of Christ by those that have been brought up under gospel light."[43]

Edwards was well aware that a familiar deist challenge to orthodox historiography concerned the timing of the Incarnation. If Christ had come to bring the truth, why had God waited so long to send him? Edwards reflected on this at every stage in his career and adopted two strategies for his response. One focused on the historical conditions necessary for such an advent, and the other emphasized God's appeals to the heathen in the centuries preceding that advent.

First, the historical conditions. Edwards argued that Christ could not have come before the Flood because the full extent and gravity of sin had not become visible; so the need for a savior from sin would not have been recognized (HWR, 297). Nor would it have been proper for Christ to have come after the Flood because there were still too few people in the world, and the great apostasy of the heathen world had not yet occurred. Thus a redemption by Christ attempted then would not be as "conspicuous" as the world's redemption ought to be (ibid.). Besides, histories of the world were not being written in these times, so the record of a redemption would have been lost and doubted by later ages (HWR, 298; Misc. 1235).

It was necessary for the heathen to continue long in unbelief in order "that there might be a thorough proof of the necessity of a savior" and so that it would be clear that human beings were "utterly insufficient to deliver themselves" from misery and subjection to the devil. Passage of time was also required to show the world that all the wisdom of the philosophers and heathen wise men could not rescue them from intellectual and spiritual darkness (HWR, 180). So it was appropriate that Christ came when Greek and Roman philosophy was at its zenith, thus demonstrating the relative vanity of human learning by comparison (HWR, 278). Finally, it was necessary for the Jews to be dispersed throughout the world (after the Babylonian exile, and then again after the destruction of Jerusalem in A.D. 70) to show the necessity of abolishing the old dispensation, which generally restricted salvation to one nation (HWR, 298).

Edwards's second strategy was to portray the history of the work of redemption as a series of revelations by God to the heathen, all of which they largely ignored. His point undoubtedly was to complement his first strategy: God waited thousands of years to send the Christ, but he did not wait to reach out to the heathen. Once again God's justice and goodness were in jeopardy, and once more Edwards fought to reconcile them with Reformed theology.

In what amounted to a condensed history of the work of redemption, Edwards devoted a section of *Original Sin* to the argument that God had used redemption

43. HWR, 373, 409–10, 427, 432, 438.

history to proclaim his truths to the entire world (chap. 1, sec, 8). Adam, for example, was alive for two-thirds of the time before the Flood, so that "a very great part" of those still alive before the Flood heard from his own mouth "the things which passed between him and his Creator in paradise." After the Flood, Noah was commissioned by God to preach to the world for 120 years (170).

God placed Abraham's family "as it were in the midst of the earth, between Asia, Europe and Africa, in the midst of those nations which were most considerable and famous for power, knowledge and the arts." Through that family and their descendants, whom he intended to be a "city on an hill . . . a light to the world," he conferred "visible tokens of His presence . . . manifesting himself there, and from thence, to the world" (171–72). As a result, Abraham was known in all the principal nations of the world. His acquaintance with Melchizedek proves that the great works of God for his family were sufficient to have awakened "the attention and consideration of all the nations in that part of the world, and to have led them to the knowledge and worship of the only true God" (172).

Similar things took place in Jacob and Joseph's time. God's wonders on their behalf "were done in the sight of the nations of the world, tending to awaken them and lead them to the knowledge and obedience of the true God" (173). In Moses and Joshua's time, God manifested himself in miracles quite publicly—"in view as it were of the whole world." The world was shaken, "the whole frame of the visible creation, earth, seas, and rivers, the atmosphere, the clouds, sun, moon and stars, were affected; miracles greatly tending to convince the nations of the world of the vanity of their false gods" (173).

Edwards continued through the principal phases of the remainder of Jewish history recorded in the Hebrew Bible. At every juncture God sought to win the attention and hearts of the heathen. News of Gideon's defeat of the vast armies of Midian, the conquests and riches of David and Solomon, and the miracles performed through Elijah, Elisha, and Jonah were intended to induce the heathen "to know that the Lord was God and that there was none else" (174). God's purpose was "to enlighten, affect and persuade them" (ibid.).

Then God undertook a "new method with the heathen world and used, in some respects, much greater means to convince and reclaim them, than ever before." He drove his people into captivity in Babylon, which had by then become "the head and heart of the heathen world," since Chaldea had been the "fountain of idolatry." Consequently, the story of the faith and bravery of the four young men in the fiery furnace was published throughout the empire (175). And when Daniel's exploits in the lion's den became known, "Darius was induced to publish to all people, nations and languages, that dwelt in all the earth, his testimony, that the God of Israel was the living God and steadfast forever, etc." (175).

After the exile came the diaspora to all parts of the Persian empire and further west. As a result Jews brought "as it were all over the heathen world" their Scriptures, synagogues, and worship of the true God. So heathen all over the world were given enough light to enjoy true religion—if they would only take advantage of it.

Thus that light, which God had given [the Jews], was in the providence of God, carried abroad into all parts of the world; so that now [the heathen] had far greater advantages to come to the knowledge of the truth, in matters of religion, if they had been disposed to improve their advantages (176).

The heathen usually did not have the right disposition to "improve their advantages," but Edwards had proven his point. Despite the postponement of the the Messiah's coming until thousands of years after the Creation, knowledge of true religion was nevertheless available during those years, and not only to the Jews. So Edwards's fairly traditional chronology could still stand against deist charges of injustice and cruelty. His God was vindicated.

There remained one more problem that had to be solved. If God had revealed His truths to the Jews (the first covenant), and news of these truths had been disseminated to much of the world before Christ, why was this covenant so different from the new covenant revealed in Christ? For the deists this difference between the covenants was evidence against a historical revelation. For a God who wanted to instruct His creation would have done so from the beginning. And the covenant which the orthodox claimed was inspired—the Old Testament—was crude and unworthy of the deity.

Over the course of his career Edwards refined responses to each of these objections. To the complaint that God should have revealed everything at the beginning, Edwards replied in effect that he did. The two covenants were different versions of a single covenant. In the redemption sermons of 1739, for example, he proposed that the religion of Israel (or the first covenant) was "essentially the same religion" as that enjoyed by the Christian church; both are built on the same foundation of divine revelation (HWR, 443).

And both teach grace. The Old Testament is not Pelagian, as deists believed; it does not teach salvation by obedience. Edwards conceded that it may appear to do so, and that the Old Testament church was mistaken about the source of true righteousness (Misc. 1354), but he maintained throughout his career that salvation by works was a surface text that God used as a pedagogical tool to point the Jews to the deeper meaning of grace. God, he wrote, used a "covenant of works" to show the Jews that by their works they could never achieve the righteousness which God demanded. "By God's contrivance of that dispensation they were led not to depend on these as works, but as [a] disposition to receive, as so many manifestations of repentance and submission" (Misc. 250). The surface text that seemed to teach works was used by God to convince its readers that they were sinners and condemned by the covenant of works, "that they might be brought to trust in the mere saving grace of God[,] which was also revealed to them" (Misc. 323).[44]

Was the Old Testament therefore self-contradictory, containing two, opposing ways to righteousness? No more so than Jesus is in the New Testament, who

---

44. Edwards makes similar points in his essays on justification in the "Controversies" notebook; Edwards Papers.

offers to the rich young ruler the covenant of works in order to teach him to "despair of it" and fly to grace (Misc. 439). The first covenant contains a "trial" (Misc. 994) or test; it highlights the "fruits of faith" rather than faith itself, but only because God in his wisdom knows that saints in that age could best come to true faith by this route.

Yet faith is not a work. Edwards recognized the dangers to Reformed theology of emphasizing faith as a condition for the reception of grace. As he put it very early in his notebooks, thinking of faith as a condition "tends to make us depend on our own righteousness" (Misc. 2). Very early in his career Edwards theorized that Christ fulfilled the second covenant's condition, which was perfect obedience and suffering. Faith is simply our reception of the gift of Christ's righteousness (Misc. 2). The covenant was made not with believers but with Christ, who is considered to be united with believers. So all that happens to Christ and is achieved by Christ, happens to and is achieved by believers (Misc. 163; Misc. 171). Later in his career, however, Edwards was willing to call faith a condition but at the same time insisted it was not a "work" that gains any merit for the believer (Misc. 1091).

Against the charge that the first covenant, found in the Old Testament, is immoral and unworthy of God, Edwards asserted that it was a type or shadow of the second covenant, presented in this manner because human understanding was in a nascent stage of development. Edwards used the metaphor of human development, referring to the Old Testament period as the childhood of the race. God's people (the "church") under the first covenant were still in an "ignorant and infantile state," he wrote at the end of the 1720s (Misc. 439); in the mid-1750s he was still referring to humanity in this period as "in a child's state" (Misc. 1354; Misc. 250; Misc. 994).

It was for pedagogical purposes that God taught people to make sacrifices for their sins, a notion that scandalized deists. Edwards explained that this primitive idea was used to teach respect for God's law and authority. If they had been permitted to "fly to God's mercy" with a simple display of repentance (this was all that deists thought was necessary), they would have learned to despise and take for granted God's holy majesty (in Edwards's mind, this was the deists' sin). But the requirement of sacrifice for sin showed them that there is no pardon without satisfaction, that sin must be suffered for, and that God hates all trespasses against his authority. This taught them a proper trust in God's mercy and an accurate view of God's majesty and jealousy, "which is the exercise of the same disposition of mind as is exercised in actually believing on Christ crucified, and is the same sort of act" (Misc. 326). Thus Edwards stated early in his career (1728) that the first covenant could produce the same saving disposition that was produced by the second covenant.

This helped explain why "the people of God under the Old Testament were kept vastly more at a distance, than now under the gospel" (Misc. 440). God's hatred for sin had not been revealed through the death of Christ, so distance was needed to impress upon the infant church God's majesty and dread for his spotless holiness. But once "the Mediator and eternal punishment [were] so plainly revealed," and it had been shown that "the sacredness of God's majesty and holiness are abundantly more effectually secured another way, and that is, by the humiliation of Christ and the eternal damnation of sinners," now the church, approaching maturity, could freely and intimately converse with God, since it was depending on the righteousness and sufferings of Christ. Such intimacy does not detract from a proper awe for God's holiness, "but only causes an admiration of his free and sovereign grace" (Misc. 440).

Once this gradual maturation of the church was understood, all other differences between the covenants were easier to reconcile. They contain different commands, and only one focuses on a mediator and teaches the gospel explicitly. But both require the same condition (true holiness, faith, and obedience) and manifest the same principle and spirit. The promises are different; one promises Canaan, prosperity, and "public tokens of favor," while the other promises eternal life (Misc. 439). But the first set of promises function as types of the second, which is dimly revealed through the shadows of the first. One covenant is the *cortex* or shell, the other the *medulla* or marrow; one contains the *putamen* or husk, the other the nucleus; one teaches the covenant of works, at least on the surface, while the other teaches the gospel; one makes impossible demands, the other makes all things possible through grace; one gives us the letter, the other the spirit; one is a ministry of law, the other of grace; the gospel is relatively hidden in one, but obvious in the other (Misc. 1353).

For these reasons expectations were different under the two covenants. Since we are in the new dispensation, we have greater obligations. We are bound to duties from which saints in the old dispensation were free, because our revelations are much clearer (Misc. 439). In fact, we are to love God "vastly more" and "in an unspeakably higher degree" because of the new manifestations God has given of himself. But we are also beneficiaries of "higher exercises of love to God" than Adam and Eve enjoyed, and "higher degrees of spiritual joys" (Misc. 894). Therefore Old Testament saints were not as accountable. Many things that would have been innocent in Adam's day would be exceedingly sinful for us. Adam might have been "earthly minded in a sense wherein it would be corrupt and abominable in Christians to be [in Edwards's day]" (ibid.).

These last remarks on how expectations depend on the degree of revelation available illustrate Edwards's developmental view of the history of religion. They also show that he believed that religious obligations are relative to historical conditions. We shall consider the implications of this thinking in chapter seven.

Final Observations

It is clear that Edwards took the deist criticisms of Reformed historiography seriously indeed. By appropriating the *prisca theologia*, he appears to have accepted implicitly their premise that it would be unjust for God to withold his revelation from the majority of the world. This move separated him from many of his Reformed predecessors. Like them, he rejected the deist and Enlightenment notion of a common religious substratum at the heart of all the world's religions.[45] But he denied the Reformed scholastic contention that only in the Christian religion can be found the marks of true religion.

The Reformed schoolmen held that all non-Christian religions were utterly incapable of leading human beings to the truth. They believed in the possibility of natural knowledge of God, but because of sin such knowledge fell far short of the knowledge that was necessary for salvation.[46] Edwards, on the other hand, seemed convinced by the end of his life that many non-Christian religions contained the condition for the possibility of saving knowledge, despite his simultaneous conviction that no nation as a whole had ever taken advantage of these "relics of truth."

If Edwards was influenced by deist criticisms, he also squared off firmly against deist and related Enlightenment understandings of the nature of religion. For the English Enlightenment religion could be comprehended by propositional moral dictates that fairly precluded worship and personal devotion in its commitment to a stoic deity largely removed from daily affairs. Edwards in contrast defended religion as worship and participation in a God who creates for his own glory and delights in praise from the creation. At issue for the two competing definitions of religion were the role of morality and the relative centrality of the human being. Enlightenment religion was a humanocentric devotion to morality; for Edwards true religion was a theocentric devotion to a transcendent God, at whose service morality played an ancillary role.

Edwards also rejected deist and Enlightenment notions of God and religion as static and unhistorical. For Edwards, humanity, religion and even the deity are in development as they enlarge and progress. Hence theology cannot be understood apart from consideration of its historical development. And the heart of theology in this life, the work of redemption, can be understood only in the historical mode. One would not be mistaken to see in Edwards a faint foreshadowing of the nineteenth century's obsession with history as the key to understanding and meaning.

But one would be mistaken to see in Edwards an incipient historicist, or to suggest with Perry Miller that Edwards was more radically modern than Robertson and Gibbon.[47] He did not scrutinize his sources for their historical accuracy in the manner of a professional twentieth-century historiographer. He was guided far less by empirical observation than theological premises. Like the deists, he was interested in the past not for its own sake but for its didactic purposes. He understood that there is unity to history, as Miller asserts, and that that unity is not transparent. But, as John F. Wilson points out, these insights were not modern but common to both ancient and medieval thinkers.[48] In these respects, Peter Gay is right to describe Edwards as intellectually and spiritually isolated from the modern world.[49]

---

45. Muller, *Post-Reformation Reformed Dogmatics*, 116.
46. Ibid., 175–85.
47. Miller, *Jonathan Edwards*, 313.
48. Ibid.; Wilson, "Jonathan Edwards as Historian," 13.
49. Peter Gay, "An American Tragedy," in *Loss of Mastery*, chap. 4.

If Edwards's historiography was not modern, however, it was not for the reason often suggested—that Edwards's reading of history was controlled by an ideological paradigm while those of modern historians are not. Hayden White's studies (and others') in the "history of narrative" have recently shown us that every historian inevitably reads the testimonies of history through the lens of one paradigm or another. There are no naked facts of history: "The historian has to interpret his material in order to construct the moving pattern of images in which the form of the historical process is to be mirrored or understood."[50] The Enlightenment model of an unbiased historian sifting through the evidence of history with pure objectivity and writing history as it really happened has collapsed. Historical narratives should therefore be understood as "symbolic structures" mediating "between the events reported" in them "and the generic plot-structures conventionally used in our culture to endow unfamiliar events and situations with meanings."[51] If Edwards was unmodern or premodern, it was not because he imposed plot-structures on his data, while more objective "modern" historians could interpret data without the taint of such plot structures. His history was certainly more theological than that of Hume or Voltaire, Gay's heroes of modern historiography, but not necessarily more ideological.

So Edwards was not a modern, but not because of his conviction that history was driven with theological purpose. Perhaps his more telling difference with modernity was his refusal to brook Enlightenment claims to universal reason. His attacks on the concept of a disinterested will were in effect assaults on the Enlightenment notion of disinterested reason that could read history without the use of a plot-structure. This eighteenth-century Augustine argued that all reason was interested, by virtue of either love of God or love of self. Hence there is no neutral reason that can adjudicate disinterestedly the claims of religion. Nor can history be interpreted properly without a vision of the divine beauty that directs it. This was a notion no less scandalous to the modern minds of the English Enlightenment than it is to modern historians two centuries later.

---

50. White, "The Historical Fact as Literary Artifact," 51.
51. White, "Historical Fact as Literary Artifact," 52. See also White, "The Structure of Historical Narrative," Metahistory, and The Content of the Form. For excellent reflections on the "poetics of history" in Christian historiography, see Zakai, Exile and Kingdom, "Reformation, History and Eschatology in English Protestantism," and "Poetics of History."

6

PARABLES IN ALL NATIONS

Typology and the Religions

Eighteenth-century deists imagined they had deflated the overweening pretensions of Christian theology. Toland, Chubb, and Tindal figured they had exposed traditional Christianity's universal claims as in fact restricted to a small corner of the planet and shown the volumes of Calvinist thought to have been the product of fanciful imaginations. The deists' challenge to orthodoxy was a formidable one: the God of orthodoxy, they avowed, had not revealed himself in history and the Bible. The true God whose will was enshrined in a few simple moral dictates could be discovered by the human mind. But the God of Calvin and Edwards was nowhere to be found in the real world because his supposed revelations were in fact chimerical. To put it charitably, he was silent.

The deists had thrown down the gauntlet. Jonathan Edwards eagerly picked it up and threw it back in the form of his typological system. God's nature, he declared through this system, is to communicate itself, that is, to flow out and diffuse itself throughout the creation so that its creatures can come to know its perfections (EW, 430–31, 434–35). Therefore God is constantly communicating Reformed truths wherever the eye can see and the ear can hear. As the psalmist proclaimed, "There is no speech nor language, where their voice is not heard. Their line is gone out through all the earth, and their words to the end of the world" (Ps. 19:3–4). Types, Edwards pronounced, "are a certain sort of language, as it were, in which God is wont to speak to us."[1] These types are words in persons,

---

1. Types, 150. "Types" is one of three notebooks Edwards devoted exclusively to elaboration of his typological scheme. The other two were "Images of Divine Things" (hereafter referred to as "Images") and "Types of the Messiah" (hereafter referred to as TM). All three are published in

places, and things—and they are found in every part of the creation. Hence there are sermons in the stones, flowers, and stars. God also speaks in history, both sacred and profane. He even speaks in the history of religions, heathen included. Indeed, every last atom of his creation pulsates with a divine melody. If the deists do not hear it, it is because they have stopped their ears.

In this chapter I will sketch briefly Edwards's typological vision of reality, and outline his arguments for its validity. We will see, as previous scholars have shown,[2] that Edwards expanded the limits of Puritan biblical typology, extending the application of its nomenclature to both nature and history. I will argue that this extension reached even to the history of religions.

Edwards's Typological View of Reality

Edwards extended the terminology of the long Christian tradition of typology, which typically saw in the Old Testament adumbrations ("types") of New Testament fulfillments ("antitypes"), to correspondences between the natural world and Reformed religious truths. He believed that the entire "system of nature" was the "voice of God to intelligent creatures," proclaiming the glories of Christ and His redemption (Misc. 1340; HWR, 218, 289; Misc. 702). No part of the natural world was exempt: "I believe that the whole universe, heaven and earth, air and seas, and the divine constitution and history of the holy Scriptures, be full of images of divine things,[3] as full as a language is of words" (Types, 152). Therefore every-

---

Typological Writings [TW], vol. 11 of *The Works of Jonathan Edwards*. Other notebooks, such as the "Notes on Scripture," the "Blank Bible," and the "Book of Controversies [BC]" (Edwards Papers) contain numerous references to typology.

2. Edwards, *Images or Shadows of Divine Things*, 1–41; Miller, "From Edwards to Emerson"; Baumgartner, "Figurative Language"; Wainwright, "Jonathan Edwards and the Language of God"; Lowance, "Typology and the New England Way" ; Lowance, "Jonathan Edwards and the Platonists," 129–51; Lowance, *Language of Canaan*, 178–207; TW, 3–33, 157–82; Knight, "Learning the Language of God"; Daniel, *The Philosophy of Jonathan Edwards*, 41–65.

3. Edwards used three words to denote things or persons in nature or history or Scripture that signify spiritual truths or realities: "types," "images," and "shadows." The latter two were subsets of the first; in other words, types could be either shadows or images. He generally seemed to think of images as more revealing than shadows; Edwards referred to images as "pictures" but said shadows were "dark resemblances." Images reveal more of the referent ("substance") than shadows do. Significantly, he spoke of the Old Testament as consisting mainly of shadows. See NS, no. 288. However, Edwards did not always sharply distinguish between images and shadows, as in his sermon on Revelation 21:18, where he refers to biblical imagery for heaven as both shadows and images (5, 15).

Wilson Kimnach suggests that Edwards seemed worried by his association of images with the traditional nomenclature of typology, pointing out that Edwards never used "types" in any of his several titles for the "Images of Divine Things" notebook (SDK, 233). But Edwards betrayed no such anxiety in the notebook entries. Throughout the notebook he used the word "types" for what the tradition had disparagingly called "allegorical" and he had labeled "images" or "shadows"; see, for example, "Images," nos. 12, 13, and 79. In Images no. 45 he explicitly associated types with natural things, usually derided by the tradition as allegories: "That natural things are ordered for types of spiritual things is evident by these texts."

thing in nature is but a pointer to something in a world beyond nature, and the second world is more real than the first: "The whole outward creation, which is but the shadow of beings, is so made as to represent spiritual things" (Misc. 362).

It was not only the natural world that Edwards saw pointing to the divine. All of history—not only what is called biblical history—is also "signification, marking the presence of something else." Each thing in nature and history can be understood only as the sign of the other to which it points. Philosophically, then, all being is communicative. As Stephen H. Daniel puts it, for Edwards communication is the condition for the possibility of (created) being rather than its consequence. Things are words, and creation is a book waiting to be read. Theologically, this means that being is God's glory because it expresses God. Grace is therefore the understanding of being as essentially communicative, and sin the denial of meaning by attempting to affirm one's significance apart from the system of divine semiotics. In the language of postmoderns, things are always already defined in terms of their intentionality.[4]

In contrast to the deist portrayal of self and world, Edwards's typological vision constitutes a living relation between humanity and its world, not the dead schematic rationalism that stripped history and nature of spiritual significance. For Edwards, all the world was alive with meaning. Each hilltop and valley contained a burning bush; every singing bird was a delphic oracle. And as Perry Miller put it, the image was no longer a detachable ornament on the surface of truth—as it had been for much of the typological tradition—it *was* truth.[5] History and nature were not simply reminders of a divinity at some remove, but in and of themselves "a manifestation and declaration of [God] to mankind . . . the effects and external expressions, and emanations of the divine perfections" (Misc. 1340).[6]

It was no wonder that Edwards believed that this typological system was for God "no trifling matter, but . . . of great IMPORTANCE" (Types, 322). It was God's imprint on the world. The expression of God's very being and his plan for the redemption of humanity were one with reality itself. God's character and humanity's future could be read in the creation, if only by those with a new sense of the heart and the Bible in their hands.

This gave a new definition to both humanity and communication. To be fully human now meant to be able to see God in "anything that being from him has some resemblance of him as the sun's majesty and green fields and pleasant flowers [have] of his grace and mercy" (Misc. 777). Seeing God in the types was now the

---

4. Daniel, The Philosophy of Jonathan Edwards, 34, 131–34, 83.
5. Miller, "Introduction" to Edwards, Images or Shadows of Divine Things, 20.
6. Edwards's use of "emanation" here and elsewhere have prompted scholars to explore the Neoplatonic influence on his thought. The most judicious assessment of Edwards's use of that tradition is Daniel's Philosophy of Jonathan Edwards. Daniel writes, "Though he borrows much of Neoplatonism's vocabulary of emanation and communication, Edwards cannot accept its implicit reduction of creation and its history to mere illusion" (The Philosophy of Jonathan Edwards, 66). Also see Watts, "The Neoplatonic Basis of Jonathan Edwards' 'True Virtue,'" and "Jonathan Edwards and the Cambridge Platonists," and Howe, "Cambridge Platonists."

"supreme act of humanity" and the highest possible form of communication.[7] No wonder Edwards said that vision is the noblest of the senses (Misc. 721).

Warrants for the System

How could Edwards believe in such a fantastic system? It was not self-evident, even to those Edwards would have considered regenerate. But to Edwards, the world was nearly as full of warrants for types as it was of the types themselves. For at one level, one regenerate seeing of the types was enough to convince the see-er of the validity of the entire system. Seeing was believing. But there were also rational warrants.[8]

The first set of rational warrants came from Scripture and validated the tradition's practice of seeing a divinely purposed relationship between Old Testament types and New Testament antitypes. The Old Testament itself, Edwards noted, often used "shadows" to typify future things: the bowing down of the sheaves of Joseph's brothers towards Joseph's sheaf foreshadowed their literal bowing to him in Egypt; Pharaoh's dream of fat and gaunt cows truly predicted fat and lean years; Daniel's four beasts accurately forecast the rise of four pagan empires; and all the Hebrew prophets' prophecies were fulfilled (Misc. 191). Paul taught us, Edwards inferred, that even so small a thing as the Bible's silence about Melchizedek's birth and death was typical. Edwards took this to be an inspired indicator of a biblical system of typology: "If so small things in Scripture are typical, it is rational to suppose that Scripture abounds with types" (Types, 151).

Paul was more explicit in other portions of his writings. In Galatians 4:21–23 he simply declared the story of Abraham's two sons to be an "allegory" for the two covenants (Types, 146). This passage was a "great confirmation" that "the history of the Old Testament in general is intended to be typical of spiritual things" (Misc. 192). Paul also wrote in 1 Corinthians that the Old Testament's admonition not to muzzle an ox was "for our sake, no doubt" (1 Cor. 9:9–10), and that the stories of the Israelites' idolatry in the wilderness "were [for] our examples" (1 Cor. 10: 1–4, 6, 11; Types, 146).

But in a move that departed in style if not substance from the Puritan typological tradition, Edwards also argued that Scripture endorses a system of types in nature. When Jesus proclaimed that he was the true light and true vine and true bread, he implied that all lights and vines and breads in this world are pointers to, or types of, their antitypes in him (Images, no. 45). Paul did the same for seed and sowing in springtime when he used them in 1 Corinthians 15 to argue for the resurrection of bodies. Unless God intended seed and planting to be types of spiritual realities, Paul's argument would not make sense: "If the sowing of seed and its springtime were not designedly ordered to have an agreeableness to the resur-

---

7. Miller, "Introduction" to Edwards, *Images or Shadows of Divine Things,* 33.
8. William Wainwright made the first detailed attempt to outline these warrants in "Jonathan Edwards and the Language of God."

rection, there could be no sort of argument in that which the Apostle alleges, either to argue the resurrection itself or the manner of it, either its certainty or probability or possibility" (*Images*, no. 7).

Scripture also indicates that human institutions can be typical of things in the spiritual world. For instance, Paul in Ephesians 5 tells us that marriage was instituted by God to typify the relationship between Christ and the church (*Images*, nos. 5, 9, 12). Paul's point was not that Christ's relationship to the church can tell us things about marriage, or simply that marriage can tell us things about Christ and the church, but that God established the human institution of marriage for the express purpose of signifying a relationship in the spiritual world.

Edwards called on the heathen world as a warrant for his system. If even the heathen, he suggested, recognize God's signature in nature, surely we should as well. "The very wiser heathens seemed to be sensible that the divine Being, in the formation of the natural world, designed to teach us moral lessons: so Ovid, concerning the correct posture of man" (*Images*, no. 134).[9]

Edwards's second major set of warrants came from the natural world itself. Its structure, he argued in a series of observations over the course of his career, points to its meaning. That is, the world is full of natural and moral analogies that by themselves suggest intelligent ordering by a Being outside the structure, and an order of being above and beyond the structure.

There is a great analogy, for example, between "works of creation and providence" (*Misc.* 651). The less perfect seems to be made in imitation of the more perfect, as an image reflects its substance (*Images*, nos. 8, 59). Animals appear to be an image of humans in many respects, plants similarly of animals, and minerals of plants.

> Thus the beasts are made like men: in all kinds of them there is an evident respect had to the body of man, in the formation and contrivance of their bodies, though the superior are more in conformity and the inferior less. Thus they have the same senses, the same sensitive organs, the same members—head, teeth, tongues, nostrils, heart, lungs, bowels, feet, etc. And from the lowest animal to the highest you will find an analogy, though the nearer you come to the highest, the more you may observe of analogy. And so plants, that are yet an inferior set of beings, they are in many things made in imitation of animals. They are propagated by seed which produce others of the same kind. The earth answers to the womb. There is something that answers to generation in the flower; there is a male part that impregnates the female part. The time of blossoming is as it were the time of love and pleasure, being the time of generation, when the seed and fruit are as it were conceived. They are like animals in their growing by nourishment running in veins, in suffering and dying by wounds, and [in] some of them there is an image of sensitiveness. (*Images*, no. 19)

If there is analogy between humans and those beings lower on the great chain of being, there is analogy between humans and beings above them as well. Angels

---

9. Ovid, *Metamorphosis*, bk. 1, ll. 84–86: "And, though all other animals are prone, and fix their gaze upon the earth, he gave to man an uplifted face and bade him stand erect and turn his eyes to heaven" (Loeb Classical Library, 1966).

are like humans in many respects, while retaining important differences. But those differences are related analogically to corresponding aspects in human beings. Even the saints manifest analogy in differences among them. Inferior and superior saints, both on earth and in heaven, are arranged hierarchically, based on the degree of their holiness. Some are higher and others are lower, and while there will be no envy or pride in heaven because the higher saints will be more loving and therefore more beloved by those below them,[10] nevertheless there will be differences between levels based on analogy (Misc. 681).

There is also an analogy to be observed in the use of language. Edwards quoted George Turnbull, a disciple of Newton, Locke, and Shaftesbury who wrote *The Principles of Moral Philosophy*, to demonstrate an analogy between the natural and moral worlds based on the correspondence between moral language and things in nature: "No words can express moral ideas, but so far as there is such an analogy betwixt the natural and moral world, that objects in the latter may be shadowed forth, pictured or imaged to us by some resemblances to them in the former."[11] Edwards reasoned that if moral philosophy needs to use language from nature to express moral concepts, and if such a use seems to be successful, there must actually be an ontological analogy between the two worlds. One must have been created with the purpose of representing the other (*Images*, no. 203).

A third warrant was teleological. Edwards reasoned from the end or purpose of creation to the character of the natural world. The fact that the purpose of mortal and natural life is spiritual made it seem reasonable that the natural world would represent spiritual truths. "Spiritual things are the crown and glory, the head and soul, the very end, the alpha and omega of all other works. So what therefore can be more agreeable to wisdom than that they should be so made as to shadow them forth[?]" (Misc. 362).

Finally, there was an aesthetic warrant. Or more accurately, a warrant drawn from the structure of beauty. Edwards argued in the *Nature of True Virtue* that earthly ("secondary") beauty is based on agreement between or union of different things, and that this kind of beauty—which we observe in things like plants and architecture and music—is an image of or analogous to the spiritual consent of different minds in a heavenly society of intelligent beings united in a benevolent agreement of heart (TV, 564–65). This in itself does not prove the typological nature of secondary beauty, but it provides further evidence that such a system may exist. Edwards argued that it would be reasonable for such a system to exist if indeed the source, pattern, and fountain of all secondary beauty is Beauty itself (TV, 550–51, 556).[12]

Since the world seems so full of analogies at so many different levels, and since Scripture corroborates what reason has inferred, Edwards concluded that "the inferior and shadowy parts" of the world indeed represent the "more real and excellent, spiritual and divine" (Misc. 362). In fact, it seemed to be God's principle "to

---

10. "Heaven is a World of Love," in EW, 374–78.
11. Turnbull, *An Enquiry*, 54f.
12. For the best survey of Edwards's aesthetics, see Delattre, *Beauty and Sensibility*.

make inferior things shadows of the supernatural and most excellent, outward things shadows of spiritual, and all other things shadows of those things that are the end of all things and the crown of all things" (Misc. 362; see also Types, 191).

Why God Uses Types

It seemed appropriate and "fitting," to use one of Edwards's favorite words, for God to use types. Edwards's God was "a communicative being" whose most overwhelming disposition was to communicate his perfections.[13] As he argues in *The End for Which God Created the World*, this was the reason for the Creation: apart from the Creation and God's continuing exercise of his attributes toward creation, many of God's attributes would lie dormant (End, 429).

But there was a problem. God is infinite, and his creation finite. How can the sublime things of infinite divinity be communicated to (relatively) tiny, finite minds? Edwards resorted to the Calvinist notion of accommodation. He said that God accommodates his truth to our finite understandings just as human adults change their manner of presentation when teaching children (Misc. 583). Ordinary discourse only distorts heavenly things because of the incommensurable gap between infinite, nonmaterial realities and human concepts expressed with words grounded in finite, material things.[14]

Therefore God uses types, which, though also employing material images to express immaterial realities, nevertheless by the power of imagery suggest to the human mind what lies beyond the visible world. So God uses types for their pedagogical value. As Edwards wrote of the expression "temple of the Holy Ghost": "By such similitudes a vast volume is represented to our minds in three words, and things that we are not able to behold directly are represented before us in lively pictures" (Misc. dd).

These pictures so cohere with human sensibilities—or, as Edwards put it, there is such an analogy or harmony between them—that the human mind is naturally led to see the substance which the types represent. "The affairs of the Jewish church are so much of a shadow, that a mind so prepared and exercised would naturally be led to the substance" if it is "of a poetical and gracious disposition" (Misc. 251).

Note, however, that the types do not have power in and of themselves to portray the spiritual world. The typological system is not transparent to all, but only to "a mind so prepared and exercised." There is no salvation by the imagination. Salvation is only by Christ and the power of his Spirit, who alone can provide the sense of the heart, which alone can read the types.

Types also have affective value. Because they are drawn from the sensory world and commonly employ material objects as images, fallen human beings, who are more familiar with the material than the immaterial world, can more easily under-

---

13. Misc. 332; EW, 434f., 438f.; see Knight, "Learning the Language of God," 543–51.
14. Calvin, Institutes, 2.11.13; 1.17.13; Misc. 931; sermon on Psalm 89:6, in SDK, 418.

stand them. They are more affected "by those things [they] see with [their] eyes and hear with [their] ears and have experience of" (Sermon on Rev. 21:18, 5).

If types are more accessible because they are grounded in sensory experience, they are also more enjoyable for that same reason. Types provide "pleasure" and "delight." We know this, Edwards argued, from the great enjoyment people derive from "the imitative arts, in painting, poetry, fables, metaphorical language [and] dramatic performances. This disposition appears early in children" (Misc. 191). Perhaps because it is enjoyable, subjects taught by types are more easily remembered, and moral lessons taught by types are received with deeper impression and greater conviction (Misc. 191).

God therefore adapted his teaching method to human nature. He instructed the human race in a way that would be best suited to the creature. Types are an aid to memory, they reinforce their lesson with extra strength and conviction, and they bring pleasure and delight.

Finally, Edwards connected types to the arts. Both, he explained, appeal to the same aesthetic and erotic capacities. Each uses the principle of *mimesis* and fulfills human desires for the dramatic and the beautiful. Types, then, are a part of the divine aesthetic, or a way in which God unites pedagogy and aesthetics.

Reading the Types

Obviously, if types are divine pedagogy, human beings must be able to comprehend them. If the typological system is "a certain sort of language, as it were, in which God is wont to speak to us," we must be able to understand that language.[15] Edwards was convinced that we are—if we possess a (regenerate) sense of the heart.

He was also convinced that the entire cosmos is stocked with types: "I am not ashamed to own that I believe that the whole universe, heaven and earth, air and seas, and the divine constitution and history of the holy Scriptures, *be full of images of divine things*, as full as a language is of words" (Types, 152; emphasis added). Hence life is a school for learning the types, so that one can ever be receiving communication from the Creator: "The multitude of those things that I have mentioned are but a very small part of what is really intended to be signified and typified by these things: but that there is room for persons to be learning more and more of this language and seeing more of that which is declared in it to the end of the world without discovering all" (ibid.).[16]

How does one learn the language? Edwards left a somewhat cryptic answer to this question. He said that while God has not explained all the types in Scripture, those that have been explained are enough to show us how to interpret the rest (Types, 151). In other words, biblical precedent is to be the primary guide. So if

---

15. Types, 150. The portions of this notebook which I quote in this section were composed in Northampton during the middle 1740s; "Notes on the Manuscript of 'Types,'" in TW, 145.
16. Therefore there is no indication that Edwards "stopped identifying particular images" (SDK, 236).

Paul has already explained that Hagar and Sarah represent the two covenants, we should learn several lessons, chief among them being that the antitype is always related to the work of redemption by Christ. Presumably, Edwards's typological notebooks would also provide indications of hermeneutical principles he thought we should follow in interpreting the types.

Edwards added that there are several methods for learning any language. Sometimes one is "naturally trained up in it, learning it by education," which might mean in this case being taught the divine idiom by God himself, as in Adam's case before the Fall. Edwards hastened to explain that "that is not the way in which corrupt mankind learned divine language" (Types, 151). They received the divine language in the forms of hieroglyphics and dark symbols without interpretation, which explains in part why human history was dominated by idolatry (Misc. 193; NS, 400–410).

The best way to learn the divine idiom is "by much use and acquaintance together with good taste or judgment, by comparing one thing with another and having our senses as it were exercised to discern it" (Types, 151). Here Edwards was both alluding to his descriptions of regeneration as a "taste" and "sense of the heart"[17] and invoking Hebews 5:14, which describes mature Christians as "those who by reason of use have their senses exercised to discern both good and evil." His point seems to be that a person with the sense of the heart is to use the biblical precedents and his or her own sense of what is harmonious with the work of redemption to discover and then interpret a type.

Edwards warned that this work of interpretation must be conducted with special care. Without such care, the divine idiom will not be learned, and one's interpretation of the types will miss their "proper beauty" (ibid.). So there is an aesthetic test: if one's interpretation of a type does not display the divine beauty, one has missed its meaning. The interpretation then will sound "very harsh in the ears of those that are well versed in the language" (ibid.).

Edwards's Place in the Tradition

Up to this point we have tried to understand Edwards's typology synchronically—in the context of his own period. We have seen that his typological system was an intricate response to the eighteenth-century deist challenge that the Calvinist God had never revealed himself. Now we shall explore its diachronic context—the history of Christian typology—and consider the significance of Edwards's system within that history.[18]

Historically, typology has been contrasted with allegory, which stems from the Greek words *allos* (other) and *agoria* (speaking) and means, literally, speaking other-

---

17. See RA, 282–83, and Misc. 782.

18. On the history of Christian typology, see Bercovitch, *Typology and Early American Literature*, especially Thomas M. Davis, "The Traditions of Puritan Typology"; Lowance, *Language of Canaan*; Brumm, *American Thought and Religious Typology*; and Lewalski, *Protestant Poetics*.

wise than one seems to speak. Generally it has meant a figurative representation of some generalization about human existence. It goes back to Homeric scholars who allegorized certain passages in Homer which they felt to be unworthy of the bard.[19] Philo (c. 20 B.C.–A.D. 40) and other Alexandrian Jews adopted this allegorical technique in order to render the Hebrew Bible less offensive to Greek culture. According to most interpreters, Philo discarded the historical context of Scripture, arguing that the abstracted meaning of a text was more real than its historical referent.[20]

Origen and other Alexandrian Christians followed Philo's example. Their Philonic allegorization permeated much patristic exegesis for more than a thousand years.[21] This hermeneutic was systematized by John Cassian in the fourth century to consist in four stylized levels of meaning: each text was believed to have a literal (historical) meaning, a tropological (moral) meaning, the allegorical (spiritual) meaning, and the anagogical (eschatological) meaning.

It was not until the sixteenth century that William Tyndale began the trend back to the centrality of the historical meaning. He insisted that all interpretations, including the typological (which usually saw the Old Testament as a series of foreshadowings of the New, but which had been overwhelmed in the medieval period by Origenist allegory) and the allegorical, must arise from the historical sense and be proved by it. This was the position taken by Luther, Calvin, and the Puritans, all of whom argued that the Bible uses similitudes and allegories only to clarify the literal, historical sense.

But the Reformers nevertheless still used typology to interpret the Bible. Luther condemned only "Alexandrian allegory" and used what he called the "literal" and "spiritual" senses to claim that "every bit" of the Old Testament applies to Christ. Calvin said that the cultus of the Old Testament law would be ridiculous unless it was understood typologically. The angel of the Lord in the Old Testament was in fact Christ; indeed, typology is the key to opening up the Old Testament.[22] Like Luther, Calvin denounced the Alexandrians' and medievals' use of allegory, but testified to the continuing importance of the trope nonetheless. He rejected Origen's and Cassian's tropological and anagogical levels, while retaining their literal and spiritual levels, and explained that Protestant allegory was based on extensive analysis of the typological event. In contrast, he argued, Origen and the Alexandrians either said that types could be understood only at the literal level or discarded them completely. Protestants generally limited allegory to what could be found in the

---

19. Davis, "Traditions of Puritan Typology," 14.

20. In *Allegorical Readers and Cultural Revision in Ancient Alexandria*, however, David Dawson has challenged this interpretation as far too one-sided.

21. There was an important minority report, however, that is often overlooked. The Antioch "school" of interpretation was founded in direct opposition to the "excesses and fantasies" of Origenist allegorical interpretation; Johannes Quasten, *Patrology: The Golden Age of Greek Patristic Literature, From the Council of Nicaea to the Council of Chalcedon* (Westminster, Md., 1963), 3:121, cited in Davis, "Traditions of Puritan Typology," 25. And as Beryl Smalley has argued, the literal sense was by no means ignored in the medieval period; interpreters did not limit themselves to the spiritual sense of a text; Smalley, *The Study of the Bible in the Middle Ages*, 83–195. For an example of how a leading medieval exegete used three levels, see Chase, *Angelic Wisdom*, 1–27.

22. Calvin, Institutes, 2.10.20.

Bible, for the most part considering nature an illegitimate source unless something from nature was already used as a type in Scripture. So the rock which Moses struck, but not every rock in nature, was a type.

By the seventeenth century a clear demarcation had been drawn between allegory and type. Allegory was Greek (Platonic) and dealt with essences, types were Jewish and concerned with existence. In allegory the physical world was a symbol of the spiritual universe discovered by a human mind, while a type was a historically true symbol instituted by God to perform a specific function. The difference between the two could be seen by the concept of linear time. The allegory was simply the Platonic representation of one thing by another; time was irrelevant. But the type by definition preceded the antitype in time, one instituted by the divine author to foreshadow the other. According to Erich Auerbach, this century's most influential interpreter of these phenomena, the type (which he called a "figural interpretation") "deals with concrete events whether past, present or future, and not with concepts or abstractions."[23]

In the seventeenth century Puritans disagreed about the relative importance that could be given to each of these two modes.[24] All agreed that typology should predominate over allegory, but the extent to which one could use allegory within a larger context of typology was at issue. Preachers were tempted to indulge a fondness for allegory as the winds of new doctrine began to blow at the end of the century, and they felt "obliged to entice and cajole their people instead of handing down dogmas."[25] Conservative typologists argued that only Old Testament events and figures should be employed. Samuel Mather, their intellectual leader, vigorously defended the literal historicity of types and attacked allegories drawn from nature and multiple levels of meaning emerging from the same biblical text.[26] But liberal typologists employed Platonic, unhistorical symbols as well as biblical historical types.

Edwards sided with the liberals. He was not afraid to mix allegory with traditional biblical typology. For instance, he wrote in his notebooks that the church of God in Scripture is represented by palm trees, and that trees in general represent God's people. He could also see in Scripture types that pointed not to the work of redemption clarified by the New Testament but to general truths of human exis-

---

23. "Figura," in Godzich and Schulte-Sasse, *Scenes from the Drama of European Literature*, 53. William G. Madsen helpfully adds that the "type looks forward in time, not upward through the scale of being" ("From Shadowy Types to Truth," 99–100).

Recently some interpreters have tried to bridge the gap between allegory and type, arguing for a formal similarity of the two. See, e.g., Dawson, *Allegorical Readers and Cultural Revision*, 15–17, and Boyarin, *A Radical Jew*. Thomas H. Luxon goes so far as to charge that the effort to distinguish typology from allegory in Protestant thought has been contradictory because it "others the self and the world into God's allegory of himself and his kingdom." This approach, while interesting and perhaps fruitful for other agendas, nevertheless fails to collapse the real distinctions in the literature I have discussed between two different genres. That is, if Protestants allegorize at a level they themselves do not recognize, they nevertheless "allegorize" in two quite distinguishable ways. See Luxon, *Literal Figures*, 26 and passim.

24. See Lowance, in Bercovitch, *Typology and Early American Literature*, 210–43.
25. Miller, "Introduction" to Edwards, *Images or Shadows of Divine Things*, 13.
26. Samuel Mather, *The Figures or Types of the Old Testament*.

tence. God's making Eve from Adam's rib, for example, was a type of the "near relation and strict union of husband and wife." And human life in nature could point to spiritual truths: temporal death represents the spiritual death the sinner deserves.[27]

He could hardly do otherwise. His vision of reality had so unified scripture and nature that any hard and fast separation of the two would be incoherent. All the world—biblical and beyond—was typical. As Wilson Kimnach puts it, Edwards wanted a "vertical typology . . . something to link the 'true' and 'real' worlds in a simple, 'sensible' idea." He retained a version of the traditional hierarchy of being but transposed it within a new "monistic cosmos." Unlike the Platonic allegorists, he insisted on "the actual organic unity, temporal and spatial, of the cosmos."[28]

While Edwards's typology pointed to general truths as well as events in the historical work of redemption, his typological schema folded all general truths into that work of redemption. The union of husband and wife, for example, was a picture of Christ's union with the church, while the death of a sinner found its final meaning in the absence of redemption.[29] So while Edwards mixed allegory and traditional typology, both fitted into the organic unity of the work of redemption.

If Edwards felt free to incorporate allegory within typology, he nevertheless saw the danger of letting allegory go too far. He portrayed himself as walking a middle road between the rationalists and deists on the left, who "cry down all types," and the Catholic and Anglican exegetes who were "for turning all into nothing but allegory and not having it be true history" (Types, 151). Deists and other rationalists such as William Whiston, Toland, Tindal, and Collins ridiculed traditional typology as mystical and therefore irrational connections that were unreliable because they were based on obscure prophecies and miracles that violated the natural laws of the cosmos. Edwards believed that Catholic and Anglican exegetes like Lancelot Andrewes and Jeremy Taylor ignored the plain historical sense of biblical narrative in favor of "witty" tropes full of "human invention."[30]

Edwards took what he believed was a middle road between the two extremes, but he dramatically expanded the breadth of the road "by which men might perceive the will of God." He was devoted to the primacy of historical reference, unlike the Anglicans he mentioned and the Neoplatonists, who tended to reduce creation and history to illusion. Yet for him the antitypes were not just New Testament persons and events but the entire drama of redemption, from eternity through time and back into eternity.

For this reason it can be said that Edwards departed from the early Protestant practice of giving utter centrality to the literal sense of the biblical text.[31] As Stephen

27. TM, 196; Misc. 646.
28. SDK, 229f.; see Kimnach's entire discussion, in SDK, 192–251.
29. Lowance, in Bercovitch, *Typology and Early American Literature*, 234; Images, nos. 5, 1, 51.
30. See Anderson, "Editor's Introduction," in TW, 11–24.
31. By "literal sense" I mean the most immediate historical referent in historical narratives and prophetic works and the most immediate literary referents in poetic works such as Song of Solomon and Psalms. Edwards often interpreted historical, prophetic, and poetic texts as referring to events in the future work of redemption far removed from the apparent intent of the biblical authors.

Stein has suggested, Edwards's ultimate interest was in the spiritual sense of Scripture, which was not simply a translation of the literal text but a redaction of the text by an inspired exegete. Edwards so emphasized Christ and his work of redemption that the biblical account of Jewish history at times could seem compromised. His biblical exegesis was not so much induction from biblical dicta as a convenient mode for expressing fundamental theological convictions.[32]

Indeed, like many before him, Edwards did not take the Old Testament text at face value. Like Augustine, who confessed the literal sense "killed" him spiritually, and Calvin, who called it "ridiculous" without the help of typology, Edwards said much in the Old Testament is "wholly insignificant and so wholly impertinent and vain" unless it is understood typologically. Typology gave him the tool he needed to unify the biblical testaments, particularly at those junctures where the literal sense by itself could not fulfill the theological vision which he believed united the Scriptures.[33]

Media

This theological vision, which he entitled the "work of redemption," was typified in Scripture, nature, and history—even, as we shall see, the history of religions.

Like his predecessors in the typological tradition, Edwards believed that the prototypical and archetypal standard for the entire system was to be found in the Bible. Not only were the sharpest and clearest images found there—that is, the antitypes of Christ and his redemption, and the most pointed Old Testament types as well—but the Scriptures also remained the hermeneutical standard against which all the other types in nature and history were to be measured.[34]

If anything, Edwards saw even more typological import in the Old Testament than many of his predecessors had. The Hebrew Bible did not just contain types here and there; nearly every stroke of the pen made by the biblical authors was typical in some way of "Christ and his redemption" (HWR, 289).

> Thus almost everything that was said or done that we have recorded in Scripture from Adam to Christ, was typical of Gospel things: persons were typical persons, their actions were typical actions, the cities were typical cities, the nation of the Jews and other nations were typical nations, the land was a typical land, God's providences towards them were typical providences, their worship was typical worship, their houses were typical houses, their magistrates typical magistrates, their clothes typical clothes, and indeed the world was a typical world.[35]

---

32. Stein, "The Spirit and the Word," 123, 124. See also his "Quest for the Spiritual Sense."
33. Augustine, *Confessions*, 5.14; Calvin, *Institutes*, 2.7.1; TM, 306, 305, 219.
34. Thus it is not true that Edwards exalted nature "to a level of authority co-equal with revelation." Miller, "Introduction" to Edwards, *Images or Shadows of Divine Things*, 28.
35. Misc. 370; see also Misc. 173, Misc. 251, Misc. 359, Misc. 362, Misc. 710, and Misc. 1353.

Like Luther, then, and other Christian theologians in the tradition, Edwards found the Christian gospel in the Hebrew Bible. Early in his career, he said that God's providences to the Jews, David's history, the temple and the prophets were all "full of the gospel" (Misc. 359). Later in his career, in his sermons on the work of redemption, he detailed some of what he had meant by this early claim. The redemption by Christ was typified by the exodus of the Jews from Egypt and their miraculous return from Babylon (HWR, 175, 263). The waters of the Flood were typical of the blood of Christ that washes away the sins of the world (HWR, 151). The cultus of the law that included "all the precepts that relate to building the tabernacle that was set up in the wilderness and all the forms, and circumstances, and utensils of it" were directed by God "to show forth something of Christ" (HWR, 182). The following entry from his *Notes on Scripture* is an example of the hundreds of entries Edwards made in his notebooks to document the ways in which the law prefigured the gospel.

> EXODUS 25:23–40. Concerning the SHOWBREAD TABLE and the Golden CANDLESTICK. These both were to stand continually in the holy place before the veil of the holy of holies, one on the north side, and the other on the south. Each of these seems to represent both a divine person and also the church. Each represents a divine person. The show-bread represents Christ, and was set on [the] south side at God's right hand, as Christ is often represented as being set at God's right hand in heaven, being next to God the Father in his office, and above the Holy Spirit in the economy of the persons of the Trinity. The candlestick, or at least the oil and lamps of it, represent the Holy Spirit, and is set at the left-hand of God's throne. Christ is as it were "the bread of God"; he is so called, John 6. 33. He is the portion of God the Father in whom is his infinite delight and happiness; and as our Mediator and sacrifice, he is as it were the bread of God, as the ancient sacrifices, that were only typical of Christ, are often called the "bread of God." This bread is called the show-bread, in the Hebrew, *Lechem Panim*, "the bread of God's face," or "presence." So Christ, in Is. 63: 9 is called *Malak panim*, "the angel of God's face," or "presence." This bread had pure frankincense set on it, which undoubtedly signifies the merits of Christ, and so proves the bread that had the pure frankincense on it, to be a type of Christ. (NS, 475)

These figures in the cultus of the law represented only one of three kinds of types. These were institutional types; but there were also providential and personal types (HWR, 204). The greatest institutional type was the practice of sacrifice, the greatest providential type was the Exodus, and the greatest personal type was David (ibid.).

David was a type of Christ both in his humiliation (typified by David's suffering and exile from Jerusalem) and his militant state, at war with his enemies (typified by David's wars against his opponents) (HWR, 227). Solomon typified Christ in his triumphal state, reigning in peace (ibid.). The altar that Noah built to the Lord after the floodwaters had receded typified Christ's sacrifice (HWR, 152–53). Moses' burning bush represented both the sufferings of Christ in the fire of God's wrath and also Israel's sufferings in Egypt; just as the bush burned without being destroyed, both Israel and Christ suffered without perishing (HWR, 175; TM, 197).

The building of the temple represented not only the human nature of Christ but also Christ's church and heaven (HWR, 224). And so on. Edwards seemed to delight in finding divinely appointed types in the Old Testament, which shadowed fulfillments in the New Testament.

Edwards did not limit typology to the Bible, as the conservative exegetes of his era did, but looked to "the whole outward creation" for "shadows of beings . . . made to represent divine things" (Misc. 362). Thus "the pattern of the cosmos" became for him one of "infinite representation." Every last part of the creation was emblematic of the divine, an effulgent crystal with supernatural meaning—even the tiniest leaf in a flower is a word from God, the sun shows forth God's glory, the clouds and mountains bespeak God's majesty, and the green fields and pleasant flowers testify to "his grace and mercy."[36]

The great markers of the days and seasons fairly burst with meaning. The sun, for example, which makes plants flourish when it shines after rain, is a type of the Sun of Righteousness who heals the soul's afflictions; the stars are types of the saints in glory, and the moon is an image of earthly glory and all the good of earthly life, which like the moon ever changes, rising and falling, waxing and waning (Images, nos. 83, 86, 139).

Birds flying in the sky are also types of the saints in heaven, but "to a fainter degree" than the stars (Images, no. 86). Another image for the saint is a tree, which grows so large from such tiny beginnings in a little twig. "Hence it may be argued," Edwards noted cryptically, "that infants do belong to the church" (Images, no. 99).

Not all of Edwards's images were so pleasant. The snake that slithers on its belly is a type of the curse God put on the devil. And human excrement represents the "corruption and filthiness that the heart of man is naturally full of," just as "the many foldings and turnings in the bowels . . . [denote] the great and manifold intricacies, secret windings and turnings, shifts, wiles and deceits that are in [human] hearts" (Images, nos. 109, 115).

If types are in nature, they can also be found in nonbiblical history. Edwards wrote in his enormous miscellany "Types of the Messiah"[37] that "many things in the state of the ancient Greeks and Romans" were typical of gospel things (TM, 191). For example, his "Images" notebook contains a long entry comparing the celebration of a military triumph in the Roman empire to Christ's ascension. Just as the Roman emperor's triumphal chariot was followed by senators and ransomed citizens, Christ was accompanied on his return to glory by principalities and powers and ransomed citizens of heaven. The Roman procession was closed by the sacrifice of a great white ox; so too Christ at the ascension entered the holy of holies with a sacrifice of his own blood. The Roman emperor treated the people in the capitol with gifts, and Christ did the same for his church (Images, no. 81; see also Misc. 1308).

The experience of the saints in history could also be typical. For instance, all the saints' enjoyment of family and friends is but a shadow of the joy they will

---

36. Miller, "Introduction" to Edwards, Images or Shadows of Divine Things, 27; sermon on Psalm 14:1, December 1752, 4; Misc. 777.

37. This is Misc. 1069, published separately in TW, 191–324.

experience in God, who is the substance. Their delight is but a scattered beam from the sun of Infinite Delight—a stream or drop taken from the fountain and ocean called God.[38]

Now this was not an entirely new system of typology simply because some of its natural types resembled Platonic allegories pointing to timeless truths.[39] Most of the natural types still pointed to the work of Christ's redemption, and even those that did not make explicit reference to that work were developed within his generally christological frame of reference.[40] Some of Edwards's most important Puritan predecessors made similar, if not as extensive, use of nature. John Flavel used natural metaphors and allegorized a few of his biblical types in his *Husbandry Spiritualized: Or, the Heavenly Use of Earthly Things* (1654). While Cotton Mather emphasized historical correspondences, he nevertheless showed occasional interest in spiritualized symbols from nature and history in his *Magnalia* and "Biblia Americana."[41] Both he and his uncle Samuel Mather endowed Old Testament types with moral value outside the Bible.[42]

But Edwards did expand the boundaries of scriptural typology. Far more freely than his predecessors, he used its nomenclature to identify types in nature and history. Others had dabbled, but Edwards pressed this new application with enthusiasm and creative vigor. He never developed in treatise form a systematic rationale for his system. But his notes to himself over the course of his career represent careful reflection on the implications of his proposition that all the world was typical.

Edwards pressed those implications even further by proposing that God had planted types of true religion even in religious systems that were finally false. God outwitted the devil, Edwards suggested, by using diabolically deceptive religion to teach what is true. In an early entry in the *Miscellanies*, Edwards suggested that the heathen practice of human sacrifice was the result of the devil's mimickry of the animal sacrifice God had instituted after the Fall.

Sacrifice was taught not by the light of nature but by God's express commandment immediately after he revealed the covenant of grace in Genesis 3:15 ("And I will put enmity between thee and the woman, and between thy seed and her seed; it shall bruise thy head, and thou shalt bruise his heel").[43] The skins with

---

38. Sermon on Hebrews 11:13f., in Gerstner, *Rational Biblical Theology*, 402–3.
39. Lowance suggests such a radical break in *TW*, 161.
40. Miller may have been right to charge that sooner or later Edwards's veneration of nature would be secularized in the nineteenth century, but he was wrong to imply that it would have been by Edwards's influence; Miller, "Introduction" to Edwards, *Images or Shadows of Divine Things*, 35. The typological notebooks did not see the light of published day until the twentieth century.
41. Lowance, *Language of Canaan*, 177. See also Lowance, "Typology and the New England Way," 15–37.
42. Lowance, *Language of Canaan*, 87. On Puritans who taught that God communicates through nature, see Maclear, "The Heart of New England Rent"; Nuttall, *The Holy Spirit*; and Knight, "Learning the Language of God," 535, 544n.
43. "In those words of God there was an intimation of another surety to be appointed for man after the first surety had failed. . . . It was an obscure revelation of the gospel and was not made to Adam or Eve directly but it was in what God said to the serpent. . . . One of those great things that were designed to be done in the Work of Redemption is more plainly signified here than the rest, viz. God's design of subduing his enemies under the feet of his Son" (*HWR*, 132–34).

which God clothed the first couple in verse 21 were taken from animals sacrificed by God, who taught them thereby that only the righteousness of Christ won by his sacrifice could cover their sins (HWR, 134–36).

Edwards insisted that animal sacrifice, the main type of Christ in the Old Testament but revealed to all the heathen, taught the necessity of propitiatory sacrifice to atone for sin. Imitating this divine type, the devil led the heathen to sacrifice human beings, even their own sons. Satan believed he had "promote[d] his own interests," outsmarting God; but God outflanked the devil. He permitted this diabolical deception, because through it "the devil prepared the Gentile world for receiving . . . this human sacrifice, Jesus Christ." Similarly, the devil induced human beings to worship idols and think that the heathen deities were one with their images. But God used this deception for his own purposes as well, to prepare the Gentile mind for the concept of incarnation, perfectly realized in Christ: "And so indeed was [the] heathenish doctrines of deities' being united to images and the heathenish fables of heroes being begotten [by] gods, a preparation for their receiving the doctrine of the incarnation, of the Deity's dwelling in a human [body], and the Son of God's being conceived in the womb of a virgin by the power of the Spirit of [God]" (Misc. 307).

Twice, then, in the history of religions, God used false religion to teach the true. In each case the devil's machinations were overruled ironically by divine wisdom. Practices considered by all Jews and Christians to be abominable—human sacrifice and idol worship—were transposed by a divine stratagem into pedagogical devices to prepare the heathen for true religion. In both cases God used non-Christian religions typologically to point to Christian truths.

The practice of sacrifice taught far more than simple propitiation. It also showed the heathen that God would not pardon without satisfaction being made, that sin "must be suffered for." It demonstrated God's jealousy and hatred for sin, indicated the need to fear God and respect the glory of his holiness and suggested to sinners that they must trust in God's mercy (Misc. 326).

At the beginning of his career, when he was a pastor in New York in the spring of 1723, Edwards told his congregation that the heathen did not understand the purpose of sacrifice. Then, and throughout the rest of his career, he made it clear that only those with a regenerate "sense of the heart" were able to read the types in creation and, we can now add, in the history of religions. As we shall see in the next chapter, he intimated at times that there were some heathen who might have taken advantage of the light they had been given through the Jews and from their own forefathers and with the light of the Holy Spirit been able to understand the types. But his conviction that most of the heathen would probably never understand did not keep him from noting the wealth of religious knowledge that could be known in non-Christian religions.[44]

There were several reasons why the false religions abounded with types of the true. The first was that most religions shared a common linguistic source. Edwards

---

44. Sermon on Hebrews 9:12, in SDK, 594.

followed Chevalier Ramsay in believing that both Christian and heathen religions could be traced back to a universal language of hieroglyphics which represented "the divine mysteries of our holy religion, which the first heathens had learned from the antient tradition of the Noevian patriarchs" (*Misc.* 1255). Over time the meaning of the signs was forgotten. Human beings attached themselves to the letter and the signs without understanding the spirit and the things signified. Because there were no tenses in these hieroglyphics, the future was often taken for the past. The symbols representing Christ's suffering and triumph were confounded into one and interpreted to mean imaginary heroes or conquerors. This was why the structure of so many heathen myths resembled the Christian drama.

This was also a reason for the prevalence of "types, figures and enigmatical speeches" in other religions. The fathers of the nations received their wisdom chiefly by tradition from wise men of the church of God, to whom divine instructions had been given in the form of "symbols and emblems." The holy men "in all nations" imitated this manner of representing divine things in "parables" and "types," so they delivered their own wisdom in "allegories, enigmas, [and] symbolic representations." This was why "it became so universally the custom among all ancient nations for their priests, prophets and wise men to utter their auguries and to deliver their knowledge and wisdom, in their writings and speeches, in allegories and enigmas, and under symbolic representations." And this was why the Egyptians and others used "hieroglyphics to represent divine things or things appertaining to their gods and their religion" (TM, 193–94).

It is striking that Edwards linked Egyptian sacred writings with "holy men [who] were led by the Spirit of God." Even if, as he makes clear elsewhere, he regarded most of Egyptian religion as abominable, nevertheless he clearly believed that there were significant formal similarities between Christianity and other religions of the East. The relationship between these religions was not one of qualitative discontinuity, but of continuity along several lines. They shared common mythical structures, common linguistic origins, and a common typical form of representation.

There was also continuity in content. As we saw above, Edwards believed that the heathen were given (by the devil!) inchoate understanding of propitiatory sacrifice and incarnation. And as we have also seen, Edwards filled his *Miscellanies* with hundreds of pages recording the doctrines that the heathen shared with Reformed Christians. These truths ranged from the Trinity and a "middle" God who expiates sins to eternal punishment and the notion that "all things owed their beginning and production to love."[45] All of these heathen notions were slightly distorted or incomplete versions of the full antitypical truth. But to the extent that they pointed to the work of redemption, in all of its intricately woven parts, they were as typical as human sacrifice was typical of Christ's oblation.

Therefore one could rummage through the religions to find traces of the drama of redemption through the Jews and the Christ. One could discover, for example, that Saturn in heathen myths was a distorted refashioning of Noah—or in fact a

---

45. See, for example, *Misc.* 151, *Misc.* 326, and *Misc.* 1181.

"shadow" of Noah. Or that Bacchus was a heathen conflation of the stories about Nimrod, Moses, and the Hebrew God. For the "blind heathen" had heard Moses' exploits attributed to God, whom they called Bacchus. Or one could determine that Hercules was really Joshua, Neptune actually Japheth, and Fohi—the legendary father of the Chinese—in fact Noah, who settled after the Flood near Ararat (NS, nos. 400–410, 455).

Concluding Observations

Jonathan Edwards was determined to defend Reformed Christianity against deist attacks that would reduce the Bible to just another expression of the religion of nature. His typological system attempted to show that the true religion of nature was but a pointer to the full and final revelation of the Bible. Yet Edwards's expansive use of typology, combined with his understanding of the limitations of language that typology is forced to use, intimated with new forcefulness the broken character of our understanding of that revelation.

The Christian faith could now be seen not as completely separated from other religions but as the end of a continuum that included religious others. It was a terminus because it alone pointed unambiguously to the true antitype, Christ's work of redemption. But like every other type it could never replace the substance, and like every other religion it was mediated by language, which, as Edwards often complained, so imperfectly approximated the divine. He thus held in tension the divine incomprehensibility and the fact of revelation. The deity was finally beyond understanding, yet this same deity had accommodated itself to broken language. Given the nature of types and the limitations of language, on the one hand, and the deist denial of revelation, on the other, this was a tension Edwards could live with.

This was also the price Edwardsean typology had to pay for trying to fold within itself both true and deceptive religion, both biblical types and extrabiblical shadows nearly obscured by darkness. Perhaps it was inevitable, given Edwards's indefatigable ambition to relate every datum of experience—no matter how apparently discordant—to his typological vision. Driving that ambition was his stubborn faith that in the midst of all discordances was persistent symmetry. Scripture and nature were finally harmonious in his system; so were history and the religions. The great pattern was made to synchronize even with minds that broke the pattern. The Evil One who tried to subvert the symmetry unwittingly promoted an even greater symmetry.

Strangely, contemporary physics is finding a similar symmetry that harmonizes apparent discordances in nature. Chaos theory has uncovered geometries and symmetries at every level of nature. More telling, it has discovered that even in the tension between ideal patterns and deviations from those patterns, which exist nearly everywhere in nature, there lurk equally ubiquitous symmetry and balance. There is a greater and deeper symmetry in which both chaos and order are enmeshed and intertwined. If Edwards's attempts to reconcile polarities seem far-fetched, it mirrors a dynamic of nature which is nearly as incredible.

What, then, are we to make of typology? It would seem at first blush to be the quaint and insular attempt of premoderns to reconcile the irreconcilables of biblical religion. And Edwards's system was so idiosyncratic that it ran the risk of solipsism, since even the regenerate would have difficulty following it without access to his private notebooks. It could hardly claim to be a system available to the church at large. Yet literary critic Northrop Frye has reminded us that our modern confidence that the future will reveal the meaning of the past is probably a legacy of biblical typology. He has also pointed out that attempts like Edwards's to see non-Christian religions as types of the true biblical antitypes are warranted by the biblical materials themselves.[46]

But the bigger problem with typological visions like Edwards's seems to be their distance from what we normally consider to be "objective reality" as defined by the scientific method. Yet here again recent developments in thought give pause. Philosopher Richard Rorty, hardly a sympathizer with such a project as Edwards's, nevertheless warns us that the true distinction is not between subjective and objective reality but normal and abnormal discourse. Normal discourse, a generalization of Thomas Kuhn's notion of "normal science," is any discourse (scientific, political or theological) which embodies agreed-upon criteria for reaching agreement; abnormal discourse is any which lacks such criteria. Rorty argues that the attempt of traditional philosophy to explicate "rationality" and "objectivity" in terms of conditions of accurate representation is a self-deceptive effort to eternalize the normal discourse of the day.[47] In a way not unlike Rorty's, Edwards wanted to remind thinkers of his day[48] that their vision of reality's patterns depended as much on their perspective as the world they thought they were perceiving.[49]

---

46. Frye, *The Great Code*, 92.
47. Rorty, *Philosophy and the Mirror of Nature*.
48. Through published works such as *Religious Affections* and the "Divine and Supernatural Light," which demonstrated the epistemology necessary for understanding his typology.
49. Rorty refers only to perspectives on the world, while Edwards spoke of not only perspectives but a world that God constructed typologically. But the point remains that what separates Edwards (or Rorty, for that matter) from later thinkers is not so much different worlds—-objective or not—-but difference in perspective (vision, if you will), that determines whether or not the world is typological.

7

A POSSIBILITY OF RECONCILIATION
Salvation and the "Heathen"

Most students of early New England remember the Robert Breck affair as a bizarre episode in which western Massachusetts ministers in 1735 arranged to have a young preacher from Harvard arrested and carried off to jail on charges of heresy. Students of Edwards also know that the Northampton theologian agreed that Breck was preaching dangerous heresy and publicly defended the ministers' actions. What most historians have overlooked, however, is that one of the three Breck doctrines deemed to be heretical concerned the eschatological destiny of the "heathen," and that it was this doctrine that seemed to bother Edwards the most.[1]

According to his accusers, Robert Breck (1713–84) had told his Windham County (Connecticut) auditors that some portions of the Scriptures were not inspired, that predestination gave "no Encouragement to Duty," and that "the heathen doing what they could would entitle 'em to salvation." It was this last accusation to which Edwards devoted the majority of his attention in his published account of the heresies.[2]

Deism and the Scandal of Particularity

Edwards was probably not surprised to learn that Breck was a disciple of Thomas Chubb,[3] the most accessible guide to deism in the 1730s. For as we saw in Chap-

---

1. For the most recent overview of the affair and relevant bibliography, see *EccW*, 4–17.
2. *A Letter to the Author of the Pamphlet Called An Answer to the Hampshire Narrative* (orig. 1737), in *EccW*, 91–163. Edwards discusses Breck's objectionable teachings in 155–61.
3. *A Narrative*, 5; *EccW*, 6, 159.

ter 1, it was the deists who most prominently raised the issue of the heathen's eschatological destiny. In the seventeenth century the Cambridge Platonists also challenged the view, usually attributed to Calvinism, that those who had never heard the gospel were damned. But the deists were bolder, seemed more relevant, and were far more popular than the Cambridge Platonists. Beginning with Lord Herbert of Cherbury, they suggested that the Calvinist God who sent people to hell because they didn't believe in one of whom they had never heard, and who created human beings knowing beforehand that they would burn in hell forever, was a monster.

For many deists, the scandal of particularity was the greatest theoretical problem of Christian orthodoxy.[4] That the Jewish and Christian God revealed himself to only one-sixth of the world seemed manifestly unjust,[5] particularly if eternal happiness depended on knowledge of that revelation. Lord Herbert, typically regarded as the father of the movement, developed his five "common notions," supposedly common to all religions, because he was scandalized by the suggestion of many church fathers that most human beings were doomed because they lived outside the light of Christian revelation. No revelation, he concluded, could be normative unless it is known and promulgated to the whole world. "Otherwise the Gentiles must be supposed to be universally lost and damned, which it were cruel and injurious to God to imagine."[6]

Charles Blount, John Toland, and Anthony Collins agreed with Lord Herbert that God must have no favorite nations or parts of the world, and hence a religion must be generally known if God expects it to be generally subscribed to. The plight of those who have not heard the gospel runs throughout the argument of Matthew Tindal's *Christianity as Old as Creation* (1730), sometimes called the Deists' Bible. As we have seen, Tindal argued that if God is good, then all would know his revelation; but if he reveals himself to only a part of the world, God is "cruel and unmerciful." This proves that God, whom Tindal knew to be good, reveals himself by the light of nature to all, and has done so since the Creation.[7] Thomas Chubb, Thomas Gordon, and John Trenchard, with all of whom Jonathan Edwards was familiar, were similarly disturbed by the implications of Calvinist soteriology for those who had not received Christian revelation.[8]

---

4. As we saw in Chapter 1, there were also practical problems, such as the avarice and self-indulgence of the clergy and persecution by the state of those who did not toe the line.

5. This was a figure used in the late seventeenth and first half of the eighteenth centuries by many of those who reflected on the religious state of the heathen. See, for example, Turner, *History of All Religions*, 606, and Broughton, *Bibliotheca Historico-Sacra*, 116. It seems to have come from a mid-seventeenth-century geographer.

6. Quoted by Leland in *Principal Deistical Writers*, 17. For Lord Herbert's distaste for Calvinism's treatment of the heathen, see his *On Truth in Distinction from Revelation*, 77, and *Antient Religion of the Gentiles*, 2–3, 29, 119.

7. *CAO*, 401; see also 5, 11, 48, 64, 242, 256, and 391–93.

8. It cannot be determined whether Edwards's reflections on the destiny of the heathen were provoked by deist speculation on the same or simply by his own confrontation with what seemed to be remarkable convergences between Christianity and heathen religions. But it is clear that he used these reflections to support his attacks on deism.

Heterodox Soteriologies

Some of Edwards's favorite authors were also disturbed.[9] They speculated explicitly or discreetly implied that the heathen could be saved and often chose to hypothesize how they could find salvation. Two of them believed that God would use transmigration of the soul to help the heathen find heaven. Philip Skelton (1707–1787), a Church of Ireland divine whose anti-deist work *Deism Revealed* (London, 1751) Edwards used extensively, suggested that the merits of Christ's death may be extended to those heathen who use reason rightly and live moral lives by the transmigration of their souls into the bodies of those born under the light of the gospel.[10] Edwards also quoted copiously from Chevalier Ramsay, the Scotsman who held that all humans sinned in a preexistent state, are reborn into earthly bodies, and eventually receive universal pardon. He believed that pagans can live in the bosom of paganism without partaking spiritually of the idolatry and superstition that surrounds them.[11] Other writers known to Edwards praised certain heathen for their worship of the true God[12] and often constructed an inclusivist ladder to heaven for them.[13] That is, they believed it was possible to go to heaven without having confessed Christ on earth.

Dispositional Soteriology

Edwards never came close to accepting transmigration of the soul or universalism, but as we saw in Chapter 5, he used the *prisca theologia* to help respond to the scandal of particularity. He agreed with the deists that the problem could not be ignored and disagreed with earlier Reformed scholastics who saw nothing beyond knowledge of God the Creator in non-Christian religions. Calvin, for example, taught that the unregenerate have an "awareness of divinity" and can sense God's love, and that some of the pagan philosophers had remarkable insight into God's law and attributes, but that none of them had been given knowledge of God's redeeming designs in Christ. Hence none possessed true righteousness or experienced God as Father or Savior.[14] Edwards, on the other hand, filled hundreds of pages in his notebooks with evidence that the pagans had received knowl-

---

9. If we can judge "favorite" by the amount of space he devotes in his private notebooks to their writings. But of course Edwards was eclectic; simply because he quoted these authors at length does not mean that he approved of all that they proposed. He thoroughly rejected, for example, Ramsay's universalism and transmigration of the soul.

10. Skelton, *Deism Revealed*, 1:171, 2:155.

11. Ramsay, *Philosophical Principles*, 1:347, 410–11, 430, 2:457.

12. Turner, *History of All Religions*, 4, 15ff., 323; Defoe, *Dictionary*, passim; Broughton, *Bibliotheca Historico-Sacra*, vi; Shuckford, *Sacred and Profane History*, 15; Sale, *The Koran*, v, 97.

13. According to Isaac Watts, for example, experience tells those without written revelation that they are sinners. If they fear God and work righteousness, and hope in a merciful God, they shall be accepted through an unknown (to them) mediator. Watts, *Harmony of All the Religions*, 92–94.

14. Calvin, *Institutes* 1.3.1; 3.2.10–12; 2.2.22–24; 4.10.3; 4.18.15; 3.8.4; 3.10.4; 3.20.34; 3.14.3; 2.2.18–27.

edge about God the Redeemer from the Jews and the *prisca theologia*. As far as he knew, the vast majority of the heathen had failed to take advantage of this knowledge, and so this knowledge was used for their condemnation rather than salvation. But the question of God's fairness that deists had posed could now be answered with integrity. God had not limited his revelation to a minority of humankind, as Calvin and his successors had suggested, but had generously displayed throughout history his redemptive purposes for (most) all the world to see. If non-Christians had not received grace, blame could not be laid at God's feet. It was, as Edwards might have put it, their own damned fault.

If Edwards differed from Calvin on the extent of revelation, he also viewed salvation differently—in a way that contains intriguing implications for the salvation of non-Christians. This new approach to soteriology emerged not from a history of religion but from his philosophical reflections on being. To be more precise, Edwards applied his own dispositional ontology to soteriology.[15] This move helped him determine what distinguishes saved heathen from unsaved ones.

For Edwards, the essence of all being is disposition or habit. Drawing on a tradition that originated with Aristotle's *hexis* and developed through Thomas's *habitus* and Reformed scholastic permutations, Edwards held that "[a soul's] essence consists in powers and habits" (*Misc.* 241). By disposition[16] he meant an active and real tendency, not merely custom or regularity. This tendency has ontological reality even when it is not exercised; indeed, its exercise is necessary and inevitable when the opportunity for exercise presents itself. So when Edwards spoke of a "holy disposition," that is, the disposition of the regenerate, he meant "an active and causal power" that, if it were exercised, would certainly produce holy effects. As Edwards put it, "All habits [are] a law that God has fixed, that such actions upon such occasions should be exerted" (*Misc.* 241).

What are these actions or effects? In other words, if a regenerate disposition is an active tendency that constitutes the essence of what it means to be regenerate, what is it an active tendency *toward*? Very early in his career Edwards answered this question and never diverged from its basic outline. In *Misc.* 39 he concluded that "conversion under the old testament was not only the same in general with what it is commonly under the new, but much more like it as to the particular way and manner, than I used to think." In what amounts to a phenomenology of true religious experience, Edwards declared what he thought to be common to Christians, Old Testament Jews, and all other true religionists "from the beginning of the world": "a sense of the dangerousness of sin, and of the dreadfulness of God's anger . . . [such a conviction of] their wickedness, that they trusted to nothing but the mere mercy of God, and then bitterly lamented and mourned for their sins."

---

15. For the importance of habit or disposition in Edwards's thought, see Lee, *The Philosophical Theology of Jonathan Edwards*.

16. When discussing being in general he usually uses the term "habit," but in reference to salvation he prefers "disposition." In other contexts he uses the following synonyms: "tendency," "propensity," "principle," "temper," and "frame of mind." See *RA*, 206–7, 283–84; Lee, *The Philosophical Theology of Jonathan Edwards*, 15–46; *SPW*, 124–29.

Just a short time earlier Edwards had written that it is this inner religious consciousness (disposition) that is the only prerequisite to salvation. No particular act, even the act of receiving Christ, is necessary: "The disposition is all that can be said to be absolutely necessary. The act [of receiving Christ] cannot be proved to be absolutely necessary. . . . 'Tis the disposition or principle is the thing God looks at." For an illustration of this point Edwards used the Old Testament Jews. They did not receive Christ in any conscious or explicit manner, but they had the proper disposition, which alone is necessary for salvation:

> It need not be doubted but that many of the ancient Jews before Christ were saved without the sensible exertions of those acts in that manner which is represented as necessary by some divines, because they had not those occasions nor were under circumstances that would draw them out; though without doubt *they had the disposition, which alone is absolutely necessary now, and at all times, and in all circumstances is equally necessary.* (Misc. 27b; emphasis added)

Now Edwards in this passage was not considering the heathen. His point was that in conversion the most essential ingredient is a certain disposition, and the manner of expressing that disposition is secondary. Only the disposition is primary, and the Old Testament Jewish saints are a case in point. Edwards also used the illustration of a man who dies suddenly, "not in the actual exercise of faith." This man is still saved, because "'tis his disposition that saves him." Yet this entry reveals an important structure in Edwards's thinking about salvation: faith is subsumed by the category of disposition. As becomes clear elsewhere in Edwards's writings, disposition functions as the ontological ground of forensic imputation.[17]

Seven years later Edwards made it clear that the disposition is more important than religious and moral behavior, for while the character of a saving disposition is constant, religious and moral expectations differ according to the degree of revelation available. The obedience required under the Old Testament era was "in considerable part different" from that required under the New. "And so there are duties that respect the Messias and his salvation and another world that are necessary now to salvation, that were not then, by reason of the different state of the church and of revelation. Though they could not be saved without the same principle and spirit of old, yet they might be saved without such explicit exercises and explicit acts thereof" (Misc. 439). The inner disposition, not any particular acts and exercises, is the only essential prerequisite to salvation. Therefore, Edwards added at the close of his Northampton sojourn, God "was pleased in a great measure to wink at and suffer (though he did not properly allow) . . . under that dark and imperfect, and comparatively carnal dispensation"[18] polygamy, divorce, blood revenge, and worship at the high places. God could overlook ungodly behavior in his saints because their disposition was pleasing.

God also overlooks faulty religious knowledge. Early in his pastorate at Northampton Edwards conceded privately that the Jewish saints of the Old Testament did not

---

17. Morimoto, *Jonathan Edwards and the Catholic Vision*, 78–101.
18. *Humble Inquiry*, in *EccW*, 281.

know about love for enemies, universal love for all humanity, monogamy, or loving one another as Christ has loved us (Misc. 343). Yet they were saved. In Edwards's last decade he became convinced that some heathen had more religious knowledge and even virtue than many Old Testament saints. Greek and Roman moralists, for example, knew that we ought to love and forgive our enemies, return good for evil, and be monogamous (Misc. 1023). Other pagan philosophers knew about infused grace, the necessity of grace for virtue, the Trinity and the Incarnation, and redemption by the suffering of a mediator (Misc. 1355). "Socrates, that great Gentile philosopher, . . . worshipped the true God, as he was led by the light of nature," and Seneca "had in many respects right notions of the divine perfections and providence" (Humble Inquiry, 300). Even the (Muslim) Persians and Turks knew true humility and disinterested love for God (Misc. 1257). In the margins of an extract describing Plato's vision of God's beauty, Edwards scribbled, "Right notions of God and religion." At the end of an extract detailing many pagan ideas, he added, "All the chief philosophers have right views of virtue and religion."[19]

These reflections on the religious knowledge and virtue of the heathen may have caused Edwards to rethink, or at least refine, his thinking on justification and regeneration. In a Miscellanies entry from the mid-1730s, he began to think about justification and regeneration as phased, and in one respect life-long, processes rather than instantaneous events. Jesus' disciples, he pondered, were "good men *before*" they met Christ, "already in a *disposition* to follow Christ" (Misc. 847; emphasis added). The same was true, Edwards thought, of Zacchaeus and the women of Canaan.[20]

If some are "good" because they have a regenerate disposition before they are outwardly converted to Christ, then perhaps conversion in those cases comes *after* they are already regenerate: "Conversion may still be necessary to salvation in some respect even after he is really a saint." In these cases justification is already a fact in one sense but in another sense depends on "these after works of the Spirit of God upon the soul" (Misc. 847). That is, the condition of justification still remains to be fulfilled after conversion. Hence saints are still in a state of probation until the end of their lives.[21]

---

19. This note is significant because it comes at the end of Misc. 1355, which immediately follows a long series of extracts from Philip Skelton ridiculing pagan notions of God (Misc. 1354). This is an illustration of how Edwards took some Reformed polemics against the heathen with a grain of salt. He believed that the heathen were generally lost in darkness but nevertheless was convinced that "the wiser heathen" possessed considerable religious and moral truth.

A similar pattern can be seen in the contrast between Misc. 965 (in which Gale scores the spiritual pride of heathen philosophers) and Misc. 1357 (an extract from John Brine that criticizes pagan philosophers for their lack of humility and failure to depend on God for virtue), on the one hand, and Misc. 986 and 1028, on the other, where Edwards praises Socrates for showing humility by not trusting in himself, and Xenophon, Plato, and Seneca for knowing that virtue is impossible without divine grace.

20. This was simply an application of the principle he articulated in 1729—that "a person according to the gospel may be in a state of salvation, before a distinct and express act of faith in the sufficiency and suitableness of Christ as a Savior" (Misc. 393).

21. Edwards also speaks of God justifying, "as it were," a person being received into the visible church on the "presumption" and "supposition" that the person is sincere, which is proved by later "faithfullness" (Misc. 689). This "visible covenant" is different from the "covenant of grace," but in

If in a certain sense justification occurs in stages and is finally complete only at death or the end of one's probation on earth, then regeneration can be viewed similarly: "The whole of the saving work of Gods [sic] Spirit on the soul in the beginning and progress of it from the very first dawnings of divine light and the first beginnings of divine life until death is in some respect to be looked upon as all one work of regeneration.... There is as it were an unregenerate part still in man after the first regeneration that still needs to be regenerated" (Misc. 847).

These views show startling similarity to the Roman Catholic view that justification is a long and gradual process of transformation that includes sanctification. Several caveats are in order. First, Edwards qualifies his statements by inserting the pregnant phrases "in some respect" and "as it were," as a reminder that these remarks should not be taken in isolation from his other, extensive discussions of these topics. Second, Edwards's understandings of justification and regeneration are exceedingly complex. It is impossible to do justice to them here; it is far better to refer the reader to several studies of these subjects.[22] But an observation relevant to our purposes can nonetheless be made: Edwards's soteriology seems in some respects to depart from distinctive Reformation emphases. Martin Luther's salvation by faith *alone* becomes for Edwards salvation by faith *primarily*.[23] While Luther emphasizes that in justification sinners are *counted* as righteous, Edwards insists that sinners are actually *made* holy in the act of regeneration.[24]

It should be said that Edwards did not follow the Protestant scholastic tendency to collapse all of soteriology into justification, and that he saw no contradiction or inconsistency between justification by Christ's righteousness and justification by good works.[25] In addition, Edwards followed the "Lombardian tradition" (of positing the radical contingency and dependence of the created virtues on God) far more consistently than most of his Reformed predecessors.[26] But his emphasis on disposition as primary and faith as secondary and the dispositional structure of his soteriology undermine the Reformation contention that salvation is the justification of the ungodly.[27] It is for this reason, in part, that Thomas A. Schafer concludes that Edwards "went beyond the doctrine of justification."[28]

It is also for this reason that Edwards's soteriology resembles Roman Catholic theology in ways that make it easier for him to consider the salvation of the hea-

---

each case there is a condition to be fulfilled. In the covenant of grace, however, God covenants "with those that before his allseeing eyes perform that condition of the covenant of grace" (ibid.).

22. Cherry, *Theology of Jonathan Edwards*, 90–106; Schafer, "Jonathan Edwards and Justification by Faith"; Morimoto, *Jonathan Edwards and the Catholic Vision*, 71–130.

23. I am indebted to George Hunsinger for this characterization.

24. See Morimoto, *Jonathan Edwards and the Catholic Vision*, 82, 153.

25. Misc. 793, Misc. 996; see also Morimoto, *Jonathan Edwards and the Catholic Vision*, 115, 113.

26. Morimoto, *Jonathan Edwards and the Catholic Vision*, 60–61.

27. In Misc. 218 faith is subsumed under the category of disposition; there is one disposition with many names: faith, hope, love, and obedience. In Misc. 315 and 412 faith is subtly relativized by statements that both faith and works are conditions for salvation, though Edwards is quick to note that works are secondary and follow faith inevitably as fruit. In Misc. 712 Edwards says there is real goodness in the human subject prior to justification. On this last point, see Morimoto, *Jonathan Edwards and the Catholic Vision*, 93.

28. Schafer, "Jonathan Edwards and Justification by Faith," 64.

then. If regeneration and justification can be considered, at least from one perspective, as processes that unfold in stages, and if one can therefore be a saint before conversion, then theological groundwork has been laid for the position that (some of) the heathen can be saints before they come to Christ, if they have the proper dispositions. If their knowledge of Christ is incomplete, it may be because they are still in the initial stages of regeneration and justification, which may be completed in glory, just as it is for infants. Edwards never reached this explicit conclusion, at least in his published writings or private notebooks. But his own theology lays the groundwork for such an interpretation.

More suggestively, Edwards described four types of persons without explicit knowledge of Christ who may nevertheless find salvation. For all four types, disposition is the critical determinant of their eschatological destiny. Very early in his career Edwards wrote that infants can be regenerated at birth without knowledge of Christ (Misc. 78), and that salvation is based on disposition: "The Infant that has a Disposition in his Heart to believe in Christ if he had a capacity & opportunity is Looked upon and accepted as if he actually believed in Christ and so is entitled to Eternal Life through Christ" (BC, 65).[29]

When Edwards asked himself how he was to understand the salvation of Old Testament saints "when yet they had no distinct respect to [Christ]," he reasoned that it was "the second Person in the Trinity" who appeared to them "as the author of temporal salvation and benefits," and whenever God is said to have manifested himself to Israel (Misc. 663). Hence they already believed in Christ in some sense (Misc. 840) and were saved by faith in Christ (Misc. 884; Misc. 1283). In an early comment that is fascinatingly relevant to our interests, Edward wrote that conversions from wickedness to righteousness in the Old Testament era were just as "frequent" as in the New Testament era (Misc. 39). In other words, true faith was plentiful in the Old Testament era among those who did not confess the name of Christ.

New Testament saints followed a similar pattern. "Cornelius did already in some respect believe in X [Christ] even in the manner that the Old Testament saints were wont to do" (Misc. 840). Before he met Peter, that is, Cornelius in some sense believed in a Christ of whom he had not yet heard.[30] Edwards said the same about the apostles. Cornelius, Nathaniel, "probably" John's two disciples, and several others were "*good men* before [they met Christ], for they seemed to be found already in a *disposition* to follow [Christ] when [Christ] first appeared to them in his human nature and this seems to have been the case with Zacchaeus and with the women of Canaan" (Misc. 847; emphasis added). Edwards infers from this that "conversion may still be by divine constitution necessary to salvation in some respect even after [a person] is really a saint" (Misc. 847). Once again we see that Edwards is suggesting instances where a person can be regenerate before conversion to an explicit knowledge of Christ. At this point, probably in the mid to late

---

29. Misc. 492 suggests that Edwards considered the state of infants as analogous to that of the heathen, since both have less than full knowledge of revelation. In this entry he speculates that without revelation we would not know "who are liable to punishment, whether children, whether heathen."

30. Calvin, in contrast, said that Cornelius was "already illumined by the Spirit of wisdom" and "sanctified by the same Spirit" but stops short of saying that he was regenerate; Institutes 3.17.4.

1730s, Edwards is returning to an inference he had reached very early in his career (1723), that "a man may have the disposition in himself for some time before he can sensibly feel them [the exercises of that disposition], for want of occasion or other reason" (Misc. 27b).

This notion of regeneration before conversion and the similarities to Roman Catholic soteriology invite comparison to Karl Rahner's conception of "anonymous Christians." Like Edwards and unlike Luther, Rahner looks more to the human subject and its condition (rather than to God's free decision or Christ's person and work) when explaining the justification of those who never hear the gospel. Both Edwards and Rahner, then, use a dispositional soteriology in so far as they ground justification primarily in the disposition of the human person. However, while Rahner's (saving) disposition highlights obedience to one's conscience,[31] Edwards's (saving) disposition is centered in religious consciousness—awareness of sin and one's need for divine mercy. Another difference between the two is that Rahner rejects "primordial revelation" and locates revelation to non-Christians in the unreflexive and unobjectified "depths of [their own] being,"[32] while for Edwards revelation to non-Christians has come historically in propositional form through the Jews and the fathers of the Gentile nations.

A fourth class of people who enjoyed salvation without explicit knowledge of Christ were those we might call holy pagans. In his 1739 sermons on the history of the work of redemption, Edwards surmises that conversion to true religion, justification, and glorification have occurred in all ages of the world since the Fall and cited examples of such holy pagans living outside Israel: Melchizedek, the posterity of Nahor (Job and his family), Job's three friends and Elihu, and Bildad the Shuhite.[33] These were individuals outside the national covenant with Israel and of course without explicit knowledge of Christ who nonetheless seem to have been regenerate.

In correspondence during his last years, he wrote of a group of Onohquagas residing in Stockbridge for a time as excelling "in religion and virtue" and "far the best disposed Indians we have had to do with, and [who] would be inclined to their utmost to assist, encourage, and to strengthen the hands of missionaries and instructors, should [any] be sent among [them]."[34] It is not at all clear from the letters that these Indians were all converted; the opposite is more probable. But it is significant that Edwards said they excelled in both religion and virtue. In both his sermons on charity and the Miscellanies he criticized pagan moralists who sometimes had good ideas about religion and virtue but failed to live virtuous or religious lives.[35] But Edwards praised these Onohquagas not for the truth of their ideas but the quality of

---

31. Karl Rahner, S.J., "Anonymous Christians," in Theological Investigations, 6:397.

32. Karl Rahner, S.J., "Jesus Christ in Non-Christian Religions," in Foundations of Christian Faith, 315, 313; Rahner, "Anonymous Christians," 394.

33. HWR, 179. Edwards also said in these sermons that after Abraham God rejected all other nations and gave them up to idolatry. That Edwards is speaking of collective groups and not individuals is clear from several discussions in his notebooks, including the one mentioned in the next paragraph of this text.

34. Letter to Secretary Andrew Oliver, April 12, 1753, 5 in LPW, 583.

35. EW, 310–11; Misc. 1238, 1350, 1357.

their lives, just as Luke had commended Cornelius for the quality of his practice. In this letter and another during that period he described two other tribes who "have a great desire that the gospel should be introduced and settled in their country."[36] Perhaps, in the twilight of his career, Edwards thought he had found holy pagans who, like Cornelius, were sincerely seeking the gospel.

God's Expectations

If there were grounds to think that these different sorts of people could be saved without explicit knowledge of Christ, and if salvation is based on dispositions, what does God expect of a saving disposition? We have already seen that a sense of sin and trust in God's mercy are required. But how was that to be manifested? For Edwards God's expectations vary according to the degree of revelation available. All human beings have received revelation, but revelation is progressive.[37] Its principal lineaments were given to the fathers of the nations, who handed them down to their descendents, but at any given time its extent varied from other times because of the law of religious entropy: different times and different places were affected by different degrees of corruption.

Hence while the basic conditions for salvation remain the same in every place and period, God's expectations vary according to the conditions of extant revelation. "Though holiness or spiritual image of God be in its principle and habit the same[,] yet the circumstances . . . the different relations to God . . . different manner of God's dealing with us and discovering himself to us and the work he appoints us and the views and expectations given us and pursuits that are appoint'd us . . . the exercises of it be most diverse" (Misc. 894). Therefore the "duties" pertaining to salvation differ because of the "different state of the church and revelation" (Misc. 439; Misc. 246). God expects the same principle and spirit, but varying exercises and explicit acts.

Edwards states as a general rule that God's expectations are always in "just proportion" to the degree of revelation present. Since eighteenth-century New England had been so flooded with revelation, God expected "vastly" more than even in New Testament times.

> A man now in order to a being perfectly holy or coming up to his duty now must be vastly more holy[,] must love God in an unspeakably higher degrees [sic]. . . . Then a man is perfectly holy when his love to God bears a just proportion to the capacities of his nature under such circumstances with such manifestations as God makes of his loveliness and benefits that he receives from him. (Misc. 894)

Edwards went on to say that more is expected of us than of Adam. If Adam were transported across time to the modern era, he would be considered "earthly minded in a sense"; if modern Christians were to behave as he did, they would be thought "corrupt and abominable."

---

36. Letter to Reverend John Erskine, April 14, 1753, in LPW, 595.
37. HWR, passim; Misc. 160; Misc. 439; Misc. 489.

Because God's expectations depend on the degree of revelation available, and the heathen have received so much less than those in the Christian world, the heathen are nowhere so displeasing to God as the unregenerate in Christian lands. After all, Edwards preached, the heathen never had a choice to receive Christ explicitly; they are not as hardened and are more free from prejudice. They have "a principle of enmity against God and rebellion against God," but a "gospel sinner" has a "habit" of rejecting God. Sinners who have heard the gospel, then, have a habit or disposition to reject the gospel, but sinners in heathen lands do not.[38]

Just before he was ejected from his pulpit, Edwards told his congregation that most of them were "more provoking enemies to that Lord they love and adore, than most of the very heathen." Nearly a decade later he wrote that the Christian world is more "hateful to God and repugnant to true virtue, than the state of the heathen world" before Christ.[39]

A Possibility of Reconciliation

In Edwards's view a saving disposition was nearly always a disposition to receive Christ; but he also considered explicitly several classes of persons who can have a saving disposition without faith in the historical Christ. And he surmised that some heathen knew more about virtue and religion than Old Testament figures who were saved. After Edwards reached these conclusions, he reflected late in his career, tentatively but positively, on the possibility of salvation for the heathen. In Misc. 1162, after explaining that heathen philosophers had said "such wonderful things concerning the Trinity [and] the Messiah," he asked whether they might have been inspired by the Holy Spirit. Yes, he figured, but then reminded himself that this is not so high "an honour and priviledge as some are ready to think." For "many very bad men have been the subjects of it." Some were idolators such as Balaam. Nebuchadnezzar, "a very wicked man," received a revelation about the Messiah and his future kingdom. Even the devil at the oracle at Delphi was "compelled to confess Christ."

But in any event, of what use were the revelations given to Socrates and Plato "and some others of the wise men of Greece," who were just as inspired as the wise men from the East? These philosophers did not use these revelations to lead their nations toward the truth, so God must have had other intentions. Edwards suggested four: to dispose heathen nations in the future to converse with and learn from the Jews, to prepare the Gentiles for their future reception of the Gospel, to confirm the truths of Christianity, and (in what is one of Edwards's most cryptic comments in the thousands of pages of his private notebooks) to benefit their own souls: "We know not what evidence God might give to the men themselves that were the subjects of these inspirations that they were divine and true . . . and so we know not of how great benefit the truths suggested might be to their own

---

38. Sermon on Matthew 11:21, 13.
39. Humble Inquiry, in EccW, 255; OS, 183.

souls." Edwards is hesitant and tentative, but he nevertheless clearly opens the possibility that these heathen could have used revelation for their own spiritual benefit—a notion that is incoherent unless it means they can be saved. When we recall that Edwards wrote this entry during a period in which he was frequently quoting from writers who explicitly argued for the salvation of the virtuous heathen, it is difficult to believe that Edwards did not include salvation among the possible benefits to heathen souls.[40]

Near the very end of his life, in a notebook entry (Misc. 1338) arguing against deist notions of reason, Edwards asserted that reason can confirm many religious truths but cannot discover them on its own. Then he considered the deist objection that most humans have not had the benefit of revelation. There is a "possibility," he replied, of the heathen being "reconciled" to God and thus receiving the benefit of divine revelation, for "the greater part of the heathen world have not [been] left meerly to the light of nature." They had received revelation by tradition from their ancestors and have borrowed from the Jews. Since the means of revelation were available, it was theoretically possible that some could have had a saving disposition and been reconciled to God. But their "extreme blindness [and] delusion" suggests that few had taken advantage of the "benefit of revelation."

Once again, we see Edwards's familiar response to deists: revelation is both necessary and pervasive. God has revealed himself to humankind, and not just to the Jewish and Christian worlds. The history of the world is the history of the work of redemption, the exploits of which were reported to most human ears. Because of this transmission of the good news to almost all human societies, salvation was available for heathen who would pursue the leads they were given from the *prisca theologia* and the Jews.

A Comfortable Agnosticism

But if Edwards was convinced that, *contra* deism, God's revelation had been made available to most of the world, he was not sure that it had indeed reached every last person. On this point he was agnostic. But his agnosticism did not bother him. For he was convinced, on other grounds, that the Scriptures were true and therefore that God was just and good. Edwards was never persuaded by the deists that God's justice had to be completely comprehensible in human terms, or that divine justice must be coordinate to human justice by some rational calculation. He was so convinced by the beauty and coherence of the Christian drama of redemption that he was happy to permit divine justice—which he conceded is finally incomprehensible to human minds—to serve as the standard by which human justice and goodness are to be judged.

---

40. Cambridge Platonist Henry More, who according to Wallace Anderson had "an early and lasting influence upon Edwards' thought," wrote that the heathen can be saved by grace through "Faithfulness to that Light and Power which God has given them." *SPW*, 21; More, *Mystery of Godliness*, bk. 10, chap. 6, 352.

At the end of his career Edwards twice reflected at some length on this question. In Misc. 1299 he acknowledges that for most of those who don't have the Scriptures reconciliation with God is "very improbable." The preacher of "Sinners in the Hands of an Angry God" was too convinced of general depravity to think otherwise. But reconciliation was not impossible, for if people really sought the truth, they could find it. If for some it was "next to impossible" (here he seems to concede that some are bereft of truth and perhaps even revelation), however, one must not hastily conclude that God is not good or just. For if God's distribution of spiritual benefits does not seem equitable, neither does his distribution of temporal benefits. Different people have different foods and animals and kinds of clothing. Some have no glass or "loadstone" (an eighteenth-century word for a piece of iron used as a magnet) at all. Even rain and sun are apportioned unequally.

Hence the mere fact that God's gifts are not distributed universally does not prove God's meanness to some. It shows only that God is discriminate in how he demonstrates his goodness. Edwards refused the deist inference that God must be unjust if his gifts are not distributed equally. By his lights, the goodness of the world in general and the objective reality of redemption in Christ have already proven God's good intent. If we cannot calculate how God's goodness coheres with distributive justice that is not by our reckoning absolutely equal and universal, so be it. The God of the spider may seem arbitrary to human eyes, but Edwards was so taken by this God's beauty that he could not imagine that this God was not also finally just to all.

A short time later (Misc. 1340) Edwards responded to the deist insistence that what is mysterious cannot be believed. "It may be expected that as in the system of nature, so in this system of revelation, there should be many parts whose use is but little understood, and many that should seem wholly useless, yea and some that should seem rather to do hurt than good." In fact, Edwards allowed, some parts of Scripture seem to do more harm than good.

But such problems should not be surprising, Edwards replied. This is to be expected in a revelation that unveils a reality that is infinitely complex and often paradoxical. Like Joseph Butler, whose *Analogy of Religion* was perhaps the most effective response to deism in the eighteenth century, Edwards argued that the difficulties and mysteries of revelation are analogous to their counterparts in nature, to whose pedestrian clarity the deists religiously appealed. "It may well be expected, that there should be mysteries, things incomprehensible and exceeding difficult to our understanding; analogous to the mysteries that are found in all other works of God, as the works of creation and providence."

So Edwards did not presume to explain all the mysteries of revelation and salvation. Instead he claimed that the vision of Christian redemption is so compelling that we are obliged to work within the bounds of that vision, reconciling as best we can its features with the world we experience. In the process we will make new discoveries because the Spirit continues to give new illumination of written revelation. But we must not insist on full understanding of every part, as the deists did, because revelation, like life, abounds with mystery and paradox impervious to human comprehension.

A Curious Tension

We are left with a curious tension in Edwards's thinking about the salvation of the heathen. On the one hand, in most of his explicit commentary on the topic, he took a negative view characteristic of his Reformed predecessors. While appreciating the religious truth known by the "wiser heathen," Edwards never tired of recording the "absurdities of the worship of the heathen." The later Miscellanies contain frequent references to human sacrifice, religious prostitution, fornication, sodomy, castration, and cannibalism. At times it seems that Edwards reveled in the titillating details. From Skelton's two-volume work Edwards was careful to copy passages that poked fun at the Greek philosophers who made dangerous journeys by sea to visit the "celebrated Prostitutes of their time," let out their own wives "for Hire," kept mistresses, and gave the world "the strongest reasons to think them guilty of greater crimes, than it was possible to commit with the other sex." Aristotle, Edwards dutifully recorded, was a fob, a debauchee, and a traitor to Alexander his master. Xenophon kept a boy lover. Sometimes Edwards's choice of extracts borders on the ridiculous: "The most solemn act of worship performed to the Syrian Baal by his ordinary devotees, was to break wind and ease themselves at the Foot of his Image" (*Misc.* 1350).

Edwards was his most uncompromising in his sermons. In an early Northampton sermon (on Revelation 3:15, before 1733) he identified immorality and idolatry as characteristically "heathenish" (13). God had forsaken and withdrawn his gracious presence from heathen lands. They were "Lost Nations" and the heathen were the devil's people (30). In a particularly vivid passage, Edwards said "the devil nurses them [the heathen] up as swine in a pen that he may fill his belly with them in another [world]. . . . They are his prey when they die. That dragon[,] that old serpent[,] then Got 'em into his own den and sucks their blood and feeds upon their bowels and vitals" (30). And there seems no hope, for "those that die heathen he will prey upon and Exert his Cruelty Upon forever" (31).

Even in his last decade at Stockbridge preaching to Indians, Edwards held out little hope for the heathen. While in these sermons he emphasized those heathen who had heard the gospel and rejected it, the implication in most discussions was that "heathen" and "lost" are synonymous. In a sermon on Proverbs 15:24, for example, he proclaims, "They that Trust in graven Images or in mahomet or Pagan priests to save them . . . take a sure course to destruction" (4). And in a sermon on Matthew 7:13–14 he declares that "all they are going in the way to destruction who are Heathens and worship the sun and moon and worship the devil and dont worship the true God" (2).

But that is not the whole picture. Edwards made a series of important theological moves beyond his Reformed predecessors that could have opened the door for a more hopeful view of the salvation of the heathen. The advances he made in typology, the extensive use he made of the *prisca theologia*, and his development of a dispositional soteriology prepared the theological way for a more expansive view of salvation. Edwards used these developments primarily to argue for a greater knowledge of religious truth among the heathen than his favorite Reformed predecessors—Francis Turretin (1623–87) and Petrus van Mastrict (1630–1706)—had allowed.[41] On the question of salvation, he usually only conceded the *possibility* that heathen could be saved and never spoke in the expansively hopeful terms of a Watts, Ramsay, or Skelton, or even a Baxter or Wesley.[42] So while he built the theological foundations upon which a more hopeful soteriology could quite naturally have been erected, he himself never chose to do so.

Perhaps Edwards reasoned that such concessions would yield too much ground to the enemy. Robert Breck had concluded that since there can be salvation without profession of Christ, it was not absolutely necessary for people to believe that Christ died for sinners. Their motive did not matter as long as they "forsake sin and lead moral lives."[43] Edwards knew that this was the deist and Arminian position, which proposed a self-determining will and considered sincerity sufficient in the absence of disinterested virtue. He retorted that mere sincerity was not enough (Misc. 1153). Self-love and fear of damnation could produce a sincere desire to be virtuous without a will to virtue. To affirm the salvation of the heathen on the grounds of moral sincerity alone would have conceded the argument to the Arminians and deists on the freedom of the will.

This may explain Edwards's puzzling reversal in his interpretation of John 1:9 ("That was the true Light, which lighteth every man that cometh into the world"). In the early 1730s, before the Breck incident, Edwards explained the meaning of John 1:9 in universal terms. Every one who was ever enlightened, he wrote in his Blank Bible, was enlightened in no other way "but by Jesus Christ." This light enlightened not only the Jews but "indifferently Every man[,] Let him be of what nation soever." Hence this was a "general" light. Edwards reminded himself at the close of the entry to "see a parallel Expression Col. 1.23 'the gospel . . . which was preached to every creature which is under heaven.'" The upshot of this comment is that non-Christians who had religious truth had been given it by Christ himself.

But nearly a decade later, after the Breck controversy had subsided, Edwards restricted the meaning of this text (John 1:9) to groups of people rather than individuals. In his "Book of Controversies" (BC, 135), he wrote, "What is really intended is only universal with Respect to Kinds and without limitation by any Rule. Or being limited or Restrained from any one Individual Person by any Rule Given." It was as if Edwards worried that William Turner may have been right, that undisciplined speculation about "the Variety which appears in Religion" might lead indeed to "Scepticism and Atheism and Impiety in the world."[44] Breck had demonstrated what damage mischievous reference to other religions could do.

---

41. Turretin, *Institutes of Elenctic Theology*, 1:9–16; Mastricht, *Theoretico-practica theologia*, 1.1.xxii–xxv.

42. Baxter forthrightly granted salvation to those (outside the "Jewish church") who did not have "knowledge of Christ incarnate," and Wesley said pagans just need to live up to the light they are given. Richard Baxter, *The Reasons of the Christian Religion* (London, 1667), 201–2; John Wesley, sermon 68, "The General Spread of the Gospel," in *Works*, 9:234; see Pailin, *Attitudes to Other Religions*, 48.

43. *A Letter*, in EccW, 159.

44. Turner, *History of All Religions*, "To the Reader" (no pagination).

Breck's position was also perilously similar to that taken by Edwards's opponents in the communion controversy that led to his ouster from Northampton.[45] Not coincidentally Breck sided with these opponents and cast the deciding vote on the clerical council. Edwards's opponents also argued for moral sincerity without full-hearted "ownership" of Christ as sufficient for admission to the sacrament. Edwards kept insisting that the conviction that one possesses Christ and therefore true virtue is necessary for such admission. Once again, to preach the salvation of the heathen based on an internal disposition without profession of Christ could too easily be co-opted by his opponents, to the ruin of his church. Ironically, the integrity of his church was ruined anyway, and he was banished to preach to the heathen.

More likely, however, Edwards saw no irony or tension in this position. For him there was no inconsistency whatsoever between the possibility of reconciliation for the heathen (because of the *prisca theologia*, God's types in the religions, and a dispositional soteriology) and the probability that only a precious few of the heathen had ever been saved. For this was the testimony of Scripture as he understood it. The sacred authors of the Bible, by the inspiration of the Holy Spirit, portrayed a world in which God had shown himself directly through Jewish history and Jesus Christ. Salvation was available to all, but only through the events of that Jewish-Christian history. News of those events had been heard by most of the world, but few had listened. Hence the world's darkness and delusion were tragic but not unfair. History was a mirror of the human soul: able to perceive cosmic truths but disinclined to appropriate them.

Furthermore, the beauty of God that he saw in the history of redemption convinced him of the justice of God the Redeemer. The aesthetic ecstasy he had experienced as a teenager had been repeated and confirmed in the years since as he contemplated the deity's manifold excellencies displayed throughout the history of the work of redemption.[46] For Edwards, seeing the beauty of God in the work of redemption was the best proof possible that this deity was true and real.[47] And since for him the beautiful was the good—the drama of redemption as climaxed in Christ was aesthetically excellent precisely because it described the apogee of love—there was no quarrelling with God's redemptive maneuverings. Every question (such as, Why was full revelation not given to every last heathen?) did not have to be answered. A glimpse of the divine glory was intrinsically self-validating. This deity was beautiful and therefore just. To demand that it stand before the bar of human justice was unconscionable hubris. It made no philosophical sense.

Therefore the fact that God had provided revelation for the majority of the heathen was sufficient to exonerate divine justice. We should be content with that peek into the otherwise inscrutable sanctum of the divine wisdom and trust that the balance of the divine economy—while baffling to the canons of human probity—was finally just. Hence the deist reproach, Edwards reasoned, had been turned back, and the deity's glory but further magnified.

---

45. The most accurate review of the controversy is Hall's introduction to EW, 1–90.
46. "Personal Narrative," in Simonson, *Selected Writings of Jonathan Edwards*, 40–41.
47. McClymond, *Encounters with God*, chaps. 1–2.

III

STRATEGIES APPLIED

8

JUDAISM

A Light among the Nations

The eighteenth century marked the beginning of a reevaluation of Judaism. For the first time since Marcion, Jews were regarded as religiously unrelated to Christians. The deists, who dominated intellectual life in England at the beginning of the century and were the leaders of this reappraisal, portrayed Judaism as essentially pagan, unspiritual, unnecessary to Christianity, and in fact the source of all that was wrong with traditional Christianity. They learned from Johann Buxtdorf the Elder (1564–1629), whose guide to synagogue life depicts Judaism as a "confused" and "disorderly" religion obsessively devoted to empty ritual. Voltaire, who studied the deists when in London in the 1720s, Bolingbroke, Gibbon, and other Enlightenment thinkers began to regard Jews as simply another political entity, unprotected by divine covenant. Pogroms against them were considered natural consequences of their creation of a cruel and irrational god. Gibbon, for example, argued that Rome fell because of the Jewish character in the Christian religion which had infected the empire.[1] It was against this background of deist severance of the religious link between Christians and Jews that Jonathan Edwards argued for one covenant binding the two religions. But in order to appreciate the contrast which Edwards's covenant struck, we must look more closely at deist objections to Judaism.

---

1. For eighteenth-century attitudes to Judaism, see Manuel, *The Changing of the Gods*, and *The Broken Staff*; Goldman, *Hebrew and the Bible in America*; and Pailin, *Attitudes to Other Religions*. For this paragraph, see Manuel, *The Broken Staff*, 85–90, 166, 175, 291, and Gibbon, *Decline and Fall*, 1:384–91, 446–48; 2:804, 807.

Judaism Unnecessary and Unspiritual

Lord Herbert of Cherbury first undermined Jewish claims to uniqueness by arguing that all the wise Gentiles were monotheists.[2] The deists then asserted that the Chinese, Egyptians, and even Greeks were monotheists before the Jews.[3] Lessing suggested not only that Judaism was superseded by Christianity but that Christianity was now superseded by the Enlightenment.[4] More radically, Chubb charged that the Jewish law was completely unrelated to the Gospel.[5] The logical end of this thinking was Tindal's proclamation that since Christianity is as old as the Creation, Judaism was unnecessary.[6]

Deists were particularly inspired by the classical authors of antiquity, especially the Romans, who treated Jews with contempt and portrayed them as fanatical zealots. Deists were also persuaded that miracle-stories were self-serving inventions of priestcraft, and that the Old Testament prophets were raving madmen. With both traditional supports for the divine authority of the Old Testament thereby subverted, it appeared self-evident that the Jewish religion was of human origin.[7]

William Warburton's *Divine Legation of Moses Demonstrated* (1737–38) was a favorite source for deists attacking Judaism. Warburton contended that Jews came to believe in the immortality of the soul only after the Babylonian exile. Encouraged by Warburton, deists portrayed Judaism as a "carnal law" that brought only "bondage" and permitted ghastly atrocities such as child sacrifice.[8] Its god was jealous and cruel (commanding innocent Amalekites and Canaanites to be slaughtered), and required ordinances such as the sabbath that could not be supported by reason.[9] Jewish heroes were controlled by their passions (David was an adulterer and murderer, and Solomon was a slave to lust) and did ridiculous things (Isaiah paraded around naked, Jeremiah carried his girdle, and Hosea married a whore).[10] David Hume added that it was inevitable that this unphilosophical monotheism lapsed into the worship of idols and concrete objects.[11] He and other deists repeated Richard Simon's argument that Moses could not have written the Pentateuch since it describes Moses' death.

---

2. Herbert, *Antient Religion of the Gentiles*, 8–11, 21, 31.

3. Most were students of Cudworth's *True Intellectual System of the Universe* (1678), one of whose central themes was that the wise heathen were monotheists.

4. Lessing, *The Education of the Human Race*, in Chadwick, *Lessing's Theological Writings*, esp. 93–96.

5. *AF*, 111.

6. *CAO*, 2–4, 8, 271.

7. See Ettinger, "Jews and Judaism in the Eyes of the English Deists," and Pelli, "Impact of Deism."

8. William Warburton, *The Divine Legation of Moses Demonstrated* (1737–38; London, 1838), 2:323–47, 1:686; Manuel, *The Broken Staff*, 186; *IW*, 1:328; *CAO*, 96–97.

9. *CAO*, 251; *AF* 29; *CAO*, 96–97, 116.

10. *CAO*, 242, 255.

11. Hume, *The Natural History of Religion*.

Just like the Barbarous Pagans

The eighteenth century's radical recasting of Judaism as a strange religion was also influenced by the seventeenth century's proliferation of encyclopedias of religions, which represented the crude beginnings of what we have come to call comparative religion. These compendia compiled reports from the fifteenth- and sixteenth-century explorers who had brought back stories of strange peoples with even stranger religions. Deists were struck by what seemed to be extraordinary similarities between Jewish religious rites, on the one hand, and the sacrifices and idol worship of pagan "savages," on the other. Deists then concluded that the Jews were borrowers rather than originators. This confirmed what they had read in their classical Roman sources—that the Jews learned from the Egyptians while in slavery. Their religion was no longer a unique source of religious inspiration, but another example of blind barbarism.[12]

In his effort to communicate this message to the world, John Toland translated La Créquinière's book showing the similarity of Judaism to the religion of the East Indians.[13] Thomas Morgan wrote that the god of Israel was an idol like many others, a local god for a single people, and a cheat to boot.[14] Others suggested that the sacrifices of Iphigenia and Jephthah's daughter demonstrate that the Jews were like the wild Picts of Europe and the primitive Greeks. David was a ruthless and sensual leader of brigands.[15] Thomas Chubb argued that their religious rites were as superstitious as the most ridiculous pagans ceremonies. Moses' ceremonies and observances "eat out, as a canker, the life and spirit of true religion and introduce superstition and false religion in its stead."[16]

If the Jews were no different from their barbarous neighbors and in fact imported to Christianity unspiritual pagan notions, then it stood to deist reason that Christianity must be purged of its Jewish elements in order to get back to its original purity. As Morgan put it, Judaism was the foul source of everything in Christianity contrary to a pure, simple, and reasonable natural religion.[17] An enormous distinction needed to be made between the gentle Christ and "the savage remnants of Judaism in Christian doctrines and practices."[18] Little wonder that Frank Manuel traces the rise of "scientific" anti-Semitism at the end of the nineteenth century to deist attacks on Jewish religion a little less than two centuries earlier.[19]

---

12. Manuel, *The Broken Staff*, 125–26, 178–79, 168, 172.
13. La Créquinière, *The Agreement of the Customs*.
14. Morgan, *The Moral Philosopher*, 147.
15. Manuel, *The Broken Staff*, 185.
16. *AF*, 19.
17. Morgan, *The Moral Philosopher*, 19.
18. Manuel, *The Broken Staff*, 291.
19. Ibid., 166.

Edwards on Jewish Identity

The deists bear some responsibility for modern anti-Semitism, but the orthodox Christian tradition is not exactly blameless in this regard. There seems to have been no end of pogroms launched against Jews in the name of Christ. The Holocaust has caused several generations of Christians to re-examine their complicity in institutional anti-Semitism, and the debate continues over the responsibility which Christian theology bears for the disasters of the Nazi era.[20] Yet the Reformed tradition which Edwards inherited and developed contained resources for at least stemming the tide of anti-Semitism, and Edwards cultivated those resources more than most. It may have been those resources, particularly the Reformed doctrine of the covenant, that resulted in attitudes toward Jews that Manuel has called "more open and positive" than in other Christian traditions.[21] We shall look closely at Edwards's conception of the covenant soon, but first we must discuss what is more primary—Edwards's understanding of Jewish identity.

Like most players in the Edwardsean theological drama, the Jews take on their identity only in relation to the grand scheme of redemption and within the historical narrative of that scheme. In the early stages of the drama, God raised up a people for himself in the midst of the world. But "the sons of the church joined in marriage with others, and thereby almost all soon became infected and the church was almost brought to nothing" (HWR, 159). God then chose to save the church by drowning the world in the Flood. But then the pattern repeated: by the time of Abraham the world had become corrupt again. So God "took another method." Instead of destroying the wicked world once more, he commanded Abraham's family to separate itself from the rest of the world, so that he might entrust to them "these types and prophecies that were needful to [be] given of Christ to prepare the way for his coming" (ibid.).[22]

Hence the Jewish nation was called into being to give collective witness, in a visible manner apart from the rest of the planet's population, to God's truth and purpose for the world. In particular the Jews were to point the world to its messiah, by holding forth their inspired utterances and foreshadowing in their own existence the coming messianic realm. This was the destiny for which Israel was brought into being; consequently this was her meaning and identity. The tragedy, according to Edwards, was that she had not yet acknowledged this identity.

---

20. The international uproar provoked by Daniel J. Goldhagen's *Hitler's Willing Executioners: Ordinary Germans and the Holocaust* (New York, 1996) is evidence that the relationship between Christian theology and anti-Semitism is still contested.

21. Manuel claims that the Reformed were more positive than Lutherans, whose official encyclopedia asserted that Jews spit when they utter the name of Christ. "How often they have slaughtered Christian children, crucified them, battered them to pieces! . . . They rouse disgust and horror. . . . Verily, they killed the Son of God." *Grosses vollständiges universal Lexicon* (Leipzig and Halle, 1735), 1499–1500; cited in Manuel, *The Changing of the Gods*, 108.

22. Edwards elaborated on this in "Types of the Messiah," where he explained that Israel's existence was for the purpose of preparing the way for the Messiah and his kingdom. This was clear, he explained, in God's first promise to Abraham: "In thee shall all families of the earth be blessed" (Gen. 12:3). TM, 204–5.

Yet if Israel did not understand her mission, God would continue his plan nonetheless. When he chose Israel, he "visibly" rejected all the other nations of the world, giving them up to idolatry so that it would be evident that they needed a savior. Then human beings would know that "all the wisdom of the philosophers and the wisest men . . . could not deliver [them] from their darkness" (HWR, 179–80).

Even Israel's punishments were used by God to serve the grand plan. The captivity in Babylon cured the Jews "of their itch after idolatry." Although some fell into this sin in later years, never again did the nation as a whole succumb to it. Furthermore, the loss of their political and religious treasures (self-government, "the glory and magnificence" of the temple, the ark containing the two stones on which were written the Ten Commandments, the Urim and Thummin, and the Shekinah cloud of glory over the mercy seat) promoted the divine drama by dimming the glory of the first dispensation in order to prepare the way for the greater glory of the second (HWR, 251–52). The diaspora after Babylon raised a general expectation of a messiah throughout the world (Virgil, for example, wrote a poem "in the language of the prophet Isaiah" about a great prince to be born[23]), showed the necessity of abolishing the old ceremonial law and worship, and helped spread knowledge of Jesus Christ when diaspora Jews in the time of Christ and after traveled each year to Jerusalem for religious feasts (HWR, 255–59). Therefore not only was Israel's identity created by its role in the divine outworking of history's purposes but every stage of Israel's history was used providentially to further those purposes.

A City on a Hill

Edwards employed a number of images for Israel's role in the work of redemption, but all of them were variations on the theme of adumbration: Israel was a shadow of the truth, a pointer to sacred glories that were outlined in her own history but fleshed out more fully in times to come. Early in his career Edwards used the image of light, which curiously enough was his favorite image for revelation more generally and Christ in particular. Judea, he writes in Misc. 350 (1728–29), was a "a sort of light amongst the nations, though they [the nations] did not know it." Judea's "practices and principles" reminded the nations of traditions they had received from their forefathers[24] and so prevented them from "degenerating as much as otherwise they would have done." Heathen philosophers, he reminded himself, obtained what they knew of "truth" from their forefathers, who had received it from the sons of Noah, or from the Phoenicians, who mediated Jewish truths to their contacts abroad.

The Jews were also a light because they prepared the heathen world for the introduction of the messiah. Jewish sacrifices, which demonstrated the necessity

---

23. Virgil prophesied a grand era of peace, to be inaugurated by the birth of a boy. See Virgil's *Eclogue* 4.

24. Once again we see evidence of Edwards's use of the *prisca theologia*.

of blood atonement for the forgiveness of sin, prepared Gentiles for understanding Christ's sacrifice.[25]

Near the end of his career, Edwards returned to the light image. In *Original Sin* he chronicled once more—albeit in short compass—the history of redemption, relating again the failure of God's first "method" to preserve a holy people (planting individuals in the midst of the world), and the new method of raising up a family and then a nation separate from the rest of the world. His purpose was for this people to "stand as a city on a hill, to be a light to the world." The light illuminated, but the failure of the surrounding world to learn from its radiance was further evidence of the traditional Christian doctrine of original sin (OS, 171–73).

True Religion under a Veil

A second image Edwards employed to describe Judaism was a direct repudiation of deist dismissals of Jews as inventors of barbarous idolatry. Edwards insisted that Judaism was true religion, if under a veil. The Jews, he wrote in his notebooks, had the "true worship and communion of the one great and holy God" (*Misc.* 378). It was "as clear as the sun at noonday" that the Jews alone had had the truth, and no other nation had come close. In fact Edwards drew support for his contention from records the deists had dismissed—"all the histories and prophecies of the Old Testament" (*Misc.* 378).

This was true religion under a veil. The full implications and clearest development of the truth had not yet been revealed. For instance, the sacrifices commanded by the Old Testament were not proper gifts, since they were God's already; they were not propitiatory and made no real satisfaction to divine justice but simply showed the Jews that by themselves they could not make atonement; there was no moral goodness in these sacrifices, so their holiness was only typical; what pleased God was the substance (Christ's sacrifice) not the shadow (the Old Testament sacrifices).[26]

Nevertheless, the sacrifices were "full of gospel doctrine."[27] The greatest and most central truths of the gospel were hidden under a veil, even in the sacrifices. They showed God's holy hatred of sin and trespasses against his authority, invoked a "sense of the heinousness of sin . . . [and] the glory of holiness," and thereby led to "trust in the mere mercy of God" (*Misc.* 326). Indeed, this was the same sensibility found in Christian believers: "[It] is the exercise of the same disposition of mind as is exercised in actually believing in Christ crucified, and is the same sort of act" (ibid.).

---

25. Edwards, "Sacrifice of Christ Acceptable," in *SDK*, 448.
26. *SDK*, 443, 445, 449, 445.
27. Ibid., 448.

Types of the Christian Religion

"True religion under a veil" was but another way for Edwards to denote what was perhaps his favorite image for Israel—a type of Christ and his kingdom. As we saw in Chapter 6, Edwards had a typological vision of all reality, which means that earthly existence appears at once as objective presentation and divinely appointed shadow of spiritual reality. This was no less true of Israel, the most vivid of all earthly shadows. It was also the richest, for *everything* in the "Jewish church" was a "shadow and representation" (Misc. 251, Misc. 282). Through the Jews God "shadowed forth and taught as under a veil" all future glorious things of the gospel (Misc. 359).

The sacrifices, for example, prepared the Jews for understanding the coming perfect sacrifice of Christ (Misc. 307). The Exodus from Egypt was a shadow of Christ's redemption from slavery to sin (Misc. 28, Misc. 160). David and the temple were "so full of the gospel" (Misc. 359): David was a type of Christ as prophet and king (HWR, 209) and "spoke abundantly" of Christ's incarnation, life, death, resurrection, ascension, satisfaction for sin, intercession, priestly office, and union with the church (HWR, 210). He also spoke of the calling of the Gentiles, the future glory of the church near the end of the world, and the final judgment (HWR, 210–211). David was a type of Christ in his humiliation (because of his wars and personal troubles), while Solomon was a type of Christ in his exaltation and triumph (because of his long peaceful reign) (HWR, 227). The temple was a type not only of Christ's human nature and the church of Christ but also of heaven (HWR, 222). The prophets' principal subject was not the Israel in which they lived but Christ, his redemption, and the glorious times of the gospel in the latter days (HWR, 238).

Edwards wrote that the Hebrew Bible contained three different kinds of types: personal, providential, and instituted. The greatest personal type was David; the greatest providential type was the redemption from Egypt; and the greatest instituted type was the Jewish sacrificial system. All of Israel's history and cultus was typical, just as, ultimately, all of the natural world was typical of the spiritual world. Edwards used Basnage's *History of the Jews* (1708) to argue that the Jews themselves believed that all things that happened to their fathers were "types and figures of the Messiah" (TM, 208–9).

Since Israel was typical of Christ's kingdom, true Christians were the New Israel. Of course this claim was not uncommon in Christian thought and had become routine in the Reformed tradition,[28] but Edwards added a graphic dimension. In an early burst of supersessionist enthusiasm, he declared that the majority of Christians in the eighteenth century probably had some Jewish blood in them, since so many Jews in Judea had become Christians. Most eighteenth-century Jews, he

---

28. Cotton Mather, for example, even wore a yarmulke in his study and liked to call himself a rabbi. Arthur Hertzberg, "The New England Puritans and the Jews," in Goldman, *Hebrew and the Bible in America*, 105.

added, had some Gentile blood as well, as David did by Ruth. This meditation on bloodlines was Edwards's basis for saying that Christians could be called Israel because they had the "essentials of Israelites"—the circumcision of the heart. Hence they were the spiritual Israel of God, and the Israelite nation was therefore but the type pointing to them, the true antitype. Therefore Jews are shadows of the real substance, which is the Gentile church (Misc. 49).

Later in his career Edwards appealed to Jewish practice to support his contention that Christians "are to be looked upon as God's people Israel" (Misc. 597). The prophets themselves, he argued, implied as much in "the intent and meaning" of their words. And the Old Testament text contains many indications of the same. Exodus 12 and Deuteronomy 20 suggest that proselytes were always regarded as "being of the same people, of the congregation or church of Israel." Elsewhere in the text strangers who worshiped the true God according to his institutions were considered "as ones born in the land." There was to be one law for the native-born and the stranger. Edwards went so far as to list Old Testament figures who were from other nations but came to be included in the people of Israel: Uriah the Hittite, Obil the Ishmaelite, Araunah or Ornan the Jebusite, Zelek the Ammonite, Ithmah the Moabite, Obed-edom the Gittite, Ittai the Gittite and his six hundred, the Jebusites, the Kenites, and the Gibeonites. And, of course, there was Ruth.

Edwards also appealed to the Talmud, which, he claimed, requires that a Gentile proselyte be circumcised and baptized and then welcomed as "an Israelite in all things." Finally he turned to Jewish-Christian history. The Jews in Christ's time were of mixed descent, evidenced by Herod who was an Edomite. If it be objected that Christians do not follow the old Jewish ordinances, there are two replies. First, God changed the ordinances at the coming of Christ, and second, Christ himself brought new ordinances for the Jews. Unfortunately, most of the Jews did not welcome the change.

One Covenant for Jews and Christians

Edwards used what was probably the most common Reformed resource for understanding Judaism—the concept of the covenant—and returned to it time and again in his notebooks throughout his career.[29] Calvin and his successors had departed from the Lutheran bipolar separation of law and gospel (which at the popular level sometimes divorced the Jewish Old Testament from the Christian New Testament) by proposing that the two covenants—Jewish and Christian—were simply two "modes of dispensation" of "one and the same" covenant.[30] Edwards's development of this concept was not remarkably different from that of his predecessors among the Puritans and Reformed, but his was among the more nuanced.

---

29. For more extensive treatments of Edwards and covenant, see Cherry, *Theology of Jonathan Edwards*, 107–23, and passim, and Bogue, *Covenant of Grace*.

30. Calvin, Institutes, 2.10.2.

Edwards followed Calvin and his heirs by portraying the two covenants (the Jewish "covenant of works" and the Christian "covenant of grace")[31] as different but integrally related modes of a single plan of redemption. As we saw in Chapter 5, he used an anatomical image to represent the relation between the two. Drawing on the distinction between the "cortex" ("shell" or "husk") of an organ and its "medulla" (central parts or "nucleus"), he played on the contrasts between outer versus inner, and letter versus spirit. The covenant of works was the cortex or shell that "envelops" the medulla of the "gospel" or covenant of grace. The first is comparable to the letter of the law, whose true meaning is communicated obscurely and indirectly, while the second may be likened to the spirit of the law, delivered more simply and directly.[32]

If the covenant of works was the outer shell containing an inner core of grace, it was also a means God used to secure the end of grace in biblical times. Edwards saw the same pattern working in his own day: just as the covenant of works was "proposed" to Israel in the wilderness, "the same is now proposed in the course of a sinner's convictions in these days." Sinners are first confronted with God's demands in the covenant of works, and only by trying to meet those demands do they discover their inability and need for grace (Misc. 1353). Hence the history of covenants in the work of redemption is reproduced in the religious psychology of the person coming to faith.

This pattern is by design, not default. It is God's method to use veils to protect the inner pearls of the gospel from being trampled by reprobate swine. The cortex of the covenant of works is at once the means to lead the elect into the nucleus and God's manner of hiding the inner mystery from the careless and the carnal, who do not deserve to see it. God uses the cortex to blind the minds of the proud and serve as an occasion for their self-righteousness (Misc. 1353).

---

31. By the covenant of works Edwards meant generally what he learned from the *Westminster Confession* and its interpreters, who drew a distinction between "the covenant of works made with Adam and his posterity on the condition of perfect obedience and the covenant of grace made in Christ with believers, offering the gift of salvation on the condition of faith in [Christ]." William Klempa, "The Concept of the Covenant in Sixteenth- and Seventeenth-Century Continental and British Reformed Theology," in Donald K. McKim, ed., *Major Themes in the Reformed Tradition* (Grand Rapids, Mich., 1992), 95. See also Calvin, Institutes, 2.11.1–8; 2.10.1–6, and Heppe, *Reformed Dogmatics*, chaps. 13–16.

32. The cortex actually consisted of two covenants, the covenant of works (which God established with Adam and his posterity) and the national covenant (which God "made with external Israel or the seed of Abraham"). The national covenant is "an appendage" to the covenant of works that typifies or shadows forth the covenant of grace and is therefore "subservient" and "subordinate" to the covenant of grace. All of its institutions were external and point to the internal spirit of the covenant of grace. Hence it consisted of an "external temporal society . . . an external earthly countrey . . . an external carnal priesthood . . . a worldly sanctuary . . . carnal sacrifices; an external altar; an external holy of holies, & an external mercy seat . . . external conformity to the law of God; an outward conformity to the moral law, and a conformity to an external and carnal law." Even pardon and sanctification were external: "freedom from guilt as it excluded from external priviledges, and a sanctification that consisted in the purifying of the flesh, delivering from carnal pollutions, & qualifying for carnal priviledges." *Misc.* 1353. For a full explication of the meaning and dynamics of Edwards's understanding of national covenant, see McDermott, *One Holy and Happy Society*, 11–36.

This is one way of explaining why in the Old Testament the gospel is imperfectly and seldom revealed, but demonstrated fully and directly in the New. The people of God in the old dispensation "could not bear" a clear revelation of the covenant of grace because they were not convinced of their inability to establish their own righteousness, just as the sinners of Edwards's day did not know their own sin and so could not appreciate the covenant of grace.

Therefore the Ten Commandments had the appearance of a covenant of works in order to teach the Israelites their inability to keep it. Yet the commandments also revealed, albeit indirectly, the covenant of grace, which it was their true intent to establish. This is evident from internal clues, according to Edwards. First, they are called "tables of the covenant," which suggests God's initiative in choosing Israel. In fact, he chose to be "married" to Israel and unilaterally constructed a covenant by which to effect the relationship. Further, Edwards wrote, the preface indicated that God had already become their God and redeemer before they had shown whether they would obey. So the commandments were instructions on how to cleave to and trust a heavenly Spouse, not terms that had to be fulfilled before a marriage would begin. Edwards claimed that in the ancient world a god was not only an object of reverence and ritual observance but also (and "especially") an object of trust, and source of defense and salvation.

In addition, Edwards pointed out, God in the Ten Commandments proclaims that he shows mercy to thousands (in the second commandment) and orders the decalogue to be covered by the mercy seat in the wilderness tabernacle. Finally, "these ten commandments . . . were seal'd with the blood of the sacrifice, which typified the blood of [Christ]." This demonstrated that God's relationship to his people was based not on human obedience but divine mercy.

This was not demonstrated but nevertheless "insinuated to [Israel] & proposed under covert" because of Israel's spiritual immaturity. Another reason that grace was not revealed more directly was that Christ and his kingdom had not yet been revealed fully. God's hatred for sin had not been illustrated in the sufferings of the Messiah and his promises of eternal punishment for the wicked were still unclear. In the absence of these clear demonstrations Israel needed tangible and severe punishments in order to maintain "the honor of the divine greatness & majesty & the dread of his spotless holiness." This was the reason God kept his people at a distance and used graphic and brutal punishments in the Old Testament but allowed the saints of the New Testament to converse with him "most freely and intimately" (Misc. 440).

Yet this difference notwithstanding, the two covenants are actually different phases or ways of performing the same one covenant. As Edwards put it early in his career, "The gospel was preached to the Jews under a veil."[33] The process of conversion was the same for Jews in the Old Testament as for Christians in the New. They were "convinced so much of their wickedness that they trusted to nothing but the mere mercy of God." This included the antediluvians, and indeed all those who lived since "the beginning of the world." Even the rate of conver-

---

33. "Profitable Hearers of the Word," 1728–29, in SDM, 247.

sion was the same. There were wicked and godly then, and conversions were just as frequent then as in Edwards's day (Misc. 39). Christ saved the Old Testament saints just like their cohorts in the New (Misc. 1283), and they believed in Christ, but under the name of the "angel of the Lord" or "messenger of the covenant" (BC, 213). In fact, Christ appeared to Old Testament Jews; Moses saw his back parts on Mount Sinai, and he appeared in human form to the seventy elders (Exodus 24: 9–11) as well as to Joshua, Gideon, and Manoah (HWR, 197). For that matter, every time God is said to have manifested himself to humans in a voice or otherwise tangible form, it was always through the second person of the Trinity (HWR, 131).

Though the two covenants had two federal heads, Adam and Christ, and one was a "dead" way but the other "living" (Misc. 35), "in strictness of speech" they were not two but one. For they shared the same mediator (Misc. 875), the same salvation (which means the same calling, justification, adoption, sanctification, and glory), and the same medium of salvation: the incarnation, suffering, righteousness, and intercession of Christ. The Holy Spirit was the same person applying Christ's redemption in both dispensations, and the method of obtaining salvation was the same—faith and repentance. The external means (the word of God and ordinances such as prayer and praise, sabbath and sacraments) were not different. Nor were the benefits (God's Spirit by God's mere mercy and by a divine person—the angel of the Lord or Mediator) and future blessings. For both the condition was faith in the Son of God as Mediator, expressed with the same spirit of repentance and humility (Misc. 1353). This is why all parts of the Old Testament point to the future coming of Christ (HWR, 283). In sum, the religion of the church of Israel is "essentially the same religion with that of the Christian church" (HWR, 443).

Jewish Prophecies of the Messiah

By the eighteenth century Jewish prophecy had become the last vital textual link between Christianity and Judaism. Miracles and prophecy had been the two strongest pillars of support for the authority of the Bible before the seventeenth century. But Old Testament miracles had lost probative power under assaults from skepticism and rationalism, particularly in the non-Catholic world because of Protestant denunciations of Catholic appeals to miracles by their saints. William Whiston, for example, had reduced miracles to natural occurrences romanticized by imaginative primitives.[34] Toland claimed the pillar of fire in the wilderness was only an ambulatory beacon carried about by Israelite sentries.[35] Hume finally did away with miracles entirely.[36]

---

34. This and the next several paragraphs are indebted in part to Manuel, *The Broken Staff*, 181–84.
35. John Toland, "Hodegus; or the Pillar of Cloud and Fire, that guided the Israelites in the Wilderness, not Miraculous," in *Tetradymus*.
36. David Hume, "Of Miracles," in *An Inquiry Concerning Human Understanding*, 117–41.

The emphasis then shifted to Hebrew prophecy, which also came under fire. Deists like Collins denied the connection between their prophecies and the coming of the Messiah. He argued that they didn't expect a messiah till nearly the end of the Old Testament period, by which time they had come under renewed persecution—an experience which in human history frequently inspires its subjects to fantasize their deliverance. He likened the Hebrew prophets to Huguenot enthusiasts who spoke in tongues and held seances predicting the end of the world.[37]

Edwards stubbornly held on to what deists tried to pull away—the prophetic ladder from Judaism to Christianity. He insisted that the prophets, no less than their Jewish predecessors, knew of religious realities at one with those of Christians. They knew of the same "way of acceptance with God" and identical "conditions of salvation." Like stars that reflect the light of the sun, their prophecies reflect the brighter truths of the new dispensation. Albeit less clearly, they nevertheless prophesied Christ and his redemption and the glorious times of the gospel in the latter days (Misc. 874; Misc. 202; Misc. 238). Edwards refused to sever the historical link between Judaism and Christianity.

Inspiration for the Heathen

If Edwards insisted on the historical connection between the Jewish and Christian faiths, he also proposed a historical link tying Jewish revelation to heathen philosophy and religion. Theophilus Gale, Isaac Barrow, and Samuel Shuckford persuaded Edwards that the best insights of the heathen philosophers were borrowed from the Jews. From Gale he learned that Pythagoras "transferred many things out of the Jewish institutions into his own philosophy,"[38] and that Aristotle had studied with a Jew in the "maritime regions of Asia" (Misc. 953; Misc. 969). He recorded Humphrey Prideaux's claim that Zoroaster and the Persian magi derived some of their ideas from ancient Jewish patriarchs and Barrow's conjecture that the heathen learned tithing from the Jews (Misc. 969; Misc. 973). Grotius convinced him that the Roman legal system and "ancient Attick laws" were both indebted to the laws of Moses (Misc. 1012).

Heathen religion was also inspired by Jewish mythology. Edwards wrote in his Blank Bible that many heathen myths were distortions of Hebrew legends. The Phoenicians, for example, confounded the stories of Adam, Noah, and Abraham and applied them all to one deity whom they called Saturn. The same dynamic was responsible for the similarity between the biblical stories of Joshua's wars and the heathen fables of Hercules. For the same reason, the Egyptian deities Apis and Serapis were symbolic representations of the biblical Joseph.[39]

---

37. Even some Protestants, such as Pierre Jurieu, dismissed Hebrew prophecies as a link between Judaism and Christianity. Jurieu believed that the Hebrew prophecies spoke of a Jewish figure who would bring world peace, not the Messiah per se. Manuel, *The Broken Staff*, 181.

38. He recorded in his notebooks Grotius's claim that Pythagoras had lived among the Jews; Misc. 963.

39. Blank Bible, 6; see also NS, no. 402.

In the eighteenth century deists and others began to repudiate the Jewish provenance of Greco-Roman religion and philosophy, suggesting instead that Jews were responsible for whatever seemed absurd in the Old Testament, and that Egypt, Greece, and Rome had inspired all that was noble and true—in other words, the natural religion of freethinkers. Edwards refused to brook this new trend, insisting to the end that anything true in natural religion came from Jewish revelation.

Evidence for Revelation

Thomas Chubb was among the deists who denied the link between Judaism and natural religion. He also took public issue with the claim made by seventeenth-century polemicists that the survival of the Jewish people over the millennia was a miracle. In Chubb's words, the "Jews continuing a distinct and separate people, as not having been lost or swallowed up, in, and by the several nations where they have had their residence, this was the *natural* produce of their original constitution . . . [for] they were strictly required . . . not to mix themselves by marriages with the people of any other nation" (AF 163; emphasis added).

Edwards seems to have been agitated by Chubb's disclaimer, for he composed a 2500-word essay in his notebooks designed to prove that the survival and religious integrity of the Jewish nation "has been from their very beginning a standing evidence to the truth of Revealed Religion" (Misc. 1335).[40] His opening sallies seem aimed at Chubb's presumption of the Jews' isolation from their neighbors. Quite the contrary, Edwards replied. Throughout their history they were surrounded by "the grossest pagans and the worst of idolaters." Yet they preserved their religion "till this day," with its "knowledge & worship of the true God, and rational & true notions of his being, attributes & works, & his relation to mankind & our dependence upon him[, and] the worship & regards due to him" (Misc. 1335). This was a miracle.

Preservation of the truth about God was particularly miraculous when it was considered that the rest of the world had "forgotten" the true God and "forsaken" his worship. (Behind this statement was Edwards's conviction that all the ancients had received knowledge of the *prisca theologia* from Adam and Noah and their sons.) The Jews were not geographically separated from this heathen world. They had spent more than two hundred years in Egypt, "the fountain of idolatry," where they had "continual intercourse & daily concern with [idolatrous Egyptians]." Then they were exiled to Babylon, another center of heathen idolatry. After their return from Babylon, idolatrous Persians, Greeks, and Romans repeatedly "swarmed" through their land. Through all these centuries the Jews for the most part preserved their religion despite its being "infinitely diverse" and "repugnant" to their neighbors—the Egyptians, Canaanites, Philistines, Moabites, and Ammonites.

Besides, the Jews were not naturally given to sublime religious thoughts. They had no schools of philosophy like the Greeks, they were not remarkably different

---

40. If this essay was not a response to Chubb, it was at least a response to arguments identical to Chubb's.

from other nations in genius or natural abilities, and they were "a comparatively small people." Yet they had "far better, more sublime and purer notions of God and religion . . . than the best of the philosophers."

It was more surprising when one could see from Jewish history that they were "exceedingly prone" to idolatry and at times felt it was "honorable" to imitate their corruptions. So they often fell into idolatry themselves, but even here the miraculous was at work: they never completely abandoned their religion.

The preservation of the integrity of the Jewish religion despite such temptation was the first miracle. The second was the preservation of the Jewish *people* from destruction. Throughout their history they teetered on the edge of annihilation, and this went all the way back to the patriarchs. Jacob and his family were nearly destroyed by Esau, then Laban, and finally the Canaanites. Joseph was nearly killed by his brothers, and those brothers and their father almost perished by famine. The whole nation of Israel in Egypt was nearly destroyed by Pharaoh during the Exodus; only a series of the greatest miracles saved them. Then they were rescued from what appeared to be slaughter at the hands of the Amalekites, Moabites, Amorites, and Og, king of Bashan. They took possession of Canaan despite the opposition of nations "greater and stronger than they" because of another series of miracles. During the time of Judges they were saved only by the special providence of God from the Canaanites (under the leadership of Deborah and Barak), the Midianites (because of Gideon's faith), and the Philistines. In their later history they were threatened by Moab, Edom, Ammon, Assyria, Babylon, Haman, and then Antiochus.

Their geographical location invited attack from all sides. Israel was in the middle of three continents, on the road connecting Asia and Africa, and between Egypt and the great eastern and northern kingdoms. Edwards thought it extraordinary that all the nations near Israel were destroyed (Midian, Moab, the seven nations of Canaan, Philistia) while Israel alone survived.

The Roman era was no different. In Titus's time the "greatest part" of the Jews was destroyed, and the rest were dispersed all over the world. Under Trajan and Hadrian in the Jewish wars one thousand cities and fortresses were destroyed, and more than 580,000 men were slaughtered.

Since that disaster the Jews have lived "in total dispersion over all the world, mixt everywhere with other peoples, without anything like government or civil community of their own, & often extremely harassed by other nations." But they survived, and with their religious culture intact: in "clear & perfect distinction still, from all other people." This was the second miracle.

In an early notebook entry Edwards had written that circumcision was evidence of the divine origin of the Jewish identity, for no religion of human origin would ever invent a rite that so wounded pride and diminished lasciviousness (*Misc.* 311). But in this long essay written near the end of his career Edwards reflected in less trivial fashion on the astonishing survival of both the Jewish people and their remarkable religion. For Edwards there was no "Jewish problem" that suggested Gentiles should preside over their disposal. Instead the Jews challenged the world by their faith and very existence to consider their claims to divine revelation.

Under God's Judgment

If Edwards distanced himself from the freethinkers of his century by defending the divine character of Judaism, he joined the legions of Christians who for centuries had criticized Jews for failing to accept Jesus as their messiah. Even liberal Christians in the eighteenth century remarked that the Jews were still suffering punishment for their rejection of Jesus long ago.[41]

Edwards rang the changes on this theme. He began with the insistence that Judaism was meant to dissolve in the face of its successor Christianity. The destruction of the temple in A.D. 70 and the resulting diaspora made it "impracticable" for Judaism to continue as a religion distinct from its Christian offshoot. After all, it was a religion for "a single nation" and not the world (Misc. 443). Its ceremonial law was burdensome and too peculiar for Gentiles to follow. Christ's resurrection made it clear that this law had been abolished (HWR, 362); Christians were now free to ignore parts of the Old Testament that had no relation to God's beauty (Misc. 79).

If the Jews held on to their old religion, they were unreasonable. God had clearly revealed himself to the world through their religion, but now that further revelation had come in Christ, the Judaism that rejected Christ was missing the "essence of religion." By rejecting this great revelation in the new covenant of Christ, it failed to "state the highest end & happiness [of man], his chief business, and his greatest misery, and the pure worship of God, right" (Misc. 129). This was a sin against reason, which showed that the Christian religion is "rational."[42]

It was also a sin of the heart. Edwards made what had become a routine charge that Jews in the Christian era were proud and hard-hearted. In a very early sermon he accused the Jews of having a "national pride" that refused to acknowledge their own sin and claims "even to this day . . . a natural right of being masters of the whole world, and expect[s] actually to be made such when their master comes."[43] Religiously, their pride resulted from trying to establish their own righteousness before God by works of the law instead of submitting to the righteousness that comes by faith.[44] In his 1739 sermons on the work of redemption he complained that Jews have been "obstinate" for 1700 years because a thick veil has blinded their eyes. Their hearts are hard (HWR, 469). Near the end of his career in *Original Sin* he repeats the charge. Jews in Paul's day, he wrote, boasted of their law as if possession of it made them a holy people and God's children. In the abstract they accepted the doctrine of original sin but in fact did not believe that it applied to themselves. They were prejudiced against the doctrine of universal sinfulness and the notion that humans are under God's wrath because of their sinful nature (OS, 337, 335). In his notebook on the types of the Messiah, he catalogued what he took to be Jewish sins:

---

41. Arthur A. Chiel, "Ezra Stiles and the Jews," in Goldman, *Hebrew and the Bible in America*, 156–67, esp. 158–59.
42. "The doctrines of Christianity are in themselves most rational, exceeding congruous to man's natural reason." "True Nobleness of Mind," 1727, in SDM, 231–32.
43. "Wicked Men's Slavery to Sin," in SDK, 340.
44. "None Are Saved By Their Own Righteousness," in SDM, 347.

According to the prophecies, the sins for which that people should be rejected from being God's people, and so given over to blindness of mind and hardness of heart, and at last so terribly destroyed, would be their unbelief, pride, self-righteousness, exalting themselves as better than others, their notorious hypocrisy and superstition, teaching for doctrines the commandments of men, and their perverseness and obstinacy in these things, attended with a persecuting spirit and practices.[45]

But the cardinal Jewish sin was denial of Jesus' messianic identity. Hence the Jewish people now constituted a "visible monument of [God's] displeasure, for their rejection and crucifying the Messiah" (AW, 135). What's more, they persecuted Christians and so had become enemies of Christ.[46]

Because of these sins God had "cast off" the Jews from being his "visible people."[47] Since most of them rejected Christ "with extreme pertinaciousness of spirit," divine wrath broke out upon them with greater ferocity "than in the days of Nebuchadnezzar." This was why Jerusalem was destroyed by the Romans, and Jews were dispersed throughout the world "in the most abject and forlorn circumstances" (OS, 182). They had been under a "curse" for the seventeen hundred years since, in what had become "the worst judgment on any people ever" (HWR, 382–83).

Now they were no longer a seed of Abraham, "no more than Ishmaelites or Edomites." Edwards believed that their rare conversions to Christianity and continued refusals to accept Christ were two clear signs that "the Spirit of God left them and their day of grace was past."[48]

Future Christians

But there was to be a second day of grace. God would not reject them forever. God had abandoned them because their idolatry had moved him to jealousy, and now he was moving them to jealousy by casting them off and taking another people for himself (HWR, 189). Just before the millennium commenced, God would remove the veil over their eyes and soften their hearts with grace. All Israel shall be saved. "Nothing is more certainly foretold than this national conversion of the Jews in the eleventh chapter of Romans" (HWR, 469).

Edwards was not innovative on this score. Increase Mather and Joseph Mede had both predicted that Israel would be restored, politically and spiritually, before the millennium would begin.[49] Cotton Mather spent his life yearning for the conversion of the Jews.[50] But Edwards seemed as energized as any. He made entries

---

45. TM, 322n.
46. Jewish persecution of Christians is a recurring theme in HWR, 352, 353, 372, 381–82, 384, 386, 388, 444, 448.
47. Pressing into the Kingdom," in Hickman, 1:661; HWR, 383.
48. HWR, 383; "Living Unconverted under an Eminent Means of Grace," in SDM, 369.
49. Manuel, The Broken Staff, 160–61.
50. Goldman, Hebrew and the Bible in America, xvii.

into his notebooks of articles in the press reporting conversions of Jews. In 1748, for example, he noted that a Jew was baptized in London, a German Christian had led six hundred Jews to the Christian faith, and fifty-three Polish Jews and one rabbi had converted in Germany.[51] He calculated the timing of this national conversion; it would be before the wholesale conversion of the heathen, and after the "first main" destruction of the Antichrist (*AW*, 140, 195–96).

Edwards also determined that the Jews would return to their homeland. This was inevitable, he reasoned, because the prophecies of land being given to them had been only partly fulfilled. It was also necessary in order for God to make them a "visible monument" of his grace and power at their conversion. At that moment religion and learning would be at their respective peaks, and Canaan once again would be a spiritual center of the world. Although Israel would again be a distinct nation, Christians would have free access to Jerusalem because Jews would look on Christians as their brethren (Blank Bible, 806; *AW*, 135).

Arrogance among Siblings

According to Arthur Hertzberg, this American linkage of Jewish conversion to the millennium was why "American intellectual anti-Semitism never became as virulent as its counterparts in Europe."[52] Christians in Europe believed the End was in the indefinite future. But in America the End seemed near, and Jews were needed here and now to help usher in the return of Christ. So in the colonies the Jewish question moved "to center stage."[53]

If Edwards was among those Americans who did not evidence an anti-Semitism as virulent as some European strains, he was nonetheless not particularly friendly to the Judaism of his day. He could never accept it on its own terms but always demanded that it be swallowed up by the religion to which it had given birth. He judged Jews to be proud, assuming that their reluctance to convert was obstinate rejection of the obvious.

Yet Edwards declined the invitation of the intellectual elites to minimize Christianity's debt to Judaism. If Christianity was the logical end of Judaism, its meaning could be found only through Judaism. The antitype was to be fully understood only by reference to its types. Hence tension in the the Jewish-Christian relationship was a family quarrel. Edwards may have exercised hubris by claiming that his Jewish brothers and sisters were less favored by their common Father, and indeed had been disowned. But he knew they would someday be reconciled to their divine Parent and regain their status as children in full favor.

---

51. "Events of a Hopeful Aspect on the State of Religion," in *AW*, 287, 292–93, 295–96.
52. Hertzberg, "The New England Puritans and the Jews," 116.
53. Ibid. This question is not settled, however. As Avihu Zakai has recently pointed out, many English thinkers in the sixteenth and seventeenth centuries also taught an imminent millennium, and there is no clear indication that such belief reduced anti-Semitism. See Zakai, "Poetics of History," and Felsenstein, *Anti-Semitic Stereotypes*.

9

ISLAM

The Left Arm of Antichrist

Toward the end of his life Jonathan Edwards launched a series of diatribes against Islam. This was not the first time, of course, that a Christian thinker had regarded Muslims with dismay. Edwards was continuing a long tradition of anti-Islamic sentiment that combined fear and loathing with curious fascination. Yet Edwards's hostility toward Islam evinced a new fervor and a new motive. His denunciations of the followers of Muhammad were unusually vitriolic because he considered Islam to be a foil for Reformed Christianity's most dangerous enemy: deism.

Aggravated Condemnation

In some respects, Edwards regarded Islam with a certain ambivalence. While he seemed to feel visceral hostility toward everything Islamic, he also wrote that Muslims are less blameworthy than wayward Protestants because the latter were brought up with greater light about Christ and true faith.[1] Since God's judgment of Muslims will be "proportioned to their light," their condemnation will be less severe than that of those who knew more.[2] Edwards also believed that Muslims have far more light about Christ than many "heathen" thinkers whom he roundly praised. The Qur'an, Edwards seemed happy to note, accurately portrays Jesus as a great prophet and messenger of God who was born of a virgin and without sin,

---

1. HWR, 489–90; MNB, 250.
2. "On the Medium of Moral Government," in Hickman, 2:488.

healed the blind, and raised the dead. "The Alcoran" even recognizes Jesus as the Messiah "foretold in the law and the prophets." "Now, owning this," Edwards claimed, "is in effect owning the whole. This is the foundation of the whole, and proves all the rest."[3]

Yet, in typically Reformed fashion,[4] Edwards believed that the light given to Muhammad and Muslims only aggravated their condemnation. For they had shamelessly ignored or abused this light. Hence they deserved only contempt. Islam, he snarled, had a tendency "to debase, debauch, and corrupt the minds of such as received it." Muslims were "an ignorant and barbarous sort of people." The propagation of Islam showed "the extreme darkness, blindness, weakness, childishness, folly and madness of mankind in matters of religion . . . [and] how helpless mankind are, under ignorance and delusion in matters of religion." The Islamic faith contained things that "are too childish and ridiculous to be publicly mentioned in solemn assembly."[5]

The "heathen" philosophers, on the other hand, were given less light about the true God but taught it more faithfully. Despite conceding that they did not love God and were full of pride, Edwards fairly gushed with admiration for the religious truth they shared with Christians. Plato, he wrote, delivered "very noble and almost divine truths concerning the nature and attributes of the supreme God." Cicero was "the greatest and best philosopher that Rome or perhaps any other nation ever produced." Epictetus was an "admirable moralist." For a true sense of virtue, he had "no superior in the heathen world." Confucius knew by divine light that the heavens are not self-existent, and Lao-zi that God is eternal and cannot be comprehended. Edwards believed that the Chinese knew of a Christ who would suffer and die to save the world.[6] Yet even they did not know, as Muhammad did, that *Jesus* was the Christ.

Regression, Sensuality, and "Pretences"

Edwards took up Islam's remarkable world-wide expansion in a section of his private notebooks (the *Miscellanies*) that was probably written after 1747—that is, in the last decade of his life. In one essay he attempted to rebut the charge that "the propagation of Mahometanism" was "parallel with the propagation of Chris-

---

3. "Mahometanism compared with Christianity—particularly with respect to their propagation," in Hickman, 2:493; hereafter referred to as "Mahometanism." These quotations are taken from a slightly edited transcription of a 2,500-word discussion of Islam in *Misc.* 1334. See note 8.

Most scholars of Islam would hold that affirming Jesus as the Messiah does not "prove all the rest." For Muhammad did not mean by "messiah" what Edwards did. Besides denying both the crucifixion and resurrection, Muhammad denied that any third party, even a messiah, could save anyone from his or her sin; Qur'an 82.17–19; 40.18–20; 4.157–159; 4.158–59. The Qur'an teaches that Jesus was "raised up" to Allah. A common Muslim interpretation is that he never died a human death but was translated to Paradise, like Enoch; Qur'an 3.55–58; 4.157–59.

4. See for example, Calvin, *Institutes*, bk. 1, chap. 4.
5. "Mahometanism," in Hickman, 2:492, 493; MNB, 249.
6. *Misc.* 979; *Misc.* 1162; *Misc.* 1181; *Misc.* 1236.

tianity."[7] More than half of his data are taken, both directly and indirectly, from Johann Friedrich Stapfer, the German Reformed scholastic whose five-volume *Institutiones theologiae polemicae* (1743–47) served as one of his principal sources of knowledge about Islam. Edwards picked and chose from Stapfer to suit his own polemical purposes.[8] But while the form of his argument was somewhat creative, its content was conventional. Edwards was advancing nothing that contemporary orthodox controversialists had not already proposed.[9]

Edwards's first line of argument was that Islam represented intellectual regression and the suppression of free thought. Whereas Christianity advanced knowledge, Islam retarded it. Any increase of knowledge brought by Islam was "borrowed" from Christianity. Christianity was propagated in Jerusalem, "one of the greatest and most public cities in the world," among the Greeks and Romans, "the most knowing and learned in the world." The gospel encouraged "reasoning and inquiry." In contrast, Islam was developed in Arabia, "a dark corner of the earth" peopled by "an ignorant and barbarous sort." Their religion was promoted by "forbidding inquiry . . . [and] discouraging knowledge and learning."[10]

Second, Muhammad won followers because of the enticement of sensual rewards. While Christianity taught self-denial, Islam gratified human sensuality. Early Christianity did battle with ancient mores, but Islam simply accommodated itself to seventh-century cultural sensibilities. It encouraged the worst of human de-

---

7. The differences between Edwards's original *Miscellanies* entry and its transcription in nineteenth-century editions of his *Works* are largely stylistic. When the nineteenth-century editor thought Edwards's language too coarse, he substituted a new word or eliminated Edwards's word: e.g., "promulgated" was substituted for "sounded out," "existed" for "was," and "blinding the eyes" for "hoodwinking mankind and blinding the eyes." Only one section, of approximately three-hundred words, is omitted from Edwards's notebook. It does not contain anything substantially different from the printed text but it amplifies and dramatizes Edwards's conviction that Islam opposes critical inquiry and was propagated by the sword. In the omitted section, for instance, Edwards quotes Stapfer: "Omnes enim infideles, qui religionem illam non amplecterentur interficere jubet Mahamet" [For Mohammed ordered the destruction of all those who did not embrace that religion]. The result is that Edwards's printed comments on Islam are less vitriolic than what he actually wrote in his private notebooks. All quotations from this section are identical to Edwards's original words.

8. Stapfer's section on Islam is fifty-two pages, approximately 16,000 words. In contrast, Edwards's discussion in no. 1334 of the *Miscellanies* takes up about 3,000 words. But while Stapfer treats many aspects of Islamic belief and history, no. 1334 focuses exclusively on Islam's propagation.

9. Many of the authors whom Edwards included in his "Reading Catalogue" were hostile to Islam: Philip Skelton, *Deism Revealed* (1749); James Miller, *Mahomet the Imposter. A Tragedy* (1744); Robert Millar, *History of the Propagation of Christianity* (1731); Daniel Defoe, *Dictionarium Sacrum or a Dictionary of All Religions* (1704); Thomas Broughton, *Bibliotheca Historico-Sacra* (1737–39), reissued as *An Historical Dictionary of All Religions* (1742); George Sale's translation of and preface to *The Koran* (1734); and the above-mentioned Stapfer theology. See "Jonathan Edwards' Reading 'Catalogue.'" We don't know if he read all of these works, but his arguments are very similar to theirs.

10. "Mahometanism," in Hickman, 2:492. In NS, no. 241, he writes, "The Arabs were above all nations a wild People and have been so through all ages . . . [with] fierce qualities . . . [they] have ever lived in professed Enmity with all mankind . . . and they have continued in a state of perpetual Hostility with the Rest of their Brethren." He goes on to note that no one has been able to subdue them—neither the Romans nor the Parthians, nor any of their successors.

sires by permitting divorce on demand, blood revenge, and polygamy.[11] (This was several decades before Edward Gibbon's observation that in comparison to Solomon's appetite for wives, Muhammad was commendably modest!)[12]

Third, because it appealed to base human desires, Islam never encountered much opposition. Christianity, on the other hand, contended against the "strongest empire ever." But while the gospel triumphed by the power of meekness, Islam won conversions only by the power of the sword.[13]

Edwards's last line of argument was an appeal to the standard orthodox assumption (at least until the middle of the eighteenth century) that miracles were the best authentication of revelation.[14] He wrote that "Christianity is built on certain great and wonderful visible facts" such as Christ's resurrection and other miracles, but Islam has "no facts for its proof and foundation, . . . only Mahomet's pretences to intercourse with heaven, and his success in rapine, murder, and violence." While Christ's miracles were performed publicly and attested to by people writing near the time and places of those miracles, Muhammad's miracles were private and lacked "public attestations of heaven."[15]

Islam in Eschatology

Other religious leaders of the eighteenth century also showed considerable interest in Islam.[16] In part, this interest was the continuation of a long tradition in Christian apologetics, beginning with Thomas Aquinas's *Summa Contra Gentiles* (1259–64), a manual for Christian missionaries in Spain. It was also stimulated by traders' contacts with Muslims at Constantinople and in Hungary, the Turkish empire, Syria, Persia, and the East Indies. War had also played a role: in 1453 Constantinople fell to the (Muslim) Turks, and in 1683 Turkish forces were defeated outside Vienna. And there had been a general growth of interest in foreign cultures, particularly the mysterious and exotic East.

But why did leaders such as Edwards show such hostility to Islam?[17] There was little or no fear of Muslim military power, or of conversions in the West to Islam.

---

11. Ibid.
12. Gibbon, *Decline and Fall*, 3:116.
13. "Mahometanism," in Hickman, 2:492.
14. John Locke, "A Discourse of Miracles," in *The Works of John Locke*, 4:226–27. See Pailin, *Attitudes to Other Religions*, 86.
15. "Mahometanism," in Hickman, 2:492–93. The notion that Muhammad was an imposter was common to Christian attacks on Islam and was spread most widely by Humphrey Prideaux's *True Nature of Imposture*.
16. See, for instance, Wesley, sermon 68, "The General Spread of the Gospel," in *Works*, vol. 9; and more generally, Pailin, *Attitudes to Other Religions*.
17. Wesley, for instance, found "all the principles of pure religion" in a story written by a Muslim, but determined Muslims themselves to be "as void of mercy as lions and tygers, as much given up to brutal lusts as bulls or goats; so that they are in truth a disgrace to human nature." George Sale, a London lawyer who translated the Qur'an in 1734, said that Muhammad gave the Arabs the best religion that was possible in the circumstances—monotheism to replace idolatry and some moral

There was the historical memory of the Crusades, but this seemed to play little or no role in Edwards's thinking.[18] What *did* figure in Edwards's thinking, however, was eschatology. Edwards believed that Islam was one of the devil's two world-historical forces stalking the earth in the latter days. It was one of the two great works fashioned by the devil in the Middle Ages (the other, of course, was the Roman papacy) that had become, since that time, twin Antichrists. Catholicism had taken over the Western empire, while Islam had swallowed up the Eastern empire. The first is the kingdom of the "beast" and the second is the kingdom of the "false prophet," both described in John's Revelation. "Heathenism" is the kingdom of the "dragon," a third demonic power in Revelation. This false trinity will work in concert near the end of the world to destroy the truth but will finally be vanquished at the battle of Armageddon (HWR, 410–11, 463).[19]

In the meantime one could scan secular history with Bible in hand to plot the course of the eschaton. Edwards did just that, of course, and recorded his copious observations in his notebooks. There he wrote that the Turks, who "have been the most terrible scourge to Christendom, that ever divine providence made use of" were the 200 million mounted troops who, according to John, were released to kill a third of humankind by three plagues of fire, smoke, and sulfur (HWR, 415f.; AW, 407). At the very beginning of that same chapter in Revelation Edwards found Muhammad himself. He was the star that fell to the earth (for Edwards, this described Muhammad's fall from Christianity) in verse 1 and released locusts which sting like scorpions. Those stung, writes John, would seek death but not find it (AW, 103).

For Edwards, it was clear that Muhammad and Islam were the referents of this passage. After all, it was a wind that blew from Arabia to bring locusts to Egypt, so Arabia was obviously the country of locusts. The poison in the tail of the locusts was therefore Islam, because Muhammad's religion would kill the soul. The tormenting pain was the pain of the afflicted conscience being tempted to convert to Islam. Seeking death, then, was wishing to be convinced of the truth of Islam so that the painful cries of the conscience would no longer be heard (AW, 103).

If that interpretation seems tortured, Jonathan Edwards was simply the latest in a long line of Western interpreters to be so pained. As early as the ninth century two Spaniards, one a priest and the other a layman (Eulogius and Paul Alvarus), devel-

---

and divine virtues "not unworthy even a Christian's perusal." But he also said that its conquests by the power of the sword provide "one of the most convincing proofs that Mohammedism [sic] was no other than a human invention." Wesley, sermon 68, "The General Spread of the Gospel," in *Works*, 9:234; see Pailin, *Attitudes to Other Religions*, 48, and Sale, "Preliminary Discourse," in *The Koran*, 45, 77, 35.

18. Edwards by and large ignored the Crusades. Of the twenty-five or so discussions of Islam that I have found in his published writings and *Miscellanies*, only two have any reference to the Crusades. One is unclear; the other, an explicit reference to the Crusades, does not mention Islam but criticizes the papacy. Hickman, 1:471; AW, 237–38. In Edwards's reviews of redemption history in both his *History of the Work of Redemption* and *Apocalyptic Writings*, there is no mention of the Crusades.

19. For surveys of Edwards's eschatology, see Stein, "Introduction" to AW, and McDermott, *One Holy and Happy Society*, 37–92.

oped the idea that the rule of Islam was a preparation for the final appearance of the Antichrist. In the eleventh century, Abbot Joachim of Fiore proclaimed that the end of the world was at hand and the Antichrist's chief instruments were the Saracens. Martin Luther also believed the end was at hand, but was perhaps even more pessimistic about Islam. It was Gog (the papacy was Magog), Muhammad was the little horn in Daniel's vision (7.8), and the expansion of Islam was the little horn's crowding of the other horns. Christendom, Luther despaired, would probably be engulfed by Islam. Interestingly, although Calvin judged Muhammad to be an apostate, he refused to speculate about the eschatological significance of Islam. But then Revelation was one of the few books on which Calvin never wrote a commentary and the only book on which Edwards did![20]

Edwards's eschatological vision of Islam differed in two respects from that of most of his predecessors. First, he did not believe the end of the world was imminent. Instead, he foresaw two-and-a-half centuries of conflict and revival to come before the millennium.[21] Intriguingly, he predicted that the two most formidable religious forces still on the scene in the twentieth century would be Roman Catholicism and Islam[22]—not far from the truth.

Second, as I have argued elsewhere, eschatology was more important to Edwards than to most Reformed thinkers. Though not the center of his theology, it was consistently prominent in, and even essential to, much of his thought.[23] Therefore his designation of Islam as the Antichrist of the East means that "Mohametanism" played a larger role in the history of redemption for Edwards than for others in his tradition.

The Deist Stick

Islam's role in eschatological history, however, does not fully explain Edwards's hostility. After all, other Christian thinkers had known this eschatological tradition but nevertheless regarded Islam with considerable favor. Pope Gregory VII, for example, speculated that because of their obedience to the Qur'an, Muslims might have eternal salvation in the bosom of Abraham.[24] Dante placed Avicenna, Averroës, and Saladin in limbo as the only moderns among the sages and heroes of antiquity.[25] William of Tripoli said that Muslims were not far from salvation.[26]

---

20. Southern, *Western Views of Islam*, 22–26, 40–42; George Huntston Williams, "Erasmus and the Reformers on Non-Christian Religions and *Salus Extra Ecclesiam*," in Rabb and Seigel, *Action and Conviction*, 344; Southern, *Western Views of Islam*, 105; Williams, "Erasmus and the Reformers," 361.
21. McDermott, *One Holy and Happy Society*, 50–60, 77–90.
22. Ibid., 82. Edwards believed that evangelical Protestantism would also be on the scene, struggling with these two religions.
23. Ibid., 41–50, 90–92.
24. Letter (ca. 1076) to the Moorish ruler al-Nasir ibn Alennas, in Migne, *Patrologia Latina*, 148, cols. 450ff.; cited in *The Declaration on Non-Christian Religions*, in Abbott, *The Documents of Vatican II*, 663 n. 14.
25. *Hell (L'Inferno)*, in *The Comedy of Dante Alghieri*, trans. Dorothy L. Sayers (Baltimore: Penguin, 1949), iv, 129, 143–44.
26. William of Tripoli, *Tractatus de Statu Saracenorum*, cited in Southern, *Western Views of Islam*, 62.

For John Wycliffe, the church was full of the same vices as Islam, but to a greater degree. Muslims could be saved if at the moment of death they "believe in the Lord Jesus Christ."[27] Some of the Radical Reformers saw Muslims as members of an interfaith church of spiritual Semites with three covenants—Judaic, Christian, and Muslim. Andreas Carlstadt, for example, allowed some Muslims into his purgatory.[28] And seventeenth-century Reformed divine Richard Baxter was willing to grant salvation to those (outside the "Jewish church") who did not have "knowledge of Christ incarnate." In the case of Islam, however, Edwards was not so willing.[29]

What made Edwards unwilling were the deists, who were using Islam as a stick to shake at their orthodox opponents. Thomas Chubb, for instance, argued that "the great prevalence of *Mahometanism*" was not due primarily to the sword, but that the sword may have assisted its later growth. Then, in a move that perturbed his orthodox readers and may have incited Edwards's criticism of Islam's propagation, Chubb alleged that Christianity's propagation was no different.[30] Matthew Tindal celebrated the "*Moammarites*, a famous sect among the *Mahometans*,"[31] who knew that reason is the only reliable tool for interpreting the metaphors and allegories of the Qur'an. If other Muslims ignored the Law of Nature (given to humans by reason alone) in blind submission to the words of the Qur'an, Tindal went on, they were no worse than Christians who made the same mistake. John Toland concluded that Muslims were really "a sort or sect of Christians" and closer to the original gospel than the historical church. An anonymous author in a 1745 issue of *The American Magazine* wrote that Christians' treatment of other religionists was no better than that of Muslims. Christianity had "prov'd as brutal, bloody and inhuman as Mohametanism."[32] By the last decades of the century, it had become a characteristic deist move to quote Islamic sources or praise Islam in contradistinction to Christianity.[33]

---

27. Southern, *Western Views of Islam*, 80–82; Wycliffe, *De Fide Catholica* (*Opera Minora*), 112, cited in Southern, *Western Views of Islam*, 82.

28. Williams, "Erasmus and the Reformers," 363–65.

29. Baxter, *The Reasons of the Christian Religion*, 201–2; see also Rooy, *Theology of Missions*, 89.

30. The notion that the propagation of Islam and Christianity were very similar was fairly common in the eighteenth century. William Paley, for example, pronounced that the success of Islam is "the only event" in the history of humanity that bears comparison with the spread of Christianity. Thomas Stackhouse added that "of all false Religions, the *Mahometan* came nearest to the *Christian* in the swift Manner of its Propagation; for in a small Time it over-ran a great Part of the *eastern* World." According to William Robertson, "There is nothing similar in the history of mankind" to the rapidity of Islam's spread. It was probably because of the prevalence of this claim that Edwards tried to refute it. Paley, *Evidences of Christianity*, 341; Stackhouse, *Compleat Body of Divinity*, 720; Robertson, *Historical Disquisitions of India*, 92; both Stackhouse and Robertson cited in Pailin, *Attitudes to Other Religions*, 100.

31. The Moammarites were probably Mu'tazilites, since Mu'ammar was the oldest of the four principal founders of the Mu'tazili school. Watt, *Islamic Philosophy and Theology*, 59, 69.

32. Chubb, *Posthumous Works*, 2:48; *CAO*, 202–3; John Toland, *Nazarenus: or Jewish, Gentile and Mahometan Christianity* (1718), 4; "Eusebius," "The Unreasonableness of Persecution," *The American Magazine* (June 1745), 256.

33. Morais, *Deism in Eighteenth-Century America*, 144. In 1771 Ezra Stiles met Theophilus Cossart, a German printer who had lived in Cairo, who appeared "to be a Freethinker & Philosopher" and thought "the morals of the Mahometans superior to those of the Christians in general" (Dexter, *The Literary Diary of Ezra Stiles*, 1:179–80).

If the intellectual atmosphere of the eighteenth century is evidence that Edwards may have had deism in the back of his mind when he was writing about Islam, his actual arguments against Islam contain compelling internal evidence that his thinking about—and therefore hostility toward—Islam was shaped in large part by deistic challenges to Protestant orthodoxy. In a long series of intricate arguments against deism in his *Miscellanies*, Edwards makes two principal arguments. For each argument he uses Islam as a star witness to substantiate his claims.

As we have seen, the deists were claiming the capability of human reason alone to discover the truths of natural religion, which are sufficient for salvation. Therefore, they said, revelation is not needed to guide humans to virtue in this life and happiness in the next. The first argument Edwards used to counter these claims was the assertion that pagan religion was derived from revelation—via the *prisca theologia*.

For Edwards, Islam was a perfect illustration of this pattern. It was only because of the revelation provided by Christianity that the Islamic world condemned polytheism, and all the truth found in Islam was taken directly from Christianity. Whatever light the pre-Islamic Arabian tribes had was derived from "the glimmerings of the gospel which had been diffused over great part of the world." Islam itself had no truth of its own; hence the propagation of Islam may be considered a part of the propagation of Christianity. Therefore, Edwards concludes, "the great propagation of the Mahometan religion," far from being evidence of natural religion, "is confirmation of revealed religion."[34] Edwards thereby turned the deists' appropriation of Islam upside down to prove that deist claims could not stand.

The second argument Edwards used to rebut deist claims was that nature and reason can never produce true religion. Edwards charged that reason is unreliable in matters of religion. The philosophers searched for clear knowledge of God for thousands of years, but in vain. Their search was relatively fruitless because unassisted reason will lead only to absurd notions. Many great philosophers, for example, have concluded that the world is eternal. This absurd conclusion is evidence that it is almost impossible for naked reason to prove a creation. Even Cicero, the "greatest and best philosopher," said good and evil persons have the same destiny in the next life. If he was so wrong, Edwards asked, what about the rest of humanity who are far less intelligent than he?[35]

But even if natural reason were somehow able to penetrate the divine mysteries, it would be overwhelmed by the human "inclination to delusion in things of religion" (MNB, 250). Human nature is such that it tends to pervert what little religious truth it is given and turn it into idolatry. As evidence for this claim, Edwards pointed to American Indians, Tartars, and Chinese peasants who still worshiped "stocks and stones and devils"[36] despite trying to perfect their religions for five thou-

---

34. "Observations on the Facts and Evidences of Christianity," in Hickman 2: 464; *Misc.* 1334.
35. "Observations on the Facts and Evidences," 461; "Observations on the Scriptures," in Hickman 2: 475, 476, 478; *Misc.* 979.
36. "Observations on the Scriptures," 476. This was an idiomatic expression common in the eighteenth century; Edwards may have derived this argument from Skelton's *Deism Revealed* (p. 76), to which he referred repeatedly in his *Miscellanies*.

sand years. There is no innate sense of God, at least "clear and sure knowledge of his nature and relation to us." Nature may be able to teach us how to continue in favor with God, but not how to regain it after we have lost it.[37]

Edwards argued that history had demonstrated this tendency of human nature to turn revelation into idolatry. This happened after the Flood, and after revelations had been given to Abraham and Isaac, Melchizedek, Job, Jacob and Joseph, and Moses. It also happened after the apostolic era. And the cardinal example in church history was Islam. The Islamic part of the world had been given revelation through the Christian church and had accepted it to such a degree that it became largely Christian. After Muhammad, however, this region turned to the idolatry of Islam. In Edwards's words, it "fell away to Mohametanism" (MNB, 249). Once more, then, Islam was used by Edwards as a principal illustration for his most important arguments against the deists.

Apologetics and Distortions

Jonathan Edwards's hostility to Islam, fired by his struggle against deism, demonstrates that his view of significant religious others was shaped in large part by internal apologetic demands. That Islam deserved appreciation as a living faith seemed to be beyond his ken. He looked at Islam through the eyes of a determined apologist for strict Reformed doctrine and New Light experience in a culture that was making enlightened reasonableness the criterion of faith.

Edwards's treatment of Islam also suggests the remarkable degree to which Western knowledge of Islam since the eighteenth century has been distorted. Edwards slavishly followed his sources, who were seventeenth- and eighteenth-century controversialists. Their reports contain an astonishing number of inaccuracies and distortions. For example, their term for Islam—Mahometanism—reflected the mistaken belief of some in that era that Muslims worshiped Muhammad. They tiresomely repeated the misleading charge that most or all Muslim conversions occurred at the point of a sword.[38] They ignored the distinguished tradition of Islamic learning that sometimes encouraged rational inquiry,[39] and the fact that Jews and Christians have often been treated tolerantly and respectfully by Muslims, perhaps more so than could be said of non-Christians in predominantly Christian lands over the same centuries or even of minority Christian bodies that lived independently of Rome.[40] Edwards's sources never mentioned that most

---

37. "On the Medium of Moral Government," in Hickman, 2:491.
38. Islamicist Frederick M. Denny writes, "Throughout the Near East and North Africa, conversion was generally a voluntary affair, but at times non-Muslims suffered persecution, discrimination and other indignities" (*Islam and the Muslim Community*). See also Daniel, *Islam and the West*; B. P. Smith, *Islam in English Literature*; Donner, *Early Islamic Conquests*; Shaban, *Islamic History*; and Hourani, *History of the Arab Peoples*.
39. See Watt, *Formative Period of Islamic Thought*.
40. One thinks, for example, of Rome's persecution of the Patari, Humiliati, Waldensians, Albigenses, and Huguenots. On Muslim treatment of other religions, see Denny, *An Introduction to*

Muslims were not polygamists, and that in Muslim folklore lustful looking at another person is equivalent to fornication in precisely the same sense Jesus intended in the Sermon on the Mount.[41]

They never mention that Muslim restrictions on polygamy were not simply indulgences to Arab passion, but also restrictions on the loose and unregulated practices of the Jahiliya period in Arabia. Nor do they recognize that divorce was said by Muhammad to be the most detestable of permitted things, or that the Qur'an counsels immediate arbitration between spouses when there is danger of a split. Muslim laws on marriage and divorce cannot be rightly considered mere accommodation to Arab sensuality.[42]

Islam was not the only cultural other concerning which Edwards was misled. He also relied uncritically on his sources for much of his knowledge of Greco-Roman culture, and for that reason came to some inaccurate conclusions. But his attitude toward Greece and Rome was considerably more positive.

Islam, 125–29; Lavtzion, *Conversion to Islam*; and Bell, *Origin of Islam*, 185–86. A new minority report, however, is being written by Bat Ye'or, who argues that the actual condition of the dhimmi—indigenous Jews, Christians, and other non-Muslims under Islamic law as a result of conquest—was one of fundamental subjection that permitted only the private exercise of religion. See her *Decline of Eastern Christianity under Islam: From Jihad to Dhimmitude* (Madison, N.J., 1997).

41. Denny, *Introduction to Islam*, 302.
42. Ibid., 303, 305; Qur'an 4.35.

10

GREECE AND ROME

Very Noble and Almost Divine Truths

In the seventeenth- and eighteenth-century polemics waged over the origin of true religion, Greece and Rome were weapons of choice. Both orthodox and deists used the classical writings of the Greeks and Romans to defend their positions and to attack their adversaries' accounts of how the ancients came to know God. The classics were ubiquitous in the literate society of the period. Original language editions and competent translations were widely available for the works of Plato, Aristotle, Plutarch, Tacitus, and Cicero. All of these writers had written about religion, both its nature and origin, and they were used by most of those who joined the modern debate.[1]

The Orthodox: The Superiority of Hebrew Culture

For centuries the Christian church had dismissed Greek and Roman religion as largely inspired by demons, while at the same time drawing upon Greek philosophy not only to confirm but also to construct Christian theology. Augustine, for example, regarded Neoplatonism as capable of serving as a preparation for Christianity, while Aquinas's theology was based partly on Aristotelian metaphysics. In

---

1. Champion, *The Pillars of Priestcraft Shaken*, 182. For example, *Cato's Letters*, a popular series of political tracts written by deists John Trenchard and Thomas Gordon from 1720 to 1723, frequently alluded to classical texts. Francis Hutcheson, the Scottish moral philosopher who influenced Edwards, was chiefly inspired by Cicero; M. A. Stewart, "Rational Dissent in Early Eighteenth-Century Ireland," in Haakonssen, *Enlightenment and Religion*, 45.

the seventeenth and eighteenth centuries, however, as more Western Christians began to consider non-Christian religions and their relationship to Christianity, influential orthodox writers tried to prove that all religions—including those of Greece and Rome—had their source in Hebrew revelation. Gerhard Van Voss (1577–1649) and Samuel Bochart (1559–1667) made titanic efforts in the seventeenth century, for instance, to trace the migrations of the gods from one part of the Mediterranean to the other.[2] They used etymology to determine that the Iliad, for example, was a reworking of Joshua's assault on Jericho and the Odyssey a story about wandering Jewish patriarchs. Vossius's magisterial De Origine ac Progressu Idololatriae (1641) was used by Lord Herbert of Cherbury to argue that all the wisest pagans recognized that there was one supreme God. Then Samuel Shuckford in the early eighteenth century synthesized Greco-Roman mythology with Hebrew history by euhemerizing[3] the former. One of Shuckford's many examples was Zeus, whom he presented as a wise Cretan patrician and contemporary of Moses.[4]

Later in the eighteenth century some thinkers began to dispense with the theory that all religion was descended from Judaism and suggested instead that non-Christian religions originated in Egypt, Babylon, and Phoenicia.[5] But there was still the same reliance among most of the orthodox on the basic assumptions of the *prisca theologia*—that true religion was given by revelation to the sons of Noah, who disseminated its lineaments to the fathers of the nations. These teachings were distorted by corrupt admixtures—perhaps from Egypt or Babylon—but the remnants of truth they still contained were derived from Hebrew sources, either by revelation or tradition. The upshot was that Hebrew culture was superior to that of Greece and Rome. What was true in Plato and Cicero was not original to them but came ultimately from Hebrew revelation.

Deists and the "Beautiful" Moral Philosophy

If the orthodox used Greece and Rome to defend the priority of their own theology, deists plundered the classics for authoritative refutations of orthodoxy. We have already seen how Lord Herbert used what he learned from Vossius to subvert hyper-Calvinist assumptions about the eternal destiny of the "heathen," a term that for nearly everyone in this period stood primarily for the Greeks and Romans. Charles Blount attacked classical religion, but the astute reader could discern a veiled

---

2. Bochart, learned oriental linguist, was best known for his etymological work in *Geographia Sacra* (2 vols., 1646, 1651); Van Voss (Vossius is the Latinized version), a Dutch humanist theologian, wrote De Theologica Gentili, et physiologia Christiana sive de origine ac progressu idoltariae (Amsterdam, 1641).

3. Euhemerus was a Sicilian writer (c. 315 B.C.) who developed the theory that the ancient beliefs about the gods originated from the elaboration of traditions about actual historical persons.

4. Shuckford, *Sacred and Profane History*. The History begins with the assertion, "All the ancient Religions of the World were originally the same" (3d. ed., 1743, p. 313) and argues both that ancient histories were generally conformed to Mosaic history, and pagan mythologies were all about the same things: important events in the first ages of the world.

5. Manuel, *The Eighteenth Century Confronts the Gods*, 104–13.

critique of Christian orthodoxy. He charged that fear created the gods, and sacrifices were enjoined by priests for the purpose of enhancing their own power. John Toland admired some classical authors for their elegance and disdain for superstition but alleged that Christianity was corrupted by incomprehensible mysteries coming from Platonic philosophy and repugnant morals stemming from Epicurus, Aristotle, and Plato. Anthony Collins claimed that neither Cicero nor Seneca believed in life after death, and Matthew Tindal praised Greeks and Romans for their ability to disagree about religion without fighting. Tindal agreed with Samuel Clarke that Plato spoiled his philosophy by countenancing the public practice of idolatry and that Socrates was superstitious when he offered a cock to Asklepius, but these were minor criticisms. All in all, Greco-Roman culture was a Golden Age to which Tindal thought moderns should aspire. It was an age in which reasoning and science flourished, without religious persecution or war.[6]

One of the classical authors most consistently applauded by freethinkers was Cicero. Montesquieu wrote in his *Discours sur Cicéron* (1716): "Cicéron est, de tous les anciens, celui qui a eu le plus de merité personnel, et a qui j'aimerois mieux ressembler."[7] Collins used him to argue against immortality, while Toland enlisted his support for a religiously tolerant civil theology. Tindal fairly gushed with praise: he called Cicero's moral philosophy beautiful. In his opinion it showed the necessary connection between virtue and happiness and created in us both a delight in virtue and aversion toward vice. In addition, the Roman moralist exposed the superstition of his countrymen, and (thankfully!) ridiculed the kinds of miracles that fill the annals of church priests.[8]

Nascent Psychology of Religion

Deists praised the Greeks and Romans for recognizing the truths of natural religion. But their successors in the second half of the eighteenth century became convinced that religious sentiment was not inborn but acquired in time. Religious experience was a psychological product of historical conditions in primitive times. Hence Vico, Hume, de Brosses, Boulanger, and D'Holbach regarded the Greco-Roman heritage with considerable ambiguity. Vico, for example, said the early Greeks and Romans were just as savage as the Aztecs and Incas. Rather than being wise, they were in fact stupid, not completely rational. Therefore there were no grounds for European *superbia*. Hume added that natural religion was born not of

---

6. Blount, *Anima Mundi*, 14, 42–43; Daniel, *The Philosophy of Jonathan Edwards*, 130; CNM, 127, 157ff., 125; DF, 135ff., 149; CAO, 101; CAO, 396, 101–8. The *Independent Whig* (IW, 41) also praised the Greeks and Romans for being able to disagree religiously without quarreling. The implication was that Greco-Roman culture was therefore superior to fractious and intolerant orthodoxy.

7. "Cicero is the most meritorious of all the ancients and the one I would most like to emulate." Montesquieu, "Discours sur Cicéro," in *Œuvres complètes*, 3 vols. (Paris, 1950), 2:15; cited in Champion, *The Pillars of Priestcraft Shaken*, 183–84.

8. Champion, *The Pillars of Priestcraft Shaken*, 185–95; CAO, 397.

cool reason but hot passions such as fear of death and thirst for revenge. Lucretius, he wrote, was correct to dismiss the gods as children of terror.

Vico and the other "historico-psychological mythographers," as Manuel calls them, repudiated the Vossius-Bochart assumption of massive borrowing by Greeks from Jews and rejected the diffusion theory that underlay the *prisca theologia*. As Hume put it, religion was a product neither of revelation and tradition (orthodoxy) nor of reason (deism) but of pleasure and pain. So while the religious quarreled over their differences, inspired in part by Greek philosophy, Hume called for retreat to the calm groves of skeptical philosophy, a call that was inspired by Greco-Roman polytheism's tolerance while repudiating its superstition.[9]

Edwards on Revelation in Greece and Rome

Edwards was almost as contemptuous of Greco-Roman religion as Hume. Generally, he preached, classical religion was "very absurd" and "brutish" because its devotees worshiped innumerable gods and performed human sacrifices. Nevertheless, amidst its "grossly absurd opinions" were "scraps of truth" (MNB, 250; HWR, 445).

Yet his treatment of classical philosophy and mythology was more eclectic and nuanced than that of either his seventeenth-century predecessors or the deists. Unlike Vossius, Bochart, and Shuckford, Edwards did not believe that all classical religion derived from existing Jewish religion. Nor did he believe like the deists that the best of classical thought consisted simply of the dictates of reason. For Edwards, truth in classical thinking—and there were considerable stores of it—had complex and diverse origins, ranging from Jewish borrowings to tradition from the fathers of the nations to direct inspiration by the Holy Spirit. Edwards never clearly committed himself to one theory of provenance, preferring to note the range of opinion and reflect instead on the abundance of religious truths in Greece and Rome.

Edwards was intrigued by the host of agreements between Greco-Roman and Reformed understandings; his voracious intellect no doubt derived great satisfaction from finding and reflecting on them. But his notebooks indicate that the principal use he made of these discoveries was not aesthetic or recreational but polemic. There is plenty of evidence in the *Miscellanies* that he was amassing ammunition for his war against the deists. These hundreds of pages in the notebooks also demonstrate that he was planning to use two lines of argument: (1) true religion is founded on revelation rather than reason, and (2) the very doctrines that distinguished Reformed orthodoxy from deism were in fact revealed by God.

Edwards's first line of argument was to attack the most fundamental premise of deism: that there was no revelation from God beyond what is found in the human

---

9. Vico, *The New Science*; David Hume, *Natural History of Religion* (1757), in Antony Flew, ed., *David Hume: Writings on Religion* (LaSalle, Ill., 1992), 105–82; Manuel, *The Eighteenth Century Confronts the Gods*, 131–81.

mind. He collected considerable clusters of data that appeared to show that the best Greek and Roman philosophers acknowledged their dependence on the divine for inspiration. For instance, he learned from Gale[10] and Grotius[11] that Plato and other "heathen philosophers" said they got their teachings from revelation, and that the "holy fathers of the nations" were "inspired" by God (Misc. 953). Furthermore, Plato professed to have learned about the One and the Many (hints of the Trinity) from the gods, and to have taught that law should come from the gods not human beings (Misc. 953.9; Misc. 954; Misc. 1086). According to Grotius, Edwards noted, Plato testified in the *Cratylus* that the Greeks "recieved [sic] letters [learning] from the gods by barbarians" older than themselves (Misc. 959; see also Misc. 962).

Edwards copied Gale's observations of similar remarks made by Socrates. In Plato's *Meno*, Socrates reportedly asserted the native blindness of all human beings; in the *Theaetetus* Socrates stated that God was the only efficient cause, and he merely the midwife. In the *Alcibiades* Socrates said that only those conscious of their ignorance can teach properly (Misc. 966; Misc. 967; Misc. 968). From Clarke and Shuckford Edwards was impressed by another line from Socrates that seemed to rebut deist presuppositions: we cannot reform ourselves, said the Athenian, unless God sends someone to instruct us (Misc. 979).

Aristotle also knew the need for revelation. According to Isaac Barrow, Aristotle's *Metaphysics* (12.8) attests that the ancients received words about the gods from the gods. And Cicero realized that the light of nature is insufficient: "We seem to be in error even with our nurses' milk" (Misc. 977).[12]

Edwards was persuaded by Gale's "proof" that the "heathen" (classical authors) received their doctrines from revelation. Gale claimed that the fact that the heathen taught original sin proves revelation. This teaching would not have come from the light of nature alone because so many who acknowledge only nature consider this doctrine "mysterious and unreasonable." Since deists universally denied original sin and claimed to be following the light of nature, it was unlikely that nature's light taught this doctrine. Hence it must have come from revelation (Misc. 960).

10. Gale, whom we have seen briefly, was a nonconformist tutor influenced by Grotius's hint that all ancient learning and philosophy were derived from the Hebrew scriptures. University preacher at Oxford, his massive four-volume *Court of the Gentiles* (1669–77) traced every European language to the Hebrew, and all philosophy and literature of antiquity to Hebrew traditions. *Court of the Gentiles* was a favorite resource for seventeenth- and eighteenth-century orthodox polemicists. See Fiering, *Jonathan Edwards's Moral Thought*, 183n, and Fiering, *Moral Philosophy at Seventeenth-Century Harvard*, chap. 6.

11. Hugo Grotius was a Dutch jurist and theologian whose *De Veritate Religionis Christianae* (1622) was a favorite source for Gale and other polemicists whom Edwards read. Grotius, better known as the "Father of International Law" (by virtue of his *De Jure Belli Ac Pacis* [1625]) than as a Christian apologist, was imprisoned for Remonstrant sympathies, escaped in a box of books, was banished from Holland at age forty-eight, and died after a shipwreck. His *De Veritate*, designed as a practical handbook for missionaries, sought to uphold natural theology and show the superiority of Christianity to other faiths (*Oxford Dictionary of the Christian Church*, 1983).

12. Edwards recorded Philip Skelton's observation that Socrates and Plato were the only heathen philosophers who were not corrupted because they alone acknowledged the natural blindness of human nature and need for a divine instructor. Only they "had a sense of religion, and man's inability to make hims[elf] perfect and happy" (Misc. 1238).

Plundering the Jews

Knowledge of religious truth came not only from the sons of Noah and the fathers of the nations, but also through borrowing from the Jews. Edwards recorded in his notebooks the conjecture from several of his sources that both Aristotle and Plato had had contacts with Jews. Gale posted a report from Clement and Eusebius that Aristotle had met a Jew from whom he learned much and through whom the Greeks received many of their traditions (Misc. 969). Edwards took note of Philip Skelton's claim in *Deism Revealed* that Plato had traveled to Egypt and there encountered a Jew, from whom he learned (Misc. 1350).

But the Jews had shared their knowledge with the ancient world in other ways. According to Grotius, the Phoenicians learned from the Jews and then passed on their knowledge to the Greeks. This explained why "the most antient Attick laws from whence the Roman were afterwards taken owe their original to the laws of Moses" (Misc. 1012). According to Barrow and Shuckford, whom Edwards read, this may also explain why some ancient peoples paid tithes and practiced circumcision (Misc. 973).

Cultural borrowing accounted for ancient knowledge of astrology and astronomy as well. Abraham, who had learned astrology from Enoch through his ancestors, taught astrology, astronomy, and mathematics to the Egyptians, Chaldeans, and Phoenicians, who in turn tutored the Greeks in these disciplines. This historical information came from Gale. Edwards added the following corollary in his own words:

> These things also confirm that human learning & all usefull & noble knowledg [sic] and not only knowledge in things divine & spiritual was originally from the chh [church] of God in all ages of the world as the light of the gospel has most evidently been the occasion of all such knowledge since Christ[.] So that [no] barbarous nation has recieved [sic] so much as civility but from the church of [Christ]. (Misc. 962)

Later in his career Edwards stipulated that secular knowledge came to the Gentiles through a myriad of sources, not excluding the direct inspiration of the Holy Spirit (Misc. 1162; TV, esp. 592–95). But it was enough to provide data that seemed to corroborate his contention against the deists that true religion is founded not on reason but revelation. Even the deists' favorite classical sources seemed to teach the same, and there appeared to be other evidence from history that the greatest classical thinkers had sat at the feet of notable Jews.

Orthodox Doctrine among the Wiser Heathen

The final move in his gathering of evidence against the deists—and for Edwards perhaps the most convincing and satisfying—was to show that some of the most celebrated Greek and Roman philosophers held beliefs which most particularly distinguished the orthodox from deists in the eighteenth century. Along the way

Edwards also showed Greco-Roman faith in doctrines that were staples even of the deists' vaunted "natural religion," such as monotheism and the immortality of the soul.[13] But the most telling arguments against deists would be evidence from the ancients themselves that they held to articles in the Reformed creed, such as the Trinity. It was at this point that Edwards showed how far he had moved beyond Calvin and his favorite Reformed divines, François Turretin and Petrus van Mastricht. They too had posited considerable knowledge of divine truths among the heathen, but they had restricted that knowledge to what could be known by reason and common grace. Edwards, however, made use of the *prisca theologia* to argue that the wiser heathen knew not only about God the Creator but God the Redeemer as well. From the Jews and tradition passed down from Noah's sons the wiser heathen had access to revelation which his Reformed predecessors had limited to those under New Testament gospel preaching.[14]

The Reformed orthodox had argued for three kinds of knowledge of divine things available to the heathen. They taught that all had, first, a sense of the divine (*sensus numinis*) and, second, a witness in the conscience that God is a lawgiver (*cognitio Dei Legislatoris*). Third, pagan philosophers could use reason to reflect on these first two kinds of knowledge in order to construct a natural theology. But knowledge of God the Redeemer was possible only by explicit recognition of Christ that comes through biblical revelation.[15]

Edwards agreed with the Reformed divines that the heathen can know truths, apart from revelation, through these three avenues, and that this knowledge is only of God the Creator. He also agreed that this knowledge does not establish a foundation upon which knowledge of God the Redeemer can be built, since this latter knowledge comes only by revelation. He further affirmed the Reformed doctrine that knowledge of God the Creator is good only for condemnation, since pagans invariably turn that knowledge to the service of idolatry. But he differed from his predecessors in stipulating that the heathen can gain considerable truths about God the *Redeemer*—not from the Bible but from the *prisca theologia*. The unregenerate heathen (some, at least) were without excuse not because they knew God the Creator, but worse—they knew even God the Redeemer, yet turned to idolatry. Edwards's use of the *prisca theologia* thus served only to heighten heathen guilt. At a very few places in his private notebooks Edwards hinted that some of the "wiser heathen" may have used this revelation for their spiritual benefit rather than ruin, but he suggested in strong and explicit terms that the majority of heathen were damned because they had been given revelation of God the Redeemer only to twist it beyond recognition. This despite the clear record (or so it seemed to Edwards) that some of the greatest mysteries of Reformed religion had been given to some of the most influential heathen thinkers.

---

13. Edwards collected evidence for ancient belief in monotheism in Misc. 964, Misc. 975, and Misc. 1351, and for the immortal soul in Misc. 953, Misc. 1016, and Misc. 1351.

14. Calvin, Institutes 1.6; 1.10; 2.9; Turretin, Institutes of Elenctic Theology, 1:1.4; Heppe, *Reformed Dogmatics*, 1–11; Muller, *Post-Reformation Reformed Dogmatics*, 1:167–94.

15. Muller, *Post-Reformation Reformed Dogmatics*, 1, 174, 179.

For example, Edwards was convinced by his sources that Plato and the Platonists believed in some version of a triune divinity.[16] He took Jacques Basnage's word for it that Plato spoke of the Being, the Word, and the Spirit or Soul, and that Plato

> asserted that these hypostases did necessarily exist were infinite & almighty & called all three one God. . . . Plato maintain'd that the first hypostasis begat the second & the second the third & asserted that they were of the same nature & that they necessarily existed & that the first cannot be without the second nor the second without the third, and attributed to these three hypostases the creation of all things. (Misc. 992)[17]

From Gale and Barrow he learned that Plato intimated a trinity in Epistle 6, where he talks about the Father, the word, and the soul of the world. He also inscribed Gale's note that "the Platonists in their Trias make the soul of the [world] their universal spirit to be the third [hypostasis]" (Misc. 970). At the very end of his career Edwards copied extracts from Cudworth arguing that one can find references to a trinity in the Pythagoreans, Orpheus, Parmenides, and some Roman thinkers (Misc. 1359).[18]

Another Reformed notion that flew in the face of deist doctrine was what Edwards called "infused grace"—the idea that moral and religious virtue cannot be produced by the self but must be imparted by God. Edwards drew again on Gale to proffer supposed proofs that the great philosophers held to this notion. Socrates, Gale claimed, asserted the corruption of human nature and hence that virtue cannot be taught but must be given by God (Misc. 966; Misc. 967). In Misc. 1028 Edwards turned to Philip Doddridge who found Plato saying in the *Republic* that if a man is truly good, it is because of God. Chevalier Ramsay[19] reported that Plato defined holiness as "infused grace" and in the *Philebus* places the sovereign good in a resemblance to the divine nature, which can flow from God alone (Misc. 1355). According to Cudworth,[20] God is the author of virtue in Euripides, Socrates, Plato, Epicurus, and Cleanthes (Misc. 1359).

---

16. We do not know whether Edwards read these philosophers himself. A four-volume edition of Plato's works is listed in his "Catalogue of Reading," but there is no clear sign that he either procured the volumes or read them. Of his many references to Plato and Platonists in the *Miscellanies*, all are taken from secondary sources.

17. Edwards cites Basnage's *History of the Jews*. He also refers to this work in his typological notebooks; see TW, 203, 305.

18. There is also Misc. 955, where Edwards posted Gale's description of Plato's One and the Many as evidence for the Trinity in his writings and Gale's statement that in the *Timaeus* Plato describes two kinds of ideas: a self-subsisting simple idea, and its exemplar or image, which is the offspring of the first.

19. Ramsay used Grotius and Cudworth as sources; as we shall see in Chapter 12, he was particularly interested in China.

20. Ralph Cudworth was perhaps the most distinguished of the Cambridge Platonists. Edwards used his cumbrous and incomplete *True Intellectual System of the Universe* (1678) to defend Reformed religion against deists and other detractors. Cudworth transmitted the *prisca theologia* to new generations of thinkers in the seventeenth and eighteenth centuries. For Cudworth's philosophy, see Aspelin, *Ralph Cudworth's Interpretation of Greek Philosophy*, and Passmore, *Ralph Cudworth*.

Deists were no doubt scandalized by Gale's claims that the classical authors also believed in "middle gods," deities that acted as emissaries or mediators between the human and the divine. One of their most violent objections was to the orthodox doctrine of the need for a mediator. But in passages painstakingly copied by Edwards, Gale declared that Plato wrote in his *Politics, Laws,* and *Symposium* that there are dæmons or "made gods" or "visible gods" that are mediators between the gods and humanity. They carry men's prayers to God, transmit God's gifts to human beings, and interpret the mind and will of God to earth. By this mediation there is made possible friendship between heaven and earth that otherwise would be impossible. These gods or "daemons" are "co-rulers with the great God" (Misc. 971).[21] In the late 1750s Edwards took care to transfer into his notebooks two passages from Ramsay about this idea of a middle god. From *The Theology and Mythology of the Pagans* he copied, "The traditions of all nations foretell the coming of a hero, who is to descend from heaven to bring back Astraea to the earth: the Persians call him Mythras, the Egyptians Osiris, the Tyrians Adonis, the Greeks Apollos, Hercules, Mars, Mercury, Jupiter the Conductor and Saviour" (Misc. 1351). From *The Philosophical Principles of Natural and Revealed Religion* Edwards transcribed Justin Martyr's contention that "all the fables of Mercury, Bacchus, Hercules, Perseus . . . were only disguises of some ancient traditions concerning the Messiah." Edwards paraphrased several paragraphs from Ramsay with a single sentence of his own: "mars was but another name of the middle god Humanized" (Misc. 1355).

Edwards seems to have particularly enjoyed the discoveries at the close of his career that Plato's moral philosophy and philosophical theology were, like his own, thoroughly aesthetic. This conjunction of the moral with the aesthetic also stood in sharp contrast to deist reductions of religion to pedestrian morality shorn of the sort of mystical beauty found in Plato. Edwards added his own imprimatur ("Right notions of God and religion") in the margin beside the following description by Ramsay of Plato's sense of God as the source and center of all beauty:

> That it has no perfect similitude with anything we behold upon Earth, or in the Heavens. that whatever else is beauty is only so by participation of its Beauty. that all other Beauties may increase decay change or perish, but this is still the same in all times & in all places. That it is by carrying our thoughts beyond all inferior Beauties, that we at length reach to that supreme Beauty which is simple, pure, uniform, immutable without colour figure or human Qualities and in fine that this sovereign Beauty is incorporeal, the splendor of the divine image & God himself. (Misc. 1355)

In another notebook entry, amidst twenty-two thousand other words copied from Cudworth's *True Intellectual System of the Universe,* Edwards reproduced this memorable Neoplatonic line: "God is the vast Sea of Pulchritude. All other beautiful things partake of it" (Misc. 1359). Deists would have gagged on this indulgence of panentheism.

---

21. These are invisible spirits; in Plato a daemon watches over each individual. They are not the necessarily evil beings of Christian lore. Burkert, *Greek Religion,* 179–81.

There were other characteristically orthodox propositions supposedly taught by classical authors: "moral government" or the notion that the gods have "a peculiar providence towards men, such as were at friendship with them" (Misc. 954), which according to Gale and Ramsay could be found in Plutarch, Seneca, Cicero, Plato, and Virgil (Misc. 963; Misc. 978; Misc. 1351); original sin or at least corruption of human nature, which Isaac Watts claimed to find in Virgil, Seneca, Juvenal, and Ovid (Misc. 1073; Misc. 1351; Misc. 966); incarnation, or the idea of divine nature being joined to the human, which Grotius claimed could be found in Julian, Porphyry, and the Egyptians (Misc. 1024); and "Christ's moral teaching" (Misc. 1023). Here again Edwards turned to Grotius, who suggested that Ovid denounced adultery of the heart, Plato enjoined the love of enemies and forgiveness of injuries, and Euripides taught that with food and clothing we should be content.

There was still more. The Greeks and Romans supposedly believed in future rewards and punishments. Barrow alleged this of Plato, Seneca, and Celsus, whom Barrow wrongly called an Epicurean (Misc. 973).[22] A. B. Dow proclaimed that Plato had a vision of hell (Misc. 1270). According to Gale and Grotius, the ancients knew that purity of heart was required for true religion. Pythagoras was said to have insisted that worship is to be given the gods with a chaste and pure soul (Misc. 963); Cicero apparently taught that purity of heart is the foundation of true religion, and Porphyry and Seneca taught something similar (Misc. 1022). Cudworth reported Galen's statement that true religion is not sacrifice but acknowledging God's great wisdom, power, and goodness. Epictetus reportedly agreed (Misc. 1359).

Even Creation and the Fall were in the ancients. According to Gale, "Plato in his Timaeus [spoke] of the origine of the universe . . . sometimes . . . in the same words with Moses" (Misc. 953). Edwards wrote in the Blank Bible in the margins of the Genesis 3 story that Plato learned the story of the Fall from the Egyptians. He also noted there that Plato knew that God rested after the Creation (see also Misc. 1351 and Misc. 1355).

The wise heathen held to other Reformed beliefs such as a worldwide deluge (Misc. 953; Misc. 1351), the future destruction of the world by fire (Misc. 956), the Sabbath (Misc. 961; Misc. 1013), the resurrection of the body (Misc. 963, 1018; Misc. 1351), tithing (Misc. 973), circumcision (Misc. 973), end-time revivals, the ascension of Christ, providence for the saints, original righteousness before the Fall, and redemption by a messiah (Misc. 1351).

By the end of his career Edwards appears to have been convinced by most of these authors. Although he noted discrepancies among them and never gave unqualified support to any single theory of the origins of true religion, he concluded in one of his last notebook entries that "all the Chief philosophers placed virtue primarily in devotion[,] spiritual knowledge[,] & union with God & believed God to be the Creatour[,] universal orderer & moral governor of the [world] & the

---

22. Celsus was actually a Middle Platonist critic of Christianity who wrote the *Alethes Logos* (True doctrine) about A.D.178. He was known as an Epicurean perhaps because Origen made the mistake originally and was not corrected. *Encyclopedia of Philosophy*, ed. Paul Edwards (New York, 1967), 2:66.

Immortality of the soul & spiritual Happiness of Heaven" (Misc. 1355). He had been persuaded that under God's common grace God had given true knowledge of himself and his ways to the wiser "heathen," particularly those with whom he was most familiar—the published philosophers of Greece and Rome. They represented the heathen world's "greatest glory of strength, wealth and learning" (HWR, 279). He agreed with Samuel Clarke that their best and brightest were unparalleled. Plato delivered "very noble and almost divine truths concerning the nature and attributes of the supream [sic] God." Cicero was the greatest and best philosopher that Rome ever produced, and Epictetus was an "admirable moralist" whose sense of virtue "seems to have had no superiour in the heathen world" (Misc. 979).[23]

They Gloried in Their Virtue

But there were superiors in the Christian world. Edwards had great respect for Greco-Roman philosophy, yet his respect was tempered by a series of piercing criticisms. His primary reproach was that the best Greek and Roman philosophers were benighted by pride. They displayed many Christian virtues but seemed to be motivated more by love of self than love of God.

> Many heathens were very eminent for many moral virtues, and wrote excellently of them; as of justice, and of generosity, and of fortitude and others. But they were far from a Christian poverty of spirit, and lowliness of mind; they sought their own glory, and gloried exceedingly in their virtue, and said nothing about such a walk as the gospel commands, a walking in self-emptiness, poverty of spirit, self-diffidence, self-renunciation.[24]

Edwards quoted Gale, who charged that even the Cynics, who decried the pride of others and seemed the most modest, were guilty of this vice. The Pythagoreans, Gale added, were the worst. Citing Augustine, he said that the philosophers' virtues were "splendid sins" (Misc. 965).

Edwards also recorded Samuel Clarke's criticisms that the Roman philosophers did not know how to be restored to God after sin (they knew sacrifices were not enough), and that they lacked certainty. Neither Cicero nor Epictetus were sure of the immortality of the soul or a future state and so conceded that their philosophies were not capable of reforming the world (Misc. 979).

In one of his last notebook entries Edwards transcribed John Brine's thoughts on "the defects of the pagan philosophers' morality" (Misc. 1357). Most of Brine's criticisms seemed to address Roman moral philosophy and to cluster around the charge that it was humanocentric. Virtue was taught not as a duty owed to one's maker but as good and beautiful in itself, abstracted from the will of God. There was no regard for the glory of God or true humility; instead virtue was thought to

---

23. Edwards here was quoting, with apparent approbation, from Clarke's 1704–5 Boyle lectures, *Evidences of Natural and Revealed Religion*. See *The Works of Samuel Clarke* 2:661.

24. *Charity and Its Fruits*, sermon 10, in EW, 310f.

be a product of the human agent. "Therefore they deny that thanks are due our Maker for virtue wherein they make human happiness to consist[,] so that according to them God made us & we make ourselves happy." To make matters worse, they added to their immorality (Cicero taught that fornication is permitted to young men) religious ignorance (Seneca said that prayer is unnecessary) (Misc. 1357).

Unreliable Sources

If Edwards was critical of the philosophers of Greece and Rome, he was largely uncritical of the secondary sources he was using.[25] He never seemed to bother checking whether Gale, Grotius, Ramsay, and Cudworth had the ancients right. If he had, he might have discovered that while there was usually some textual basis for their claims, they often ignored context, especially in their readings of Plato. Typically their interpretations were literal and ignored the surrounding text. As a result the statements they proffered for evidence took on meanings and implications often removed from what seems to have been their original intent.

A good example is the long train of passages attributed to Socrates and Plato that reputedly demonstrate the philosophers' belief in revelation coming from the divine to human beings. There are indeed statements to that effect in Plato's dialogues. In the *Philebus* Plato has Socrates say, "The men of old dwelt nearer the gods and passed on . . . [a] saying" (16c–e), namely that all things consist of one and the many. In the *Timaeus* Socrates refers to "dark sayings and visions" (71e), and in the *Theaetetus* he insists that he has no knowledge but is only a midwife, "constrained by heaven," to help others gain knowledge: "The delivery is heaven's work and mine. . . . I can myself bring nothing to light because there is no wisdom in me" (149a–150d).

But there are problems with a flat declaration that Socrates and Plato believed in a doctrine of revelation comparable to that of Reformed thinkers in the eighteenth century. Shuckford's reference to the *Laws*, where Plato supposedly said that no man should institute a law, is obscure. Plato speculated at great length on what the most rational system of laws should be, but never appealed to divine revelation. He supported the use of stories about the gods to win popular support for legislation (*Laws* 887b) and called them "most true" (881a), but he argued that the myths about the gods contain some untruths which must be discerned and repudiated by reason (*Republic* 379c–383c), and "the gods themselves have no existence in nature, but are a product of human artifice, and vary according to local conventions."[26]

In addition, Gale and Grotius crowed that in the *Cratylus* Plato announces that the Greeks received their learning from the gods through barbarians older than themselves. In fact this is the position that Plato ridicules, deriding it as a "con-

---

25. This section is indebted to philosopher Hans Zorn of Roanoke College.
26. W.K.C. Guthrie, *The Later Plato and the Academy*, vol. 5 in Guthrie, *History of Greek Philosophy*, 361.

trivance" and conceding "these are not reasons but only ingenious excuses for having no reasons concerning the truth of words" (425d–426a).[27]

Socrates claimed to have a divine commission and an inner voice that warned him when he was doing wrong. But he never claimed inspiration in the sense of receiving a body of revealed truths, as Edwards himself suggests in Misc. 1162.[28] Aristotle's view was not dissimilar. Barrow had suggested that Aristotle regarded as inspired the forefathers' notions that the heavenly bodies are divine and that the divine encloses all nature (Misc. 973). But Aristotle also considered the Greek myths to be fictions devised for the consumption of the unphilosophical multitudes (Metaphysics 12.8, 1074b 1–14).[29]

Gale's and Grotius's treatments of the Trinity follow a similar pattern. They uncovered ideas in Plato and the Platonists that bear a dim resemblance to some elements of trinitarianism but not the close correspondence they claimed. For example, Gale suggests that Plato's comments in the Philebus about the One and the Many are hints of the Trinity (Misc. 955). Yet the One and the Many are principles of earthly things, not divinity. Gale also wrote that Plato referred to this as strange. However, Socrates called strange not this doctrine but the method of inquiry that was given by the gods. More precisely, he said it was difficult to practice: one had to first search for the unity in things, and then investigate their multiplicity (16b–c).[30]

Gale also confused a Platonic distinction in the Timaeus, where Plato spoke not of two kinds of ideas (as Gale put it, the independent idea and its image) but the difference between an invisible form and its visible instantiation—a familiar concept for students of the middle dialogues, but quite different from Christian ideas of God and God's Image (Timaeaus 51d; Misc. 955).[31] On the other hand, Gale is correct in his ascription of Trinity-like ideas to the Neoplatonists (Misc. 970). Plotinus described a triad of the One, the Nous, and the World Soul, with the World Soul linking God and the world. According to Plotinus, the ideas in the Nous are reflected in the World Soul, and it is through the World Soul that things in the world participate in those ideas. This is how human souls can derive from the World Soul.[32] Hence the Grotius material (on God as three hypostases), which Edwards cites in Misc. 992, is more a summary of Plotinus than Plato. Plato spoke of triads and in the Timaeus describes the World Soul as composed of unchanging being, changing being, and their combinations, but again these are descriptions of the World Soul not God. God placed intelligence into the World Soul (30b), but this was not God's nature receiving intelligence. Furthermore, the idea of

---

27. On the sources of knowledge for Plato, see W.K.C. Guthrie, Plato: The Man and His Dialogues: Earlier Period, vol. 4, in Guthrie, History of Greek Philosophy, 160–63, 168–70, 256–58, 261–64.

28. W.K.C. Guthrie, Socrates (Cambridge, 1971), 19, 79, 80n, 81, 82–5.

29. Isaac Barrow (1630–77) was an Anglican divine, classical scholar, and mathematician, whose Works (probably the 1683–87 edition edited by Tillotson) Edwards used at Northampton.

30. See Guthrie, The Later Plato and the Academy, 60–61, 148–49, 206–7.

31. See ibid., 267–68, 270.

32. See Philip Merlan, "Plotinus," in Encyclopedia of Philosophy, 6:351–59; Rist, Plotinus, esp. 84–129.

emanations ("the first hypostasis begat the second & the second the third," *Misc.* 992) is neoplatonic rather than Platonic.[33]

There were comparable errors made on other claims for Christian ideas among the classical authors. For example, Edwards cited Gale's claim that Plato used the same words as Moses in a description of the Creation (*Misc.* 953). Plato did indeed speak of the beginning of the world in the *Timaeus*, but with words and ideas quite different from Moses'. God, he said, created by imposing form and order on preexisting matter (53b).[34]

Grotius also maintained that Plato and Socrates taught original sin. In fact they taught a kind of defective human nature, but nothing like the Christian conception of fallenness. There is no mention of a fall in the Platonic corpus. Plato said that no one sins intentionally, since no one purposely chooses what is not good. Hence in the *Timaeus* evil is the product of ignorance, which comes from "an ill disposition of the body and bad education," both of which occur against one's will (86e). Yet the connection of the soul to the body suggested to Plato that there was an original defect in human nature, which may have come from the fact that the human soul was made from the same elements as the World Soul, but "diluted to the second or third degree" (41d).[35]

Gale did not distort egregiously every Greek view, however. For example, he was generally accurate in his ascription of a belief in middle gods to Plato. The *Symposium* speaks of spirits as halfway between gods and humans, mediating between them: "envoys and interpreters that ply between heaven and earth, flying upwards with our prayers, and descending with the heavenly answers and commandments" (202e–203a). The *Laws* testify that gods and spirits, whose property we are, are our allies in our fight against evil (906a) and mention the custom to dedicate sacrifices to "gods, spirits and sons of gods" (910a). These spirits, however, do not play a major role in Plato's system of beings.[36]

Gale also got Socrates right on the idea that virtue comes only by divine assistance. In the *Meno* Socrates asserts that people are not naturally good because goodness requires wisdom, which not all human beings possess (89a). Socrates also suggests that virtue cannot be taught, so those who are good must have become so by divine influence or inspiration (89d–96d).

In general, however, Edwards's sources were often less than accurate in their reporting of what classical authors said about morality and the divine. They usually reproduced something that possessed some degree of correspondence to the texts in question, but typically that correpondence was not strong enough to bear the theological weight that seventeenth- and eighteenth-century Christian apologists sought to place on it.

---

33. See Gilbert Ryle, "Plato," in *Encyclopedia of Philosophy*, 6:314–33, esp. 320–24; Merlan, "Plotinus," and Rist, *Plotinus*, 66–83.

34. Yet in *Timaeus* 37e-38c Plato suggests that before the creation there was no time, so that the beginning of creation was the beginning of time.

35. See Guthrie, *The Later Plato and the Academy*, 92–97.

36. Ibid., 357, 386.

The Migration of the Gods

Edwards was enamored with Greek and Roman *philosophy* because of an often distorted view of what the ancient philosophers believed. He was also intrigued by Greek and Roman *mythology*, but precisely because he believed it was distorted. That is, Edwards considered Greco-Roman mythology theologically and historically significant because of its relationship to Christian revelation. Ancient mythology confirmed Christian revelation by its distortions of revelation. The deists believed that all true religion derived from sources independent of revelation, but ancient mythology seemed to Edwards to confirm the existence of historical revelation by the manifest connections between pagan myths and biblical stories.

Edwards followed Vossius, Gale, and Shuckford in postulating a migration of gods from Israel through Phoenicia and Egypt to Greece (and later to Rome) by three vehicles: (1) euhemerism (the notion that pagan gods are inflated versions of historical figures), (2) linguistic confusion (conflating several different figures into one because of similarity in words, or dividing exploits of one person among several new names because of verbal similarities), or (3) hermeneutical confusion (attributing the works of a human figure to God because of a failure to understand the biblical text). The result was a profusion of deities and myths, all betraying derivation from Hebrew biblical legends. So the God of Israel was given new names when his legends were taken abroad, and the stories of his people in Canaan took on new life and ontological meaning (humans often became divinities) when they traveled through the Mediterranean world.

According to Gale, the Hercules legend was an example of both euhemerism and hermeneutical confusion. Joshua became Hercules because

> such ancient things that were taken originally from different persons, and handed down by tradition, and handed from one nation to another, [were] at length come to be understood of the same person. . . . [for] Hercules, or Melicarthus, which was Hercules' name among the Phoenicians, was probably first not a proper name, but an appellative, a word that signified any great hero, or a general name for all mighty and valiant leaders in war, that in length of time might be taken for a proper name, and especially by the Grecians, that did not understand the signification of the word. (NS, no. 402)[37]

The Bacchus myth was also a result of linguistic and hermeneutical confusion. Bacchus was said by Bochart, whom Edwards transcribed assiduously in his *Notes on the Scriptures*, to be a pagan distortion of Nimrod and Moses. This confusion of Moses, for example, with the God who acted through him and then with the god Bacchus, was "very natural." For the Greeks, according to Gale, had other names for Bacchus (Iao, Adonai, El Eloah, and Jehovah Sabaoth) that were identical to the Jewish names for their God. These Greeks made the same mistake that the

---

37. According to Hadas and Smith, Gale was right: Hercules was "the prime example of a man raised above ordinary humanity by his services to mankind. . . . Quite probably there had been a real Heracles [Hercules], who ruled at Tiryns and won high esteem for extraordinary prowess or service" (Hadas and Smith, *Heroes and Gods*, 22).

residents of Lystra made when they called the apostles Paul and Barnabas Hermes and Zeus (Acts 14:12).

Bochart and Edwards believed there were good reasons for believing that the Bacchus legends were based on the stories of Nimrod and Moses. They believed the name Bacchus to be derived from the Hebrew *Barcush*, or son of Cush, and Cush was the father of the biblical Nimrod.[38] This belief was reinforced by several correspondences. Both Bacchus and Nimrod were styled "mighty hunters," and Bacchus's "other name" was Nebrodes, which "is the very name of Nimrod among the Grecians" (NS, no. 401). The Bacchus story also contained remarkable similarities to Mosaic attributes and legends. For, as Bochart pointed out, both Bacchus and Moses were born in Egypt, shut up in an "ark," and put on the waters. Both fled from Egypt toward the Red Sea and had serpents (in Moses' case, a bronze serpent). For both, water flowed from a rock and milk and honey were provided. Both were called legislators, turned sticks into snakes, saw light in the darkness, and had unknown tombs (NS, no. 401). Incidentally, Gale added, the Egyptian myth of Osiris is the Bacchus legend under a new name. For the Greeks called Osiris Dionysus, which is another Greek name for Bacchus (NS, no. 407).[39]

Another Egyptian myth, the saga of Apis and Serapis, was really the Joseph story. According to Vossius, whom Gale used extensively as a source, this was clear for a number of reasons. First, the symbol used by Egyptians for Apis was a bullock that represents a "husbandman" or farmer, which was how Egyptians remembered Joseph because he provided them with grain during their drought.[40] In fact Joseph is compared to a bullock in Scripture (Deut. 33:7). Second, Apis is a derivative from the Hebrew word for father, which Joseph called himself in Genesis 45:8. Finally, Serapis was also represented by a bushel on its head, once again a symbol of Joseph's providing food. The word "Serapis" comes from Apis and the Hebrew word for ox or prince, both of which were applicable to Joseph (NS, no. 407; Blank Bible: Gen. 41).

Cudworth, Bochart, and others fascinated by mythology saw many connections between Hebrew legends and Saturn as well. Cudworth noted, in words reproduced by Edwards, that both Noah and Saturn had three sons among whom the world was divided. Saturn had a son (Jupiter) who cut off his father's genitals, which according to Cudworth was probably a reworking of the story of Ham seeing his father Noah's nakedness (NS, 400). Bochart thought that the Adam stories were also attached to the name of Saturn, for both Saturn and Adam were said to have known a paradisical time, and both were driven from their kingdoms and later taught humanity the arts of husbandry. Bochart, citing Eusebius, even attrib-

---

38. Nothing of the sort is indicated by modern scholars I consulted; the closest was Burkert's hypothesis that "Bacchus" might be "a Semitic loan-word meaning wailing; the Greek women who search for Dionysos would then correspond to the women of Israel who bewail Tammuz" (Burkert, *Greek Religion*, 163).

39. According to Burkert, Osiris was identified with Dionysus "from the start" (*Ancient Mystery Cults*, 6).

40. In this Vossius was right: Serapis was the Egyptian bull-god Apis; Morford and Lenardon, *Classical Mythology*, 453. Bacchus was also "bull-horned"; Morford and Lenardon, 244.

uted some tales of Saturn to the stories of Abraham in the Bible. Both Saturn and Abraham offered their only sons, circumcised them, and forced their companions to do the same (Blank Bible: Gen. 1–3).

There were plenty of other connections to lesser-known deities. Jupiter was said to be a warmed-over Ham (NS, 400); Silenus, "so famous among the poets," was really Christ because both were known as great doctors, were carried on an ass, and worked a wine press (Christ was said in Revelation 19:15 to tread the winepress of the wrath of God [NS, no. 403]); Pan and Faunus, the gods of shepherds, were really God going among the Israelites in the wilderness, when they were shepherds (NS, no. 404); Neptune was Japhet, the son of Noah (NS, no. 405); and the Greek philosophers' obsession with being came from the divine self-pronouncement, "I am that I am" (Exod. 3:14; NS, no. 412).

Concluding Thoughts

All of these migrations and subsequent transmutations among the Greeks and Romans of the Jewish and Christian stories seemed to delight and fascinate Edwards. Many, if not most, of the etymological connections were strained, and it was clear that many of the gods had changed significantly since their first incarnations in Palestine.[41] But instead of being disturbed by the increasing gap between the biblical stories and their so-called counterparts in Greece and Rome, Edwards was invigorated, for two reasons. First, he was either unaware of or overlooked the historiographical problems with these etymological claims and happily concluded that what seemed to be remarkable correlations in fact confirmed the reality of biblical revelation. Second, he regarded the eclipse of the Greco-Roman imperial cultus and its mythology as Christ's triumph over the gods. Indeed, it meant the defeat of heathenism, an event of world-historical proportions: it was the "greatest revolution that ever was; the most like creating the [world] anew" (Misc. 1327). Hence the gods of Greece and Rome both testified unwittingly to the God of the Jews and were slain by that same God's Messiah. In their apparent victory in Greece and Rome the gods were merely aping their future conqueror, whose victory was foreshadowed during the classical period by their very worship and brought crashing to its ruin the empire they served. Edwards could therefore regard the mythologies of Greece and Rome as broken types of the great Christian antitype.

Edwards's understanding of Greco-Roman philosophy was similarly triumphalist. He didn't bother checking his sources, preferring instead to take them at face value and exult in their value for refuting those who challenged Reformed theology. As a result he came to see the "wise philosophers" of Greece and Rome as inspired by

---

41. Deist conclusions about Greece and Rome were also questionable. For instance, there is considerable evidence that the classical world was not free of religious persecution, as Tindal claimed (note 7 above). One of many examples is that bacchanals, devotees of Isis, and Caldean soothsayers and horoscopists as well as Christians were imprisoned and killed by the Romans because of perceived offenses against the state cult. Frend, *Martyrdom and Persecution in the Early Church*, 76–93.

the Holy Spirit, "which led em to say such wonderful things concerning the Trinity the Messiah &c" (*Misc.* 1162). He reminded himself that even the wicked can be so inspired, such as Balaam and the devil at the oracle of Delphi who was "compelled to confess Christ." Nevertheless some of these wise heathen seemed to Edwards to share knowledge of the highest mysteries of Christian faith. That did not mean that they were necessarily regenerate, but it did mean that that was conceivable. These revelations from the Holy Spirit may have been of "great benefit . . . to their own souls" (*Misc.* 1162).

Even the heathen gods, then, could serve as instruments of salvation for the elect. In their first incarnations they were instruments of the devil that led their devotees astray. But in the Edwardsean work of redemption, they could be used, ironically, to participate in their own conquest by Christ. The history of the work of redemption, as sketched in Edwards's notebooks, reached further than his contemporaries would have ever imagined.

11

AMERICAN INDIANS

The Devil Sucks Their Blood

Jonathan Edwards felt little but contempt for Native American religion. When trying to refute English Nonconformist John Taylor's notion of an innate human capacity for religious knowledge, he used American Indians as a trump card. What did Europeans find when they came to America and discovered a people who had had the benefit of thousands of years to develop this capacity for religious truth? Nothing but "the grossest ignorance, delusions, and most stupid paganism" (OS, 151).

The Devil's People

Like many colonials, Edwards regarded Native American religion as peculiarly satanic.[1] He accepted the prevailing assumption that the Indians were a remnant of the Ten Lost Tribes of Israel that had lost all knowledge of true religion and somehow made their way eastward across Asia and then by ice floes or land bridge to North America—led all the way by Satan for the purpose of removing them from the gospel.[2] Once settled in America, they had become Satan's peculiar people, and their religion nothing more than devil worship.[3] Despite considering themselves free, they were in reality "the devil's captives"—even more than the rest of

---

1. David S. Lovejoy argues that the seventeenth century "perfected the image of the American Indian as a subject of the Devil's kingdom" ("Satanizing the American Indian," 621).
2. HWR, 155, 433–34. This was something of a consensus among colonial religious leaders such as Cotton Mather. DB, 11–12; Hutchison, *Errand to the World*, 39; Vaughan, *New England Frontier*, 20.
3. Sermon on 1 John 3:10, March 1756; HWR, 472. On the assertion that the Native Americans worshiped the devil, see also DB, 261.

the heathen world, which Edwards referred to more generally as the "kingdom of Satan."[4] Not only were they owned by the devil and therefore rightly called "the devil's People," but they were being devoured unwittingly by the prince of darkness. As the minister of an angry God put it, "The devil sucks their blood."[5] They could look forward only to the misery of hell.[6]

Why the invective? What led Edwards to assume demonic inspiration and compare Indians to "beasts"?[7] One factor was the overwhelming consensus among whites that native culture was inferior and despicable. Even John Eliot, the "apostle to the Indians," referred to them as "doleful creatures," the very ruins of mankind.[8] Edwards had been raised on tales of "Indian" ritual torture and cannibalism. They told of the Hurons, for example, who urged all the members of their villages to participate in the torture of captives.[9] Both Hurons and Iroquois believed that if their victims did not exhibit terror, their gods would be displeased and send misfortune to the captors. Sometimes the captives' bodies were cut up, cooked, and eaten in an effort to replace a tribal member lost to war or disease and to "devour" what they symbolized as the source of their rage.[10]

Edwards no doubt also recalled the Indian murder of one of his aunts and two cousins, and the captivity of an uncle and four more cousins.[11] There was also

---

4. Sermon on Luke 19:10, June 1751; sermon on Acts 14:26 ("Private meeting on occasion of missionaries W—ges & Hawley going into the Country of the six nations May 1753").

5. Sermon on Revelation 3:15, spring 1729, 30. This sermon is about the "heathen," who for Edwards and his contemporaries consisted of people who worshiped deities others than the god of Christianity, Judaism, and Islam. When Edwards thought of the heathen, he thought first of the Greeks and the Romans, and then of various tribes around the world. It is clear from this sermon that he was thinking of tribes of his own day (since he used the present tense and described religious practices foreign to the Greeks and Romans with whom he was familiar), and that the most probable referents were the North American Indians, the only "heathen" he knew firsthand.

6. All those who "worship the sun & moon & worship the devil & dont worship the true G. that made the [world] & J.X. his Son" go to hell; sermon on Matthew 7:13–14, January 1751.

7. Lecture on 2 Peter 1:19, August 1737, 29–30.

8. Cotton Mather, *Magnalia Christi Americana*, 1:504; cited in DB, 26.

9. Bowden, *American Indians and Christian Missions*, 71.

10. Dennis, *Cultivating a Landscape of Peace*, 89f. For more "routine" tortures inflicted on captives, see John Demos, *The Unredeemed Captive: A Family Story from Early America* (New York, 1994), 80–81, and Richter, *Ordeal of the Longhouse*.

One can imagine that fewer stories were told of white atrocities inflicted on Indians. On white atrocities, see Jennings, *Invasion of America*, 160–70, esp. 160: "There were no Indians in Ireland when Cromwell's armies made it a wilderness, nor were there Indians with Wallenstein and Tilly during the Thirty Years' War in central Europe. If savagery was ferocity, Europeans were at least as savage as Indians. . . . Many of the aspects of so-called savage war were taught to Indians by European example." For white use of torture and savagery in warfare in King Philip's War, see Lepore, *The Name of War*. For British torture of their own soldiers, see Jennings, *Empire of Fortune*, 208–9. Indians apparently invented scalping, but whites encouraged the practice by paying for scalps; see Axtell, *The European and the Indian*, 16–35, 207–41.

11. On February 29, 1704, Kahnawake Indians from near Montreal killed 48 people at Deerfield, Massachusetts, and took another 112 as captives to Canada. Among the killed were Reverend John Williams's wife and two children. He and his four other children were taken captive; all were eventually returned to Massachusetts except Eunice (age four at capture), who chose to remain for the rest of her life among the Kahnawake. See Demos, *Unredeemed Captive*.

Indian "idolatry"—reverence shown for the numinous in nature—that Edwards and the rest of the Reformed interpreted as sinful worship of the creature rather than the Creator.[12] As a result, Edwards and most Protestant missionaries failed to see anything in Indian religion that could serve as common ground or a point of contact in evangelism. They studiously discounted similarities between Indian and Christian religion, such as moral government, retribution, heaven and hell, and the necessity of a moral life.[13]

Jesuits missionaries, on the other hand, looked for elements of Indian culture that could be used as foundations on which to build understanding of Christian doctrine. They regarded apprehensions of divinity among the Indians as inchoate adumbrations of truths that were clarified by Christian revelation. For example, the French Jesuit Jean de Brébeuf, martyred by the Iroquois in 1649, believed that by the grace of God Indian superstitions might be turned into true religion "like spoils carried off from the enemy."[14]

Not coincidentally, Catholic missionaries were more successful than their Protestant counterparts.[15] While Protestant missionaries often forced their prospective converts to choose between Christ and their culture,[16] Jesuits showed respect for native culture. Indians were also more impressed by French (Catholic) willingness to intermarry with and to live among them (Protestant missionaries generally lived with other whites), and by Jesuit flexibility on morals. According to Henry Warner Bowden, "Instead of insisting on a single moral standard without regard to local contexts, they used cultural realities to set realistic goals for behavioral change."[17]

God's Extraordinary Graces

If Edwards was profoundly uninterested in Native American culture and regarded native religion as unmixed satanic brew, he nevertheless was singularly intrigued by what seemed to be God's saving work among the devil's people. This intrigue

---

12. See, for example, Edwards's sermon on Deuteronomy 32:29, July 1752.

13. Winslow, *Jonathan Edwards, 1703-1758*, 29; Hutchison, *Errand to the World*, 32. Most Europeans did not expect to learn anything from "heathen" religions. Jennings, *Empire of Fortune*, 53; Bowden, *American Indians and Christian Missions*, 122.

14. Grant, *Moon of Wintertime*, 32f.

15. James Axtell reports that after the fall of New France, most of the 10,000 Indians (largely adults) who had been evangelized by missionary priests kept practicing their Catholic faith despite the absence of clergy. Axtell, *The Invasion Within*, 277.

16. Grant, *Moon of Wintertime*, 263. Of course, it was not only Protestants who confused Christianization with Europeanization. Jesuits forced the Montagnais of Quebec in 1633-1634, for example, into European-styled agricultural communities. The Montagnais felt that if they stayed they would lose their identity. Ronda, "The Sillery Experiment."

The primary reason why Indians rejected the claims of Protestant missionaries seems to have been their fear that becoming Christian would mean losing their lands. By legal and illegal means the English had gradually acquired most Indian land in New England. Hankins, "Bringing the Good News," 200, 438; Ronda, "We Are Well As We Are."

17. Bowden, *American Indians and Christian Missions*, 116; Axtell, *The Invasion Within*, 277; Bowden,

seems to have been inspired in part by Solomon Stoddard and David Brainerd. Stoddard, Edwards's grandfather and senior pastor under whom Edwards served as assistant for three years, had long envisioned a multiracial American church, with Indians in full communion with whites.[18] In 1723 Stoddard published a blistering attack on New Englanders for their failure to heed God's command to evangelize the Indians.[19]

David Brainerd, whose legend far exceeds his accomplishments,[20] nevertheless was so convinced of God's extraordinary graces shown to his "Indians" that his diary persuaded Edwards that "something very remarkable" was occurring among these subjects of Satan (HWR, 434; letter to Rev. Hollis, July 17, 1752).[21] Brainerd had related the stories of Susquehannas who manifested a "disposition" to hear the gospel and natives on Juniata Island who were remarkably free of prejudice against Christianity (DB, 294). He had written of an Indian medicine man, clad in bearskin and mask, beating a rattle and dancing "with all his might," who felt his fellow Indians had become corrupted and sought to restore their ancient religious ways. He opposed their consumption of alcohol and affirmed many but not all of Brainerd's Christian doctrines. Brainerd believed that he was "sincere, honest and conscientious" and concluded "there was something in his temper and disposition that looked more like true religion than anything I ever observed amongst other heathens" (DB, 329–30).

Brainerd's converts seem to have impressed Edwards as well. One woman was a textbook example of Edwardsean spirituality. "She has seemed constantly to breathe the spirit and temper of the new creature . . . [and manifested] a true spiritual discovery of the glory, ravishing beauty, and excellency of Christ" (DB, 371). Another, a medicine man, had been a "murderer" and "notorious drunk-

---

American Indians and Christian Missions, 84. See also Peter A. Dorsey, "Going to School with Savages: Authorship and Authority among the Jesuits of New France," *William and Mary Quarterly*, 3d ser., 40, no. 3 (July 1998): 39–420.

18. Paul R. Lucas, "'The Death of the Prophet Lamented': The Legacy of Solomon Stoddard," in Stephen J. Stein, ed., *Jonathan Edwards's Writings: Text, Context, Interpretation* (Bloomington, Ind., 1996), 75–78.

19. Stoddard, Question, esp. 6–12. It must be added, however, that earlier Stoddard had evinced a less than generous attitude toward Indians. In 1703 he wrote to Governor Dudley suggesting the English might hunt Indians "with dogs . . . as they doe Bears" because Indians don't fight fairly, "after the manner of other nations." They are thieves and murderers, he wrote, who "don't appear openly in the field to bid us battle, . . . [and] use those cruelly that fall into their hands." Stoddard concluded that since they act like wolves, they should be treated like wolves. Stoddard, "Letter to Gov. Dudley."

20. Bowden observes that Brainerd's evangelism was confined to a small area around today's Trenton (New Jersey) where he spent only sixteen months, converting no more than fifty Indians, to whom he administered communion only three times. Bowden, *American Indians and Christian Missions*, 154; see also DB, 338. On Brainerd's legend, see Conforti, *Jonathan Edwards, Religious Tradition, and American Culture*, 62–86.

21. According to Norman Pettit, there is "little doubt that Brainerd's example eased [Edwards's] decision to take up the Stockbridge mission. . . . he took up the cause of the Indians and defended them against exploitation with a zeal that must have been inspired by Brainerd's work." DB, 16.

ard" who had purposely steered other natives away from Brainerd's preaching. Brainerd compared him to Simon Magus and confessed that he had secretly wished for his death. But then the medicine man had a "lively, soul-refreshing view of the excellency of Christ," challenged another to embrace Christ, and like Saint Paul spent his days preaching the faith he once attacked.[22]

Brainerd's greatest boast was in his own Indian congregation, made up of those who had welcomed his preaching. Here, Brainerd claimed, was Christian love of greater strength than in the early church (DB, 387) and a sense of the presence of God stronger than in any white congregation: "I know of no assembly of Christians where there seems to be so much of the presence of God, where brotherly love so much prevails, and where I should take so much delight in the public worship of God, in the general, as in my own congregation" (DB, 367–68).

Edwards believed these events had great significance. In his appendix to Brainerd's *Life*, Edwards speculated that the "wonderful things which God wrought among [the Indians] . . . are but a forerunner of something yet much more glorious and extensive of that kind" (DB, 533). By this he meant a "general revival of religion" that would be "very glorious . . . special and extraordinary" and would produce the "flourishing of Christ's kingdom on earth" (DB, 532). In other words, Brainerd was underestimating the importance of his work when he concluded that "the living God, as I strongly hoped, was engaged for [the Indians' salvation]" (DB, 255). Not only was God acting in demonstrative ways to redeem the devil's people, but this redemption had world-historical significance. It would presage a last, mighty work of the Spirit across the world at the end of time.[23]

In the meantime "something remarkable" was appearing among the natives of New England (HWR, 434). Their approach to things of the Spirit was not following the usual Reformed pattern. Even their moral character was different, for they displayed far less ingenuity in evil than the Europeans did: "The poor savage Americans are mere babes and fools (if I may so speak) as to proficiency in wickedness, in comparison of multitudes that the Christian world throngs with" (OS, 183). But of far more significance was their religious sensibility. Beginning in his sermon series on the history of redemption in 1739, and continuing into the 1740s and then intensifying during the Stockbridge years, Edwards was repeatedly struck by what seemed to be a regenerate disposition among otherwise unconverted Indians. In the 1740s he was commenting on what he had heard from Brainerd, but in the 1750s he reported his own observations from his frontier mission outpost.

Edwards first made public comment about "remarkable" things among the natives in a 1739 sermon on the work of redemption. There he noted that among "many Indians" there was a "remarkable . . . *inclination* to be instructed in the Christian religion" (HWR, 434; emphasis added). His use of the word "inclination" is suggestive if not determinative because of his later use of the same word

---

22. Ibid., 308, 391–95.
23. See chapter 2 of McDermott, *One Holy and Happy Society*, for Edwards's end-time scenario.

in the *Religious Affections* (1746) for the central orientation of the self, which signals the basic direction of the soul, either toward or away from God (*RA*, 12–13, 100, 107, 310, 312, passim).

Whether or not Edwards meant in 1739 that this promising inclination was evidence of a regenerate disposition, his choice of a text for his first sermon to the Indians at Stockbridge suggests that in 1751 he was considering that possibility.[24] The new missionary pastor chose to preach on Acts 11:12–13, the story of the Roman centurion Cornelius, who is described by Luke as a God-fearing "devout man" whose prayers and alms were approved by God (Acts 10:2–4)—and whom Edwards had regarded as regenerate (just before Peter told him about Jesus) at least as early as 1740.[25] Edwards told his auditors that Cornelius "had heard something of the true G. before Peter came to Him but he knew but little[.] he did not know anything about J[esus] X[Christ]." But Cornelius "was willing to be instructed" and "had a mind to know more." Therefore he "prayed to G. that he might be brought into the Light."

After explaining how Cornelius and his family were converted through Peter's preaching, Edwards proclaimed, "Now I am come to preach the true Relig. to you & to your Childr. as Peter did to Cornelius & his family that you & all your chil. may be saved" (Sermon on Acts 11:12–13; January 1751). We don't know if anyone that day was "willing to be instructed" and "had a mind to know more," but we do know that Edwards was convinced shortly thereafter that Native Americans at Onohquaga[26] had such a mind. In the following year he wrote the Reverend Isaac Hollis that "many" members of that tribe "that used to be notorious drunkards and blood-thirsty warriors, have of late strangely had their *dispositions* and manners changed through some wonderful influence on their minds." They were now uninterested in war and had forsaken drunkenness. What's more, they had "a *disposition* to religion and a thirst after instruction."[27] Once again, Edwards's vocabulary was suggestive. "Disposition" was a word Edwards used synonymously for "inclination," both in sermons and in his most developed analysis of religious experience, the *Religious Affections*. To say that the Onohquagas had a disposition to religion and a thirst after instruction recalls the nearly identical description of Cornelius and therefore suggests that the Spirit was working in these people to prepare them for conversion.

A similar suggestion is made in his 1753 letter to Andrew Oliver, the secretary of the Board of Commissioners for Indian Affairs. Edwards told Oliver that "sachems of the Conneenchees" had informed him that the Onohquagas were more religious and virtuous than "their own tribe" and then claimed that he had found this testimony to be true. "They have appeared to be far the best *disposed* Indians

---

24. This was a congregation of between one and two hundred Mahican and Mohawk Indians.
25. *Misc.* 840 (spring 1740); see Chap. 7.
26. This was the name for several villages along a ten-mile stretch of the Susquehanna River. By the mid-1750s there were Tuscagoras, Mahicans, Shawnees, and Oneida Indians living in these villages. Calloway, *The American Revolution in Indian Country*, 108–11.
27. Letter to the Reverend Isaac Hollis, July 17, 1752.

we have had to do with, and would be inclined to their utmost to assist, encourage and to strengthen the hands of missionaries and instructors, should [any] be sent among [them], and do all they can to forward their success among themselves and other Indians round about."[28] Two days later Edwards wrote a Scottish minister that another group of Indians had a Cornelian desire to hear and assimilate the gospel: they "have a great desire that the gospel should be introduced and settled in their country."[29]

Edwards apparently pondered these things in his heart and deduced that the Indians would have a glorious future in the work of redemption. His optimism was not shared by many. In fact, Samuel Kirkland, "the most effective Protestant missionary to the Iroquois," concluded that they were under the curse of Ham and as a people would never be called to God at the millennium.[30] Edwards, in contrast, added no qualifications when he predicted that the natives of America, along with "the nations of Negroes and others," shall "serve the true God and praises shall be sung to the Lord Jesus Christ" (HWR, 472).

Therefore he was confident that God would work through preaching to redeem the devil's people. During his seven years at Stockbridge he preached more than 190 sermons, only 27 of which were repetitions of sermons delivered earlier.[31] It is clear from the extant manuscripts that Edwards worked hard to adapt his rhetoric to the abilities of his hearers. As Rachel Wheeler has noted, the Stockbridge sermons tell more stories than the Northampton sermons;[32] they are also simpler in presentation and employ more imagery derived from nature. For example, a 1751 sermon on 2 Peter 1:19 ("We have a more sure word of prophecy") illustrates all three of these devices:

> When G. first made man He had a principle of Holiness in his Heart. That holiness that was in Him was like a Light that shone in his Heart so that his mind was full of Light[.] But when man sinned against G. He lost his Holiness & then the light that was in His mind was put out.... Truly good men ... not only have the light Shining round about em but the Light Shines into their Hearts.... wicked men ... altho the Light shines round about em yet it dont Shine into 'em but are perfectly dark within.

The imagery is of light and darkness, there is the story of the Fall, and the difference between the regenerate and unregenerate is put in starkly simple terms.

Imagery drawn from rustic life can be seen in another sermon from the same month. Preaching on Genesis 1:27, Edwards declared that "the Holiness of God is like the brightness of the Sun & Holiness in men is as when you hold a Glass in the light of the Sun whereby the Glass shares with some Image of the suns Brightness" (Sermon on Gen. 1:27, August 1751). Perhaps referring to the native sus-

---

28. Letter to Oliver, April 12, 1753.
29. Letter to Reverend John Erskine, April 14, 1753.
30. Axtell, *The Invasion Within*, 272.
31. Davies, "Prepare Ye the Way of the Lord," 200. However, most of the sermons at Stockbridge were "not original but outlines of Northampton sermons" (SDK, 66).
32. Wheeler, "'A Heathenish, Barbarous, Brutish Education': Jonathan Edwards and the Stockbridge Indians" (unpub. paper loaned by the author), 6.

ceptibility to drink, Edwards compared humans to swine: "Men when they are drunk do vile [things] & behave thems[elves] in a Beastly manner like a pig that wallows in the mire" (ibid.). Describing regeneration, he used the graphic images of snakes, toads, and excrement: "That which is filthy like a toad or serpent is made to shine bright with some of [Christ's] beauty & brightness. That which is like a Heap of dung is made a[s] one of G[o]ds precious Jewels" (ibid.).

If Edwards preached more simply to his Indian audience, accommodating the form of his message to unsophisticated ears, he did not sacrifice content. The aesthetic dimension of his theological vision, for example, was not an elitist mystery reserved for learned adepts but stood at the heart of his understanding of true religion, to which even the most rusticated soul was given access. He told the Stockbridge Indians in his first sermon, for instance, that they must have "their Eyes opened to see how lovely [Christ] is."[33] In an October 1751 exposition of Psalm 119:18 ("Open thou mine eyes, that I may behold wondrous things out of thy law"), he explained that the "chief things" that our eyes must be opened to see are Christ's "Glory and Excellency." In a sermon on the two ways of life—one that leads to life and happiness, and the other that leads to death and misery—he explained that even those who go to church may be headed for death. This is true for all those who attend meetings but into whose hearts the Light has not shone, so that they "are blind & dont see the Glory & Loveliness of G[od] and [Christ]."[34] And in a communion lecture in Stockbridge he asserted that a good man "Loves G[od] above all else for his own Beauty."[35] Hence if Edwards preached a gospel at once aesthetic and mystical, he considered his Stockbridge Indian parishioners capable of understanding such rarefied themes. His outlines were less complex and his imagery earthier than in his sermons to white audiences—but the vision he tried to evoke no less sublime.

Native Humanity

The Jonathan Edwards who disdained native religion nevertheless held an extraordinarily positive view of the spiritual status of (some) Native American individuals and tribes, considered them to be less morally culpable than their white, nominally Christian counterparts, and entertained an exalted conception of their eschatological destiny. Perhaps as a result of his seeing a spiritually receptive disposition in so many of them, he also held a more positive view of their humanity than most of his fellow colonials. Few of them desired anything but the extermination of Indians, and certainly not their salvation.[36] Oft-repeated legends of native cruelty and laziness were taken as *prima facie* confirmations of their

---

33. Sermon on Acts 11:12–13.
34. Sermon on Matthew 7:13–14, January 1751.
35. Lecture before the sacrament, Psalm 27:4 [2], 1.
36. According to Samuel Hopkins (the elder), writing of the Stockbridge mission in the early 1750s, many would as soon kill as convert the Indians; Hopkins, *Historical Memoirs Relating to the Housatonic Indians* (Boston, 1753). My thanks to Rachel Wheeler for this citation.

infernal destiny. Edwards was raised with the same legends and had familial experience that might have corroborated some strains of these stories, but he was also convinced that "remarkable" acts in the drama of redemption were being performed on the New England colonial stage. So he looked forward to the final scene in which those currently being held prisoner by Satan would be triumphantly liberated. And since current scenes were providing dramatic previews of the final act, it was easier for Edwards than for his benighted contemporaries to imagine the fullness of the *imago dei* hiding in *potentia* behind the camouflage of what whites considered native brutishness.

Many of those contemporaries "distrusted and even opposed the missionary endeavor,"[37] judging Indians to be something less than fully human, "Satan's associates in his intensifying war against Christian order."[38] Because of Edwards's proleptic view of redemption history, he could see more blessed realities unfolding beyond the demonic present, but for many of his *confrères* service to Satan meant loss of humanity—or at least barbarism, with all of its attendant blindness to what makes life humane. Bowden has suggested that American colonials transferred their loathing for Irish "barbarians" to the Native Americans.

> Since Elizabethan times the English had viewed the truculent Irish, who followed a separate religion and culture, as barbarians who would not accept the manifest advantages of British control. In America that preconception transferred easily to the Indians, who indicated a similar reluctance to acknowledge the superiority of English life.[39]

For most colonials, then, the natives were savages of the lowest sort. One needed to respect no scruples against invading their lands, since their domain lay outside the sanctions of morality and law.[40] Even Francis Parkman, the nineteenth-century American historian, blamed the destruction of the great Native American nations in his century on their "ferocity" and "intractable indolence" and referred to the native character as "homicidal" and "demoniac."[41]

Edwards, in contrast, proclaimed to his Indian hearers, "We are no better than you in no Respect." His forefathers, he asserted, were once in spiritual darkness like the Indians, and were given light only by the kindness of God. So the English too had been heathen once and now had religious knowledge only because of God's grace. Now it was the Indians' turn to receive that same kindness and light.

In fact, the New England colonials were guilty of greater sins than the natives because the colonists had sinned against greater light. Their failure to teach native children to read was "shameful neglect," which "undoubtedly" has made "the great God . . . very angry." New Englanders had shamefully neglected their duty;

---

37. Douglas E. Leach, *The Northern Colonial Frontier 1607–1763* (New York, 1966), 190.
38. Morrison, *Embattled Northeast*, 50.
39. Bowden, *American Indians and Christian Missions*, 113–14; see also Canny, "The Ideology of English Colonization."
40. Jennings, *Empire of Fortune*, 59f.
41. Parkman, *The Jesuits in North America*, 418; cited in Jennings, *Empire of Fortune*, 85; Jacobs, *Dispossessing the American Indian*, 110; Jacobs, "Some Social Ideas of Francis Parkman."

they had not behaved like Christians because they had shown so little love for the souls of Indians. For that matter, all who "call thems[elves Christians] & have wicked Hearts & live wicked lives, are the devils People as well as the Heathen. They are on the devil's side not on [Christ's] side."[42]

For many New Englanders, this would have been a scandalous statement. To say that white colonials were just as much the devil's people as Indians was a logical but distasteful deduction from Christian theological premises. But to go further and assert that there was no metaphysical distinction between whites and Indians, and to suggest that Indians could attain the same spiritual status as whites was socially dangerous. Would that encourage resistance to the juggernaut of white land development?

Edwards seems to have developed genuine affection for his Indian congregation. Early in his tenure at Stockbridge, shortly after being ejected from the Northampton pulpit by parishioners who complained of his "unsociable" ways, Edwards seemed encouraged that "the Indians seem much pleased with my family, especially my wife."[43] Later he referred to them as "my people" and noted happily that they "steadfastly adhere to me" despite the concerted efforts of the Williams family—his own relatives—to alienate them from him.[44] Edwards also included the white Stockbridge congregation in the company of his supporters, but he preached a kinder and gentler message to the native congregation. In her careful study of the Stockbridge sermons, Rachel Wheeler notes that while Edwards told the Native Americans repeatedly of Christ's desire to save them, he spent far more time in his sermons to the "English" congregation at the mission warning them of God's wrath. The missionary preacher emphasized to his native auditors not God's judgment but the divine invitation; he was careful to apprise them that God's election did not depend on skin color or nationality. There is "forgiveness offered to all nations," he assured them.[45]

In the last decade of his life, then, Edwards signaled a change in emphasis. No longer did he automatically consider Native Americans stellar members of Satan's kingdom. The majority of them may still have been damned, but they were no more prominent in that infernal realm than legions of white hypocrites. Among the worst were the greedy English and Dutch traders, who purposely kept the natives from instruction "for the sake of making a gain of you. For as long as they keep you in Ignoran[ce] tis more easy to cheat you in trading with you." Of course the French weren't any better. According to Edwards, they made sure the Indians didn't learn to read so that they would not see that French ways "are not agreeable to the Scriptures. . . . When the Bible is hid from em they cant cheat em & make em believe what they have a mind to."[46]

---

42. Sermon on 2 Peter 1:19; sermon on 1 John 3:10.
43. Letter to the Reverend Timothy Edwards, in *LPW*, 420.
44. Letter to Reverend Thomas Gillespie, in *LPW*, 610.
45. Rachel Wheeler, "Disappointment: The Stockbridge Indians and Jonathan Edwards," chap. 3 in Wheeler, "Living Upon Hope"; sermon on Luke 24:47, October 1751.
46. Sermon on 2 Peter 1:19.

To confer moral equivalence on English and French sins was, for many New Englanders, a kind of communal treachery. Of course Edwards would in the same breath join his compatriots in denouncing the French as benighted pawns of the papal Antichrist. Yet his willingness to condemn both English and French exploitation of the natives underscores the relative singularity with which he showed respect for their humanity in ways that most of his compatriots did not. He never came close to the fraternal humility of John Woolman, who respected their religious *knowledge* and considered their condition as (in some respects) superior to his own.[47] But he showed some affinity for the spiritual sensitivity of Roger Williams, who said that Indians had not sinned against gospel light and were closer to grace than the "unchristian Christians" of the Massachusetts Bay Colony.[48]

Practical Service

Edwards demonstrated his respect for Indians as fellow human beings in a number of ways during his seven years of service as a missionary on the Massachusetts frontier. In one respect, however, his Indian congregation might have sensed something less than respect. He adamantly refused to learn their language, claiming that his time would be spent more profitably teaching them English and that they themselves agreed with his decision. One wonders if those who disagreed felt free to voice their disapproval to one who was director of the mission compound on which they lived. Perhaps some of them also wondered why Edwards encouraged his own son to learn Mahican, and how such an industrious scholar could not make some effort to learn the language of those he hoped to win.[49]

Nevertheless Edwards expended considerable time and effort defending his native parishioners against greedy whites who were manipulating the Stockbridge mission for their own aggrandizement. Despite recurrent physical distress and public vilification of his efforts, Edwards wrote numerous letters to Boston and London pleading the natives' rights to education and justice. He obtained land and had it plowed for native families, for example, so that they could send their children to school and made sure that five native boys found lodging in white homes so they could receive an education. Edwards took at least one of the boys into his own home.[50]

In 1751 Edwards wrote to the Speaker of the Massachusetts Assembly to urge that body to honor its treaty obligations to the Housatonnuks.[51] When a friend of one of the whites seeking to exploit the mission struck a native child on the head with a cane, it was Edwards who managed to convince the offender to pay dam-

---

47. John Woolman, *The Journal of John Woolman and A Plea for the Poor* (1774; Secaucus, N.J., 1972); cited in Hutchison, *Errand to the World*, 33.
48. Hutchison, *Errand to the World*, 36–37.
49. See letter to William Pepperrell, January 30, 1753, and the letter to Jonathan Edwards, Jr., May 27, 1755.
50. Letter to Thomas Prince, May 10, 1754.
51. This was the name given by white settlers to the Stockbridge natives, most of whom were Mahicans, a branch of the Algonquins. Davies, "Prepare Ye the Way of the Lord," 196.

ages. After a native was killed by two whites, he labored to obtain indemnity money to pay the grief-stricken family.[52] Edwards spent hours listening to the broken English and sign language of native children and asking questions in broken Indian dialect, so that he could accurately report to Boston Commissioners[53] that his Indian scholars did not have enough blankets or food, that some boys had no breeches and many were going ragged to meetings, and that all the boys were being forced to work six days per week. Once a week he sat the children down for instruction in religion, experimenting with new methods that emphasized narrative and Socratic questioning instead of rote learning, which until then had been the method of choice. Edwards was concerned that the lessons would "cease to be a dull, wearisome task, without any suitable pleasure or benefit."[54] Sadly, Edwards and others (John Sergeant and Timothy Woodbridge) who fought for Indian rights "were all but powerless against the aggressive [Ephraim] Williams [ironically, a relative of Edwards] and his supporters . . . [who] cheated the Indians out of their land and drove them from their town."[55]

Edwards also showed concern for Native Americans outside his own acquaintance. Before he arrived at Stockbridge he had worked with John and David Brainerd trying to get fresh land in New York for natives near Cranberry, New Jersey, who were being pushed out by white settlers (DB, 65). Edwards had long taken interest in missions to the natives and came to serve as something of a clearinghouse for both foreign and Boston correspondents seeking news of their religious and political loyalties.[56]

Final Remarks

Typically in studies of colonial relations between Native Americans and the European settlers, attention has focused exclusively on European influence on the natives. Some scholars, however, are now probing the influence that went in the other direction, from the Indians to the whites. Richard W. Pointer, for example, has recently shown how the Delaware River Valley Indians helped shape David Brainerd's spirituality.[57] As I have suggested, Indians may have influenced Edwards as well. Although he gave little indication of seeing any value in their religion and

52. Letter to Sec. Josiah Willard, May 27, 1754.
53. These men were commissioners of the "Society in London, for Propagating the Gospel in New England, and the Parts Adjacent." Dwight, *The Life of President Edwards*, 449.
54. Letter to William Pepperrill, in *LPW*, 407–8.
55. Miles, "The Red Man Dispossessed," 74–75. This was the same Williams family that engineered Edwards's expulsion from Northampton. Ephraim Sr., head of the Stockbridge branch of the family, was an uncle to Solomon Williams, who wrote a challenge to Edwards's *Humble Inquiry* on communion qualifications—the material issue that led to Edwards's removal.
56. See, for example, his letter to the Reverend John Erskine, May 20, 1749, in *LPW*, 268–71, and his report to the Speaker of the Massachusetts House of Representatives in 1751 on an Albany conference between the English and the natives, in *LPW*, 394–405.
57. Pointer, "'Poor Indians' and the 'Poor in Spirit.'"

culture, he was clearly impressed by what God seemed to be doing among them. They seemed to him a divinely determined bellwether of the future direction of redemptive history. They may also have prodded him to think more deeply about the relationship between regeneration and conversion. Among the natives of the Connecticut and Hudson River valleys he found unconverted souls who displayed signs of what may have appeared to him to be regeneration. One wonders if they helped inspire his speculation in the twilight years of his life that God had given religious truth to the heathen to "benefit their souls" (*Misc.* 1162).

But if he was not convinced that they were saved, he was certainly struck by what Rachel Wheeler has called their common humanity. These American heathen, whom he once called "beasts," had now become souls with names—and parishioners whose interests he protected against those who would exploit them.[58] Even those Indians who never embraced Edwards's Christ showed their pastor a respect and gratitude that Edwards remembered was so sorely lacking among many of the "saints" at Northampton.[59] The uncivilized natives showed more civility and common virtue than the educated English. Little wonder that Edwards's private notebooks evidence continual rethinking of the spiritual knowledge and state of the heathen. On this subject, in the last eight years of his life Edwards was a work in progress. His untimely death interrupted what was gradually emerging as a reconsideration of traditional understandings of the limits of grace. Edwards's Indian parishioners may have played a role in that reformulation.

---

58. See Wheeler, "Disappointment."
59. Letter to Reverend Thomas Gillespie, October 18, 1753, in *LPW*, 610; see also notes attached to sermon on Luke 1:77–79, December 1753.

12

THE CHINESE PHILOSOPHERS

Shadows of the Trinity

In the eighteenth century China became the focus of an international religious and philosophical debate over the origins of true religion.[1] Did God reveal morals and salvation through historical revelation or innate reason? Both sides in the debate appealed to Chinese culture. Deists claimed that China was a living prototype of deist ethics, while traditionalists pointed to traces of orthodox theology in the Chinese Classics, which supposedly evidenced revelation passed down to Chinese patriarchs from the sons of Noah. Jonathan Edwards followed this debate from his frontier outpost in New England and used China to support his own attacks on deist claims.

Jesuits and the Most Blessed Nation

The eighteenth-century debate was dependent on travelogues written by Jesuit missionaries to China in the sixteenth and seventeenth centuries.[2] The Jesuit pioneer in East Asia, Francis Xavier, died in 1552 just off the coast of China while waiting to enter the country. In 1583 Matthew Ricci settled in Chaoch'ing, a provincial capital, and then in 1601 reached the imperial capital. Ricci's clock-repair

---

1. I am grateful to Li Wang of the University of Iowa for help on this chapter.
2. Christianity had come twice before to China and both times had completely disappeared: first in the seventh century in the T'ang Dynasty, and then in the thirteenth century during Mongol rule. Latourette, *Christian Missions in China*, 51–55, 61–77. For surveys of the Jesuit missions to the Far East, see Pinot, *La China*; Etiemble, *Les Jesuits en China*; and Charles E. Ronan and Bonnie Oh, *East Meets West: The Jesuits in China, 1582–1773* (Chicago, 1988).

and map-making skills won the respect of the emperor, and his gracious conversational skills opened doors for further Christian missions. At his death in 1610 the church in China was said to have two thousand members.[3] Ricci's successor, Johann Adam Schall von Bell (1591–1666), further improved the Jesuits' reputation at the imperial court by predicting eclipses. By 1664 254,980 Chinese had been baptized.

Success bred opposition. In 1664 court officials charged that the Jesuits were preparing the country for Portuguese occupation; five Chinese Christians were executed as a result. Then Catholic opponents back in Europe alleged that the Jesuits, in their desire to be accepted by Chinese nobility, had compromised essentials of the faith. The ensuing Rites Controversy raged over funeral customs, ancestor worship, and the name of God. Ricci had permitted his Chinese congregations to use the word *shen* ("holy") for anything venerable, including the person of Confucius. He also believed that the reverence paid to ancestors was only symbolic and so left it to indigenous church leadership to decide its theological propriety for themselves (the first Chinese bishop Lô Wen-Tsao permitted its practice during his episcopate from 1685 to 1691). Finally, he was persuaded that the ancient Chinese terms *Tian* (Heaven) and *Shang-di* (Supreme Ruler) could be used by Christians as names for God. Missionaries from other Catholic orders, however, believed that Ricci and his fellow Jesuits had introduced their converts to a semi-pagan Christianity. In 1693 the French vicar apostolic Charles Maigrot, who had lived in China for ten years, decided that the Jesuits had misunderstood the Chinese rites and issued orders that Chinese Christians were neither to participate in ancestor reverence rites nor to refer to God with traditional Chinese terms.[4]

It was in this context that the Jesuits defended Chinese culture as incipiently Christian. They argued that Chinese philosophy and religion contained elements that pointed to key elements of Christian faith, and therefore Chinese terms for God and traditional ancestor rites could be used by Christians. Louis Lecomte's *Nouveaux Memoires sur l'etat présent de la China* (1696)[5] was the most widely distributed Jesuit apology to appear in Europe. Lecomte claimed that Fohi,[6] the first emperor of China, was descended from the children of Noah, and that the Chinese had preserved knowledge of the true God for two thousand years before Christ in a manner that could serve as "both an Example and Instruction to Christians themselves."[7] No nation had been more blessed than China, for the founders of the

---

3. Neill, *A History of Christian Missions*, 138–41; see also Dunne, *Generation of Giants*, and Rowbotham, *Missionary and Mandarin*; Jonathan D. Spence, *The Memory Palace of Matteo Ricci* (New York, 1984).

4. Neill, *A History of Christian Missions*, 140f., 160–63; Latourette, *Christian Missions in China*, 134; Rowbotham, *Missionary and Mandarin*, 119–75.

5. This was translated into English the following year and published as *Memoirs and Observations: Topographical, Physical, Mathematical, Mechanical, Natural, Civil and Ecclesiastical, Made in a Late Journey Through an Empire of China, and Published in Several Letters* (London, 1697).

6. This may be a reference to Fu Hsi, first ancestor of humankind according to Chinese legend.

7. Lecomte, *Memoirs and Observations*, 317.

Middle Kingdom had learned true religion from Shem and his sons and had preserved their people from idolatry until the time of Christ.[8]

Another French Jesuit, Joachim Bouvet, claimed that the I-Ching follows a numerical pattern revealing monotheism, seven days of creation, the Incarnation, and redemption by a savior.[9] His confrère Joseph Prémare declared that Jesus is the soul of the Chinese Classics.[10]

The Jesuit narrative that had the greatest impact on the European mind was Jean Baptiste Duhalde's four-volume *Description géographique, historique, chronologique, politique, et physique de l'empire de la Chine et de la Tartarie chinoise* (1735).[11] Duhalde had never been to China himself but had collected Jesuit anecdotes highlighting the moral excellence of Chinese emperors and officials. According to Arnold H. Rowbotham, his work more than any other source "created an eighteenth-century tradition of benevolent despotism in China.... No single work on the Far East, before or since, has had such a profound influence on European thought." Duhalde told his readers that some of Noah's descendants settled in China about two hundred years after the Flood and taught there by tradition the principles of true religion, moral government, and true virtue. Unlike the Greek and Roman moralists and philosophers, Chinese thinkers emphasized humility and denied the eternality of matter. Duhalde cited a passage in the Dao-de-jing which he suggested points to the Trinity and quoted Confucius as prophesying the coming of a Most Holy person in the West.[12]

"Good Old Confucius" among the Deists

The Sorbonne eventually condemned the Jesuits' interpretation of Chinese culture. To the theologians at Paris, the Jesuits' claims for China undermined the uniqueness of Israel's election; God could save a few heathen, but it was implausible that a whole nation would be so extraordinarily favored.[13]

Precisely, replied the deists. China is only a clear example of what is germinating in every human breast and could be developed with proper nuture. She is liv-

---

8. Rowbotham, *Missionary and Mandarin*, 141–44. Le Comte used Philippe Couplet's long preface to the first Latin translation of Confucius's works, produced by Couplet and three other Jesuits in 1687; Walker, *Ancient Theology*, 200.

9. Walker, *Ancient Theology*, 220–23.

10. Rowbotham, "Jesuit Figurists," 479.

11. My references are to the English translation, P. Duhalde, *The General History of China. Containing a Geographical, Historical, Chronological, Political and Physical Description of the Empire of China, Chinese-Tartary, Corea and Thibet. Including an Exact and Particular Account of their Customs, Manners, Ceremonies, Religion, Arts and Sciences*, 3d ed. (London, 1741).

12. Rowbotham, "Jesuit Figurists," 264, 257; Duhalde, *General History of China*, 3:15–21; 3:27, 28, 30, 35. If the Jesuits were liberal theologically and culturally, they were conservative in their politics. Couplet imagined Confucius coming to France, recognizing in Louis XIV the ideal monarch, and admiring most his revocation of the Edict of Nantes. This caused Pierre Bayle to remark that if the Jesuits gained China, they would make it "toute catholique." Walker, *Ancient Theology*, 229.

13. Walker, *Ancient Theology*, 203.

ing proof that one does not need God to be moral, as Bayle put it, and that religion and morality are independent of one another. They were inspired by Leibniz's publication of Jesuit letters from China in *Novissima Sinica* (1697), in the preface to which he suggested that Chinese missionaries ought to be sent to the West to teach natural religion.[14]

Encouraged by Locke's remark that Confucius knew some of the precepts of Jesus' gospel, John Toland declared that the Chinese sage was among the "Votaries of Truth," along with Socrates, Plato, Xenophon, Cato, Cicero, and Parmenides. Charles Blount used Jesuit travelogues on China to decry "particular religions" and argue that revealed religion cannot be true because it is not known to all human beings.[15]

In the "Deists' Bible" Tindal lauded Confucius for recognizing that it is wrong to love our enemies and that God does not love evil men. Although he granted that the maxims of Jesus and Confucius do not differ substantially, Tindal praised Confucius for being "plain and simple," a refreshing contrast to the "more obscure" teachings of Jesus in the New Testament. Tindal apparently believed that "the humanistic basis of the Confucian canon was . . . an antidote to the obscurantism of the Christian scriptures." David Hume and William Warburton were also impressed by the clarity and luminosity of Chinese ethics.[16]

Outside England deist reactions were similar. Voltaire was so persuaded by Duhalde's reports of Chinese virtue that he pronounced Duhalde one of the great men of his age and portrayed China as a utopian state, ruled by wise men. Montesquieu used Duhalde's descriptions of the Chinese in his *L'Esprit des lois* (1748), finding in its system honor and virtue, the characteristics of the monarchy and the republic. The freethinker La Mothe le Vayer is reported to have exclaimed, "Sancte Confuci, ora pro nobis!"[17]

The American deists were also enthusiastic. The *Independent Whig* reported that "good old Confucius" had a "more Christian spirit," and that the Chinese were happier and held to a more virtuous paganism than their counterparts in the West. In China, John Trenchard declared, "all men of any eminence for learning or dignity" were deists. Trenchard therefore wished that all men would become "rational and sober Chinese."[18]

Benjamin Franklin was eager to get news of the virtuous Chinese out to his American readers. A. Owen Aldridge reports that Franklin was fond of reading about China and as a young man had wanted to visit that country. In 1735 he

---

14. Rowbotham, *Missionary and Mandarin*, 251. Leibniz's writing on China, which was based on Le Comte, moved August Hermann Francke, the German pietist, to establish a mission in China, and philosopher Christian Wolff to develop a rational natural morality dependent on neither religion nor revelation. Francke had Wolff dismissed from the faculty at Halle for teaching what Francke took to be "atheism." Rowbotham, *Missionary and Mandarin*, 251, 253; Davis, "China," 536.

15. Locke, *The Reasonableness of Christianity*, 173; Toland, *Pantheisticon*, 64; Blount, *Modern Brachmins*, 81, 89, 198; Blount, *Great Is Diana*, 3.

16. *CAO*, 341; Rowbotham, *Missionary and Mandarin*, 253; Davis, "China," 538–42.

17. Rowbotham, *Missionary and Mandarin*, 250.

18. *IW*, 2:56.

published an analysis of Confucian thought in his newspaper and nine years later printed portions of Duhalde in the *American Magazine and Historical Chronicle*.[19]

Chevalier Ramsay and the Key to Heathen Mythology

Chevalier Ramsay was as excited about China as the deists, but for the purpose of defending, not discrediting, revelation. Ramsay was one of the most interesting intellectuals of the eighteenth century. Raised in the Church of Scotland by a Presbyterian father and an Episcopalian mother, he converted to Roman Catholicism after a personal audience with French mystic Archbishop Fenelon, whom he later served as literary executor and biographer. He lived with the French Quietist author Madame Guyon for two years and came to be persuaded that Origen's metempsychosis and universalism were the best responses to challenges from Celsus and Bayle. Toward the end of his life he wrote an *Apology for the Free and Accepted Masons* (1738).[20]

Ramsay used China to prop up a tottering *prisca theologia* that he had learned from Ralph Cudworth.[21] Seventeenth-century scholars had shown that traditional sources for the *prisca theologia* such as the *Hermetica* were probably Christian forgeries written well after the centuries when Plato and other philosophers were said to have read them.[22] But Ramsay followed Cudworth in contending that the Chinese Classics were completed long before Plato and the other philosophers of Greece and Rome emerged. Hence the *prisca theologia* was vindicated: the original deposit of revelation containing Christian truths was indeed passed down from the biblical patriarchs to the founders of the heathen nations.

China was Ramsay's trump card. No other culture could be traced back so far as China's; no civilization was nearer to the origin of the world. In fact, the Chinese language was never distorted by Babel, since the Chinese patriarchs were safely removed from that linguistic catastrophe. Hence its "hieroglyphs" (characters) represent humanity's original language, perhaps going back to the dialect of Eden, and the mythology depicted by those hieroglyphs is therefore clearer than all other heathen mythologies that are "less ancient and more obscured by succession of time."[23] Ramsay concluded that Chinese mythology provided a hermeneutical "key" to the explication of all other non-Christian mythology. Since China was earlier, and all mythologies derived from the same revelation distributed by patriarchs descended from Noah, the earliest rendition was the most accurate and thus most useful for interpreting the true meaning of later myths that presumably were more distorted by the sinful vicissitudes of time.

---

19. Aldridge, *The Dragon and the Eagle*, 8, 26, 28, 77.
20. Walker, *Ancient Theology*, 231–53. See also G. D. Henderson, *Chevalier Ramsay* (London, 1952).
21. Cudworth, *True Intellectual System*. Ramsay got what he knew of China from Boyer D'Argens, *Lettres chinoises*, 5 vols. (La Haye, 1739–40) and Duhalde. Henderson, *Chevalier Ramsay*, 206–7, 219–20.
22. Harrison, "Religion" and the Religions, 136f.
23. Ramsay, *Philosophical Principles*, 2:176–80.

Ramsay claimed to find plenty of Christian truth in the Chinese Classics. In the "Y-King [I-Ching]," for example, there is a minister of the supreme God "whom they call the holy or saint by excellence," and who reunites in one person all the divine attributes and human qualities. Tian gave this minister "out of love the whole universe to govern" because "the instructions of the saint are these of the supreme God himself." In fact, the saint is "TIEN [Heaven] speaking with a human voice. . . . He has the form of a man, but the heaven and the earth are re-united in him." This "HEAVEN-MAN" existed before anything was produced.[24]

This saint was not only an apparent incarnation of God, but also an atoning sacrifice. By his "justice . . . the world shall be re-established in the ways of righteousness." And by his sufferings and death, he would offer a sacrifice to "save the world." The I-Ching "Messiah" would banish all sin and suffering and "turn his eyes to the west." His suffering was necessary to undo the effects of the Fall, which was instigated by a woman and the pride of the devil—"the rebellious and perverse dragon."[25]

Because of these revelations found in coded form in the Chinese Classics, there were undoubtedly Chinese like Cornelius of the early church, whose prayer and almsgiving were accepted by God despite his ignorance of the name of Jesus. "May God not by his internal universal Grace have many Cornelius's in Africa, Asia and America who have never heard of the historical facts of the Bible, nor of the visible church, nor of the sacramental signs and symbols? . . . such as Socrates, Heraclitus, Epictetus and many others, as St. Justin Martyr assures." Just because heathen reside within the "bosom of Paganism" does not mean that they have partaken of its "impious, idolatrous, and superstitious worship." One must look at the heart's intent not the outward act, no matter how "inhuman." Even those who offer human sacrifice may have done so out of a genuine "submission to what they thought was a divine command." In any event, it was no worse than Christian "princes and priests [who hunt down] . . . Turks, Pagans and heretics, ravage their countreys, enslave their persons, burn, rack and torture their bodies [and] sacrifice millions of our fellow creatures in religious wars."[26]

Unfortunately, even the Chinese eventually confused the original revelation. Like all other heathen, they too "attached themselves to the letter, and to signs, without understanding the spirit and thing signified, and thus fell, by degree, into the grossest idolatry, and wildest superstitions." This semiotic mistake resulted in confusing the prophetic future (of the Messiah) for the legendary past. Redemptive actions of the future Messiah were thought to be exploits of their own mythic heroes. Thus the transcultural Messiah was turned into a tribal champion serving national pride. Then their own nation was reified as the elect one, a "peculiar favorite of heaven." Like other elect nations, China also came to regard the rest of the world as "profane, wicked and reprobate."[27] So despite the fact that she pre-

---

24. Ibid., 2:176–80.
25. Ibid., 2:445, 447.
26. Ibid., 2:104f., 457, 397–400.
27. Ibid., 2:14–16, 279, 16.

served true religion and its revelations longer and in purer form than anyone else, eventually China too went the way of all flesh.

Jonathan Edwards on China's "Many Religious Truths"

Early in his career Jonathan Edwards became convinced that China was more civilized and religiously aware than other nations because she had been ruled by Noah for "many hundreds of years" and was isolated from the corrupting influences of other civilizations (Misc. 350).[28] Then in the 1740s he encountered a serious claim to China's significance in the *prisca theologia*. Three times during that decade he made mention in his reading catalog[29] of Samuel Shuckford's *Sacred and Profane History of the World Connected*,[30] which attempted to refute deist arguments by proving an original revelation made to the fathers of the nations. Edwards had possession of Shuckford's volumes by 1747 and copied from them the contentions that China's language was uncorrupted by "the confusion of Babel," and that Noah was the first king of China. Noah's ark landed north of India, Shuckford explained, and Fohi, the legendary first Chinese king, was said to have lived in the same period. In fact, he was supposed to have lived in northwest India, near Ararat. Fohi had no father and Noah's ancestors perished in the Flood; Fohi's mother was said to have conceived him encompassed by a rainbow; Fohi was reputed to have bred seven kinds of animals, and Noah took animals into the ark by sevens. Hence Fohi and Noah were probably one and the same. Edwards gave little indication whether he believed this particular claim, but he took it seriously enough to record it in his Notes on the Bible at Genesis 8:4 under the heading, "CONCERNING THE MOUNTAIN ON WHICH THE ARK RESTED, AND FOHI, OF CHINESE, HIS BEING THE SAME WITH NOAH."[31]

Just before Edwards left Northampton for Stockbridge, he made note in his reading catalog of John Lockman's *Travels of the Jesuits into various Parts of the World compiled from their letters* (1743), which drew from Lecomte and Duhalde. It is not clear whether Edwards ever procured a copy. But it *is* clear that he secured a copy of Ramsay's *Philosophical Principles*, and that he spent a good part of the Stockbridge years delighting in its evidences of an original deposit of revelation made to the patriarchs of Israel and transmitted to the founders of the nations through Noah's sons. Edwards copied no less than sixteen thousand words from Ramsay,[32] and a significant portion of what he copied described the religious knowledge of the Chinese.

Edwards overlooked Ramsay's unorthodox denunciations of predestination, original sin, the satisfaction theory of the atonement and God's infinite foreknowl-

---

28. Misc. 350 was composed in 1728 or 1729. *Miscellanies, a-500*, 101.
29. "Jonathan Edwards' Reading 'Catalogue,'" nos. 421, 450, 481.
30. Shuckford, *Sacred and Profane History*. My references are to the second edition, published in 1731.
31. Ibid., 1:98–104; NS, no. 455.
32. Most of his copying from Ramsay went into Misc. 1351 (3867 words) and Misc. 1355 (approx. 13,000 words). Word count courtesy of Kyle Farley.

edge, and his arguments for purgatory, metempsychosis, and universal pardon.[33] But he seemed intrigued by Ramsay's insistence that the Chinese knew about the coming Messiah. In 1751–1752 he copied passages from Ramsay focusing on (among many others) the passages from the I-Ching that supposedly describe "the saint" who has a human voice but through whom *Tian* will speak. This "heaven-man" would "labour and suffer much" in order to make a worthy sacrifice to the Lord. In another passage "Laotsee"[34] predicted that this heaven-man would proclaim, "He that takes upon him the filth and dust of the Kingdom shall be king of the universe." "Isemakonank" said that "the Saint dies to save the world . . . he loses himself to save others." In still another both "Laotsee and Confucius" predicted that the heaven-man was to come from the West.[35] In another *Miscellanies* passage from the same period Edwards copied from Jackson's *Chronological Antiquities* the assertion that Confucius taught the future coming of a "perfectly holy man" who would reintroduce the practice of virtue (Misc. 1200).

Just before the end of his career Edwards copied into his private notebooks large portions of Ramsay's *Discourse Upon the World and Mythology of the Pagans* (1727), a comparative study of religions that sought to prove their unity and common origins. Ramsay concluded his synthesis with a statement that Edwards records: "We see then that the doctrines of the primitive perfection of nature, its fall, and its restoration by a divine Hero, are equally manifest in the Mythologies of the Greeks, Romans, Egyptians, Persians, Indians and Chinese" (Misc. 1351).[36] Edwards added in the margin his own conclusion that there are "many religious truths" in Chinese and other "heathen" traditions. In this extract Edwards recorded Ramsay's documentation of three states of the world (paradise, fall, restoration) and evil's etiology in sin against God in the I-Ching. Edwards also noted here Ramsay's claim that the Chinese Classics prophesy the coming of the hero "Kiun Tse" who would be a shepherd or prince and perform the same role played by Mithras, "Brama," and Osiris. According to Ramsay, ancient traditions common to all nations taught that the "middle god" would expiate sin by suffering (Misc. 1351).

Edwards was also impressed by "hints and shadows of the Trinity" in the writings of the Chinese philosophers. He recorded Ramsay's paraphrase of the "Tonchu" [Dao-de-jing] passage, "The source and root of all is one. This self-existent Unity produces necessarily a second. The first & second by their union produce a third. In fine these three produce all."[37] Not long after he copied Philip Skelton's citation of the same passage.

33. Ramsay, *Philosophical Principles*, 1:151, 200–220, 347, 410, 430, 471, 477, 2:21.
34. A common eighteenth-century designation for Lao-zi.
35. All of the statements in this paragraph are from Misc. 1181, which is a long extract from the April 1751 issue of the *Monthly Review* that featured selections from Ramsay's *Philosophical Principles*.
36. This long Misc. entry is misleadingly titled "Travels of Cyrus" by Edwards, probably because *Travels* and the *Discourse* were published together. A small portion of this long entry contains extracts from *The Travels of Cyrus*, 2 vols. (London, 1727), but the majority of the entry comes from the *Discourse*. The original was *Les Voyages de Cyrus, avec un discours sur la mythologie* (Paris, 1727).
37. Misc. 1181. The passage Ramsay paraphrased is number 42 in the Dao-de-jing: "The Way produces one; one produces two, two produces three, three produce all beings." *Tao Te Ching*, in Lao-zi, *The Essential Tao*, 35.

Edwards became convinced that the Chinese also knew about regeneration.[38] Quoting Ramsay, he wrote that they were aware that Tian must "[restore] in us that primitive light & purity which the soul received from heaven upon its first creation which it has lost by sin & which heaven alone can render to it by its internal irradiations and influences" (Misc. 1181).

Edwards also recorded Ramsay's misogynist interpretation of the Fall—that "a woman threw us into slavery . . . [but] the wise husband raised up a bulwark of walls" (ibid.). The devil was the woman's co-conspirator; the I-Ching supposedly describes a "rebellious and perverse dragon" that was thrown down to earth to punish his pride and ambition, whose effects spread to all nations "and deluged the earth with crimes" (ibid.).

These last notebook entries, penned in the months before his death, show that Edwards shared Ramsay's conclusion that Chinese culture contained more pointers to religious truth than any other and in fact was the best validation of the prisca theologia. He recorded extracts that include mention of Lecomte and Duhalde and stated that all nations outside Greece and Italy "except China" are profoundly ignorant of religious truth (Misc. 1350). It is clear that he was aware that traditional sources for the prisca theologia such as the Chaldean Oracles and the Hermetica were spurious, but that he agreed with Cudworth and Ramsay that China provided independent confirmation of the tradition and therefore was a hermeneutical key to non-Christian mythology (Misc. 1355). When he started his presidency at Princeton, then, he was prepared to tell his students that the Chinese possessed all the essential truths of the Reformed religion, but in "mythological" form (Misc. 1351).

Concluding Remarks

Not all of Edwards's contemporaries shared his enthusiasm for Chinese culture. Richard Walter and George Anson's *A Voyage Round the World in the Years 1740–44* (1748) ridiculed China's morals and labeled its people "corrupt" and "thievish." Evangelicals almost uniformly rejected Confucius as an unbeliever and felt they could neither admire nor learn from him.[39] Daniel Defoe read Lecomte and concluded that China may have been a "wise nation among the foolish ones," but that it was now "a nation of fools among the wise ones." Confucius' maxims were "without consistency . . . [and] with very little reasoning" in them. China's religion showed "absurdity and ridiculous folly," and its philosophy was much inferior to that of the Greeks and Romans. They had gunpowder and guns, but their failure to make "bombs, carcasses [and] hand-grenades" showed them to be "unaccountable blockheads that they have made no farther improvement." Even their

---

38. Presumably by tradition from the sons of Noah.
39. Aldridge, *The Dragon and the Eagle*, 24. Aldridge's conclusion that Edwards "made no comments at all" about the Chinese reflects the tendency of scholars to overlook Edwards's unpublished manuscripts, particularly the notebooks that contain enormous extracts from Ramsay, Cudworth, Skelton, and other authors.

arts and handicraft were copied indirectly from exiled Jews who had wandered east.[40] Although the eighteenth century has been called by one historian the "Age of Respect" in its attitude to China,[41] some important Protestant evangelicals later in the eighteenth century were as contemptuous as Defoe. During his public attack on deism Timothy Dwight, for example, condemned Confucius as a symbol of infidelity because the Chinese sage was celebrated by deists as an example of ethics in the absence of religion. So while Edwards was one of many European religious thinkers in the century to admire Chinese culture, he was one of the few orthodox who did.[42]

It also must be pointed out that Edwards was misled on the nature of Chinese religious thought by his sources—Ramsay, Cudworth, and even the French Jesuits. The vast majority of supposed evidence for Christian concepts in the Chinese Classics simply does not exist. For example, *Tian*, the Chinese word for Heaven, in its earliest uses referred to a personal god but in much of the later literature lost its personal reference, indicating instead the impersonal divine.[43] In addition, the I-Ching contains very little if any indication of a personal god, and the passages that Edwards's sources interpreted as messianic were almost certainly intended to describe the "superior person," an entire class of human beings who manifest Confucian virtue.[44] The earliest Western interpreters of the Chinese Classics—the Jesuits—may have taken advantage of the hermeneutical freedom that Chinese characters provide because they were not representations of words but symbols of ideas. Translation of characters therefore may have made it easier to pass off eisegesis as exegesis.

For our purposes, however, it does not matter what the Chinese Classics actually mean. What is significant is that Edwards, the century's greatest theologian in a tradition that had customarily dismissed non-Western religions as unambiguously uninformed, believed that the Chinese had received extraordinary light from God. Their ancient religious masters had taught true religion, albeit in veiled form. This meant that vestiges of Reformed doctrine could be found not only in the Bible but also (and even!) in the religious culture of Asia. Edwards never spoke directly to the religious state of actual Asians, but he made it perfectly clear that there was religious truth in Asian culture, and that it was the product of God's acts of revelation in history.

---

40. Defoe, *Serious Reflections*, 3:123–31.

41. Isaacs, *Images of Asia*. Ezra Stiles, for instance, viewed Chinese culture as a benevolent humanism; Aldridge, *The Dragon and the Eagle*, 265. Isaacs refers to the nineteenth century as the "Age of Contempt."

42. Aldridge observes that the Protestant orthodox as a rule "did not welcome alien strains." Aldridge, *The Dragon and the Eagle*, 265.

43. Fung Yu-Lan, *A Short History of Chinese Philosophy*, 192–93; Julia Ching, *Chinese Religions* (Maryknoll, N.Y., 1993). In general, the Chinese never bothered to define their terms for the divine with any precision, so claims to find a personal god in uses of *Tian* and *Shang-di* impose determinate meaning where the Chinese were at best vague. See Dunne, *Generation of Giants*, 283, and Rowbotham, *Missionary and Mandarin*, 128.

44. *The I Ching*, trans. James Legge, esp. appendix 2, hex. 7–64.

CONCLUSION

Confounding the Enlightenment

Deism was the most crystallized version of Enlightenment religion in the eighteenth century. It expressed clearly and cogently quintessentially Enlightened thinking about God and God's relation to humanity. The French and German Enlightenment thinkers also talked about God, religion, and humanity's moral obligations to God, but none conceived of religion so programmatically as their deist counterparts in England. When either the *philosophes* or the German philosophers departed from deist thinking, the departures were more in degree than kind; they extended the reach of deist claims and broadened their implications, but their differences were more quantitative than qualitative. Therefore when Jonathan Edwards set his sights on deism and confronted its claims, he was doing battle with Enlightenment *religion*. The contest between Edwards and the deists was a contest of religions.

Yet deism was more than just a set of religious claims. Its interests and influence extended further—to epistemology, ethics, ontology, and even politics. For that reason it is instructive to look at Henry May's analysis of the American Enlightenment. May has shown that the Enlightenment in America was not one thing, but a series of interrelated movements with diverse emphases and perspectives. What makes his analysis relevant to our purposes is the discovery that deism's reach extended to each phase of the American Enlightenment.

May has distinguished four phases or categories of Enlightenment thought that influenced American minds in the eighteenth and nineteenth centuries. The Moderate or Rational Enlightenment, inspired by Newton and Locke, preached balance, order, and religious compromise. It carried the day until the middle of the eighteenth century. Then the skeptical Enlightenment developed in Britain and

France about 1750. It culminated in Hume's epistemological skepticism and d'Holbach's materialism. The Revolutionary Enlightenment, which called for the rise of a new heaven and earth out of the destruction of the old, was launched by Rousseau and carried to its climax by Thomas Paine and William Godwin toward the end of the century. Finally, the Didactic Enlightenment was a challenge to both the Skeptical and Revolutionary Enlightenments. Beginning about mid-century and centered in Scotland, it flourished at the beginning of the nineteenth century by proclaiming an intelligible universe, clear and certain moral judgments, and historical progress.[1]

Deists reflected and anticipated features of all four phases of Enlightenment. They called for the theological simplicity of the Moderates, flirted with the materialism of the Skeptics,[2] would have agreed with the Revolutionaries that the existing political order was defective,[3] and supported the Didactic confidence in moral clarity and certainty. In method, they would have cheered Kant's exhortation "*Sapere aude*" [Dare to know!].[4] Their program highlighted what Jürgen Habermas has defined as the permanent sign of Enlightenment: domination over an objectified external nature and repressed internal nature.[5] Neither matter nor spirit contained mystery for deists; they believed that they could be controlled by the proper application of commonsense reason.

Child of the Enlightenment

Although in his encounter with deism Edwards was battling different modes of Enlightenment thinking, he was a child of the Enlightenment himself. He cut his teeth at Yale on the New Learning of the first stages of Enlightenment[6] and showed in his writings through the course of his career that in both method and content his mind was shaped by Enlightenment sensibilities. There are indications, for example, that even in his thinking about God Edwards worked in part with Enlightenment presumptions.

The Enlightenment could not brook an arbitrary God. After the intellectual and social violence of the seventeenth century, the Age of Newton felt more secure with a God bounded by laws similar to the gravity that kept the planets from spinning off wildly into the cosmos. Edwards would not dispense with arbitrariness

---

1. May, *Enlightenment in America*. The literature on the Anglo-American Enlightenment is burgeoning. The works I have consulted include Ferguson, *The American Enlightenment*; Howe, *Making the American Self*; Anderson, *The Radical Enlightenments of Benjamin Franklin*; Sher and Smitten, *Scotland and America*; Walters, *The American Deists*; Haakonssen, *Enlightenment and Religion*; Frei, *Eclipse of Biblical Narrative*; Redwood, *Reason, Ridicule and Religion*; Oberg and Stout, *Representation of American Culture*; Stromberg, *Religious Liberalism*; Mossner, *Bishop Butler*; Cragg, *Reason and Authority*; Commager, *Empire of Reason*; Meyer, *The Democratic Enlightenment*; and Koch, *Religion and the American Enlightenment*.
2. Toland was a materialist; see Sullivan, *John Toland and the Deist Controversy*, 174.
3. This is a central theme in Champion, *The Pillars of Priestcraft Shaken*.
4. Immanuel Kant, "What Is Enlightenment?" in *Kant on History*, 3.
5. Habermas, *Philosophical Discourse*.
6. See Morris, *Young Jonathan Edwards*.

as the deists did. His God was arbitrary (or "sovereign," as he put it) at times, particularly at the beginning and end of the world, and at the top and bottom of the Great Chain of Being (Misc. 1263). But Edwards, influenced by Newton's disciple Samuel Clarke, also said that God acts according to the natural fitness of things, and that being is a network of laws that prescribe actions and events. As Fiering has observed, Edwards's God was no *Deus absconditus*.[7] Even the operations of the economic Trinity proceed according to the fitness and decency of things (Misc. 1062); the divine has made itself subject to Enlightenment ideals of order and beauty.[8]

The reader of Edwards's private notebooks can look over his shoulder, as it were, to see how through the course of his career he struggled to reconcile the Reformed doctrine of original sin with Enlightenment insistence that God must be fair. In 1727 Edwards concluded that God did not put any new sin into original human corruption to make it sin, but simply withdrew supernatural controls on self-love (Misc. 301). A year or two later he added that infants "consent" to their original corruption (Misc. 384). About a decade after that he suggested that God was not unjust in making Adam our representative because Adam stood a better chance than we of passing the test, since he was spiritually mature and we are only spiritual babes (Misc. 997).[9]

Benjamin Franklin once wrote George Whitefield that human affairs are below the notice of God, and that this was an "uncomfortable" thought. After receiving the letter the great evangelist penned a note to himself, "Uncomfortable indeed! And, blessed be God, unscriptural."[10] Jonathan Edwards would have added, "And unreasonable as well!" For Edwards as for Enlightenment thinkers, the truths of faith and reason were one. As he declared in his 1739 sermons on charity and its fruits, "There is the most sweet harmony between Christianity and reason."[11] He tried to demonstrate at the end of his career in *The Nature of True Virtue* that there is a natural morality which reason can discern without the aid of revelation. It is no surprise that for Edwards and Enlightenment thinkers, all of whom contended that true faith and right reason agree, light was the metaphor of choice for illumination of reality. To see was to know. For Newton, Locke, Tindal, Toland, and Edwards, new "light" had dawned in the Age of Reason, showing as never before the harmony of reason with faith. Edwards disagreed sharply with most Enlight-

---

7. Fiering, *Jonathan Edwards's Moral Thought*, 343.

8. Compare Tindal's declaration that God "acts in constant conformity to the Reason and Nature of things" (*CAO*, 26). Hence May's characterization of Edwards as rejecting in wholesale fashion the balance, order, and reason of the Moderate Enlightenment is inaccurate; May, *Enlightenment in America*, 49.

9. A good bit of Edwards's popular notoriety is due to his claim that God holds not love but hatred for the wicked, a claim not necessarily innovative for a Reformed theologian but certainly consistent with Enlightenment notions of fitness. Tindal, for example, made nearly the identical claim; *CAO*, 342.

10. Franklin to Whitefield, September 2, 1769, *Papers of Benjamin Franklin*, 16:192; cited in Howe, *Making the American Self*, 25.

11. "Charity Contrary to a Censorious Spirit," in *EW*, 286–87.

enment thinkers over the *nature* of both reason and faith, but he agreed that they were correlative and could now be seen more clearly than in past ages.

Edwards's treatment of religion also showed striking similarity to, and perhaps influence from, Enlightenment assumptions. Deist and other Enlightenment thinkers were generally engaged in the critique of religious appearances, as Robert Jenson has pointed out; Edwards's theological project could be characterized with considerable accuracy as directed to the same end—most pointedly in his magnum opus, the *Religious Affections* (1746). Like the deists, Edwards sometimes railed against priestcraft but confined his vituperation to the medieval priesthood, whose crime was twofold: they were ignorant and they took the Scriptures out of the hands of the laity in order to promote their own interests and privileges (HWR, 414).

Tindal and most other Enlightenment critics of traditional Christianity insisted that a faith was to be judged by the works it produced.[12] Edwards was more interested in the nature of the faith that produced works and disagreed with deists over what constituted a good work, but he nevertheless affirmed the Enlightenment presumption that true religion will have social value—and reached a somewhat cynical conviction of the truth of the last notion after what he witnessed in the Great Awakening. Edwards also joined with deists and other Enlightenment critics in their skepticism over religious "enthusiasm." David Hartley defined enthusiasm in words that nearly replicated passages from the *Religious Affections*: "a mistaken persuasion in any person that he is a peculiar favorite with God; and that he receives supernatural marks thereof."[13] In the *Affections* Edwards lambasted all those who relied on "impulses and whispers . . . of the favor and love of God to them" and denounced the validity of religious experience that arose from a sense of being a divine favorite (RA, 246, 245).

If Edwards shared Enlightenment distaste for religious narcissism, he also was sensitive to the Enlightenment suspicion of appeals to tradition. John Toland boasted in his epitaph that he was "no man's follower."[14] With similar protestation of intellectual independence (and perhaps deferring to enlightened repudiation of the "Calvinistic" system), Edwards told readers of *Freedom of the Will*, "I utterly disclaim a dependence on Calvin, or believing the doctrines which I hold, because he believed and taught them; and cannot justly be charged with believing in everything just as he taught" (FW, 131).[15]

Jenson was right to note that Edwards could sound like "the unchastened rationalists of his period," for he professed to agree with Tindal and Chubb that reason must judge "whether there be any revelation & whether any pretended revelation be really such" (Misc. 1340).[16] As we have seen in an earlier chapter,

---

12. CAO, 52; DCR 73.
13. Cragg, *Reason and Authority*, 10.
14. Daniel, *John Toland*, 13.
15. According to Hopkins, Edwards's Boswell, "Tho' his Principles were Calvinistic, yet he called no Man, Father. He thought and judged for himself, and was truly very much an Original" (Samuel Hopkins, *The Life and Character of the Late Rev. Mr. Jonathan Edwards* [Boston, 1765], 41).
16. Jenson, *America's Theologian*, 22.

Edwards used what he called regenerate reason to "prove" that revelation is necessary and that the Bible is that revelation. Enlightenment thinkers would never have granted the distinction between regenerate and unregenerate reason, but it is significant that Edwards allowed them their insistence that reason must and can prove the validity of revelation.

Edwards was not always so clear on the difference between these two kinds of reason. Near the beginning of his career he seemed to concede the Enlightenment claim that natural reason ("the light of nature") could adjudicate differences over God's character. Edwards wrote in his private notebooks that "it don't seem congruous, and in itself it is not congruous" for God to forgive sin in the absence of repentance. "This now seems to me evident," he added, "to the very light of nature" (Misc. 244). At this point Edwards opted for the Enlightenment's source of authority rather than Scripture, which indicated that Jesus forgave his murderers despite their lack of repentance. Later, Edwards came to understand reason and revelation with far more sophistication than this entry alone indicates, but the point remains that he confronted the Enlightenment not from without but from within its thought-world.

So Edwards spoke in terms understood best by other children of the Enlightenment. In the process of debating its method and conclusions, he conceded some premises to his antagonists. Another example can be found in Edwards's long arguments for revelation. Deists proclaimed *ad nauseam* that our obligations cannot extend beyond our abilities. In a late *Miscellanies* entry (Misc. 1304), Edwards supposed that since we are obligated, God must have provided the means (revelation) to meet our obligation to practice true religion.

It was also a presumption of the Age of Enlightenment, pronounced most vigorously by deists, that happiness is the end of creation. Edwards was not so simplistic, for he made happiness coincident with God's glory.[17] Nevertheless, he was no less insistent than Tindal and Toland that human beings are intended for felicity. After all, he did share with the deists some Enlightenment presuppositions. By the end of his life Edwards was entertaining conceptions that earlier Reformed thinkers would have abhorred: that there are common elements in most non-Christian religious traditions; Cudworth's notion that these involve a kind of monotheism and Trinity among most "pagans"; the Jesuits' contention that true religion had existed for thousands of years among the Chinese; and the postulate that a certain monotheism remained among the best Indians and Greek polytheists.

Reconfiguring the Enlightenment

If Edwards looked out on the world with some Enlightenment presuppositions, he was not completely captive to the Enlightenment paradigm. In fact he turned other Enlightened axioms on their heads by reconstituting the nature and role of

17. His final elaboration of this was in *The End for Which God Created the World*, in *EW*.

central Enlightenment metaphors: religion and morality, God and world, truth and mystery, reason, happiness, and nature.

Perhaps most important, he always resisted the deist move, and for that matter the tendency of a surprising number of "orthodox" divines, to make true religion more or less synonymous with moral virtue. Edwards insisted instead that true religion always issues from aesthetic vision. It produces moral virtue, but not the kind produced apart from such vision. That is, if a seeing of divine beauty was not at the heart of religious experience, the virtue produced was secondary rather than primary.[18]

Therefore moral sincerity, which for deists and most Enlightenment thinkers was sufficient, was not enough for Edwards. Sincerity does not save unless it is the appeal of true virtue. A non-Christian without the gospel may have a saving disposition, but no natural disposition can truly repent and love God and therefore supply the defects of natural virtue (*Misc.* 1304). Hence without an infusion of grace the heathen were damned.

In other words, Edwards cared more about internal states than external works, for if the internal disposition was right, works would take care of themselves. He agreed with Enlightenment religion that works have evidential value, but he did not equate religion with morality in Enlightenment fashion and wanted to pay far more attention than the deists did to the nature of the religious sensibility which inspired works. The nature of the affections was critical—far more important than social manifestations of affections. Hence the conversion of one soul was "a more glorious work of God than the creation of the whole material universe," and of greater benefit to the planet "than all the temporal good of the most happy revolution in a land or nation amounts to, or all that a people could gain by the conquest of the world."[19] The *Religious Affections*, in which Edwards asserts that the last and chief sign of true religion is Christian practice, argues that all such practice arises from spiritual influence that gives the soul eyes to see the beauty of holiness. This suggests that the work of redemption for Edwards was ultimately more important than either the study of the material universe or the promotion of social reform. It also means that Edwards focused preeminently on the mysteries of the soul while the Enlightenment calculated benefits to society.

While Edwards articulated a different view of the nature of religion, he also challenged Enlightenment views of other religions. This study has shown that he rejected the Enlightenment idea of a common substratum at the heart of all the world religions. We have also seen that he rejected the move to sever Christianity's covenantal tie to Judaism. His attitudes toward other religions reflect a dialectical relationship to Enlightenment views of the same. On the one hand, like many Enlightenment thinkers he moved toward a universal history of religion that took interest in non-Christian religions and sought to configure them in such a way that God showed care for more than just the one-sixth of the planet that practiced

---

18. *TV*, chap. 1, sect. 2.
19. Jonathan Edwards, *Some Thoughts Concerning the Revival*, in *The Great Awakening*, vol. 4 of *The Works of Jonathan Edwards*, 344–45.

Christianity and Judaism. Unlike many of his orthodox predecessors and contemporaries, he made room for the work of the Holy Spirit among "pagan" philosophers in China and Greece and began to imagine the work of redemption among Native Americans who remained unconverted to Christianity. On the other hand, Edwards used the cultural tools available to him—the *prisca theologia*, for example—to serve the interests of Christian theology and a particularistic vision of God's revelation to the world. At the time of his death he was in the process of fashioning a system that embraced all of world history and religion in a way that not only showed Enlightenment-like concern for all peoples but also supported Reformed insistence on the particularity of Christian revelation. Unlike most theologians of his day, Edwards took seriously the notion of religious truth among other religions and exercised theological daring capacious enough to include peoples and gods far removed from orthodox Christianity.

Edwards finally broke with Enlightenment views of religion, however, because of a different god and world. Deists proposed a static but beneficent Newtonian hero who designed a system of secondary causes. Edwards, however, argued that it is the being—not simply the will—of God that is the universal and immediate Cause of all. There are no secondary causes because, as Hume was to say later, there is no inherently necessary connection between what goes before and what follows. Edwards rejected both natural law and mechanistic causation in favor of the continuous immediate creation of God from moment to pulsating moment. Creation was not from nothing so much as from the "inexhaustible depths of God's infinity."[20] The world was not a giant machine as the Enlightenment portrayed, but a living organism shining with divine brilliance and throbbing with the energy of the living God.[21]

Edwards also overturned Enlightenment notions of truth. He said the deist bar of common sense failed to admit truths of life that even deists affirmed. For life, like religion, abounds with mystery and paradox. Edwards believed that the Enlightenment restriction of truth to propositions that could be understood comprehensively presumed a one-dimensional view of the human person. Propositions are functions of affections, which are grounded in aspects of personality that transcend thinking. Edwards believed that religion is born not of mere rational perception (as deists supposed) but the complex mixture of passion (which Hume was to emphasize), interest, and ratiocination. So salvation cannot be by proposition alone; it must come not simply by cognitive assent but by the infusion of grace into the whole person—thinking, willing, and feeling.

Enlightenment thinkers who reduced religion to self-evident propositions consequently redefined or eliminated the power of evil and therefore salvation, church and worship, sacraments and mysteries, Incarnation, Atonement, and mediation by Christ. Because Edwards refused to divorce truth from mystery, he was able to accept some Enlightenment premises without surrendering these distinctive doctrines of Reformed theology.

---

20. Elwood, *Philosophical Theology of Jonathan Edwards*, 58.
21. See chapter 3 in Jenson, *America's Theologian*, for a rich exposition of this theme.

As Hans Frei has shown, Enlightenment thinkers wanted to fit the biblical story into another world framed by what they thought to be self-evident and commonsensical propositions.[22] But Edwards understood all the world—including the worlds of other religions—in terms of the biblical story. The Enlightenment—particularly deism—was nervous if by its lights some questions went unanswered. Edwards was not. He came to acknowledge that there was something more to the salvation of the heathen than previous Reformed divines had allowed, and more to non-Christian religions than most Christians had granted. At the time of his death he was still unsure of how to explain fully the abundance of revelation given to the heathen. Yet he rejected simplistic resolutions and seemed to feel no need for a fully rationalized calculation of salvation's mechanisms. His vision of the beauty of divine things was self-validating, and this assured him of God's goodness and justice to all.

Edwards told the deists their understanding of reason was too limited. They had arbitrarily reduced reason to immediate intuition, which could never provide a complete system of knowledge. He agreed with them that reason can and must determine the possibility of revelation but proceeded immediately to show them why unregenerate reason could never understand regenerate arguments for revelation. The power of reason in which they boasted was real but beyond their reach.[23]

Their view of reason was not only too small but also naive. In a move that is familar to postmoderns, Edwards demonstrated the interested nature of all reasoning. Edwards usually failed to concede the sinful interest in his own reasoning, but he rarely failed to point out that there is no disinterested reasoning among the unregenerate.

He also showed that the deist attack on Christianity's lack of uniformity was doctrinaire. Like Bishop Butler, he argued that in no other discipline of life is there uniformity. Diversity not uniformity is the rule of existence. Edwards contended that by definition revelation is a massive concatenation of interrelated parts, no one of which can be isolated from the whole. He used empirical as well as abstract reason to make his case; for Enlightenment thinkers who relied almost entirely on abstract reason, this was a crippling blow.

His reconfiguration of nature was also a strike against the Enlightenment paradigm. Edwards resisted his age's fondness for regarding the cosmos as a giant mechanism whose motion was started by God at the creation. He replaced this picture with the image of the physical universe as (almost) God's body. Space is God, he declared.[24] Not only was God the beating heart of the cosmos, whose every atom was God's thought, continuously rethought and therefore recreated,

---

22. Frei, *Eclipse of Biblical Narrative*, esp. 51–85.

23. Ironically, Edwards, who supported Spirit-led "enthusiasm," had more confidence in reason than John Locke, whom enthusiasm terrified. Locke confessed he could not reconcile divine omnipotence and human freedom, in both of which he believed; Edwards was confident that he had proven their reconciliation in *Freedom of the Will*.

24. Edwards, "Of Being," in *SPW*, 203.

but nature was also a sign—a massive system of divine communication.[25] The cosmos was bursting with divinely implanted types pointing to the antitypes of God's history of redemption. Edwards's typology was light-years from the modern scientific method based on empirical experience alone. It exploded Enlightenment conceptions of rationality and objectivity, which have been, in Rorty's words, "normal discourse" until recently. Edwards reminded the Enlightenment, as we are being reminded by postmoderns, that objectivity is in the mind of the beholder, and there is no neutral point of view except in God.

Edwards's view of the cosmos, then, was radically theocentric. Because the Enlightenment was just as radically humanocentric, its preachers had difficulty talking about sin and evil and often were obsessed with happiness and its pursuit. Since God's purpose was human happiness and not his own glory, the Enlightenment either dismissed or minimized traditional notions of hell. Even Bishop Butler, who wrote the most perceptive response to deism in the eighteenth century, found no place in that work for discussions of sin or atonement.[26]

Edwards was also interested in human happiness. It emerged as a common theme in both his sermons and discourses, and this no doubt was an index of his immersion in the age. But while he stated that happiness is part of the end for which God created the world, it is coordinate to God's glory, which comprehends and finally defines human fulfillment. This was one final instance of Edwards's grand synthesis of Enlightenment themes with classical Reformed doctrines. It and the other themes we have developed in this study demonstrate how Edwards was capable of incorporating Enlightenment metaphors—such as nature, reason, and happiness—into a theological system that not only reconfigured them but related them meaningfully to traditional Christian notions of judgment, atonement, incarnation, Trinity, and mystery.

The Enlightenment after Edwards

In 1790 Edmund Burke triumphantly asked, "Who, born within the last forty years, has read one word of Colins [sic], and Toland, and Tindal, and Chubb, and Morgan, and that whole race who called themselves Freethinkers? Who now reads Bolingbroke? Who ever read him through?"[27] Burke would have been disturbed to discover that deism, while moribund in England toward the end of the century, was alive and well in the American republic he admired.[28]

American deism was not a powerful force during Edwards's lifetime. But in the decades after his death, particularly near the end of the century, it borrowed

---

25. Daniel, *The Philosophy of Jonathan Edwards*.
26. Butler, *The Analogy of Religion Natural and Revealed*.
27. Burke, *Reflections on the Revolution in France*, 135.
28. Thomas Jefferson, for example, copied 10,000 words of Bolingbroke into his private notebooks and told John Adams that he had read Bolingbroke though six times. He was steeped in Chubb and other deist writers. Benjamin Franklin was converted to deism as a teenager by reading deist writers; Gaustad, *Sworn on the Altar of God*, 22, 25.

from the American Revolution a passion that it had previously lacked and enjoyed considerable popularity among the cultural elite. The majority of students at Yale, Dartmouth, and Princeton were said to have become skeptics because of its influence.[29] Edwards's cousin Joseph Hawley was so affected by it that he soon distrusted "any Doctrine upon the mere authority of God's word."[30] Benjamin Franklin, Thomas Jefferson, and other leaders of the new republic were proponents of Enlightenment religion.

Was Edwards's critical confrontation with the Enlightenment to no avail? Did his creative interaction with Enlightenment and deist thinking have no impact upon cultural leaders and other thinking Americans? We know that many of Edwards's arguments against Enlightenment religion and philosophy were found in his notebooks by his son, Jonathan Edwards Jr., and published in Edinburgh in the last decade of the century. But his American readers were probably few.[31] There were plenty of orthodox divines in America who declaimed against deism, both from the pulpit and in the press, and some perpetuated the *prisca theologia* tradition, but none was able to reverse the movement of cultural elites to the Scottish moral philosophy that was at odds with Edwardsean ethical theory.[32]

It is beyond the scope of this study to explain the demise of the Edwardsean vision among intellectual culture after Edwards's death. No doubt it is related to the inaccessibility of Edwards's notebooks (although his major treatises on sin, the will, ethics, and the work of redemption were published within several decades after his death), and to the overwhelming American obsession during and after the Revolution with personal freedom. Although Edwards refused to call himself a Calvinist, his theology falls loosely within that tradition and was perceived that way by later generations, who grew increasingly disenchanted with what they perceived to be Calvinism's denial of freedom and (human) dignity. In

---

29. Walters, *The American Deists*, 1–3.

30. Joseph Hawley, *Confessions of His Belief in Arminianism*, cited in Morais, *Deism in Eighteenth-Century America*, 67.

31. Edwards, *Miscellaneous Observations on Important Theological Subjects*; Edwards, *Remarks on Important Theological Controversies*.

32. Howe, *Making the American Self*, 46. The *prisca theologia* tradition was more resilient than historians have realized. It did not perish with Chevalier Ramsay or John Webb, as D. P. Walker and Peter Harrison have suggested, but enjoyed continued life in eighteenth-century America as well as in Britain and on the continent; Walker, *Ancient Theology*, 248–49; Harrison, *"Religion" and the Religions*, 155. There are signs in fact that it passed into the nineteenth century through Edwards's disciples and others. Samuel Hopkins wrote in the first indigenous American systematic theology, "There are many things generally believed and practised in the heathen world, in their religion, which evidently depend on tradition, and, though in many respects corrupted, had their original in divine revelation, handed down from Noah and his sons, or taken from the Jews and the revelation given to them. But one instance shall be mentioned, namely, the practice of sacrificing beasts." Hannah Adams, in her early-nineteenth-century encyclopedia of religions, spoke of the "primitive theology" carried to India by Noah or a descendant of Shem and then corrupted by descendants of Ham. Remains of this theology were "still apparent in India, and are contained in the Vedas." Hopkins, *System of Doctrines* (1792), in *The Works of Samuel Hopkins, D.D.*, 1:30–31; Adams, *A View of Religions*, 406.

contrast, Enlightenment religion's concentration on self-determination was welcomed by Americans, who thought they knew how to make themselves free.[33]

Edwards may have failed to stem the tide of radical Enlightenment thinking in America, but he was among the few who foresaw the gravity of its threat to Christianity. He was also among the few who tackled the challenge of the radical Enlightenment head-on and brought to bear on the debate some of the best resources of the Christian theological tradition. His confrontation with the gods was not the most successful when judged against later intellectual history, but it may have been America's most profound in that age of light.

---

33. See May, Enlightenment in America, esp. 153–251; Hatch, Sacred Cause of Liberty; and Noll, Princeton and the Republic. On the rise and fall of the Edwardsean tradition in the eighteenth and nineteenth centuries, see Conforti, Jonathan Edwards, Religious Tradition, and American Culture.

SELECTED BIBLIOGRAPHY

PRIMARY SOURCES

Manuscripts

Edwards, Jonathan. Edwards Papers. Beinecke Rare Book and Manuscript Library, Yale University. New Haven, Connecticut.
———. "Jonathan Edwards' Reading 'Catalogue' with Notes and Index." Edited by L. Brian Sullivan. *Works of Jonathan Edwards* office, Yale Divinity School. New Haven, Connecticut.
———. Miscellanies. Typescript by Thomas A. Schafer. Beinecke Rare Book and Manuscript Library, Yale University. New Haven, Connecticut.
———. Miscellanies. Typescript on disk. *Works of Jonathan Edwards* office, Yale Divinity School. New Haven, Connecticut.

Published Works

Adams, Hannah. *A View of Religions, in Two Parts*. 3d ed. Boston, 1801.
Basnage, Jacques. *The History of the Jews, from Jesus Christ to the Present Time*. London, 1708.
Baxter, Richard. *The Practical Works of Richard Baxter*. 4 vols. London, 1864.
Beiser, Frederick C. *The Sovereignty of Reason: The Defense of Rationality in the Early English Enlightenment*. Princeton, N.J., 1996.
Blount, Charles. *The Miscellaneous Works of Charles Blount, Esq*. London, 1695.
Broughton, Thomas. *Bibliotheca Historico-Sacra: or, an Historical Library of the Principal Matters Relating to Religion Antient and Modern: Pagan, Jewish, Christian and Mohammedan*. London, 1737.
Burke, Edmund. *Reflections on the Revolution in France*. London, 1790. Indianapolis, 1955.
Butler, Joseph. *The Analogy of Religion Natural and Revealed to the Constitution and Course of Nature*. 3d ed. London, 1887.
Calvin, John. *Institutes of the Christian Religion*. Translated by Ford Lewis Battles. Edited by John T. McNeill. Philadelphia, 1960.

Chadwick, Henry, ed. and trans. *Lessing's Theological Writings*. Stanford, Calif., 1972.
Chambers, Ephraim. *Philosophical Dictionary*. London, 1728.
Chubb, Thomas. *A Collection of Tracts on Various Subjects*. 2 vols. 2d ed. London, 1754.
———. *A Discourse Concerning Reason*. London, 1733.
———. *The Posthumous Works of Mr. Thomas Chubb*. 2 vols. London, 1748.
Clarke, Samuel. *A Discourse Concerning the Being and Attributes of God, The Obligations of Natural Religion, and the Truth and Certainty of the Christian Revelation*. Sixteen sermons preached in 1704–5 for the Boyle lectures. In *The Works of Samuel Clarke*. 2 vols. New York, 1978.
Collins, Anthony. *A Discourse on Freethinking*. London, 1713.
Cragg, Gerald C. *The Cambridge Platonists*. New York, 1968.
Cudworth, Ralph. *The True Intellectual System of the Universe*. Andover, Mass., 1837.
Defoe, Daniel. *A Dictionary of All Religions*. London, 1704.
———. *Serious Reflections During the Life and Surprising Adventures of Robinson Crusoe*. 3 vols. New York, 1907.
Dexter, Franklin B., ed. *The Literary Diary of Ezra Stiles, D.D., LL.D*. New York, 1901.
Dyche, Thomas. *A New General English Dictionary*. London, 1725.
Edwards, Jonathan. *Charity and Its Fruits*. Edited by Tyron Edwards. Edinburgh, 1969.
———. *Images or Shadows of Divine Things*. Edited by Perry Miller. Cambridge, Mass., 1947.
———. *Miscellaneous Observations on Important Theological Subjects*. Edited by Jonathan Edwards Jr. Edinburgh, 1793.
———. *The Nature of True Virtue*. Edited by William K. Frankena. Ann Arbor, 1960.
———. *Remarks on Important Theological Controversies*. Edited by Jonathan Edwards Jr. Edinburgh, 1796.
———. *Treatise on Grace*. Edited by Paul Helm. Cambridge, 1971.
———. *The Works of Jonathan Edwards*. John E. Smith, general editor. New Haven [Yale University Press], Conn., 1957– .

Vol. 1: *Freedom of the Will*. Edited by Paul Ramsey. 1957.

Vol. 2: *Religious Affections*. Edited by John E. Smith. 1959.

Vol. 3: *Original Sin*. Edited by Clyde A. Holbrook. 1970.

Vol. 4: *The Great Awakening*. Edited by C. C. Goen. 1972.

Vol. 5: *Apocalyptic Writings*. Edited by Stephen J. Stein. 1977.

Vol. 6: *Scientific and Philosophical Writings*. Edited by Wallace E. Anderson. 1980.

Vol. 7: *The Life of David Brainerd*. Edited by Norman Pettit. 1985.

Vol. 8: *Ethical Writings*. Edited by Paul Ramsey. 1989.

Vol. 9: *History of the Work of Redemption*. Edited by John F. Wilson. 1989.

Vol. 10: *Sermons and Discourses, 1720–1723*. Edited by Wilson H. Kimnach. 1992.

Vol. 11: *Typological Writings*. Edited by Wallace E. Anderson and Mason I. Lowance. 1993.

Vol. 12: *Ecclesiastical Writings*. Edited by David D. Hall. 1994.

Vol. 13: *The Miscellanies, a-500*. Edited by Thomas A. Schafer. 1994.

Vol. 14: *Sermons and Discourses*. Edited by Kenneth P. Minkema. 1997.

Vol. 15: *Notes on Scripture*. Edited by Stephen J. Stein. 1998.

Vol. 16: *Letters and Personal Writings*. Edited by George S. Claghorn. 1998.

Publication of this edition is continuing.

———. *The Works of President Edwards*. 2 vols. Edited by Edward Hickman. London, 1834. Reprint. Edinburgh, 1974.

———. *The Works of President Edwards in Eight Volumes*. Edited by Edward Williams and Edward Parsons. Leeds, 1806–11.

———. *The Works of President Edwards: With a Memoir of His Life, In Ten Volumes*. Edited by Sereno E. Dwight. New York, 1829–30.

Faust, Clarence H., and Thomas H. Johnson, eds. *Jonathan Edwards: Representative Selections*. New York, 1962.

Gale, Theophilus. *Court of the Gentiles*. 3 vols. London, 1669–71.

Gardner, H. Norman, ed. *Selected Sermons of Jonathan Edwards*. New York, 1904.

Gay, Peter. *Deism: An Anthology*. Princeton, N.J., 1968.

Gibbon, Edwards. *The Decline and Fall of the Roman Empire*. 3 vols. New York, n.d.

Gordon, Thomas, and John Trenchard. *The Independent Whig*. 2 vols. 7th ed. London, 1736.

Grosart, Alexander, ed. *Selections from the Unpublished Writings of Jonathan Edwards*. Ligonier, Pa., 1992.

Grotius, Hugo. *De Jure Belli et Pacis*. Paris, 1625.

Heppe, Heinrich. *Reformed Dogmatics*. Grand Rapids, Mich., 1978.

Herbert, Lord of Cherbury. *The Antient Religion of the Gentiles*. 2d ed. London, 1705.

———. *Lord Herbert of Cherbury's De Religione Laici*. Edited and translated by Harold R. Hutcheson. New Haven, Conn., 1944.

———. *On Truth in Distinction from Revelation, Probability, Possibility, and Error*. 3d ed. Translated by Meyrick H. Carre. Bristol, 1937.

Hopkins, Samuel. *The Works of Samuel Hopkins, D.D.* Boston, 1865.

Hume, David. *Dialogues Concerning Natural Religion*. Edited by Norman K. Smith. Indianapolis, 1985.

———. *An Inquiry Concerning Human Understanding*. Edited by Charles W. Hendel. Indianapolis, 1955.

———. *The Natural History of Religion*. In *David Hume: Writings on Religion*. Edited by Antony Flew. LaSalle, Ill., 1992.

The I Ching. Translated by James Legge. 2d. ed. In *The Sacred Books of the East*, vol. 16. F. Max Müller, general editor. New York, 1963.

Kant, Immanuel. *Kant on History*. Edited by Lewis W. Beck. Indianapolis, 1963.

Le Créquinière, de. *The Agreement of the Customs of the East-Indians, with Those of the Jews, and Other Ancient People*. Brussels, 1704.

Lao Tzu. *Tao Te Ching*. In *The Essential Tao*, ed. Thomas Cleary. San Francisco, 1991.

Law, William. *The Case of Reason*. London, 1731.

Lecomte, Louis. *Memoirs and Observations: Topographical, Physical, Mathematical, Mechanical, Natural, Civil and Ecclesiastical, Made in a Late Journey Through an Empire of China, and Published in Several Letters*. London, 1697.

Leland, John. *A View of the Principal Deistical Writers*. Reprint. New York, 1978.

Locke, John. *An Essay Concerning Human Understanding*. Edited by A. S. Pringle-Pattison. Oxford, 1924.

———. *The Reasonableness of Christianity*. Washington, D.C., 1965.

———. *The Works of John Locke*. London, 1768.

Mastricht, Petrus van. *Theoretico-practica theologia*. 2d ed. Utrecht, 1724.

Mather, Samuel. *The Figures or Types of the Old Testament*. Edited by Mason I. Lowance Jr. New York, 1969.

McClymond, Michael J. *Encounters with God: An Approach to the Theology of Jonathan Edwards.* New York, 1998.

Millar, Robert. *The History of the Propagation of Christianity, and Overthrow of Paganism.* 2 vols. Edinburgh, 1723.

Miller, James. *Mahomet the Imposter. As It is Acted at the Theatre-Royal in Drury-Lane.* London, 1744.

More, Henry. *An Explanation of the Grand Mystery of Godliness.* London, 1660.

———. *The Philosophical Writings of Henry More.* Edited by Flora Mackinnon. New York, 1929.

Morgan, Thomas. *The Moral Philosopher.* 2d ed. London, 1738.

A Narrative of the Proceedings of those Ministers of the County of Hampshire, etc. That have disapproved of the late Measures taken in order to the Settlement of Mr. Robert Breck, in the Pastoral Office of the first Church in Springfield, with a Defence of their Conduct in that Affair. Written by Themselves. Boston, 1736.

Parkman, Francis. *The Jesuits in North America in the Seventeenth Century.* 1867. 2d ed. Boston, 1909.

Paley, William. *Evidences of Christianity.* 3d. ed. Cambridge, 1901.

Patrides, C. A., ed. *The Cambridge Platonists.* London, 1969.

Plato, *The Collected Dialogues of Plato, Including the Letters.* Edited by Edith Hamilton and Huntingdon Cairns. Princeton, N.J., 1961.

Prideaux, Humphrey. *The True Nature of Imposture Fully Display'd in the Life of Mahomet with a Discourse annexed, for the Vindicating of Christianity from this Charge: Offered to the Consideration of the Deists of the Present Age.* 2d ed. London, 1697.

Ramsay, Andrew Michael. *Philosophical Principles of Natural and Revealed Religion unfolded in a Geometrical Order.* 2 vols. Glasgow, 1748.

———. *The Travels of Cyrus.* 2 vols. London, 1727. Originally published in Paris in 1727 under the title *Les Voyages de Cyrus, avec un discours sur la mythologie.*

Sale, George. *The Koran, Commonly Called the Alkoran of Mohammed.* London, 1734. Reprint. New York, 1984.

Shuckford, Samuel. *Sacred and Profane History of the World Connected.* 4 vols. London, 1728.

Simonson, Harold P., ed. *Selected Writings of Jonathan Edwards.* Prospect Heights, Ill., 1970.

Skelton, Philip. *Deism Revealed, or The Attack on Christianity Candidly Reviewed in Its Real Merits.* 2 vols. London, 1751.

Smith, John. *Select Discourses.* London, 1660.

Stoddard, Solomon. "Letter to Gov. Dudley." *Massachusetts Historical Society Collections,* 4th ser., 2:235–37.

———. "Question: Whether God Is Not Angry with the Country for Doing So Little towards the Conversion of the Indians?" Boston, 1723.

Tindal, Matthew. *Christianity as Old as the Creation.* London, 1730.

Toland, John. *Christianity Not Mysterious.* London, 1696.

———. *Letters to Serena.* London, 1704.

———. *Pantheisticon: or, the Form of Celebrating the Socratic Society.* London, 1751. New York, 1976.

———. *Tetradymus.* London, 1720.

———. [L.P., Master of Arts, pseud.] *Two Essays Sent in a Letter from Oxford.* London, 1695.

Turnbull, George. *An Enquiry into the Wise and Good Government of the Moral World.* 2 vols. London, 1740.

Turner, William. *The History of All Religions in the World.* London, 1695.

Turretin, François. *Institutes of Elenctic Theology.* Translated by George Musgrave. Edited by James T. Dennison Jr. 3 vols. Phillipsburg, N.J., 1992– .

———. *Institutio Theologiae Elencticae*. 1679–85. Handwritten translation by George Musgrave Giger at Princeton Theological Seminary.
Voss, Gerhard Van. *De Theologica Gentili, et physiologia Christiana sive de origine ac progressu idoltariae*. Amsterdam, 1641.
Watts, Isaac. *The Harmony of All the Religions*. London, 1742.
Wesley, John. *The Works of the Rev. John Wesley, A.M.* 14 vols. London, 1837.
Whichcote, Benjamin. *Moral and Religious Aphorisms*. London, 1930.
Wollaston, William. *The Religion of Nature Delineated*. London, 1726.

Secondary Sources

Books

Abbott, Walter M., S.J. *The Documents of Vatican II*. New York, 1966.
Adas, Michael. *Machines as the Measure of Men: Science, Technology, and Ideologies of Western Dominance*. Ithaca, N.Y., 1989.
Aldridge, A. Owen. *Benjamin Franklin and Nature's God*. Durham, N.C., 1967.
———. *The Dragon and the Eagle: The Presence of China in the American Enlightenment*. Detroit, Mich., 1993.
———. *Jonathan Edwards*. New York, 1964.
Anderson, Douglas. *The Radical Enlightenments of Benjamin Franklin*. Baltimore, 1997.
Ashton, John. *Social Life in the Reign of Queene Anne*. London, 1919.
Aspelin, Gunnar. *Ralph Cudworth's Interpretation of Greek Philosophy: A Study in the History of English Philosophical Ideas*. Goteborg, Sweden, 1943.
Axtell, James. *The European and the Indian: Essays in the Ethnohistory of Colonial North America*. New York, 1981.
———. *The Invasion Within: The Contest of Cultures in Colonial North America*. New York, 1985.
Barth, Karl. *The Word of God and the Word of Man*. Translated by Douglas Horton. Gloucester, Mass., 1978.
Becker, Marvin B. *The Emergence of Civil Society in the Eighteenth Century: A Privileged Moment in the History of England, Scotland, and France*. Bloomington, Ind., 1994.
Bell, Richard. *The Origin of Islam in Its Christian Environment*. London, 1926.
Bercovitch, Sacvan, ed. *Typology and Early American Literature*. N.p., 1972.
Blundell, Sue. *The Origins of Civilization in Greek and Roman Thought*. London and Dover, N.H., 1986.
Bogue, Carl W. *Jonathan Edwards and the Covenant of Grace*. Cherry Hill, N.J., 1975.
Boon, James A. *Other Tribes, Other Scribes: Symbolic Anthropology in the Comparative Study of Cultures, Histories, Religions, and Texts*. New York, 1982.
Bowden, Henry Warner. *American Indians and Christian Missions: Studies in Cultural Conflict*. Chicago, 1981.
Boyarin, Daniel. *A Radical Jew: Paul and the Politics of Identity*. Berkeley, Calif., 1994.
Brauer, Jerald, ed. *Reinterpretation in American History*. Chicago, 1968.
Brumm, Ursula. *American Thought and Religious Typology*. Translated by John Hoaglund. New Brunswick, N.J., 1970.
Burkert, Walter. *Ancient Mystery Cults*. Cambridge, 1987.
———. *Greek Religion*. Translated by John Raffan. Cambridge, Mass., 1985.
Byrne, Peter. *Natural Religion and the Nature of Religion: The Legacy of Deism*. London, 1989.
Calloway, Colin. *The American Revolution in Indian Country: Crisis and Diversity in Native American Communities*. Cambridge, 1995.

Chai, Leon. *Jonathan Edwards and the Limits of Enlightenment Philosophy.* New York, 1998.
Champion, J. A. I. *The Pillars of Priestcraft Shaken: The Church of England and Its Enemies, 1660–1730.* Cambridge, 1992.
Chase, Steven. *Angelic Wisdom: The Cherubim and the Grace of Contemplation in Richard of St. Victor.* Notre Dame, Ind., 1995.
Cherry, Conrad. *The Theology of Jonathan Edwards: A Reappraisal.* Bloomington, Ind., 1990.
Cohen, Warren. *America's Response to China: An Interpretive History of Sino-American Relations.* New York, 1971.
Cole, Rosalie. *Light and Enlightenment: A Study of the Cambridge Platonists and the Dutch Arminians.* Cambridge, 1957.
Commager, Henry Steele. *The Empire of Reason: How Europe Imagined and America Realized the Enlightenment.* New York, 1977.
Conforti, Joseph A. *Jonathan Edwards, Religious Tradition, and American Culture.* Chapel Hill, N.C., 1995.
Conkin, Paul. *Puritans and Pragmatists.* New York, 1968.
Cragg, Gerald R. *The Church and the Age of Reason, 1648–1789.* New York, 1960.
———. *From Puritanism to the Age of Reason.* Cambridge, 1950.
———. *Reason and Authority in the Eighteenth Century.* Cambridge, 1964.
Crocker, Lester. *An Age of Crisis.* Baltimore, 1959.
Cummins, J. S. *The Travels and Controversies of Friar Domingo Navarrete (1618–86).* Cambridge, 1962.
Daniel, Norman. *Islam and the West.* Edinburgh, 1960.
Daniel, Stephen H. *John Toland: His Methods, Manners and Mind.* Kingston, Canada, 1984.
———. *The Philosophy of Jonathan Edwards: A Study in Divine Semiotics.* Bloomington, Ind., 1994.
Dawson, David. *Allegorical Readers and Cultural Revision in Ancient Alexandria.* Berkeley, Calif., 1992.
De Boer, John. *The Theory of Knowledge of the Cambridge Platonists.* Madras, India, 1931.
Delattre, Roland. *Beauty and Sensibility in the Thought of Jonathan Edwards: An Essay in Aesthetics and Theological Ethics.* New Haven, Conn., 1968.
Dennis, Matthew W. *Cultivating a Landscape of Peace: Iroquois-European Encounters in Seventeenth-Century America.* Ithaca, N.Y., 1993.
Denny, Frederick M. *An Introduction to Islam.* New York, 1985.
———. *Islam and the Muslim Community.* San Francisco, 1987.
Dodds, E. R. *The Ancient Concept of Progress.* Oxford, 1973.
Donner, Fred McCraw. *The Early Islamic Conquests.* Princeton, N.J., 1981.
Droze, Arthur J. *Homer or Moses? Early Christian Interpretations of the History of Culture.* Tübingen, 1989.
Dunne, G. H., S.J. *Generation of Giants: The First Jesuits in China.* London, 1962.
Elwood, Douglas J. *The Philosophical Theology of Jonathan Edwards.* New York, 1960.
Etiemble, René. *Les Jesuits en China, 1552–1773.* Paris, 1966.
Fagan, B. F. *The Clash of Cultures.* New York, 1984.
Felsenstein, Frank. *Anti-Semitic Stereotypes: A Paradigm of Otherness in English Popular Culture, 1660–1830.* Baltimore, 1995.
Ferguson, Robert A. *The American Enlightenment, 1750–1820.* Cambridge, Mass., 1997.
Fiering, Norman. *Jonathan Edwards's Moral Thought and Its British Context.* Chapel Hill, N.C., 1981.
———. *Moral Philosophy at Seventeenth-Century Harvard.* Chapel Hill, N.C., 1981.
Frei, Hans. *The Eclipse of Biblical Narrative: A Study in Eighteenth and Nineteenth Century Hermeneutics.* New Haven, Conn., 1974.
Frend, W.H.C. *Martyrdom and Persecution in the Early Church.* New York, 1967.
Frye, Northrop. *The Great Code: The Bible and Literature.* New York, 1982.
Fung, Yu-lan. *A Short History of Chinese Philosophy.* New York, 1948.
Gaustad, Edwin S. *Sworn on the Altar of God: A Religious Biography of Thomas Jefferson.* Grand Rapids, Mich., 1996.

Gay, Peter. *The Enlightenment: An Interpretation.* 2 vols. London, 1967.
———. *A Loss of Mastery: Puritan Historians in Colonial America.* Berkeley, Calif., 1966.
Geertz, Clifford. *The Interpretation of Cultures.* New York, 1972.
George, Timothy. *The Theology of the Reformers.* Nashville, Tenn., 1980.
Gernet, Jacques. *China and the Christian Impact.* Cambridge, 1982.
Gerstner, John H. *The Rational Biblical Theology of Jonathan Edwards.* 3 vols. Powhatan, Va., 1991– .
Godzich, Wlad, and Jochen Schulte-Sasse, eds. *Scenes from the Drama of European Literature. Theory and History of Literature* 9. Minneapolis, 1984.
Goldman, Shalom, ed. *Hebrew and the Bible in America: The First Two Centuries.* Hanover, N.H., 1993.
Goldmann, Lucien. *The Philosophy of the Enlightenment: The Christian Burgess and the Enlightenment.* Translated by H. Maas. Cambridge, Mass., 1973.
Grant, John Webster. *Moon of Wintertime: Missionaries and the Indians of Canada in Encounter since 1534.* Toronto, 1984.
Greenblatt, Stephen. *New World Encounters.* Berkeley, Calif., 1993.
Guelzo, Allan C. *Edwards on the Will: A Century of American Theological Debate.* Middletown, Conn., 1989.
Guthrie, W.K.C. *The Later Plato and the Academy,* Vol. 5 in *A History of Greek Philosophy.* Cambridge, 1978.
Haakonssen, Knud, ed. *Enlightenment and Religion: Rational Dissent in Eighteenth-Century Britain.* Cambridge, 1996.
Habermas, Jürgen. *The Philosophical Discourse of Modernity: Twelve Lectures.* Translated by Frederick Lawrence. Cambridge, Mass., 1987.
———. *The Structural Transformation of the Public Sphere: An Inquiry into a Category of Bourgeois Society.* Cambridge, Mass., 1994.
Hadas, Moses, and Morton Smith. *Heroes and Gods: Spiritual Biographies in Antiquity.* New York, 1965.
Harrison, Peter. *"Religion" and the Religions in the English Enlightenment.* Cambridge, 1990.
Hatch, Nathan. *The Sacred Cause of Liberty: Republican Thought and the Millennium in Revolutionary New England.* New Haven, Conn., 1977.
Hatch, Nathan, and Harry S. Stout, eds. *Jonathan Edwards and the American Experience.* New York, 1988.
Holbrook, Clyde A. *The Ethics of Jonathan Edwards: Morality and Aesthetics.* Ann Arbor, Mich., 1973.
Hourani, Albert. *A History of the Arab Peoples.* Cambridge, Mass., 1991.
Howe, Daniel Walker. *Making the American Self: Jonathan Edwards to Abraham Lincoln.* Cambridge, Mass., 1997.
Hunt, Michael. *Making of a Special Relationship: The United States and China to 1914.* New York, 1983.
Hutchison, William R. *Errand to the World: American Protestant Thought and Foreign Missions.* Chicago, 1987.
Isaacs, Harold. *Images of Asia: American Views of China and India.* New York, 1962.
Jacob, Margaret, C. *The Radical Enlightenment: Pantheists, Freemasons and Republicans.* London, 1981.
Jacobs, Wilbur R. *Dispossessing the American Indian: Indians and Whites on the Colonial Frontier.* New York, 1972.
James, Clifford, and George E. Marcus. *Writing Culture: The Poetics and Politics of Ethnography.* Berkeley, Calif., 1986.
Jennings, Francis. *Empire of Fortune: Crowns, Colonies, and Tribes in the Seven Years War in America.* New York, 1988.

———. *The Invasion of America: Indians, Colonialism, and the Cant of Conquest.* Chapel Hill, N.C., 1975.
Jenson, Robert W. *America's Theologian: A Recommendation of Jonathan Edwards.* New York, 1988.
Jochim, Christian. *Chinese Religions: A Cultural Perspective.* Englewood Cliffs, N.J., 1986.
Jordan, Louis. *Comparative Religion: Its Genesis and Growth.* Edinburgh, 1905.
Koch, G. Adolph. *Religion and the American Enlightenment.* New York, 1968.
Kramnick, Isaac. *Republicanism and Bourgeois Radicalism.* Ithaca, N.Y., 1990.
Küng, Hans. *On Being a Christian.* New York, 1976.
Lach, Donald F. *Asia in the Making of Europe.* 3 vols. Chicago, 1965–93.
Latourette, Kenneth Scott. *A History of Christian Missions in China.* New York, 1929.
Lavtzion, Nehemiah, ed. *Conversion to Islam.* New York, 1979.
Leach, Douglas Edward. *Arms for Empire: A Military History of the British Colonies in North America, 1607–1763.* New York, 1973.
Lee, Sang Hyun. *The Philosophical Theology of Jonathan Edwards.* Princeton, N.J., 1988.
Lepore, Jill. *The Name of War: King Phillip's War and the Origins of American Identity.* New York, 1998.
Lesser, M. X. *Jonathan Edwards: A Reference Guide.* Boston, 1981.
———. *Jonathan Edwards.* Boston, 1988.
———. *Jonathan Edwards: An Annotated Bibliography, 1979–1993.* Westport, Conn., 1994.
Lewalski, Barbara Kiefer. *Protestant Poetics and the Seventeenth-Century Religious Lyric.* Princeton, N.J., 1979.
Lillywhite, Bryant. *London Coffeehouses.* London, 1950.
Lovelace, Richard. *The American Pietism of Cotton Mather: Origins of American Evangelicalism.* Grand Rapids, Mich., 1979.
Lowance, Mason I., Jr. *The Language of Canaan: Metaphor and Symbol in New England from the Puritans to the Transcendentalists.* Cambridge, Mass., 1980.
Luxon, Thomas H. *Literal Figures: Puritan Allegory and the Reformation Crisis in Representation.* Chicago, 1995.
Manuel, Frank. *The Broken Staff: Judaism through Christian Eyes.* Cambridge, Mass., 1992.
———. *The Changing of the Gods.* London, 1983.
———. *The Eighteenth Century Confronts the Gods.* Cambridge, Mass., 1959.
Marshall, Bruce. *Christology in Conflict: The Identity of a Saviour in Rahner and Barth.* Oxford, 1987.
Mason, Peter. *Deconstructing America: Representations of the Other.* London, 1990.
May, Henry F. *The Enlightenment in America.* New York, 1976.
McClymond, Michael. *Encounters with God: An Approach to the Theology of Jonathan Edwards.* New York, 1998.
McDermott, Gerald R. *One Holy and Happy Society: The Public Theology of Jonathan Edwards.* University Park, Pa., 1992.
McKim, Donald K. *Major Themes in the Reformed Tradition.* Grand Rapids, Mich., 1992.
Meyer, Donald H. *The Democratic Enlightenment.* New York, 1976.
Miller, Perry. *Jonathan Edwards.* 2d ed. New York, 1949.
Morais, Herbert M. *Deism in Eighteenth-Century America.* New York, 1960.
Morford, Mark, and Robert J. Lenardon. *Classical Mythology.* 4th ed. New York, 1991.
Morimoto, Anri. *Jonathan Edwards and the Catholic Vision of Salvation.* University Park, Pa., 1995.
Morris, William S. *The Young Jonathan Edwards: A Reconstruction.* Brooklyn, 1991.
Morrison, Kenneth M. *The Embattled Northeast: The Elusive Ideal of Alliance in Abenaki-Euramerican Relations.* Berkeley, Calif., 1984.
Mossner, Ernest Campbell. *Bishop Butler and the Age of Reason: A Study in the History of Thought.* New York, 1936.

Muller, Richard A. *Post-Reformation Reformed Dogmatics. Volume 1: Prolegomena to Theology.* Grand Rapids, Mich., 1987.

Neill, Stephen. *A History of Christian Missions.* Rev. ed. New York, 1986.

Noll, Mark. *Princeton and the Republic, 1768–1822: The Search for a Christian Enlightenment in the Era of Samuel Stanhope Smith.* Princeton, N.J., 1989.

Nuttall, Geoffrey. *The Holy Spirit in Puritan Faith and Experience.* Oxford, 1946.

Oberg, Barbara A., and Harry S. Stout, eds. *Benjamin Franklin, Jonathan Edwards, and the Representation of American Culture.* New York, 1993.

Pagden, A. *European Encounters with the New World: From Renaissance to Romanticism.* New Haven, Conn., 1993.

Pailin, David A. *Attitudes to Other Religions: Comparative Religion in Seventeenth- and Eighteenth-century Britain.* Manchester, 1984.

Passmore, J. A. *Ralph Cudworth: An Interpretation.* Cambridge, 1951.

Pinot, Virgile. *La Chine et la formation de l'esprit philosophique en France, 1640–1740.* Paris, 1932.

Placher, William C. *The Domestication of Transcendence: How Modern Thinking about God Went Wrong.* Louisville, Ky., 1996.

Rabb, Theodore, and Jerrold Seigel, eds. *Action and Conviction in Early Modern Europe: Essays in Memory of E. H. Harbison.* Princeton, N.J., 1969.

Rahner, Karl, S.J. *Foundations of Christian Faith.* New York, 1978.

——— *Theological Investigations.* Vol. 6. Baltimore, 1969.

Redwood, John. *Reason, Ridicule and Religion: The Age of Enlightenment in England, 1660–1750.* Cambridge, Mass., 1976.

Richter, Daniel K. *The Ordeal of the Longhouse: The People of the Iroquois League in the Era of European Colonization.* Chapel Hill, N.C., 1992.

Rist, J. M. *Plotinus: The Road to Reality.* Cambridge, 1967.

Roberts, James D. *From Puritanism to Platonism in Seventeenth-Century England.* The Hague, 1968.

Rooy, Sidney H. *The Theology of Missions in the Puritan Tradition: A Study of Representative Puritans: Richard Sibbes, Richard Baxter et al.* Delft, 1965.

Rorty, Richard. *Philosophy and the Mirror of Nature.* Princeton, N.J., 1979.

Rowbotham, Arnold. *Missionary and Mandarin: The Jesuits at the Court of China.* Berkeley, Calif., 1942.

Rudisill, Dorus Paul. *The Doctrine of the Atonement in Jonathan Edwards and His Successors.* New York, 1971.

Said, Edward. *Orientalism.* New York, 1978.

Scheick, William J., ed. *Critical Essays on Jonathan Edwards.* Boston, 1980.

Schwartz, Stuart B., ed. *Implicit Understandings: Observing, Reporting, and Reflecting on the Encounters between Europeans and Other Peoples in the Early Modern Era.* New York, 1994.

Seznec, Jean. *The Survival of the Pagan Gods: The Mythological Tradition and Its Place in Renaissance Humanism and Art.* New York, 1953.

Shaban, M. A. *Islamic History* A.D. 600–750 (A.H. 132): *A New Interpretation.* Cambridge, 1971.

Sharpe, Eric J. *Comparative Religion: A History.* New York, 1975.

Shea, William M., and Peter A. Huff. *Knowledge and Belief in America: Enlightenment Traditions and Modern Religious Thought.* Cambridge: Cambridge University Press, 1995.

Sher, Richard B., and Jeffrey R. Smitten. *Scotland and America in the Age of Enlightenment.* Princeton, N.J., 1990.

Simonson, Harold P. *Jonathan Edwards: Theologian of the Heart.* Grand Rapids, Mich., 1974.

Smalley, Beryl. *The Study of the Bible in the Middle Ages.* Notre Dame, Ind., 1978.

Smith, Byron Porter. *Islam in English Literature.* Beirut, 1939.

Smith, John E. *Jonathan Edwards: Puritan, Preacher, Philosopher.* Notre Dame, Ind., 1992.
Southern, R. W. *Western Views of Islam in the Middle Ages.* Cambridge, Mass., 1962.
Stein, Gordon, ed. *The Encyclopedia of Unbelief.* Buffalo, N.Y., 1985.
Stephen, Leslie. *History of English Thought in the Eighteenth Century.* 3d ed. 2 vols. New York, 1949.
Stout, Harry S. *The New England Soul: Preaching and Religious Culture in Colonial New England.* New York, 1986.
Stromberg, Roland N. *Religious Liberalism in Eighteenth-Century England.* Oxford, 1954.
Sullivan, Robert E. *John Toland and the Deist Controversy.* Cambridge, Mass., 1982.
Torrey, Norman L. *Voltaire and the English Deists.* New Haven, Conn., 1938.
Tracy, Patricia J. *Jonathan Edwards, Pastor: Religion and Society in Eighteenth-Century Northampton.* New York, 1980.
Turner, James. *Without God, Without Creed: The Origins of Unbelief in America.* Baltimore, 1985.
Vaughan, Alden T. *New England Frontier: Puritans and Indians 1620–1675.* Boston, 1965.
Vico, Giambattista. *The New Science.* 1735. Translated by T. G. Bergin and M. H. Fisch. Ithaca, N.Y., 1984.
Wainwright, William J. *Reason and the Heart: A Prolegomenon to a Critique of Passional Reason.* Ithaca, N.Y., 1995.
Walker, Daniel Pickering. *The Ancient Theology: Studies in Christian Platonism from 15th–18th Century.* Ithaca, N.Y., 1972.
———. *The Decline of Hell: Seventeenth-Century Discussions of Eternal Torment.* London, 1964.
Walters, Kerry S. *The American Deists: Voices of Reason and Dissent in the Early Republic.* Lawrence, Kansas, 1992.
———. *Rational Infidels: The American Deists.* Wolfeboro, N.H., 1992.
Watt, M. Montgomery. *The Formative Period of Islamic Thought.* Edinburgh, 1973.
———. *Islamic Philosophy and Theology.* Edinburgh, 1962.
White, Hayden. *The Content of the Form: Narrative Discourse and Historical Representation.* Baltimore, 1987.
———. *Metahistory: The Historical Imagination in Nineteenth-Century Europe.* Baltimore, 1973.
———. *Tropics of Discourse.* Baltimore, 1978.
Winslow, Ola Elizabeth. *Jonathan Edwards, 1703–1758: A Biography.* New York, 1940.
Yates, Frances A. *Giordano Bruno and the Hermetic Tradition.* Chicago, 1964.
———. *The Occult Philosophy in the Elizabethan Age.* London, 1979.
Yolton, John W., ed. *Philosophy, Religion and Science in the Seventeenth and Eighteenth Centuries.* Rochester, N.Y., 1990.
Zakai, Avihu. *Exile and Kingdom: History and Apocalypse in the Puritan Migration to America.* Cambridge, 1992.

Articles and Essays

Barnes, Harry Elmer. "Romanticism and the Philosophy of History." In Barnes, *A History of Historical Writing.* 2d. ed. New York, 1963.
Baumgartner, Paul R. "Jonathan Edwards: The Theory Behind His Use of Figurative Language." *Publications of the Modern Language Association* 74 (1963): 321–25.
Canny, Nicholas P. "The Ideology of English Colonization: From Ireland to America." *William and Mary Quarterly,* 3d ser. 30, no. 4 (October 1973):575–598.
Carabelli, Giancarlo. "Deismo inglese e dintoni: alcuni studi recenti." *Rivista critica di storia della filosofia* 33 (1978): 418–51.
Davis, Walter W. "China, the Confucian Ideal, and the European Age of Enlightenment." *Journal of the History of Ideas* 44 (1983), 523–48.

Delattre, Roland. "Beauty and Politics: A Problematic Legacy of Jonathan Edwards." In Robert W. Shahan and Kenneth R. Merrill, eds., *American Philosophy from Edwards to Quine*. Norman, Okla., 1977.
———. "Beauty and Theology: A Reappraisal of Jonathan Edwards." In Scheick, *Critical Essays on Jonathan Edwards*, 136–49.
Ettinger, Samuel. "Jews and Judaism in the Eyes of the English Deists in the Eighteenth Century" (in Hebrew). *Zion* 29, nos. 3–4 (1964).
Gohdes, Clarence. "Aspects of Idealism in Early New England." *Philosophical Review* 39 (1930): 537–55.
Howe, Daniel Walker. "The Cambridge Platonists of Old England and the Cambridge Platonists of New England." *Church History* 57 (December 1988): 470–85.
Isani, Mukhtar Ali. "Cotton Mather and the Orient." *New England Quarterly* 43 (March 1970): 46–58.
———. "Edward Taylor and the Turks." *Early American Literature* 7, no. 2 (1972): 120–23.
Jacob, Margaret C. "John Toland and the Newtonian Enlightenment." *Journal of the Warburg and Courtauld Institutes* 32 (1969).
Jacobs, Wilbur R. "Some Social Ideas of Francis Parkman." *The American Quarterly* 9 (Winter 1957): 387–96.
Johnson, Thomas H. "Jonathan Edwards's Background of Reading." *Publications of the Colonial Society of Massachusetts*, 28 (1930–33): 193–222.
Knight, Janice. "Learning the Language of God: Jonathan Edwards and the Typology of Nature." *William and Mary Quarterly*, 3d ser., 48 (1991): 531–51.
Lovejoy, Arthur O. "The Parallel of Deism and Classicism." In Lovejoy, *Essays in the History of Ideas*. 1948. New York, 1960.
Lovejoy, David S. "Satanizing the American Indian." *New England Quarterly* 67, no. 4 (December 1994): 603–21.
Lowance, Mason I. "Jonathan Edwards and the Platonists: Edwardsean Epistemology and the Influence of Malebranche and Norris." *Studies in Puritan American Spirituality* 2 (January 1992): 129–51.
———. "Typology and the New England Way: Cotton Mather and the Exegesis of Biblical Types." *Early American Literature* 4 (1969): 15–37.
Maclear, James F. "'The Heart of New England Rent': The Mystical Element in Early Puritan History." *Mississippi Valley Historical Review* 42 (1956): 621–52.
Madsen, William G. "From Shadowy Types to Truth." In Joseph Summers, ed., *The Lyric and Dramatic Milton*. New York, 1965.
Miles, Lion G. "The Red Man Dispossessed: The Williams Family and the Alienation of Indian Land in Stockbridge, Massachusetts, 1736–1818." *New England Quarterly* 67, no. 1 (March 1994): 46–76.
Miller, Perry. "From Edwards to Emerson." In Miller, *Errand into the Wilderness*. New York, 1964.
Pelli, Moshe. "The Impact of Deism on the Hebrew Literature of the Enlightenment in Germany." *Eighteenth-Century Studies* 6 (1972/1973): 35–59.
Pointer, Richard W. "'Poor Indians' and the 'Poor in Spirit': The Indian Impact on David Brainerd.'" *New England Quarterly* 67, no. 3 (September 94): 403–26.
Ronda, James P. "The Sillery Experiment: A Jesuit-Indian Village in New France, 1637–1663." *American Indian Culture and Research Journal* 3, no. 1 (1979): 1–18.
———. "'We Are Well As We Are': An Indian Critique of Seventeenth-Century Christian Missions." *William and Mary Quarterly*, 3d ser., 34 (January 1977): 66–82.
Rowbotham, Arnold. "The Jesuit Figurists and Eighteenth-Century Religious Thought." *Journal of the History of Ideas* 17 1/4 (Jan/Oct 1956): 471–85.

Schafer, Thomas A. "Jonathan Edwards and Justification by Faith." *Church History* 20 (1951): 55–67.
Schmitt, Charles B. "Perennial Philosophy: From Agostino Steuco to Leibniz." *Journal of the History of Ideas* 27 (October–December 1966): 505–32.
Stein, Stephen J. "Cotton Mather and Jonathan Edwards on the Number of the Beast: Eighteenth-Century Speculation about the Antichrist." *Proceedings of the American Antiquarian Society* 84 (1974): 293–315.
———. "Providence and the Apocalypse in the Early Writings of Jonathan Edwards." *Early American Literature* 13 (1978): 250–67.
———. "The Quest for the Spiritual Sense: The Biblical Hermeneutics of Jonathan Edwards." *Harvard Theological Review* 70 (1977): 99–113.
———. "The Spirit and the Word." In Hatch and Stout, *Jonathan Edwards and the American Experience*.
Stromberg, Roland N. "Lovejoy's 'Parallel' Reconsidered." *Eighteenth-Century Studies* 1 (1967–68).
Wainwright, William J. "Jonathan Edwards and the Language of God." *JAAR* 48 (1980): 519–30.
———. "The Nature of Reason: Locke, Swineburn, and Edwards." In Alan G. Padgett, ed., *Reason and the Christian Religion*. Oxford, 1994.
Walker, D. P. "Orpheus the Theologian and Renaissance Platonists." *Journal of the Wartburg and Courtauld Institutes* 16 (1953): 100–120.
Walsh, Clement. "A Note on the Meaning of 'Deism.'" *Anglican Theological Review* 38 (1956): 160–65.
Watts, Emily Stripes. "The Neoplatonic Basis of Jonathan Edwards's 'True Virtue.'" *Early American Literature* 10 (1975): 178–89.
Wessell, Leonard P. "Rejoinder to Stromberg's 'Reconsideration.'" *Eighteenth-Century Studies* 2 (1968–69): 439–49.
White, Hayden. "The Historical Fact as Literary Artifact" In Robert H. Canary and Henry Kozicki, eds., *The Writing of History: The Literary Form and Historical Understanding*. Madison, Wis., 1978.
———. "The Structure of Historical Narrative." *Clio* 1 (1972): 5–20.
Wilson, John H. "Jonathan Edwards as Historian." *Church History* 46 (1977): 5–18.
Winnett, Arthur R. "Were the Deists 'Deists'?" *Church Quarterly Review* 161 (1960): 70–77.
Zakai, Avihu. "The Poetics of History and the Destiny of Israel: The Role of the Jews in English Apocalyptic Thought During the Sixteenth and Seventeenth Centuries." *The Journal of Jewish Thought and Philosophy* 5 (1996): 313–50.
———. "Reformation, History and Eschatology in English Protestantism." *History and Theory* 26, no. 3 (October 1987): 300–318.

Dissertations

Davies, Ronald E. "Prepare Ye the Way of the Lord: The Missiological Thought and Practice of Jonathan Edwards." Ph.D. diss., Fuller Theological Seminary, 1989.
Hankins, Jean Fittz. "Bringing the Good News: Protestant Missionaries to the Indians of New England and New York, 1700–1775." Ph.D. diss., University of Connecticut, 1993.
Lepore, Jill. "The Name of War: Waging, Writing and Remembering King Philip's War." Ph.D. diss., Yale University, 1996.
Watts, Emily Stripes. "Jonathan Edwards and the Cambridge Platonists." Ph.D. diss., University of Illinois, 1963.
Wheeler, Rachel. "Living upon Hope: Mahicans and Missionaries, 1730–1760." Ph.D. diss., Yale University, 1998.

INDEX

Aldridge, Alfred Owen, 5n7, 37n9, 210
allegory, 118–122
Anderson, Wallace, 57, 68n35
Andrewes, Lancelot, 121
Anglicanism, 23, 33
Aquinas, Thomas, 169, 176
Aristotle, 176, 180, 181, 188–189
Arminianism, 18–19, 46–50, 144
Arminians, 7, 18
atonement, satisfaction theory of, 18, 26, 31, 42, 42n20, 49n34
Auerbach, Erich, 120
Augustine, 93n18, 96, 122, 176, 186

Barrow, Isaac, 92, 160, 180, 181, 183, 188
Barth, Karl, 3, 13, 13n29
Baxter, Richard, 144, 172
Bayle, Peter, 93, 209n12, 210, 211
Bellamy, Joseph, 46
Basnage, Jacques, 183
Blount, Charles, 19, 20, 25, 28, 35n2, 131, 177, 210
Bochart, Samuel, 177, 179, 190–191

Bolingbroke, Henry St. John, Lord, 20, 35n2, 149, 225
Bouvet, Joachim, 209
Bowden, Henry Warner, 196, 197n20, 202
Brainerd, David, 197–198, 205
Breck, Robert, 130, 144–145
Brine, John, 42, 135, 186
Burke, Edmund, 37–38, 225
Butler, Joseph, 32n75, 142, 224, 225
Buxtdorf, Johann the Elder, 149

Calvinism, 26, 48, 88, 116, 131
Calvin, 57n7, 58n10, 63n26, 74, 96n24, 119, 122, 132–133, 137n30, 156–157, 171, 182, 220, 226
Cambridge Platonists, 22, 23, 63, 67, 68, 87, 92, 131
Cassian, John, 119
Celsus, 50, 185, 211
Champion, J.A.I., 24
chaos theory, 128–129
Chauncy, Charles, 6
Cherry, Conrad, 7n14, 69n39

China, 10, 11, 25, 40, 93
  Chinese philosophers, 42, 207–216
Chubb, Thomas, 20, 25, 26, 27, 28, 30, 31, 32, 33, 35–36, 42n20, 47, 63, 72, 75, 86, 88, 89, 110, 130, 131, 150, 151, 161, 172, 220, 225
Cicero, 42, 43, 173, 176, 178, 185, 186, 187, 210
Clarke, Samuel, 20, 28, 32, 35, 40, 43, 72, 92, 178, 180, 186, 219
Clement of Alexandria, 68, 93, 181
Collins, Anthony, 19, 25, 27, 30, 32, 121, 131, 160, 178, 225
Confucius, 6, 31, 92, 167, 210, 214, 215–216
Cooper, James Fenimore, 5
covenant, 9–11
Cudworth, Ralph, 22, 94, 150n3, 183, 185, 187, 191, 215, 216

Daniel, Stephen H., 7n14, 23, 112
Dao-de-jing, 92, 209, 214
Dawson, David, 120n23
Defoe, Daniel, 93, 215–216
deism, 4–5, 7–8, 10, 12, 18, 34–51
  as anticipator of the Enlightenment, 217–218
  and China, 209–211
  and the classics, 177–179
  fear of it, 37–38, 46–47
  and historical revelation, 105–109
  historiography of, 19–21
  and history, 91–92, 97–99
  integral to the Edwards corpus, 38–50
  and Islam, 171–174
  its opposition to typological interpretation, 121–122
  its view of prophecy, 159–160
  nature of, 26–32
  and opposition to Judaism, 26–28, 149–151
  origins of, 21–26
  and orthodoxy, 18–19
  and the religions, 50–51
  and revelation, 71–86
d'Holbach, Baron, 27n50
Dickinson, Jonathan, 37
Doddridge, Phillip, 183

Duhalde, Jean Baptiste, 209, 210, 211, 213, 215
Duns Scotus, John, 67

Edwards, Jonathan
  and American Indians, 194–206
  and Chinese religion, 213–216
  deism in his written corpus, 38–50
  and divine beauty, 3
  and divine wrath, 3
  and the Enlightenment, 217–227
  on epistemology, 68–70
  on Greco-Roman philosophy, 179–193
  and his battle with deists over the religions, 50–51
  and his fear of deism, 38
  and his typological view of reality, 111–122
  and his view of Israel's role in the work of redemption, 152–165
  and his war on Enlightenment religion, 34–51
  on history, 91–107
  on how God communicates through typology, 122–128
  as an infralapsarian, 39n16, 43
  and Islam's place in his eschatology, 169–171
  on John 21:25, 35–36
  the legacy of his fight against deism, 225–227
  on the limits of reason, 63–70, 80–86
  on self-determination of the will, 36, 47
  and soteriology, 130–139
  and soteriology for heathens, 139–145
  on what reason can know about God, 56–63
Enlightenment, 3–5, 7, 10, 11, 217–227
Epictetus, 185, 186
Epicurus, 178
  Epicureanism, 185
Erskine, John, 46, 47
Esculapius, 51
Euripides, 41, 185
Eusebius, 93, 181, 191

Ficino, Marsilio, 87, 93
Fiering, Norman, 5n7, 7n14, 219
Flavel, John, 125
Franklin, Benjamin, 6–7, 30, 210, 219, 225n28, 226
Frei, Hans, 224
Frye, Northrop, 129

Gale, Theophilus, 41n19, 92, 94, 135n19, 160, 180, 181, 183–184, 186, 187–189, 190, 191
Gay, Ebenezer, 6
Gerstner, John H., 7n14, 38
Gibbon, Edward, 149, 169
God
   a communicating being, 43, 112
   creation as communication of God's goodness, 89–91
   the eighteenth century as a debate over God's character, 17–19
   evidence for God's existence, 56–59
   knowledge of God the Redeemer and Creator, 65–66, 73
   relativity of God's expectations, 139–140
   and selfishness, 43–44, 48–49
   use of typology as pedagogical tool, 116–117
   what reason can know about God's attributes, 58–63, 73
Godwin, William, 218
Gordon, Thomas, 29, 131, 176n1
Greek and Roman philosophers, 9, 64, 65, 93–94, 96, 133, 135, 140, 143, 160, 167, 176–193
Grotius, Hugo, 41, 92, 94, 160, 180, 181, 185, 187–189
Guelzo, Allan C., 7n14

Habermas, Jürgen, 23, 218
Harrison, Peter, 96
Hartley, David, 220
Hegel, Georg Wilhelm Friedrich, 4
hell, 42
Herbert of Cherbury, Edward, Lord, 21, 24, 26, 28, 35n2, 131, 150, 177
Herder, Johann, 4
Hertzberg, Arthur, 165
Hinduism, 94
Hobbes, Thomas, 35n2, 73

Holbrook, Clyde A., 48
Homer, 119
Hopkins, Samuel, 201n36, 226n32
Hume, David, 35n2, 88, 100, 150, 159, 178–179, 210, 218, 223
Hutcheson, Francis, 176n1

I-Ching, 94, 209, 212, 214, 215
Independent Whig, 27, 210
Indians, American, 6, 10, 11, 12–13, 73, 138, 173, 194–206
Islam, 6, 9, 11, 46, 143, 166–175

Jefferson, Thomas, 225n28, 226
Jenson, Robert, 5n7, 7n14, 220, 223n21
Jesuits, 10, 25, 93, 196, 207–209, 216
Judaism, 9–11, 26–28, 149–165
   anti-Semitism, 150–152, 165
Julian the Apostate, 51
Jupiter, 51
Juvenal, 94, 185

Kant, Immanuel, 4, 218
Kimnach, Wilson, 60, 65, 121
Kirkland, Samuel, 200
knowledge, 55–56
   spiritual and rational, 61–62
Kuhn, Thomas, 129

Lactantius, 93
language, 82, 95, 115, 126–127, 211
Lao-zi, 42, 167, 214
law of nature, 77–80
Law, William, 32n75
Lecomte, Louis, 208, 213, 215
Lee, Sang Hyun, 7n14, 101
Leibniz, Gottfried, 7, 210
Leland, John, 35n2, 39
Lessing, Gotthold, 4, 24n37, 150
Locke, John, 5, 17, 22, 23, 28, 32, 34, 55, 60, 63, 65, 68, 72–73, 86, 210, 217, 224n23
Lockman, John, 213
Luther, Martin, 119, 123, 136, 171
Luxon, Thomas H., 120n23

Maigrot, Charles, 208
Manuel, Frank E., 27, 151, 152n21, 159n34

Mastricht, Peter van, 39n16, 144, 182
Mather, Cotton, 6, 125, 155n28, 164
Mather, Increase, 164
Mather, Samuel, 120, 125
May, Henry, 217–218, 219n8
Mayhew, Jonathan, 6
McClymond, Michael, 7n14
Mede, Joseph, 164
Middleton, Conyers, 30
Miller, Perry, 47, 112
Mirandola, Pico Della, 93
Montesquieu, Charles Louis de Secondat, 210
morality
   and Cambridge Platonism, 22–23
   and deism, 18–19, 22–23, 27–28
   and God, 73
   and Locke, 28
   and Tindal, 77–80
   and worship, 89
More, Henry, 22, 63, 68, 141n40
Morgan, Thomas, 27, 35n2, 151, 225
Morimoto, Anri, 136nn.
Morris, William S., 7n14, 68n35
Muhammad, 11, 12
Muslims, *see* Islam

Native Americans, *see* Indians, American
Newton, Isaac, 5, 22, 34, 217, 219
Nicholas of Cusa, 87
Norris, John, 60

Origen, 93, 119, 211
original sin, 47–48
orthodox, 18
   definition of, 18n5
Ovid, 41, 94, 114, 185

Paine, Thomas, 218
Pettit, Norman, 197n21
Philo, 119
Placher, William C., 88–89
Plato, 41, 44, 64, 176, 178, 180, 181, 183–186, 187–189, 210
Plotinus, 68, 188
Plutarch, 176, 185
Pointer, Richard W., 205
Porphyry, 50, 185
Prémare, Joseph, 209

Prideaux, Humphrey, 92, 169n15
prisca theologia, 8, 12, 80, 93–109, 132–133, 140–141, 145, 161, 173, 177, 179, 182, 211, 213, 215, 223

Qabbalah, 93
Qur'an, 6, 12, 93, 166–167

Rahner, Karl, 138
Ramsay, Chevalier, 42, 92, 93, 127, 132, 144, 183, 184, 185, 187, 211–215
Ramsey, Paul, 32, 35
reason, 7–8, 10, 55–70, 220–221
   abstract, 18, 31–32
   for Cambridge Platonists, 22–23
   and John Locke, 22–23, 73
   and mystery, 80–86
   and revelation, 71–77
religion, 8, 222
   for Cambridge Platonists, 22–23
   deist understanding of, 21, 31–32
   history of, 91–109
   natural, 18, 32
   nature of, 88–91
revelation, 7, 10, 34–51, 71–86
   deist rejection of, 21, 71
   in Greek and Roman philosophy, 181–186
   in Islam, 173–174
   and John Locke, 22–23
   in Judaism, 153–156, 161–162
   for pagan philosophers, 140–141
   and reason, 71–77
   of redemption in history, 99–105
   written and spiritual, 66–67
Ricci, Matthew, 207
Rorty, Richard, 129, 225
Rousseau, Jean-Jacques, 218

Said, Edward, 12
Sale, George, 93, 169n17
salvation for non-Christians, 9, 13, 26, 130–145
scandal of particularity, 7, 24, 25, 96, 131
Schafer, Thomas A., 136
Schleiermacher, Friedrich, 4

Seneca, 41, 94, 135, 178, 185, 187
Shaftesbury, Anthony Ashley Cooper, Earl of, 20, 22, 35n2
Shuckford, Samuel, 44, 92, 160, 177, 179, 180, 181, 187, 190, 213
Simon, Richard, 150
simple ideas, 68–69
Skelton, Philip, 35n2, 39, 42, 92, 93, 132, 135n19, 143, 144, 180n12, 181, 214
Smith, John, 68
Smith, John E., 68n36
Socrates, 3n3, 64, 178, 180, 183, 187–189, 210
Spinoza, Baruch, 73
Stapfer, Johann Friedrich, 40, 92, 168
Stein, Stephen, 122
Stephen, Leslie, 86
Stoddard, Solomon, 197
Stogdon, Hubert, 40

Tacitus, 176
Taylor, Edward, 6
Taylor, Jeremy, 121
Taylor, John, 48, 194
Tertullian, 70
Tindal, Matthew, 5, 20, 25, 26, 28, 29, 30, 31, 33, 35, 35n2, 36–37, 47, 60, 63, 65, 73, 75, 77–80, 86, 110, 121, 131, 150, 172, 178, 192n41, 210, 219nn8,9, 220, 221, 225
Toland, John, 5, 19, 20, 23, 24, 25, 26, 28, 30, 32, 33, 35n2, 60, 65, 75, 96n25, 110, 121, 131, 151, 159, 172, 178, 210, 220, 221, 225
 and Druidism, 26
 and Masonic lodges, 86
Trenchard, John, 29, 131, 176n1, 210

Trinity, 40–41, 42, 55, 58–59, 209, 214, 219, 221
Turnbull, George, 115
Turner, William, 144
Turretin, Francis, 39n16, 58n11, 62n20, 144, 182
Tyndale, William, 119
typology, 8–9, 45, 50, 110–129, 155–156, 225

Van Voss, Gerhard, *see* Vossius
Vicar of Brayism, 23
Vico, Giovanni Battista, 88, 178
Virgil, 94, 153, 185
Voltaire, 7, 11, 27, 100, 149, 210
Von Bell, Johann Adam Schall, 208
Vossius, 177, 179, 190, 191

Wainwright, William J., 68n35, 70, 70n42, 86n25, 113n8
Wang, Li, 207n1
Warburton, William, 150, 210
Watts, Isaac, 40, 92, 132n13, 144
Wesley, John, 48, 144, 169n17
Wheeler, Rachel, 200, 201n36, 202, 206
Whichcote, Benjamin, 22
Whiston, William, 35, 121, 159
Whitby, Daniel, 47
Whitefield, George, 37
Williams, Roger, 204
Wollaston, William, 19, 20
Woolston, Thomas, 35n2
Woolman, John, 204
worship, 89–91

Xavier, Francis, 207

Zakai, Avihu, 165n53